DATE DUE
DATE DE RETOUR

MAR 1 – 2000	
APR 7 2000	

CARR McLEAN   38-296

Critical Essays on
TED HUGHES

CRITICAL ESSAYS
ON
BRITISH LITERATURE

Zack Bowen, General Editor
University of Miami

Critical Essays on

TED HUGHES

edited by

LEONARD M. SCIGAJ

G. K. Hall & Co. / New York
Maxwell Macmillan Canada / Toronto
Maxwell Macmillan International / New York Oxford Singapore Sydney

For permission to quote from the copyrighted poetry of Ted Hughes, the editor and contributors are especially grateful to the following: Faber & Faber, Ltd., for quotation from Hughes volumes published by them: *The Hawk in the Rain*, © Ted Hughes 1957; *Lupercal*, © Ted Hughes 1960; *Wodwo*, © Ted Hughes 1967; *Crow*, © Ted Hughes 1970, 1972; *Season Songs*, © Ted Hughes 1976; *Gaudete*, © Ted Hughes 1977; *Cave Birds*, © Ted Hughes 1978; *Remains of Elmet*, © Ted Hughes 1979; *Moortown*, © Ted Hughes 1979; *River*, © Ted Hughes 1983; *Flowers and Insects*, © Ted Hughes 1986; and *Wolfwatching*, © Ted Hughes 1989. Farrar, Straus & Giroux, Inc., for quotation from their published Hughes volume, *Wolfwatching*, © Ted Hughes 1991. HarperCollins, Publishers, Inc., for quotation from Hughes volumes published by them: *The Hawk in the Rain*, © Ted Hughes 1957; *Wodwo*, © Ted Hughes 1967; *Crow*, © Ted Hughes 1971; and *River*, © Ted Hughes 1983. Ted Hughes, for quotations from *Lupercal*, © Ted Hughes 1960; *Gaudete*, © Ted Hughes 1977; *Remains of Elmet*, © Ted Hughes 1979; *Moortown*, © Ted Hughes 1980. Viking Penguin, Inc., for quotation from Hughes volumes published by them: *Season Songs*, © Ted Hughes 1975, and *Cave Birds*, © Ted Hughes 1978.

G. K. Hall & Co.
Macmillan Publishing Company
866 Third Avenue
New York, New York 10022

Maxwell Macmillan Canada, Inc.
1200 Eglinton Avenue East
Suite 200
Don Mills, Ontario M3C 3N1

Macmillan Publishing Company is part of the Maxwell Communication Group of Companies.

Library of Congress Cataloging-in-Publication Data

Critical essays on Ted Hughes / edited by Leonard M. Scigaj.
    p. cm.
    Includes bibliographical references and index.
    ISBN 0-8161-8872-6 (alk. paper.)
    1. Hughes, Ted, 1930– —Criticism and interpretation.
I. Scigaj, Leonard M. II. Series.
PR6058.U37Z636 1992   92-563
821'.914—dc20   CIP

The paper used in this publication meets the minimum requirements of American National Standard for Information Sciences—Permanence of Paper for Printed Library Materials. ANSI Z3948-1984.∞™

10 9 8 7 6 5 4 3 2 1

Printed in the United States of America

For
Gerald Hardner
Datta Wagle
Alberto Gonzalez

Contents

◆

General Editor's Note   ix
Publisher's Note   x
Introduction   1
    LEONARD M. SCIGAJ

HUGHES AS LAUREATE

    Medusa Face   41
        DEREK WALCOTT

    The New Poet Laureate   45
        SEAMUS HEANEY

STYLE AND POETICS

    Beasts/Shamans/Baskin: The Contemporary Aesthetics
    of Ted Hughes   49
        DAVID PORTER

    Wolf Masks: The Early Poetry of Ted Hughes   67
        STAN SMITH

    Poetics   82
        EKBERT FAAS

    "The Poetry Does Not Matter"   99
        KEITH SAGAR

    Animal Music: Ted Hughes's Progress in Speech and Song   109
        DON MCKAY

MAJOR POETRY VOLUMES

Ted Hughes   123
   A. E. DYSON

Thinking Animal: Ted Hughes   131
   FREDERICK GRUBB

Talking Beasts: The "Single Adventure" in the Poems
of Ted Hughes   143
   DANIEL HOFFMAN

Crow: A Mythology of the Demonic   153
   CHARLES V. FERNANDEZ

Genetic Memory and the Three Traditions of *Crow*   163
   LEONARD M. SCIGAJ

The Economy of Flesh in Ted Hughes's *Gaudete*   172
   Rand Brandes

Cave Birds: Hughes's Progress of the Masculine Soul   188
   NEIL ROBERTS AND TERRY GIFFORD

Historical Landscape in Ted Hughes's *Remains of Elmet*   205
   PATRICIA BOYLE HABERSTROH

"How Precisely the Job Can Be Done": Ted Hughes's
Moortown   222
   CAROL BERE

Ted Hughes' Quest for a Hierophany: A Reading of *River*   230
   BO GUSTAVSSON

Wolf-Masks: From *Hawk* to *Wolfwatching*   241
   ANN SKEA

FROM THE POET

Myth and Education   255
   TED HUGHES

Index   269

General Editor's Note

◆

The Critical Essays on British Literature series provides a variety of approaches to both classical and contemporary writers of Britain and Ireland. The formats of the volumes in the series vary with the thematic designs of individual editors and with the amount and nature of existing reviews, criticism, augmented, where appropriate, by original essays by recognized authorities. It is hoped that each volume will be unique in developing a new overall perspective on its particular subject.

Leonard Scigaj's lengthy introduction stresses the breadth of the poet's interests, his anthropological underpinnings, his extensive involvement with environmental issues, and his dedication to children's poetry. He divides Hughes's work into five stages, each represented by two major volumes of poetry, and interweaves his own exceptionally detailed treatment of the entire body of Hughes criticism with an ardent championing of this major voice in contemporary British poetry.

ZACK BOWEN
University of Miami

Publisher's Note

◆

Producing a volume that contains both newly commissioned and reprinted material presents the publisher with the challenge of balancing the desire to achieve stylistic consistency with the need to preserve the integrity of works first published elsewhere. In the Critical Essays series, essays commissioned especially for a particular volume are edited to be consistent with G. K. Hall's house style; reprinted essays appear in the style in which they were first published, with only typographical errors corrected. Consequently, shifts in style from one essay to another are the result of our efforts to be faithful to each text as it was originally published.

Introduction

Leonard M. Scigaj

Healer of the torn psyche, critic of religious taboos and technological exploitation, alchemist for an exhausted English language, mythographer of our spiritual soulscape, environmentalist for our imperiled globe—Ted Hughes throughout his lengthy career has synthesized in his work most of the important concerns of post–World War II Western poetry. With a more capacious grasp of world mythology than Yeats's and a redemptive vision as inclusive as Blake's, Hughes's oeuvre is as important as it is major. The quest to define the key features of his style and the stature of his art runs throughout innumerable reviews, over 150 critical essays, and a dozen or more full-length scholarly studies of his art.

Hughes is a formidable force in contemporary poetry. He is blessed with a musical ear as fine as Eliot's, a capacity for acute description and arresting metaphor unrivaled in twentieth-century literature, and an attentiveness to the wounds of our post-Holocaust world as superfine and sympathetic as one finds in Milosz and Pilinszky. His direct, unromantic scrutiny captures our attention, and he enlarges our grasp of ourselves and our world through exhilarating imagery that changes dimensions effortlessly from microcosm to macrocosm. If he occasionally produces uneven or overly theatrical lines in poems where he strains toward a vatic/apocalyptic plane that is now out of fashion, he reminds us that, as with Shakespeare's verse, an occasional excess may result from attending the creative moment and realizing its energy in words. At his best, as in the *Gaudete* "Epilogue" and in many of the poems of *River*, Hughes synthesizes style and form into a rich and complex vision, creating matchless moments that fuse the inner world of feeling and aspiration with the wonders and trials of the natural world.

At this printing, Hughes has published ten volumes of major adult poetry, more than a dozen works of children's literature, and at least eighteen radio plays. He has broadcast more than two dozen self-scripted radio talks on creative writing for adolescents, and published about three dozen reviews, two important essays on myth and literature, and many introductions to the work of other poets. His voice-overs to individual poems appear on British television, and he has introduced his poems in BBC radio readings and a Thames TV program. His poetry has appeared in essay questions for "A" level university entrance exams since the early 1960s, and he has appeared atop poetry readership polls in England as the most well-known and respected voice of his generation. His many literary prizes culminated in his being named Poet Laureate of England on 19 December 1984.

Hughes's commitment to his public extends far beyond the scope of his own writings. He is a tireless judge of children's literary competitions, including a twenty-five year stint, still continuing, as judge of the *Daily Mirror* contest, now the W. H. Smith National Literary Competition. Aware of the growing number of adolescent poets who convey great anxiety about our endangered environment in their verse, Hughes in 1989 persuaded Prince Philip, the Duke of Edinburgh, and the Archbishop of Canterbury to sponsor an international competition for religious/environmental dramas written by children, the best of which would be enacted in a festival and then published as the Sacred Earth Drama, a sourcebook of children's drama. The goal of the Sacred Earth Drama reflects Hughes's belief that adults, too readily callous to environmental information, can't help being affected and educated by works written and acted by their children, whose environmental inheritance we are squandering.

As an educator of adults Hughes first leased and then sold his Lumb Bank home in Yorkshire to the Arvon Foundation, and he continues to assist the foundation's program of offering affordable, concentrated, week-long creative writing courses taught by established writers in a unique country setting. Martin Booth called the Arvon experience "at the core of what British poetry ought to be doing these days."[1] Hughes's generous aid to other creative artists is well-known: through creative collaborations and essays, he has helped to advance the careers of many graphic artists, photographers, and British and East European poets. As an advocate for the environment, Hughes has since the 1960s donated poems or allowed fair copies of his poems to be auctioned to raise funds for saving trees, salmon, rhinos, and for other worthwhile causes. He offers first printings of some of his poems to newspapers (the London *Independent* often bids highest), and donates the proceeds to the Atlantic Salmon Trust. Hughes's interest in education and the environment grows from his belief in our potential to live in harmony with nature.

Yet for all his involvement in contemporary culture, Hughes has experienced a decline in reader and scholarly interest. Tastes have changed; English poets today often content themselves with a language that strokes the middle class with safe, cozy scenes where vision is restricted to the ordinary, while American poets often become involved in a narrow postmodern investigation of the limits of language. Hughes's reception is especially endangered in

America for two reasons. Five of his six major volumes of adult poetry since *Crow* (1970–71) are not available, for Harper-Collins and Viking-Penguin have decided not to offer second printings. At this moment, the only post-*Crow* volume available in the U.S. is the recent *Wolfwatching* (both cloth and paper from Farrar, Straus and Giroux). Equally damaging is the fallout from restrictions Hughes and his sister Olwyn placed on copyright permissions for the unpublished works of Sylvia Plath, Hughes's first wife. These restrictions regularly draw the ire of American biographers and feminists. Hughes's poetry may be undergoing a temporary decline, but not for want of intrinsic merit.

The central conviction that we live simultaneously in both the inner and the outer worlds informs Hughes's poetry. Hughes develops this idea in the second of his "Myth and Education" essays, reprinted in this volume. Although he recognizes that ours is a postmodern world where language is a very unreliable messenger, Hughes writes poems that are profound acts of faith in humans. Throughout the thirty-five years of his career, he has repeatedly asserted in both poems and essays that our imaginative gifts and our ability to communicate through language constitute our greatest resources for exploring and enjoying the moment-by-moment intersection of inner and outer worlds, and for realizing our individual and cultural potential. The consciousness that grants humans freedom beyond the rote satisfaction of instinctual desires can express itself only through language; through language one may purposefully connect inner and outer worlds, organize and direct one's life, and question and revise outdated perceptions that inhibit historical progress. Each volume of Hughes's poetry offers thematic and structural guides to achieving self-comprehension and living harmoniously in a culture that—if we work at creating it—can reflect our most worthy aspirations and goals. This sometimes entails showing us how to wrestle with psychic and cultural demons that can inhibit our progress or permanently maim the soul.

Hughes's willingness to wrestle with these demons has made him controversial. In the work of many contemporary poets today, nature is etherized by urban sameness and minimal involvement, or benignly spread out against a sky suitable only for a walk in the park, or captured with a few sprinklings of imagery that might appear in a field guide or tourist brochure. Worse, a myopic concern with the failure of language can create in poetry a hopelessness so pervasive that the historical, political, socioeconomic, and environmental forces shaping our lives are never engaged. Hughes will not sanitize experience, nor will he retreat because a devalued language occasionally fails us. He finds life eminently worth living to the fullest and the deepest, and accepts the poet's responsibility to forge a language equal to the human capacity for growth and resistant to cries of futility. The adventure quest, the structuring principle of Hughes's major poetic sequences, is indigenous to our health; throughout Western literature this quest motif has critiqued the meek and security-minded.

The integrity of Hughes scholarship rests on the willingness of the reader/critic to engage the poetry fully and deeply. Critics praised the formalism in his first two collections, *The Hawk in the Rain* (1957) and *Lupercal* (1960). But when he searched global mythology and literature for ways to tap the psyche's deepest roots and critique a corrosive and painfully uprooted contemporary culture, Hughes's formal dexterity and enormous gifts for graphic imagery and arresting metaphor caused many critics to bail out. With a degree in cultural anthropology from Cambridge (1954), Hughes became very adept at adapting themes and techniques from world folklore and mythology to poetry. He quickly outstripped both Oxbridge critics trained in Leavisite evaluations of the tradition of moral realism and American critics habituated to New Critical formalism.

According to M. L. Rosenthal, modern poetry represented a "concentrated effort to re-establish vital continuities with whatever in the past is myth-making, wonder-contemplating, and strength-giving, and to discover widened, fresher meanings."[2] In effecting this, the modern poet draws from the resources and achievements of global culture; Donald Davie stresses this point in "The Poet in the Imaginary Museum."[3] Yet many contemporary critics failed to assimilate Rosenthal's and Davie's points. Prepared for a few Chinese ideograms, Dattas and Dayadhvams, they expected almost everything else to come from their university training in the Greco-Roman-Christian tradition of Western culture.

When Hughes in the sixties developed a nonrealistic style wrought from an amalgam of Kafkaesque and Tibetan surrealism, combined the responses of Christian catechisms with invocations and metaphysical meditations from the Upanishads, and borrowed the formal extravagances, fantastical events, and instantaneous perceptual changes from Zen Buddhism, shamanistic and trickster folklore, he left faint-hearted critics stupefied. The American poets Gary Snyder and W. S. Merwin, whose poetry synthesizes similar areas of our global culture but without Hughes's graphic imagery and muscular language, have usually been more appreciated by their American critics. Nevertheless, reviews of new Hughes volumes had to be written in the haste of newspaper deadlines, and most often the result, instead of expressions of humility from those out of their depth, or provisional grapplings with the text, expressed a peevish irritability from critical emperors exposed in the threadbare clothes of outdated university educations. Reviewers and academics could identify unsettling violence in the graphic imagery, but few could move beyond their limitations to discover the causes and purposes of the violence. The convenient way out for the harried newspaper critic and stature-conscious academic was the biographical fallacy, skewed to an ad hominem pitch.

Having labeled Hughes a nihilist in the early 1970s, critics such as David Holbrook and Calvin Bedient have had little to say about the very sanguine nature poetry that Hughes published in *Remains of Elmet* (1979),

Moortown (1979) and *River* (1983).[4] After painting themselves into a corner of dismissiveness, these critics prefer either silence or a scurrilous rearguard tactic of special pleading. They justify their dismissal of Hughes by abstracting and sandwiching together poems with violent imagery from Hughes's recent work and topping the mélange with a sauce of negativism. Others, however, were willing to probe beyond the limits of their university educations.

The best Hughes criticism exists in full-length studies. Keith Sagar at the University of Manchester wrote the first critical study of Hughes. The second edition of his *The Art of Ted Hughes* (Cambridge, 1978) synthesizes most of Hughes's intellectual and stylistic influences from the beginnings through *Cave Birds* into concise, readable prose. With California librarian Stephen Tabor, Sagar has produced an elegant and exhaustive bibliography of Hughes's poetry, essays, children's work, interviews, recordings, and so on, through 1980 (London: Mansell; New York: H. W. Wilson, 1983). They plan an updated edition with Mansell in 1996.

Ekbert Faas's *Ted Hughes: The Unaccommodated Universe* (Santa Barbara: Black Sparrow, 1980) is important for several reasons. His second chapter, "Poetics," graphs Hughes's transformation "from an empathetic miniaturist of plants, animals and men into a visionary spellmaker of polyhistoric dimensions and sweeping vatic gestures," through the adoption of a "multicultural aesthetics," a combination of Oriental "flash vision," a physical language akin to tribal societies and the origins of human speech, and a belief in the "imagination's conjuring powers" that in part derives from his study of shamanistic rites. In the central chapters of his book, Faas applies his "multicultural aesthetics" to *Crow* and *Gaudete* as he focuses on the underworld journey to recover the desecrated bride—Hughes's poetic response to the deaths of his first wife, Sylvia Plath (1963), and Assia Gutmann Wevill (1969). Faas's interviews with Hughes concerning *Crow* and *Gaudete*, reprinted as appendix II of his volume, are essential for any Hughes scholar.

Terry Gifford at Bretton Hall College, Yorkshire, and Neil Roberts of Sheffield University, published *Ted Hughes: A Critical Study* with Faber in 1981. Their somewhat Leavisite approach evaluates individual poems to determine the best of Hughes's opus, responds to charges of violence in the poetry, and determines the main facets of Hughes's style. The American critic Stuart Hirschberg in 1981 published *Myth in the Poetry of Ted Hughes* (Dublin: Wolfhound Press, 1981), a helpful source study that concentrates on the shaman, Trickster, and White Goddess consort figures in the poetry. Craig Robinson found Hughes engaged in a quest to define responsible adulthood as he applied Heidegger in his *Ted Hughes as Shepherd of Being* (New York: St. Martin's Press, 1989).

My first book, *The Poetry of Ted Hughes: Form and Imagination* (Iowa City: University of Iowa Press, 1986), focused on the structure of each major volume, the Oriental influences, and concentrated upon a three-stage development from a 1950s New Critical formalism to a 1960s mythic surrealism and finally a mystic landscape poetry from the late 1970s through *River* (1983). My Twayne *Ted Hughes* volume (Boston: G. K. Hall, 1991) focused on continuities in Hughes's poetry, especially in language, nature, and environmental concerns, from the early poetry through *Wolfwatching* (1989).

Because chapters in the above-mentioned critical studies tend to be lengthy as they synthesize Hughes's enormous intellectual and stylistic influences and probe the dense textures and mythic forms of his work, and because these books are readily available in university libraries, I have resisted as much as possible reprinting chapters from them. For this *Critical Essays* volume I have concentrated on substantive, insightful journal responses to major adult poetry volumes that are not as conveniently available.

I have also resisted reprinting articles written for Sagar's two international conferences on Hughes at Manchester University in 1980 and 1990, collected in *The Achievement of Ted Hughes* (Manchester: Manchester University Press; Athens: University of Georgia Press, 1983) and *The Challenge of Ted Hughes*. *Achievement*, a first-rate collection, is available in university libraries; at this writing *Challenge* is under consideration at a British press. *Achievement* contains important essays on Hughes and Blake (Sagar), the farming poems in *Moortown* (Robinson), the trickster in *Crow* (Jarold Ramsey), and the *Cave Birds* mythology (Graham Bradshaw), as well as solid specialty studies on Hughes's relationship to Movement verse (Annie Schofield), East European poets (Michael Parker), Shakespeare (Bradshaw), Sylvia Plath (Faas), Redgrove and Heaney (Gifford/Roberts), shamanism (Michael Sweeting), drama (Fred Rue Jacobs), and children's poetry (Keith Cushman).

My strategy in this *Critical Essays* edition was to concentrate on the history of Hughes's reception in reviews and journals to delineate major lines of scholarly interpretation and controversy: the violence, complex form, history and myth, treatment of women, and the stylistic changes. Because the reviews of Hughes's work graph the waxing and waning of his acceptance and reveal the central critical issues, I attempted a balanced presentation of scholarly studies and reviews in this introduction. Research clarified five historical stages in the reception of Hughes's poetry by scholars and reviewers.

I. *THE HAWK IN THE RAIN* (1957) AND *LUPERCAL* (1960)

Every poet dreams of the sort of reception that greeted *The Hawk in the Rain*, but few garner such enthusiastic praise for a first volume. Early in 1957 the Poetry Center of the Young Men's and Young Women's Hebrew Association of New York, with W. H. Auden, Marianne Moore, and Stephen Spender as judges, chose *Hawk* over 286 other entries for first prize: publication by Harper & Brothers. In May, Faber and Faber, with congratulations from T. S. Eliot, accepted *Hawk* for their fall list. Within two months of the 18

September release date, Hughes had gleaned very positive reviews from almost every major London and New York newspaper and magazine. *Hawk* created such a splash in part because its poems towered over the timid and tidy poetry of the period, including the thin, urbane wit of Movement poets such as Larkin, Amis, and Wain. Hughes dared to treat major themes: love, war, death, and the possibility of transcendence. The reviews identified the main facets of Hughes's early style.

Most reviewers praised the fresh originality of conception, the vitality and dramatic immediacy of execution, the strength of intellectual content, the concentrated passion of feeling, and the power of the imagery and metaphors. Robin Skelton lauded Hughes's "fine control over logic and feeling"; he predicted "the emergence of a major poet" from the compression and passion of a language that, like the work of Angries writers Osborne and Sillitoe, "reflects in form and content the violence and tension of our days." John Press wrote that Hughes "has clearly assimilated the work of the best modern poets," and W. S. Merwin enjoyed the echoes of masters such as Hopkins, Graves, Yeats, and Dylan Thomas precisely because Hughes always took these echoes into original territory, so that the poems never "slipp[ed] into any of the expected varieties of contemporary poetry."[5]

Many probed even deeper and sensed in Hughes what Edwin Muir wrote in one of the very first reviews to reach print: "His distinguishing power is sensuous, verbal and imaginative; at his best the three are fused together."[6] What Muir saw as a fusion of thought and feeling, a perception echoed in the reviews by Fuller, Alvarez, Hough, and *TLS*,[7] was the very recognizable formalism of the American New Criticism, which Hughes had absorbed by reading the poetry and essays of John Crowe Ransom.[8] Fuller spoke of a "true originality of conception, and a density of execution which represents a real exploration of the complexities of the subjects." Hough perhaps came closest to the truth:

> The first impression is one of great verbal vitality not always under control; but the second is pure poetic intelligence. The phrase poetic intelligence really does mean something; it means not the kind of intelligence that condenses a few clever critical observations into verse, but the kind that can penetrate and transform. . . . [Such poems] are very unlike the current philosophic-epigrammatic mode with its anxiety to make a point—a two-line point after the statutory ration of descriptive imagery. What these poems have to "say" runs all through them . . . keeps up a high tension throughout. . . .

Several reviewers expressed reservations about unevenness—occasional lapses into heated rhetoric, or patches where the syntax becomes tortuous or where verbs clot the line or shout their energies too boisterously. These excesses resulted from Hughes's absorption of the New Criticism and the high value it placed on Shakespearean/Jacobean drama and the metaphysical poets. As a student Hughes had acquired a deep love for Shakespeare, especially the direct, passionate language of tragic heroes under stress. A few critics writing in academic journals in 1958, especially W. I. Carr and Alan Brownjohn, dismissed *Hawk* for what they saw as a violent, combative gesturing without moral commitment (Carr), a "slangy, self-consciously turbulent diction," and "a raw, sex-and-violence imagery" (Brownjohn).[9]

To have mastered at age twenty-seven the very difficult, reigning school of formalism in a first volume of poetry suggests superior talent and poetic gifts. In his second volume, *Lupercal*, Hughes revealed another facet of his talent: an unwillingness to repeat a style he had just succeeded in mastering. Like his American counterparts Lowell, Merwin, Olson, Plath, Rich, and Sexton, Hughes underwent a major stylistic renovation in the late fifties. He found that formalism distanced the expression of personal emotion and demanded a closure that resolved all onto an ahistorical aesthetic plane. This program could not express unresolved human anxiety over international crises like the Suez, Soviet suppressions of democratic revolts in Hungary, and, most of all, the Cold War's chronic threat of world annihilation.

Meanwhile, England after World War II was reduced to a second-rate world power, forced to dismantle its colonial empire in a climate of chronic unemployment and hard currency shortages, and adjusting to its slowly rebuilt cities with a tweedy resignation mixed with nostalgic memories of the past. Given his Cambridge education in cultural anthropology, Hughes found himself reading pre-conquest English history and taking the long view of the English national character. *Lupercal* reflects his appreciation of the survival abilities shared by humans and animals, and his probing, given the thirty million killed in the war, of the relationships among apathy, survival, and aggression.

Reviewers praised *Lupercal* lavishly. John Holmes best expressed the vividness and immediacy that most noted: the poet is so immersed in the freshness and vividness of the poem's experience that he "all but becomes what he observes." The most discerning recognized that Hughes was trying to discover the extent and the limits of our relationship with animals by facing squarely what Peter Davison called "the beast in all of us." Thus he could awaken a sense of the dark animal magic in us and suggest that we mimic his artistry in the volume by controlling the more ferocious, terrifying manifestations of this power. Many recognized Hughes's compassionate portraits of humans in the volume, and Graham Hough suggested a deliberate balancing of animal predation and human dignity in *Lupercal*'s organization, with the poet's compassion and feeling for the humans evidenced especially in poems like "A Woman Unconscious."[10] One further insightful step concerning these juxtapositions between humans and animals would have caused critics to recognize Hughes's belief in the human capacity to transform brute nature into enduring civilization in Nicholas Ferrer, Crag Jack, the Retired Colonel, and perhaps even the trusting tramp.

Alvarez affirmed that in *Lupercal* Hughes's violence "is now wholly contained by his artistic resources." But Hough and Skelton, while strong in their praise, worried over what they considered an obsessive concentration on violence. Of the few negative *Lupercal* reviews, only John Press, while admiring the stoic endurance in portraits of humans, accused Hughes of what he thought to be a "preoccupation with power and violence regarded almost as ends-in-themselves."[11]

Though studies of Hughes's poetry in academic journals were slow to appear until the mid-sixties, A. E. Dyson's "Ted Hughes," the first journal examination to reach print (1959), is remarkable for its delineation of some of the main characteristics of Hughes's early style, and keen in its recognition that Hughes's poems are probes and meditations, explorations to one side or the other of the boundaries between human and animal energy, with the poet sometimes wholly absorbed in the experience of the animal, or wholly concentrated within the human perspective, or resting in some intermediary position. Dyson praised Hughes's "quest for resilience and endurance" and his identification with elemental energy to triumph over circumstance and provide a guarantee of being and life. For Dyson, Hughes's powerful and unmistakably individual voice was "the most distinctive we have heard in poetry since Dylan Thomas," to be admired for its resolute desire to swim "against the prevailing currents of detachment, irony, urbanity and Neo-Augustan influences" that characterized Movement poets such as Davie, Larkin, and Wain.[12]

Two years later, however, J. M. Newton followed the complaints about Hughes's rhetoric stated in the review essays of Brownjohn and Press, and thus began the scholarly debate about "overdone virility and overdone violence." Newton grudgingly allowed "the relief of an occasional vivid experience" in Hughes's poetry, but lamented a tendency toward very ordinary description that alternates uneasily with overwriting, a "flogging [of] his inspiration" that reveals the need for "a greater inner stillness."[13]

In 1965 Frederick Grubb, however, offered a much more probing examination of Hughes's early poetry, and praised Hughes's art as one where Nature is given equal status with humans; thus Hughes rejects both the Laurentian desire to "lapse out" into an almost anti-intellectual blood consciousness, and the opposite extreme, the use of nature merely to demonstrate human concerns. Grubb concluded that Hughes "greets the intellect as in league with, though not subordinate to, nature, and his poems are often models of the ordering of experience." Especially in *Lupercal*, Grubb found that intelligence and respect for the otherness of nature and animal life play equal parts, with a very sophisticated use of feeling to guide thought to a balanced appraisal of areas of kinship. Nature and human intelligence interact without facile merging within a richly complex vision that normally includes an ample sense of a historical continuum rooted in a distinctly English environment and tradition.[14]

Stan Smith in 1975 expanded on this sense of a historical continuum in Hughes and offered the most provocative reading of the early poetry. For Smith the colorless "anaesthetized poetry of the fifties" is best understood by considering Herbert Marcuse's "one-dimensional universe." Applying Marcuse, Smith wrote that "the geo-political settlement, conceived at Yalta and Potsdam, brought to birth at Fulton, and confirmed in the Truman Doctrine, seemed to have created a social universe insulated from historical refutation, in which history itself had come to a stop. Nothing in the future, it appeared, could rescind the status quo established and consolidated by the Cold War." Nevertheless Smith found the postwar "social deadlock" and closed political and emotional universe filled with contradictions and energies repressed by the smug confidence of an "amoral meritocracy." He considered Hughes of all postwar British poets "the most honest in his attempts to come to terms with the restless and uncomprehended violence that continued to fret beneath the surface of an apparently convalescent European sensibility."[15]

For Smith "Hawk Roosting," one of the more troubling poems in *Lupercal*, is not a revelation of some Hitlerian drive within the poet, but an accurate depiction of Cold War totalitarian authority, what Orwell feared in *1984*. The hawk also embodies the "paranoia which is the normal condition of the bourgeois soul here and now, locked in a State that allows its members no privacy or autonomy." The poem's irony reveals that "the meritocratic free spirit is the more securely enslaved by its ignorance of its dependence" upon creation, time, history.

The overdeveloped superego in such a society turns instinct back upon itself, with explosive consequences, in such poems as "Macaw and Little Miss." The poet's own drive toward a return to real historical development is mediated and distanced, according to Smith, by analogies with animals. Yet most of these animal poems, such as "The Jaguar," repeatedly court deeply "ambiguous images of the tension between boundless inner potency and external limitation." Often Hughes's placing of animals and heroes in past centuries or in an archaic world reveals a nostalgia for a time where real historical developments happened, and for Smith this expresses a "nostalgia" for the *future* breakdown of the stalemated Cold War society, even while the formal artistry of the poems as wolf masks works to propitiate and control the energies released.

II. *WODWO* (1967) AND *CROW* (1970–72)

Nineteen sixty-two was a watershed year for Hughes scholarship. Alfred Alvarez, in a feisty introduction to his anthology *The New Poetry*, brought the violence issue into prominence as he lamented the British poets and critics who adhere to "the gentility principle." This he defined as "a belief that life is always more or less orderly, people always more or less polite, their emotions and habits more or less decent and more or less controllable; that God, in short, is more or less good." Behind this attitude, wrote Alvarez, sat the bored, underpaid, welfare state Englishman with his stiff upper lip. The wry ironies and urbanity of Movement poets—most of them university teachers, librarians, or civil servants—reflected this genteel attitude.

Alvarez considered "gentility" a deliberate refusal to confront the realities of the Holocaust and the millions of soldiers who died in World War II. Somehow a "muddle through" attitude would outface the evil without and the aggressive libido within. Alvarez called for a poetry that would drop this pretense and confront the historical forces without and the undisciplined energies within that wrought the carnage. He believed American modernist experimentalism was more likely to foster serious examinations of the postwar present. In his introduction, Alvarez named Hughes the only postwar British poet whose verse was equal to the task of examining the modern psyche and its violent historical context.[16]

Alvarez's introduction and his 1965 *Encounter* article placed many British critics in an uncomfortable position, for to champion Hughes's poetry seemed to sell out traditional English values. Others, retrenching to a stubborn reassertion of the worth of contemporary British poetry, were less prone to praise Hughes. A year after Alvarez's introduction, David Holbrook coupled his distaste for the salvos of critical "trend setters" with a response to Alvarez on the violence issue, and prepared the ground for subsequent negative treatments of Hughes in journal essays. Holbrook called Alvarez a "trend setter" who encourages poetry that embodies "the depressive attitude," a "histrionic indulgence in a despisal of life," and accused Hughes of sentimental self-pity that engulfs all human attempts at conscious choice and action in fogs of *hwyl*—portentous rhetorical bluff, as in the poetry of Dylan Thomas.[17]

Though many critics have noted the deep irony that indicts rather than supports the hawk's arrogant monologue in "Hawk Roosting" (*Lupercal*),[18] the poem received pride of place in a 1965 BBC Third Programme discussion of violence in poetry. Here Philip Hobsbaum asserted that the hawk embodies the poet's arrogant attitude toward his audience.[19] By the mid-1960s Holbrook and Hobsbaum had articulated the central critical response of those who did not favor Hughes's poetry: corner Hughes on the violence question and insinuate the biographical fallacy. The poems' graphic imagery thus becomes a revelation of Hughes's own blighted imagination, pure and simple. One need only ignore the many poems that evince awe and reverence for nature; separate instances of graphic imagery from formal and mythic contexts meant to control the energies released; inject the biographical fallacy; and list these instances of violent imagery as irrefutable proof of a warped mind.

In the introduction to their 1963 volume of essays on practical criticism, C. Brian Cox and A. E. Dyson, the founding editors of *Critical Quarterly*, wrote that the analysis of poetry "should aim to deal precisely with the total meaning" and avoid "that contemptuous tone of dismissal which has been one of the worst features of criticism during the last decades." For Cox and Dyson "discrimination, the ability to differentiate between degrees of excellence, can be taught as part of appreciation, not depreciation. Many analysts in the past have spent too much time explaining what is wrong with a poem. This hypercritical attitude can do great damage both to reader and poet."[20] Though Hughes is not mentioned in this introductory essay, Cox and Dyson anticipated what was about to happen in much criticism of Hughes's poetry since the mid-1960s. The biographical fallacy, raised to an ad hominem pitch, frequently substituted for penetrating analysis and patient evaluation by those who felt negative about Hughes's poetry.

While critics debated the question of violence in the mid-1960s, Hughes was extending his poetic resources to mesh his anthropology studies in Western and Oriental cultures with a new surrealistic style wrought from his reading of folklore, Kafka and Lorca, and shamanic initiation accounts recorded in Eliade. To this Hughes added much reading in Jung, Freud, Laing, and other staples of psychoanalytic criticism. The first fruits of this new and complex style appeared in *Wodwo*, Hughes's third poetry volume.

Hughes's prefatory note about employing a "single adventure" in *Wodwo* signaled what has since become his standard practice: the deliberate organization of poems in major volumes around seasonal cycles and mythic quest motifs. A. Mollema observed that "Ted Hughes's poems should not be read as separate, individual units"; they "show a considerable degree of interdependence because of the mythical elements that they share." Mollema believes that one ought to apply Northrop Frye's "encyclopaedic" thematic mode to Hughes, who speaks in more extended patterns that mark him as "a spokesman of society." Hence Mollema believes that "to rip [Hughes's poems] out of context is inevitably to deprive them of some of their meaning." While agreeing with Derwent May's observation that Hughes has an "exceptional gift for making words act out the processes they are describing,"[21] Mollema reminds us that language and other attributes of style in Hughes reinforce mythic dimensions consciously invoked by the poet to function as key determinants of meaning.[22]

The few reviewers who disliked *Wodwo* complained that the poetry was obscure, inaccessible, or even impenetrably overwritten, and that the volume lacks a coherent controlling vision.[23] Most praised Hughes's breakthrough into an original, distinctive voice, a powerfully intense blend of the surreal and the macabre, an adumbration of what Howard Sergeant called "the dark forces and energies which lurk below the surface in us all." Jeremy Robson wrote that though the social concern often "takes surrealistic somersaults into fantasy . . . , the power and brooding intensity of the vision remain riveting."[24] The few reviewers who commented on the tripartite organization of *Wodwo* expressed bafflement or found the divisions arbitrary.

Without commenting on the relevance of Hughes's cryptic "Author's Note" for the organization of *Wodwo*, Anthony Hecht in his short review perceptively suggested that the volume follows ritual initiations where "the initiate was made dramatically and terribly to confront his deepest animal nature." Hecht found *Wodwo* a demonstration of "the frightening and insoluble paradox that man at his peril . . . denies his animal nature, but at the same time that very nature, when it gets out of hand, makes him bestial and hateful and can also kill him. By the same token, man's consciousness, while useful, is also dangerous, and when divorced from his deepest nature is feeble and useless." Robin Skelton, in an equally penetrating review, says that in *Wodwo* the protagonists "come face to face with their shadow selves" to learn that "the drama of the unconscious is more potent than that of the conscious, and that our most intense experience and struggle occur on the level of instinct in the darker places of the mind."[25]

Other reviewers focused more precisely upon the animal poems in *Wodwo*, and explored the very tantalizing topic of whether these poems present some primal energy shared by humans and animals—whether the animals are metaphors for human concerns, or creatures in their own right whose struggles arouse Hughes's empathy. J. M. Newton found most poems carefully shaped to lead the reader beyond the everyday toward a "fresh perception of the other . . . and of its power and centrality" that awakens in the reader "a fuller possession of his own power and centrality." For Newton the violence in these poems was neither gratuitous nor sensational, but an attempt to awaken the reader from the world of comfort and habit. Sidney Bolt disagreed, finding only a passive lapse into the animal's instinctual automatism at the heart of the animal poems.[26]

For Derwent May the brilliant metaphors and captivating rhythms of the animal poems simultaneously present the "sensuous drama" of the animal as well as "all kinds of human striving and ease." Graham Martin believed that "the animals aren't there for their own sake but as metaphors for a particular human vision, embodying either a sometimes active, sometimes baffled primal energy, or an unthinking predatory violence, awful in both senses, whose human application should need no spelling out. Both are aspects of the one vision, sometimes worshipped for its strength, spontaneity, and delicate quickness, sometimes feared for its unreflecting automatism, its dangerous incapacity for change." Only Jeremy Robson and Donald Davie noted that the personal struggles with violent energies in animals and humans often extended to social and national issues (as in "Karma" and "Out"); Davie wondered if Hughes, like Lawrence before him, was meditating on whether anything of the English tradition survived 1918 "apart from naked and stoical violence."[27]

The most important early essay on the very difficult poems of *Wodwo*, appearing amazingly within a year of the work's publication, was Daniel Hoffman's "Talking Beasts: The 'Single Adventure' in the Poems of Ted

Hughes." Through an expert examination of Hughes's recent reviews of books on Norse mythology and shamanism, and applications of Robert Graves's *White Goddess*, Hoffman concluded that the "single adventure" organization concerned a mythic quest, a confrontation with our own often violent instinctual life, and the psychological experience of recognizing the inevitability of death. Regeneration, only hoped for in *Wodwo*, is tempered in a postwar culture that offers neither comforting beliefs in immortality, nor the security of a supportive tribe or community to return to.[28]

P. Strauss examined Hughes's struggle in *Wodwo* to locate an area in humans that is "free, undetermined," as opposed to the instinctual determinism of animals. This leads to very substantive discussions of "Wodwo," "Fern," and "The Bear" as examples of the potentially self-determining freedom of humans, which contrasts with the animal determinism of "Second Glance at a Jaguar" and the earlier "Hawk Roosting." In 1983 I graphed more closely the shamanic and surrealistic withdrawal from Western culture in Part I, a movement repeated in the Part II stories and extended to include the recognition of death and dismemberment in the Part II radio play *The Wound*. I discovered an Oriental regeneration in the more serene, Zen-influenced nature poems of Part III.[29]

Crow created quite a stir. Its publication marked both the high point of Hughes's reception by critics, and the solidification of negative opinion that foreshadowed the decline in interest in his poetry later in the 1970s. Many reviewers praised *Crow* as one of the most exciting and important books of poetry of the decade, a dazzling technical achievement combined with what Sanford Dorbin called a powerful vision of "a world sufficient to the terror and guilt that characterize this century." "The headlines are on its side," wrote Christopher Porterfield.[30]

But the substance and craft of *Crow* generated considerable controversy and contradictory responses from reviewers. The main areas of conflict included the violence, the unfamiliar style and form, authorial control, and whether myth constitutes a retreat from history. These became the main lines of scholarly divergence on the merits of Hughes's work later in the decade. Newton lauded the metaphysical reach of Hughes's thought in *Crow*, while others (Hamilton, Stanford, Utz) complained the volume contained weak thinking and crude ideas. Neil Roberts praised the growth in moral awareness in Crow, the development of conscience and acquisition of a soul, while others (Fuller, Hamilton, Holmes, Cooley, Robinson/Simms, Utz) found the poems amoral, irresponsible, lacking in sincerity or commitment to real human problems.[31] While most praised the survival imperative in Crow, some found that applications to the human world reduce all to brutish instinct or even convey a nihilistic vision.[32] Alvarez continued his divisive taunts at British poets in his review of *Crow* by stating that Hughes is the sole British poet to join "the select band of survivor-poets whose work is adequate to the destructive reality we inhabit." The Alvarez review, one of the first to reach print, prompted retorts from many subsequent reviewers of *Crow*.[33]

Opinions on Hughes's language and craft in *Crow* also diverged widely. May, Lask, and Carruth found the language banal, glib, or careless, whereas Stuart and Kessler concluded that the volume contained a very sophisticated self-reflexivity, sufficient to convey the realization that our consciousness, like Crow's, creates our world through words, and words can liberate as well as blind.[34] Some objected that, unlike Hughes's early work, the Crow poems lacked closure, control, or formal tightness. Others, mindful that poets who compose longer sequences organize them by developing themes and motifs, found Hughes in firm control of his material. A few noted the presence of American Indian Trickster mythology, but without commenting on how Hughes's use of this material itself becomes a meaning-bearing organizational principle, as I have done in the *Crow* chapter of my first Hughes book.

Stephen Spender and Marjorie Perloff, after praising some of Hughes's technical accomplishments in *Crow*, rejected the volume because they believed it presented a totally bleak vision of human nature, unrelieved by positive alternatives. Charles Molesworth complained that "we are deprived of any comforting tradition of discourse to guide or relieve our attention to tone." Yet Barry Wallenstein pointed toward Hughes's very dextrous control of form, noting that "Crow is a hero in the mock epic tradition."[35] Hughes certainly ridicules human foibles through the satiric exaggerations of Crow's escapades. Satires and mock epics offer reductive and exaggerated views of humans, but they present these reductions seriously, in the hope of awakening the reader to healthier norms. Would one expect to find positive alternatives in the closed satiric universes of *Hudibras, The Rape of the Lock*, Molière, Greek satyr plays, or Pynchon novels?

Satiric traditions guide the tone in *Crow*, as I suggest in my essay reprinted in this volume.[36] Part of the problem is that Hughes developed Crow's character to embody so many of the weaker traits of humans that he becomes "one of us," as Conrad's Marlow would have it. Crow in his guile bends satiric forms to the breaking point, as did Tartuffe in the final act of Molière's satire. But the world of Crow also owes much to the fantasy world of trickster narratives, in which hilariously broad comic exaggerations and transgressions of taboos convey at the same time an implied censure of such buffoonery.

Terry Eagleton dismissed *Crow* because he believes myth lacks historicity: it creates "a refuge from reality." Eagleton found Hughes committed "to a world view in which history can have value only in negative and caricatured form." One could readily argue the reverse: Crow's escapades critique a Western scientific and religious view of reality that, if left unexamined, constitutes our greatest barrier to historical change. Charles Fernandez, in his essay reprinted here, locates Hughes's principal target for *Crow* in Western religion, science, and technology: all attempt to suppress the demonic, which for Plato, Aristophanes, the Eskimo and Jewish traditions, was an essential force, expressed primarily as sexual love, that "not only binds man to woman but also man to God." Fernandez finds Hughes attempting more than a negative critique of history. Crow's comic escapades embody for Fernandez the first steps in an attempt to accept and harness the demonic as "the inspiration to create, procreate, and recreate."[37] Crow's actions, however hilariously misdirected, embody a force engaged in a general housecleaning of dead artifacts in a stalled Western culture, in the process awakening readers to examine their habits and assumptions.

Hughes's attention to the scientific and religious dimensions of Western culture in *Crow* helps explain his use of demonic energy and its violent aspects. The question of violence in Hughes centers on its purpose: is it gratuitous, or a self-indulgent nihilism? Does it attempt to release and accommodate natural energies deemed necessary to civilization, or to critique Western cultural assumptions that produce violence because they cannot harness demonic force for civilizing purposes *before* it becomes violent? Most major Hughes scholars contend that his graphic imagery portrays either the agonized psychic struggle to enlarge one's perceptions, or the consequences of depending upon inadequate defense mechanisms based on rational common sense, religious taboos, or scientific data. These defense mechanisms repress natural human energies to the point of explosion.

In his 1972 British Council monograph, Keith Sagar ended his discussion of *Crow* by claiming that "Hughes cannot take quite seriously any attitude to experience which takes for granted the continuance of our civilization with very much its present structure and values. . . . [for] to assume these things is to ignore or willfully misread the evidence." Sagar believes that Hughes's symbols are not narrowly literary but derive from "totemism, folklore, and the archetypes of Jungian psychology. . . . [They] magically invoke the powers they make manifest . . . [while] the myth controls the energies they release."[38] In "The Poetry Does Not Matter," his contribution to this volume, Sagar charts the development of Hughes's style as a series of attempts to harness and develop the elemental energies within humans in ways that would allow them to adapt harmoniously to the energies of the universe.

It is not difficult to locate in the major symbols of *Wodwo* and in the figure of Crow an extension of what Stan Smith saw in the early poetry: a creative imagination in tense conflict with a culture whose failed beliefs attempt to forestall historical change. Hence in *Crow* Hughes attempts to liberate purposeful energies in the reader while insisting that we reexamine our cultural assumptions. According to David Porter, whose article on Hughes's aesthetics appears in this volume, "for a deadened culture, balance must be restored by primitive recoveries in the imagination. For the poet, balance comes from the deep, energy-giving worlds whose power can be summoned along the path of language." Hence Hughes's "goal is to release the deep animations of the culture rather than to contain his private agonies."[39]

Brenda Megerle finds *Crow* a complex dialogue between Hughes and his culture. She believes that Hughes admires Crow's connectedness with nature's survival energy, but satirizes Western culture's mentalizing of experience. Here "man takes his science-ax to Nature, his mother, and pounds and hacks at her," for *Crow* expresses "Hughes's condemnation . . . of the great faith this world still invests in the analyzing mind." Lawrence Ries, in his extended study of violence in Hughes, concluded that for Hughes humans cannot control and master violence with the intellect; Hughes "offers for a solution an accommodation with [man's] violent nature that depends upon his ability to fuse the intellectual with the instinctual."[40]

A. K. Weatherhead found Hughes's emphasis upon victimization in *Wodwo* and *Crow* an advance in moral concern with "an existence fraught with pain," but rued Hughes's sacrifice of the "superb formal style of his early verse" for the extravagant tonelessness, the "flat and barren verse of *Crow*." Lawrence Kramer argued that Hughes tried to push the natural power of language for mediating and reenacting experience toward a forced, violent transcendence and in the process blurred the signification of objects in his poems. Graham Bradshaw discussed what he considered an almost cynical repudiation of language in *Crow*, and worried over whether Hughes was driving himself toward "a Beckett-like dead end"—the inexpressibility of meaning.[41]

In contrast to the nay-sayers, Seamus Heaney found a place for Hughes within the English tradition of survival and endurance. Heaney recognized in Hughes's poetry "the genius of the language itself," able "to undam the energies of the dialect" and achieve "freedom and naturalness and homeliness." Heaney praised Hughes for his emphasis upon survival and endurance, bedrock values of the English shires, and for continuing a creative dialogue with our failed culture. Hughes is willing "to explore not just the matter of England, but what is the matter with England." According to Heaney, "the loss of imperial power, the failure of economic nerve, the diminished influence of Britain outside Europe, all this has led to a new sense of the shires, a new valuing of the native English experience."[42]

Others focused on the violent energy in the early poetry through *Crow*, while excluding the larger cultural dimensions. Julian Gitzen explored transformations of energy in the early poetry and *Crow*, and David Lodge compared sadomasochistic violence in *Crow* to the caricatures and fantasy world of cartoons, but neither pressed hard enough to discover what Hughes's purpose might have been in these areas. Anthony Libby reduced Hughes to an apocalyptic survivor poet interested only in satisfying "the reptile brain, the limbic node."[43]

Calvin Bedient continued the tendency of negative Hughes criticism to become preoccupied with the violence question in his 1972 essay "On Ted Hughes." In the tradition of yellow journalism, Bedient labeled Hughes a poetic Schopenhauer of the will to live, a "worshipper of the claw" who scorns life and admires only strength. For Bedient, Hughes is a "voyeur of violence" whose cynicism "is slung out like hash" in *Wodwo* and whose nihilism appears in the "tearing mouth" and " 'nothinged' mind" of *Crow*.[44]

Three years later David Holbrook charged Hughes with nihilism a dozen times in his discussion of *Crow*, his second essay on Hughes. Holbrook found Crow a "passive victim, without . . . any power of finding meaning in his world."[45] This is largely true in the Crow sequence as published to date, but Holbrook's mistake lies in *equating* Crow's passivity with Hughes's own views. Throughout his Hughes essays, Holbrook displays a wooden incapacity to recognize how form and style function as guides to and determinants of meaning, especially in Hughes's deft use of poetic subgenres: the surrealism of *Wodwo* and *Gaudete*, and the satiric/mock epic fables and fantasy universe of *Crow*. Holbrook's whole effort depends upon collapsing authorial distance into a simplistic biographical fallacy: the despondency of the persona in Parts I and II of *Wodwo* is Hughes's despondency. For Holbrook, Crow's eyes are Hughes's eyes; therefore the blinkered vision of Crow is Hughes's blinkered vision. (Is Macbeth's or Timon's view of life therefore Shakespeare's?)

In his essays on Hughes, Holbrook specifically names Alvarez for encouraging an extremist "nature poet gone blind" because he championed the examination of violence in his aforementioned "gentility principle" introduction to his 1962 *The New Poetry*. A post hoc fallacy operates here. The subject matter and thematic development of Hughes's poetry derive naturally from his North Country English roots, his nurture in the moors and canals of Yorkshire and in those everlasting dinner conversations about the dead and the survivors of Gallipoli,[46] his Cambridge anthropology training, and his readings in depth psychology. Hughes had earned considerable stature, and with it considerable poetic freedom, after the high praise accorded *Hawk* and *Lupercal*—two years before the Alvarez introduction appeared. The biographical and poetic evidence indicates that Hughes would probably have continued his "single adventure" in precisely the way he did in *Wodwo* and *Crow* whether or not Alvarez printed a single sentence on his poetry. Recognizing Hughes's formal and stylistic craftsmanship would help Holbrook notice that Hughes pilots a course parallel to the philosophical biology of Portmann, Plessner, Grene, and others who Holbrook believes affirm a creative freedom, self-development, and wonder of the cosmos that he finds antithetical to Hughes's supposed "nihilism." Though no one questions the sincerity of his intentions, Alvarez's spotlighting of the violence question and his radical denigration of all British poetry save Hughes's has damaged the critical reception of his poetry.

III. *GAUDETE* (1977) AND *CAVE BIRDS* (1978)

Many reviewers and scholars already fatigued with complex form and graphic imagery in Hughes found the lecherous escapades of the Reverend Nicholas Lumb in *Gaudete* exasperating. The volume certainly was, as Joyce Carol Oates remarked, "the most controversial work of England's finest contemporary poet." The views of John Bayley and Thomas Lask are typical of the opposition. Bayley praised Hughes's "technical performance" and found the central narrative filled with "gripping pages in a compulsive sequence which one is unable to take one's eyes off." But he rejected the volume because "we become fascinated voyeurs" viewing Hughes's "reductive talent" that "dispenses completely with humanity and the intellect." Even though Lask found the story-telling power "compelling" and "attention-riveting," he asserted that "*Gaudete* does not manage an emotional hold on the reader," and that its violence "seems to exist for its own lurid purposes."[47]

Many reviewers made pointed comments as they dismissed a poet so strongly identified with violence. Robert Pinsky wrote that he couldn't "find anything under all that ketchup except baloney"; Peter Ackroyd complained that he "can't take all this suffering any more" every time he opens a new Hughes book; and Derek Stanford wrote that Hughes is "a walker on the wild side and younger brother to the bride of Frankenstein—who is the highbrow equivalent of our wode-and-sequin spattered punk culture." Geraldine Moyle found the plot "lurid and lascivious," "one long coital odyssey" from an "unflagging stud."[48]

Edwin Brock trashed the hardest. Though Alvarez did not review *Gaudete*, Brock assumed that with each new Hughes book "the publicity department of Hughes Inc. (the company founded by Alvarez, which now pays dividends to many smaller shareholders) goes into operation. . . . One could almost imagine a Board Meeting where a policy decision was taken that every new Hughes poem must give the consumer the expected frisson of volume and violence, blood and guts." Blunt titles often reflected the impatience of reviewers: "Smash and Bash" (Bayley) or "How to Open a Pigeon" (W. H. Pritchard).[49] In one significant case, however, continued reading of *Gaudete* prompted a reversal of opinion: four years after his negative review, Bayley wrote that "*Gaudete* has come to impress itself on me as one of the most remarkable achievements of modern poetry, an achievement in which fantasy—the very odd tale or legend that preoccupied the author—is made as real as life on the farm."[50]

Hughes had taken his late modernist passion for cultural mythography beyond the ken of most critics. Though the detractors conveyed little in the way of substantive commentary, most of the supportive reviewers could only express bafflement at this amalgam of prose poems and cryptic "Epilogue" lyrics. Except two: J. M. Newton and Irvin Ehrenpreis. Newton, comparing *Gaudete* to chapter 40 of Job, said Hughes articulated a sense of religious mystery, of the *"mysterium tremendum* of life," and realized a portion of the "wellnigh daemonic and wholly incomprehensible character of the eternal creative power." Hughes affirmed the *"intrinsic value* of the incomprehensible" in his first successful evocation of the feminine divinity of creation, whose potent glare consumes the persona's consciousness in the final "Epilogue" poems.[51]

Ehrenpreis, expert in late modernist mythography from his work on Lowell, most perceptively identified *Gaudete* as a "myth of death and resurrection," wherein Lumb and his changeling double "call up the problem of body and mind, passion and reason." In the "Prologue," the ailing priestess and her dwarf guardian "stand for the primal forces in our make-up, trying to survive and to keep in touch with our overcultivated selves." Ehrenpreis notes that if the clergyman simply tries to live out his repressions, as Lumb's double does in the central narrative, he "destroys himself and his society. But by suffering for the elemental spirits, he achieves communion with them, purifies himself, and becomes a priest-poet-savior" in the "Epilogue."[52]

The hostile responses to the violent imagery and the difficult form and subject matter of *Gaudete* reduced future journal interest in Hughes to a minimum. Edward Larrissy wrote a short, thin discussion of how Lumb accommodates the feminine and, resurrected, writes love lyrics "from a more open and chastened state of mind." Peter King discussed *Gaudete* briefly in his essay collection *Nine Contemporary Poets*: Lumb heals his divorce from his inner life and achieves wholeness through a reliance on his inner self. Neither Larrissy nor King explored the "Epilogue" poems in detail, or the cultural critique behind the violence in the central narrative.[53]

One of the most important journal articles from the *Gaudete* period is Don McKay's, reprinted in this collection. McKay graphed clearly the progress of Hughes's aesthetic from *Crow* through *Gaudete*, including the unpublished 1971 *Orghast* drama and the 1975 *Season Songs* for children. For McKay, Hughes from the time of Crow's lyric gesture in "Glimpse" strove for language that, like music, would commune with natural forces. But the mental tyrant Holdfast (cf. *Orghast*) rules society (note the technology associated with men in *Gaudete*: guns, binoculars, telescopes, artificial insemination of cattle). Lumb dispenses a renewing energy that, after a violent explosion from the senescent males, finally achieves a balance in the "Interlude," after which Lumb attempts songs of the earth in the "Epilogue." Hence McKay believes that "the central paradox of *Gaudete* is that the goddess's revenge is also her gift or blessing, as the title, meaning 'rejoice,' implies."[54]

Fortunately, major studies of Hughes began to appear after *Gaudete* to probe even deeper into the form and content of Hughes's works, and the relationship of the violence to psychology and Western culture. In the second edition of *The Art of Ted Hughes*, Sagar discussed the mythic background to

Gaudete at length—Dionysus, Isis, Hercules, and Graves's *White Goddess*. For Sagar as for Hughes, these myths express not modernist arcana, but permanent realities, relationships between humans and the cosmos that we lose contact with "under the influence of all the isms which have conditioned our culture." The sterility of the society in the central narrative depicts this. For Sagar, Lumb is "pure instinct" needing to recover "the lost sense of the sacredness of nature . . . in all its fullness of being." Sagar also offered the first extended discussion of the "Epilogue" poems, in which he found Lumb seeking atonement with nature, not possession; through his suffering he tries "to reestablish his life in the most basic realities of his nature and the world's."[55]

Faas linked the plot of *Gaudete* with the deaths of first wife Sylvia Plath and with Assia Gutmann Wevill, the woman Hughes left Plath for, and charted the hero's descent to the underworld to recover the lost bride. Connecting the "Epilogue" poems with Hughes's readings in South Indian *vacana* poetry, Faas reads these poems as deep meditations meant to realize a new divinity on the plane of Oriental Enlightenment. In my first Hughes study, I discussed the surreal dreamscape of the central narrative as the release of instinct in the celibate prelate's psyche, culminating in a final recognition of the limits of pure instinct. The "Epilogue" poems record the reborn Lumb's attempt to recognize in the realm of spirit and consciousness the vast extent of his dependence upon nature, presented as a feminine deity that controls both his inner cycles and the cycles of the natural world.[56]

Eagleton in his review of *Gaudete* argued that Hughes's language, "locked tight in the bursting fullness of its presence," lacks a self-reflexive awareness of its limits. It "mirrors" a realist problematic rather than constructs its own program.[57] While this is true of the central narrative's critique of the patriarchy, Eagleton followed the special pleading tactics of others by devoting not a single sentence to the "Epilogue." The humble self-examination and reverence toward nature of the reborn Lumb in the "Epilogue" revises the male eroticism and fetishism of the female in the central narrative, and in so doing critiques its language of power and mastery. Rand Brandes, in a new treatment of *Gaudete* included in this collection, discusses how the "Epilogue" attempts to deconstruct the central narrative's objectivization of the female by offering "a fluid, open and decentered text informed by matriarchal mythopoetics."

In *Ted Hughes as Shepherd of Being*, Craig Robinson offered an insightful discussion of the "Epilogue" poems. Robinson looks at Hughes in the context of Heidegger's assertions about language: when language withers to surfaces—facts, rational categories, and stereotypes—it loses its plenitude, its ability to embrace what Heidegger calls the holy house of Being. For Robinson the goddess in the "Epilogue" is Being itself, unencompassable, incarnate and transcendent, both concealed and revealed. As the renewed Lumb struggles to recognize his complete dependence upon the mysterious footfalls of Being, language becomes an utterly honest inquiry into this mysterious plenitude, renewed in the spare, taut poems just as Lumb is renewed.[58]

Reviews of the hermetic psychodrama *Cave Birds* (1978) were mixed. Some considered the poems obscure, puzzling, or mannered—"enigmas wrapped in riddles," according to Richard Tobias. Many claimed the work lacked unity and coherence: a plot and a realistic setting were always necessary for the generation of British critics trained in Movement verse, and *Cave Birds* seemed to offer neither.[59] Since a few critics exaggerated the violence question beyond proportion in their *Gaudete* reviews, and seemed to get away with it, others began to dismiss Hughes by trotting out prepackaged phrases without grappling at all with the poetry. Christopher Reid bemoaned the "caveman metaphysics" of *Cave Birds*; Robert Nye complained of a persistent mood of "unreflecting savagery" in the poems; and Bedient after two short paragraphs labeled the poems "sublime cartoons of nasty nihilism."[60]

Craig Raine, however, found *Cave Birds* an ambitious and successful attempt to make a psychodrama "convincingly concrete." Martin Booth, appreciating a new "mellowing towards the subject matter" in Hughes, concluded that "his range and virtuosity astonish and his fertility of vision places him not only as a poet but almost a seer" whose work widens our self-comprehension. The most penetrating observation came from Richard Murphy: "perhaps we are being told to change our lives, by giving up the false pride of our male technological mastery, and to become true to the most powerful feminine nature of our inner selves."[61]

Cave Birds received very little attention in academic journals. The most judicious, perceptive treatment appeared in the 1981 Gifford and Roberts *Ted Hughes: A Critical Study*, reprinted in a condensed, definitive version in this collection. Through a patient and balanced discussion of the central image clusters in individual poems and the alchemical dramatic form, Gifford and Roberts conclude that the poems comprise a multileveled sequence; they respond to the Baskin drawings as well as record a psychological transformation in a hero figure where "accounts of real experience—in particular, death and sexual love—" often fuse with "stages in a symbolic adventure." Most importantly, Gifford and Roberts believe that the final marriage with the feminine, brilliantly expressed in "Bride and groom lie hidden for three days," reveals not simply a psychological integration with an anima figure in a purely male quest, but union with a feminine principle "who is both his hitherto imprisoned daimon or inner self and the spirit of material nature."

In other words, the male hero learns of his utter dependence upon natural cycles outside himself; the male intellect's attempt at a cold mastery of nature is a crime that can be rectified only by learning to live in harmony with nature's superior powers and cycles. "The Guide," the "achievement of an intuition, a sure instinct for living" according to Gifford and Roberts, results from the hero's final recognition of his "subjection to the elements."

Stuart Hirschberg provides very helpful and at times intriguing material from Egyptian, shamanic, alchemical, and astrological sources, mixed in interesting ways with Castaneda and crow lore, in the *Cave Birds* section of his 1981 study *Myth in the Poetry of Ted Hughes.*[62] Though at times overwritten or esoteric, Hirschberg's book provides a fairly reliable guide to mythic sources in the poetry.

IV. *REMAINS OF ELMET* (1979) AND *MOORTOWN* (1979)

Remains of Elmet continued Hughes's emphasis upon the primacy and centrality of nature, and a number of reviewers grasped his purpose. Dave Smith noted that in these West Yorkshire landscape poems Hughes tried to effect a rebirth of language by balancing images of laboring in life's prison with "images of genesis, gestation, fecundity, and perseverance." Glyn Hughes praised the healing energies released by Hughes in poems that revealed the volume's central myth: the reclamation by maternal nature of a landscape wounded by "the deadly Platonic way": the "whole ecclesiastical-material achievement" of Methodism and mills, theology and textiles. For Richard Murphy the many uplifting poems of *Elmet*, such as "Cock-Crows," mime the mythic action of returning West Yorkshire to nature after centuries of Industrial Revolution desecration: "now the puritan god has died, and the older Celtic deity is recovering her rites of the sun and the moon." Murphy concluded that "the message of the poems . . . is that the world must be resacralized." The arresting metaphors and "brilliant evocations of moods" in the poems strive to accomplish this resacralization.[63]

Two journal studies of *Elmet* also explore the key area of Hughes's new emphasis upon material nature. Carol Bere concentrated on the biographical poems and their relation to Hughes's BBC essay "The Rock," and found in Hughes's attitude toward the landscape poems a consistent organizing principle—the poet's acceptance of time and change in the nurturing moors and valleys. Patricia Boyle Haberstroh studied the historical dimensions of Hughes's mythmaking in her very comprehensive essay on *Elmet*, and concluded that "Hughes draws a direct line from the early Christian Angles to the nineteenth-century industrialists, seeing the beginning and end of a cycle, the technological abuse of nature a final consequence of the Anglican conversion to Christianity and the latest example of turning the landscape into a waste." As "the mills and chapels crumble," nature reawakens; the poems testify that "the nature spirits . . . still lie deep in the English psyche and are beginning to reveal themselves as the valley wrestles free from the domination of the Christian mind."[64]

For Haberstroh the poems satisfy because a tense counterpoint sustains energy throughout. On the one hand, images of enclosure and paralysis (church walls, mill walls, rigid geometric shapes, and telegraph wires) "close off nature and the instinctive life." On the other hand, images of freedom, wildness, rebirth, regeneration, endurance, and sacralized nature (uplifting imagery of light, wind, wings, water, trees, trout—the naked elements and creatures of nature) create "a new kind of binding to the earth." Haberstroh believes that in maintaining this tension throughout *Elmet* "Hughes avoids the one-sided response which gave rise to the accusation that his earlier poetry celebrated violence."

Elmet, however, elicited as many negative reviews as positive. Some reviewers could locate no unifying principle or sustaining tension. Others found the language ordinary to the point of monotony, or sentimentally preoccupied with the pathetic fallacy.[65] A few refused to probe the poetry at all, preferring special pleading attacks that dwelt only on instances of violent imagery. Peter Porter asserted that the reader is "consistently battered by language"; Geoffrey Grigson alluded to a "perverse" and "indulgent nastiness in presenting a wild, savage mess"; Andrew Motion worried about how Hughes at his worst "clubs his subjects to life"; and Bedient topped all with statements about how Hughes "flogs his imagination" with "primal drum-thumping" where "everything acts violently or is acted upon."[66] In the late seventies, caricature often replaced criticism as shopworn critical clichés about the violence in Hughes's poetry substituted for honest readings of poems by a poet undergoing major stylistic changes.

For those weary of the ordeals of Hughes's mythmaking, the title sequence of *Moortown* was "a welcome relief" and "one of the best things Hughes has ever written," according to Dana Gioia, whose review represents the majority opinion. Except for a half dozen of Hughes's most stringent critics, everyone loved the opening farming poems. The consensus was that Hughes exhibited genuine sympathy for animals and for a peopled landscape in the farming poems, the elegies, and the best poems of "Earth-Numb." Instead of what John Harvey called the "magnificent dogmatizing" of a mythopoeic imagination that treated each experience as "Everything and Extinction," the poet faces "things just as they are" with an "exhilarating" and "intense but practical sympathy—without pathetic fallacy." Harvey, also synoptic, saw Hughes exhibiting a brave, unadorned clarity, a "sharp, wondering attentiveness" that "includes sympathy, humor, and a respect for the flags of dignity people keep flying even when wrecked."[67]

The varied contents in the four sections of *Moortown*—farming poems, poems of social commentary, mythic sequences—and the reprinting of "Earth-Numb" poems that date back to the early 1970s (in one case 1963) certainly included some uneven work. This prompted some reviewers to inventory Hughes's stylistic defects over the course of his career. Eric Homberger noted a strained emphasis and repetitiveness in many poems; at times Hughes too soon invests even the most ordinary subject with cosmic significance or when vision flags adds "stronger and stronger doses of metaphor . . . to keep the poems alive." Peter Scupham, whose *TLS* review was one of the few hostile to *Moortown*, accused Hughes of "verbal assault and battery" as "creation is caught in a web of multiplying verbal intensifiers. We must ride out the hurricane unquestioningly." Eagleton found *Moortown* devoid of intelligence as Hughes's formerly muscular language either "flails" with "hollow incantation" or relaxes into careless prosaic imprecision. To Eagleton's list of defects, Scupham added awkward run-ons, dangling participles, arbitrary line lengths, and cavalier metaphoric identifications.[68]

Certainly a number of poems in "Earth-Numb" are either insufficiently realized or lack the intensity one normally associates with Hughes's work. Any major poet who has achieved a distinctive style and voice occasionally parodies himself. But, as Christopher Ricks noted, Hughes has always set high standards for himself. Hence critics habituated to quality poetry in Hughes's volumes will all the more readily spot defects. For the farming poems, Hughes stated in his BBC "Moortown" program that he deliberately sought a different style. He tried not to refashion the original experience by "assault[ing] it with technical skills" in any one of the styles he had previously mastered. Technical brilliance achieved by revision and craft destroyed what he most wanted: the "fresh, simple presence of the experience."[69]

The vast majority of *Moortown* reviewers praised the farming poems lavishly and were very impressed with this new simplicity. John Bayley found the farming poems "exactly equal to the task" of "laying the visible world inexorably before us" through a simple yet "concentrated" language that achieves "power and precision." The clarity and intense directness of the farming poems helped Dick Davis to identify a unique strength: "Hughes's poems do not define but evoke—his typical poem is an act of empathy that attempts to enter the secret quiddity of its subject . . . [because] for Hughes truth is inward."[70] The best scholarly discussions of the farming poems are Craig Robinson's somewhat bucolic study in *Achievement* and my unromantic comparison of these poems with Blake's Beulah realm in my first Hughes book.

The myth sequences "Prometheus on His Crag" and "Adam and the Sacred Nine" in *Moortown* received less praise. Though Booth, Carey, and Parisi considered the volume an engrossing celebration of life and death, some found the myth sequences facile, portentous, arbitrary, or simply disappointing. According to Blake Morrison, "in these wham-bam dealings with polarities and paradox everything can equally well be its opposite . . . and I want to read something else." P. F. Robinson disagreed, and in doing so articulated another strength: Hughes's courageous tenacity of vision that "enlarges outward" toward "the psychological apprehension of the elemental nature of the universe." Robinson ended his review with the penetrating observation that Hughes's poetry is, "as Madox Hueffer once wrote about Henri Gaudier-Brzeska, . . . an adventure, an exploration; and that to refuse to consider where it may possibly get is to say 'What fine fellows those yachtsmen, lounging on the pier, are in comparison with the dirty-looking chaps whose ship is visible on the horizon, bound for the North-West Passage.' "[71]

Myth in Hughes "may possibly get" to a profound examination of the inner/outer dialogue of self and world and the grappling with one's psychic energies that is necessary for self-development. For Hughes human life is unaccommodated by any teleology. Though he finds existentialism a reductive preoccupation with conscious choice, Hughes at least agrees that humans must define their own essence and their own understanding of the universe through their actions. This happens with a believable gradualness through agonizing questioning in the myth sequences of *Moortown*, though for Prometheus the emphasis lies in understanding the role of physical pain, while for Adam the focus resides on learning to recognize and activate one's spiritual endowments. Carol Bere explored what she considered the "wide range of [Hughes's] risk-taking" and the twin poles of his "complex vision" as she examined the "new compelling generosity" of the farming poems and the "demanding" yet "rewarding" Prometheus sequence.[72]

More scholarly appreciation is needed of Hughes's highly original insights into old myths, insights that apply very directly to the world of today. Consider, for instance, his trenchant probing into how male-female relationships can self-destruct when one avoids self-development in the brilliantly concise "Earth-Numb" poem "Acteon." The attacking hounds in the poem represent not divine retribution from a guilt-oriented Western culture, but a bestialized reflex of Acteon's *own* psychic and spiritual energies that he has refused to develop and integrate. Diana's face becomes zigzagging puzzle pieces because of Acteon's inability to develop and focus his powers beyond a flaccid, inadequate chat—"talking carpet talking hooverdust." As puzzle pieces become devouring hounds, one surmises that Acteon could never appreciate Diana's uniqueness, for he has developed none of his own. Living life according to a thin rational common sense, this modern Acteon is totally unprepared for what Diana's beauty triggers in his deeper self.

Hughes's poetry may not be heavily peopled with realistic portraits, but especially in the myth sequences he offers something more important and desperately needed by both men and women in today's stressful world: "blueprints" (his term) for organizing the psyche. In my second Hughes study I discussed how language in the poetry functions to help us recognize, activate, and organize our psychic energies—to achieve an integration similar to that depicted in oriental mandalas.[73] The birds in *Cave Birds* and in "Adam and the Sacred Nine," Lumb's colloquy with the goddess in the *Gaudete* "Epilogue," Prometheus's agony and Crow's irresponsibility—these mythic elements are not evasive exaggerations of "Everything and Extinction," but failed or successful quests to integrate the inner self and to connect that self with the outer world of change and limits. As such they offer important guides toward understanding ourselves and enriching our experience.

The most substantive explication of the Prometheus and the Adam mythic sequences in *Moortown*, too lengthy to reprint here, is Craig Robinson's. He saw in both the achievement of responsible adulthood through learning how to live simultaneously in the inner and outer worlds, how to accept reality with readiness rather than habit, how to accept suffering, and how to care for other creatures. Freedom and activity, the resolutions of both sequences, occur only by becoming responsible for one's own inner development. Robinson concludes that "man has increasingly come to appear in Hughes' more recent poetry as the pinnacle of the evolutionary process— not in the sense of his being lord over creation, able to use and exploit it at his whim, but as life's latest servant, the current growing tip of a single urge. What is special about man is that the directing and furtherance of that urge seems to have been put into his own hands. . . . He himself has been charged with the task of fulfilling nature in himself."[74] In my first Hughes study I charted a Blakean alchemical movement from the Beulah world of the farming poems to the awakened creativity of Los at the conclusion of "Adam and the Sacred Nine."[75]

V. *RIVER* (1983) AND *WOLFWATCHING* (1989)

River contains some of the most spectacular poetry Hughes has written; it offers a fully realized apotheosis of two decades of his meditations on the primacy and significance of nature. Though many of the reviewers recognized the splendor of the poems, and praised a poet writing at the height of his powers, *River* attracted little scholarly interest. Mary Kinzie in her review stated best the majority position: that Hughes's purpose in composing these splendid fishing poems was "to recapture something of a prehistoric sense of awe before earth and creature." This he accomplished in a flexible style that combined the dilation of dropped lines with the "virtuoso strokes" of fresh and startling river imagery, the "galvanic harshness" and brilliance of his language, and mesmerized speakers who perceive in "a state of half-idle, horizonless trance." In agreement, Dick Davis wrote that "a Hughes poem holds its reader almost by an act of hypnosis; his celebrated empathy with the creatures of his poems is achieved by a staring concentration on their presence and uniqueness" where "the reader is drawn in and momentarily possessed by the reality Hughes evokes."[76]

Like many others, Davis found that the Peter Keen color photographs are arbitrary in subject matter and placement, and contribute little to the reader's appreciation or understanding of the poems, unlike the Baskin drawings of the flayed, afflicted spirit in *Cave Birds* or Fay Godwin's austere, brooding black-and-white photographs in *Elmet*. Elizabeth Maslin published the sole journal study of the relationship of Hughes's poetry to the visual art that often accompanies it. She found "not poetry as melody with pictures as accompaniment but counterpoint, where poems and pictures each pursue their own melodic line, creating harmony and discord within an overall unity."[77]

Reviewers of *River* often admired the evocations of wonder, awe, and the "sheer presence" (Glyn Hughes) of a poetic line that realizes "reports from an authentic frontier of reality and the imagination" (Davis). Martin Booth averred that Hughes sought to take his "readers out of their lives and into themselves."[78] The sheer number of quoted passages in reviews from *different* poems thought to be exceptional reflects the achievement of *River*.

Ron Smith recognized metaphysical dimensions behind the epic poise of poems that, of all Hughes's published work, most clearly realized the power and fecundity of the goddess of nature. Peter Redgrove, whose review wins the Covering Cherub award for obscuring the poetry with self-important remarks, applied an Elizabeth Sewell statement (from *The Orphic Voice*) in a way that adumbrates one of the key features of Hughes's late style. Hughes is one of those few poets whose work exemplifies Sewell's point that poetry can be "one of the great living disciplines of the mind, friendly to all other disciplines, and offering them and accepting from them new sources of power." Mindful of Hughes's attempt since the late 1960s to reverse the Western Christian privileging of the rational intellect over the environment (ours is the only culture in planetary history to make such a claim), I discussed the environmentally friendly Taoist metaphysics of *River* in my first Hughes book, and in my second how Hughes's attitude toward nature in the volume parallels much recent interdisciplinary work on the environment.[79]

Manly Johnson and John Mole in their negative reviews of *River* concentrated on what they considered to be a heavily foregrounded language that overwhelms and dulls the reader's senses at the same time that disengagement from the poems is difficult. Bedient suggested that in *River* "nihilism is overcome, not excluded," because throughout the volume Hughes hesitates "between prayer and frightened flight" from the drama of life and death he witnesses. Despite his many negative comments, Bedient ended his review with grudging praise about Hughes's "singular and forceful being" that resists the goddess' indifference to humans. The shifts of tone in this review reveal how difficult it is for Bedient to part with his nihilism charge.[80]

Helen Vendler, whose subtle and sensitive work on the aesthetics and epistemology of Stevens and major postmodern poets has enriched us all, descended on Hughes with a reductive club two weeks after he became poet laureate. Vendler's gifted powers could detect in *Moortown* and *River* only an intentional fallacy imputed by the critic herself, buttressed with the sort of special pleading screwed to an ad hominem pitch that one finds in Bedient and Holbrook. Hence "Hughes notices in nature what suits his purpose," and his purpose is to cast out his sadistic "poison" into "the Gadarene swine of objectified nature," where for the moment of the poem "the horror has changed places." Vendler trashes with Amazonian force; she reprints line after line of Hughes's violent imagery to prove how his "blighted imagination" finds a "perverse fascination in the stylization of victimage."[81]

In the few negative reviews of *Moortown* and *River* one detects a further waning of interest in Hughes's language and mythic enterprises. J. D. McClatchy, in his very perceptive review of *River*, correctly articulated a change in critical taste in both England and America during the eighties. As Derek Walcott noted in "Medusa Face," reprinted in the opening section of this volume, the majestic scale of Hughes's mythic vision, and the grandeur and strength of his language, are out of fashion in recent British poetry, where readers appear content with "elegaic sociology, the ordinary ordinarily recorded."[82] Perhaps that is why Blake Morrison and Andrew Motion omitted Hughes from their 1982 *Penguin Book of Contemporary British Poetry*; he is in their estimation "no longer the presiding spirit of British poetry."

McClatchy noted in America a shift of taste toward the "loose-limbed plangencies of Ashbery," while Hughes, known largely for *Crow* and ignored in the heavy shadows Plath biographers have cast over him, has ossified into a menacing statue, "a legend of himself, lurking in the biographies of Sylvia Plath as a demon-doll for feminists to stick pins in." A few of America's most influential women critics seem content to use the patriarchal privileges of their positions to train critical attention solely on Hughes's editing of Plath and the administration of the Plath estate.

The *Modern Language Association* supports this one-sided focus, allowing Hughes-bashing with each new and more sensationalized Plath biography, while at this writing not permitting a single presentation, much less a special session, solely on the poetry of Hughes. This is the response of American scholars to a writer who has published ten significant volumes of poetry over a thirty-five year career that includes eight years as England's poet laureate. Philip Larkin, however, was accorded an *MLA* special session in 1985, less than a month after a *Times* obituary (3 December 1985) dubbed him "the last neo-Georgian."[83] Such partisan scapegoating follows the binary logic of the patriarchy, which feminist theory rejects. One can only admire women such as Megerle, Haberstroh, Bere, Maslin, and Skea, who, refusing to box and label Hughes, have found very positive views of the feminine in his poetry. McClatchy in his balanced and circumspect review found no obsessive violence or poisoned Gadarene swine in *River*. Instead he found a "transparency of natural calm and meditative depth; it dispels the violence, even as it magnifies the power and fragility."

The Swedish scholar Bo Gustavsson, in his essay "Ted Hughes's Quest for a Hierophany: A Reading of *River*," saw *River* as a successful journey of the soul toward "union with the divine," a merging with "the source of being" that involves self-sacrifice and a reverence for nature. The results are spiritual renewal, a refreshing of the senses in our daily lives, and an acceptance of the purpose of the life and death cycle. Gustavsson believes that the paradoxes and ambiguities of this life and death cycle have informed Hughes's lifelong quest and are finally reconciled in *River*. Like Gifford/Roberts and Haberstroh, Gustavsson's discussion of *River* corroborates Hughes's assertions in his second "Myth and Education" essay: because in real life we live simultaneously in both the psychological world and the outer world of nature, poetry must be faithful to both.[84]

Gustavsson, like most major Hughes scholars, treats the feminine in Hughes's mythic quests as much more than an anima adjunct in a purely male quest. The male quest hero in Hughes's poetry since *Crow* learns a posture of humble fealty in the presence of a nature that governs his deepest drives and actions in the outer world. All of Hughes's personae in major sequences since *Crow* learn this important truth: Lumb in his "Epilogue"; the *Cave Birds* persona in "The Guide"; the central persona of *Elmet*; the farmer, Prometheus, and Adam in *Moortown*, and the fisherman persona of *River*.

British critics are often resistant to what Larkin once called the "myth kitty." In the shamanic flights of Hughes to the source of creation they often see what Denis Donoghue described as "a retreat from the genuine perplexities of history, time and society by recourse to an aboriginal world, nature free from the experience of history." Critics who explore Hughes's connections to tribal folklore, the shaman, Jung, alchemy, and so forth risk dismissal as either "devotees" (Graham Martin) or humorless exegetes (Roger Garfitt).[85] Yet Hughes argues in his poetry and essays that history is more than a rubble of dead facts and the spoils of patriarchal wars. Cultural values can either release or thwart libido in individuals as well as leaders; they can also promote or retard maturity in individuals as well as civilizations. Poets are public figures who can raise our consciousness of our cultural health, and act as agents in the process of developing and controlling demonic energies.

When Hughes adapts Jung, Eliade, Campbell, folklore, the occult and tribal myths to his poetry, he articulates perennial human needs and desires expressed in both oral and written literature. He believes that reducing existence to cool observation and rational common sense proves fatally inadequate when confronting the real violence that haunts every page of the twentieth-century historical record. Hughes's poetry provides a survival kit for confronting the worst that may come; Movement verse, like much postmodern poetry, leaves one hiding under Neville Chamberlain's appeasement umbrella.

The growing impatience of many critics with Hughes's evocations of awe and wonder at nature over the past twenty years parallels the extent to which we have polluted our planet over that same period with greenhouse and ozone-depleting gasses, acid rain, raw sewage, and toxic chemicals. Indifference to the natural world by our increasingly urbanized Western citizens underlies both. Tastes may change, but when they reflect a concern only with surfaces or the pleasures of the text, they expose deficiencies in our cultural orientation. When Hughes explores tribal attitudes, he evokes more ecologically sound responses to nature than our carefree, celluloid consumer culture seems able to muster.

Gustavsson suggested in his conclusion that Hughes after *River* would probably "return to everyday life" to share the elixir of knowledge from his completed quest with ordinary people. *Wolfwatching*, Hughes's most recent volume, represents just such a return to the perplexities of everyday living. Like the early *Hawk* and *Lupercal*, Hughes in *Wolfwatching* presents animals riveted in their energetic bite and hold to the actual earth. But the volume also contains contrasting portraits of relatives broken by a dispiriting culture.

What is new in *Wolfwatching* is the anguished sense of human loss at relatives dulled into submission by a failed, dehumanizing culture. Some reviewers complained of slackness in the poetic line, and wondered if the old wolf of the title poem were Hughes himself, drained by the laureateship and the children's lecture circuit. It is also possible to see a deliberateness in what Jo Shapcott called poems of "spent force,"[86] as if Hughes were trying to evoke a new vulnerability in the muscle of his masculine line. The "scrupulous calm" of the family portraits—poems "of character rather than fate"[87]— could result from a *style* scrupulously controlled to evoke a culture with all its passion spent. Carol Ann Duffy observed that the family portraits are "moving acts of reclamation" within a poetry that retains both power and generosity, for in *Wolfwatching* Hughes proves that he still "looks, smells, tastes, listens harder than anyone else; it is as if he thinks with his senses."[88]

Critics appreciated the range of Hughes's poetry in *Wolfwatching*. Stating their preferences for either the animal poems or the family portraits, they revealed Hughes's success at both. Bernard McGinley spoke for many when he extolled Hughes's "acute observation, empathy with the animal world . . . lack of sentimentalism, and above all linguistic precision." Like Peter Forbes, McGinley found Hughes's "Little Whale Song" superior to "all the recent [environmental] efforts of Heathcote Williams" in his *Whale Nation*. James Aitchison observed that the "family portraits . . . add a new strength and a new humanity to Hughes's work." Mick Imiah, though critical of what he saw as Hughes's "loss of power" in the volume, praised the two poems about uncles, for here the feeling is genuine and "sustained by working metaphor and dignified by a severe regard for the shape of individual lives. They give off not a bang but a steady hum of power. They sound like a fresh start." Edna Longley, Dannie Abse, and Forbes praised "Telegraph Wires" as a return to the tautness and succinctness of Hughes's early work. Forbes preferred the animal poems in *Wolfwatching* to those in *Moortown Diaries*, the reissued first part of *Moortown*, for he likes his Hughes not just "ticking over" but "with the turbo switched on."[89]

Aitchison noted that in *Wolfwatching* Hughes returns "to the primal encounter between the human and the animal worlds," an encounter that began with his very first volume. Yet what one makes of the encounter, and especially of Hughes's regular use of wolves in his poetry, is open to question.

Ann Skea in a new essay explores the energies and ambiguities that the wolf represents throughout Hughes's poetry. As an animal with incredible survival skills that treads the borderline between the domesticated and the predatory, and as an animal familiar that for the shaman has great "summoning force," the wolf for Skea represents both the beauty and the horror of energies that "are part of our own nature." We must incorporate these energies into our lives, and learn to transform their predatory potential into civilizing growth. Because they exist within us as well as in every quarter of life, these energies can appear threatening to the timid, vulnerable soul or society that suppresses or denies them.

Hughes's poetry since *Wodwo* offers a rich texture that invites multiple interpretations. The treatment of *River* and *Wolfwatching* in my second Hughes book emphasizes the environmental rather than the social psychological dimensions of Hughes's recent poetry. Here, as well as in my forthcoming essay "Ted Hughes and Ecology: A Biocentric Vision" in *The Challenge of Ted Hughes*, I emphasize that the major thrust of Hughes's vision since the mid-1960s has been to resurrect the power and primacy of nature, and to reorient us away from an anthropocentric tendency to quantify and exploit nature. In Hughes's late poetry, animals survive by adapting to nature's limits without degrading the planet. In proposing a more biocentric conformity to the cycles and limits of nature, Hughes's poetry since *Wodwo* parallels interdisciplinary approaches to the environment since the mid-1960s: from ethicians to theologians, ecofeminists, environmentalists, and ecologists.[90]

Scholarly evaluations of Hughes's poetry remain far from complete. More detailed examinations of his prosody, his relation to women, the environment, history, postmodernism, visual art, and connections between his mythic and his nature poetry, will provide a comprehensive assessment. Nick Bishop, with a new book at Harvester Press, and Ann Skea, with a Hughes manuscript under consideration at Faber, indicate a rekindling of interest in Hughes in the United Kingdom. Neil Roberts's graduate students at Sheffield are keen on researching Hughes, as are a few of mine at Virginia Tech. In the main, however, Hughes's research in America rests at a low ebb; senior scholars seem oblivious to Hughes's influence upon contemporary poetry. American feminists, misinformed by the sensationalized Plath biographies, have consigned him to oblivion, and the silence of senior scholars implies acquiescence.

For its intellectual penetration, stylistic virtuosity, versatility, technical finish, and unique voice, Hughes's poetry will wear as well as the Bard's. One can nitpick failed lines, graphic imagery, or inflated rhetoric in Shakespeare's as well as Hughes's poetry, and in the process miss the measure of the talent entirely. On the violence question, critical St. Georges could count corpses in the *Iliad* or *Hamlet*, or wrench torturous speeches from Shakespeare's tragedies, and begin blotting out their thousand lines, only to find the poetry in tatters afterwards. The violence in Hughes's volumes is always mediated and controlled by the structure and by journey motifs to suggest a way to decrease violence. So much is stitched into the torn richness of Hughes's verse that casting only for violence nets red herrings. Patient, diligent examination and just evaluation will provide more satisfactory results.

Notes

1. Martin Booth, *British Poetry 1964 to 1984* (London: Routledge & Kegan Paul, 1985), 25.

2. M. L. Rosenthal, *The Modern Poets: A Critical Introduction* (New York: Oxford University Press, 1960), 9.

3. See Donald Davie's title essay in Barry Alpert, ed., *The Poet in the Imaginary Museum* (Manchester: Carcanet Press, 1977), 45–56.

4. See notes 17, 32, 44, 45, 60, 79. In his review of *River* (see note 79), Bedient attempts grudging praise after many negative comments, resulting in awkward shifts of tone. Holbrook's latest essay continues his accusations of nihilism. See David Holbrook, "The Crow of Avon? Shakespeare, Sex and Ted Hughes," *Cambridge Quarterly* 15, no. 1 (1986): 1–12.

5. Robin Skelton, "Current Verses," *Manchester Guardian*, 4 October 1957, 9; John Press, "A Poet Arrives," *Sunday Times*, 3 November 1957; W. S. Merwin, "Something of His Own to Say," *New York Times*, 6 October 1957, section 7, 43.

6. Edwin Muir, "Kinds of Poetry," *New Statesman*, 28 September 1957, 391.

7. Roy Fuller, untitled, *London Magazine* 5 (January 1958): 61–64; Alfred Alvarez, "Tough Young Poet," *Observer*, 6 October 1957; Graham Hough, "Turbulences," *Encounter* 9 (November 1957): 83–87; *Times Literary Supplement*, 18 October 1957, 626.

8. See Leonard M. Scigaj, *The Poetry of Ted Hughes: Form and Imagination* (Iowa City: University of Iowa Press, 1986), 32–64.

9. W. I. Carr, "The Hawk in the Rain," *Delta* no. 14 (Spring 1958): 25–27; Alan Brownjohn, "The Brutal Tone," *Listen* 2 (Spring 1958): 20–23.

10. John Holmes, "A Poet Seeks the Limits of His World," *Christian Science Monitor*, 25 August 1960, 8; Peter Davison, "Self-Revelation in the New Poetry," *Atlantic Monthly* 208 (November 1961): 170–74; Hough, untitled, *Listener*, 28 July 1960, 159–60.

11. Alvarez, "An Outstanding Young Poet," *Observer*, 27 March 1960; Skelton, "The Rites of Lupercal," *Guardian*, 18 March 1960, 8; Press, "Violence in Verse," *Sunday Times*, 3 April 1960.

12. A. E. Dyson, "Ted Hughes," *Critical Quarterly* 1 (Autumn 1959): 219–26.

13. J. M. Newton, "Mr. Hughes's Poetry," *Delta* no. 25 (Winter 1961): 6–12.

14. Frederick Grubb, "Thinking Animal: Ted Hughes," in his *A Vision of Reality: A Study of Liberalism in Twentieth-Century Verse* (London: Chatto & Windus, and New York: Barnes & Noble, 1963), 214–25.

15. Stan Smith, "Wolf Masks: The Early Poetry of Ted Hughes," *New Blackfriars* 56 (September 1975): 414–26. A slightly altered form of this essay later appeared as chapter 7 of Smith's *Inviolable Voice: History and Twentieth Century Poetry* (Dublin: Gill & Macmillan, 1982), 150–69.

16. Alvarez, "The New Poetry, or Beyond the Gentility Principle," in Alvarez, ed., *The New Poetry* (London, Penguin, 1962), 17–28.

17. David Holbrook, "The Cult of Hughes and Gunn," *Poetry Review* 54 (Summer 1963): 167–83.

18. See Grubb, "Thinking Animal," 220; Smith, "Wolf Masks," 417–18; Jon Silkin and Anthony Thwaite, "No Politics, No Poetry?" *Stand* 6, no. 2 (1963): 7; J. D. Hainsworth,

"Ted Hughes and Violence," *Essays in Criticism* 15 (July 1965): 356–59; Peter Elfred Lewis, "The New Pedantry and 'Hawk Roosting,' " *Stand* 8, no. 1 (1966): 58–63; Allen Grant, "Ted Hughes," in Maurice Hussey, ed., *Criticism in Action: A Critical Symposium on Modern Poems* (London: Spottiswoode, Ballantyne, 1969), 101–104; Julian Gitzen, "Ted Hughes and Elemental Energy," *Discourse* 13 (Autumn 1970): 478–79; Keith Sagar, *The Art of Ted Hughes*, 2nd ed. (London and New York: Cambridge University Press, 1978), 47–50; Scigaj, *Hughes: Form and Imagination*, 72.

19. See Lewis, "New Pedantry," 58–63.

20. C. B. Cox and A. E. Dyson, "Introduction" to *Modern Poetry: Studies in Practical Criticism* (London: Edward Arnold, 1963), 20.

21. See Derwent May, "Ted Hughes," in Martin Dodsworth, ed., *The Survival of Poetry: A Contemporary Survey* (London: Faber & Faber, 1970), 162.

22. A. Mollema, "Mythical Elements in the Poetry of Ted Hughes," *Dutch Quarterly Review of Anglo-American Letters* 2 (1972): 2–14.

23. See Louise Bogan, "Verse," *New Yorker*, 30 March 1968, 133–38; Sydney Bolt, "Ted Hughes: Laureate of Leucotomy," *Delta* no. 42 (February 1968): 4–11; Hayden Carruth, "Critic of the Month: I," *Poetry* 112 (September 1968), 418–27; John Juniper, "Search for Wholeness," *Tablet*, 8 July 1967, 752; Ray Mariels, "The Single Adventure Flawed," *Northwest Review* 10 (Summer 1968): 125–130; John Press, "New Poems," *Punch* 5 July 1967, 34; Julian Symons, "Moveable Feast," *New Statesman*, 16 June 1967, 849; "Bringing Out the Beast," *Times Literary Supplement*, 6 July 1967, 601.

24. Howard Sergeant, "Poetry Review," *English* 17 (Spring 1968): 28–31; Jeremy Robson, "The Real Thing," *Tribune*, 30 June 1967, 11.

25. Anthony Hecht, "Writers' Rights and Readers' Rights," *Hudson Review* 21 (Spring 1968): 207–217; Robin Skelton, "Leaders and Others: Some New British Poetry," *Kenyon Review* 30, no. 5 (1968): 689–96.

26. J. M. Newton, "Ted Hughes's Metaphysical Poems," *Cambridge Quarterly* 2 (Autumn 1967): 395–402; Bolt, "Laureate of Leucotomy," 5, 9.

27. Derwent May, "Mid-Sixties Muse," *Times*, 13 July 1967, 7; Graham Martin, "Poets of a Savage Age," *Listener*, 6 July 1967, 22; Robson, "Real Thing," 11; Donald Davie, "As Deep as England," *Guardian*, 25 May 1967, 14.

28. Daniel Hoffman, "Talking Beasts: The 'Single Adventure' in the Poems of Ted Hughes," *Shenandoah* 19 (Summer 1968): 49–68.

29. P. Strauss, "The Poetry of Ted Hughes," *Theoria* 38 (May 1972): 45–63; Scigaj, "Oriental Mythology in *Wodwo*," in *The Achievement of Ted Hughes* (Manchester: Manchester University Press, and Athens: University of Georgia Press, 1983), 126–53; revised and repr. in Scigaj, *Hughes: Form and Imagination*, 85–121.

30. Sanford Dorbin, untitled, *Library Journal*, July 1971, 2324; Christopher Porterfield, "Demons and Victims," *Time*, 5 April 1971, 91–92.

31. J. M. Newton, "Some Notes on *Crow*," *Cambridge Quarterly* 5 (Autumn 1971): 376–84; Ian Hamilton, "Ted Hughes," in his *A Poetry Chronicle: Essays and Reviews* (London: Faber & Faber, 1973), 165–71 (originally *Times Literary Supplement*, 8 January 1971); Derek Stanford, "An Elementary Demonstration," *Books and Bookmen* 16 (December 1970): 31–32; Steve Utz, "Crow and the Stone Harp," *Southern Review* 11 (April 1975), 478–81; Neil Roberts, "The Spirit of Crow," *Delta* no. 50 (Spring 1972): 3–15; John Fuller, "Blown Up," *The Review* no. 24 (December 1970): 62–64; Richard Holmes, "A British Metamorphosis," *Times*, 17 December 1970, 15; Peter Cooley, "New Beasts, New Blessings," *Shenandoah* 23 (Winter 1972): 88–93; Ian Robinson and David Simms, "Ted Hughes's Crow," *Human World* no. 9 (November 1972): 31–40.

32. Mordecai Marcus, "Creation as a Broken Gutter Pipe," *Prairie Schooner* 46 (Fall 1972): 272–73; Calvin Bedient, "On Ted Hughes," *Critical Quarterly* 14 (Summer 1972): 103–121. See also the Hamilton and Cooley reviews in note 31.

33.   Alfred Alvarez, "Black Bird," *Observer*, 11 October 1970, 33. Reviews of *Crow* responding to Alvarez include Stephen Spender, "The Last Ditch," *New York Review of Books*, 22 July 1971, 3–4; Howard Sergeant, "Poetry Review," *English* 20 (Summer 1971): 65–68; Carolyn Kiser, "The Feast of Domitian," *Poetry* 99 (February 1972): 291–96; and the Roberts and Robinson/Simms reviews listed in note 31.

34.   Derwent May, "Bird Words," *Listener*, 29 October 1970, 603; Thomas Lask, "The Old Heaven, the Old Earth," *New York Times*, 18 March 1971, 37; Hayden Carruth, "Here Today: A Poetry Chronicle," *Hudson Review* 24 (Summer 1971): 320–36; Dabney Stuart, " 'This Has No Face, It Must Be God,' " *Mediterranean Review* 2 (Fall 1971): 51–55; Jascha Kessler, "The Inner Worlds Where Poets Wander," *Saturday Review*, 2 October 1971, 39, 50–51.

35.   Spender, "Last Ditch," 3–4; Marjorie Perloff, "Poetry Chronicle," *Contemporary Literature* 14 (Winter 1973), 120–23; Barry Wallenstein, "Crow," *Commonweal*, 17 September 1971, 483.

36.   Scigaj, "Genetic Memory and the Three Traditions of *Crow*," *Perspectives on Contemporary Literature* 9 (1983): 83–91.

37.   Terry Eagleton, "Myth and History in Recent Poetry," in Michael Schmidt and Grevel Lindop, eds., *British Poetry Since 1960: A Critical Survey* (Chatham, England: W. & J. Mackay, 1972), 233–39; Charles V. Fernandez, "Crow: A Mythology of the Demonic," *Modern Poetry Studies* 6 (Autumn 1975): 144–56.

38.   Keith Sagar, *Ted Hughes* (Longman: British Council, 1972), 37, 34.

39.   David Porter, "Beasts/Shaman/Baskin: The Contemporary Aesthetics of Ted Hughes," *Boston University Journal* 22 (Fall 1974): 13–25.

40.   Brenda Megerle, "Ted Hughes: His Monsters and Critics," *Southern Humanities Review* 11 (Spring 1977): 184–94; Lawrence Ries, "Ted Hughes: Acceptance and Accommodation," in his *Wolf Masks: Violence in Contemporary Poetry* (Port Washington, New York: Kennikat Press, 1977), 92–129.

41.   A. K. Weatherhead, "Ted Hughes, 'Crow,' and Pain," *Texas Quarterly* 19 (Autumn 1976): 95–108; Lawrence Kramer, "The Wodwo Watches the Water Clock: Language in Postmodern British and American Poetry," *Contemporary Literature* 18 (Summer 1977): 319–42; Graham Bradshaw, "Ted Hughes' Crow as Trickster-Hero," in Paul V. A. Williams, ed., *The Fool and The Trickster: Essays in Honor of Enid Welsford* (Ipswich, England: D. S. Brewer & Totowa, New Jersey: Rowman & Littlefield, 1979), 83–108.

42.   Seamus Heaney, "Now and in England," *Critical Inquiry* 3 (Spring 1977): 471–88.

43.   Julian Gitzen, "Hughes and Elemental Energy," 476–85; Gitzen, "Ted Hughes and the Triumph of Energy," *Southern Humanities Review* 7 (Winter 1973): 67–73; David Lodge, " 'Crow' and the Cartoons," *Critical Quarterly* 13 (Spring 1971): 37–68; Anthony Libby, "Fire and Light: Four Poets to the End and Beyond," *Iowa Review* 4 (Spring 1973): 111–26.

44.   Bedient, "On Ted Hughes," 103–21.

45.   Holbrook, "Ted Hughes's 'Crow' and the Longing for Non-Being," in Peter Abbs, ed., *The Black Rainbow: Essays on the Present Breakdown of Culture* (London: Heinemann, 1975), 32–54. An expanded version of this essay later appeared as "From 'Vitalism' to a Dead Crow: Ted Hughes's Failure of Confidence," in Holbrook's *Lost Bearings in English Poetry* (London: Vision Press, 1977), 101–63.

46.   Hughes's father William Hughes was one of only seventeen survivors of an entire battalion of the Lancashire Fusiliers whose total strength was replaced three times at Gallipoli. As a child, Hughes often heard surviving relatives discuss the Great War after Sunday dinner.

47.   Joyce Carol Oates, "Gaudete," *New Republic*, 28 January 1978, 32–34; John Bayley, "Smash and Bash," *Listener*, 2 June 1977, 726; Thomas Lask, "Books of the times," *New York Times*, 19 July 1978, C-21.

48.   Robert Pinsky, "English Poetry," *New York Times Book Review*, 25 December

1977, 4–5; Peter Ackroyd, "Agonizing," *Spectator*, 11 June 1977, 23; Geraldine Moyle, "Hughes' Gaudete: A Poem Subverted by its Plot," *Parnassus* 6 (Spring/Summer 1978): 199–204.

49.   Edwin Brock, "Brock Reviews Hughes," *Ambit* no. 71 (1977): 82–83; William H. Pritchard, "How to Open a Pigeon," *Nation*, 21 January 1978, 53–55. See note 47 for Bayley.

50.   Bayley, "Facts and Makings," *London Review of Books*, 21 February 1980, 14–15.

51.   Newton, "No longer 'through the pipes of Greece'?", *Cambridge Quarterly* 7, no. 4 (1977): 335–45.

52.   Irvin Ehrenpreis, "At the Poles of Poetry," *New York Review of Books*, 17 August 1978, 48–50.

53.   Edward Larrissy, "Ted Hughes, the feminine, and *Gaudete*," *Critical Quarterly* 25 (Summer 1983): 33–41; Peter King, "Elemental Energy: The Poetry of Ted Hughes," in his *Nine Contemporary Poets: A Critical Introduction* (London: Methuen, 1979), 107–51.

54.   Don McKay, "Animal Music: Ted Hughes's Progress in Speech and Song," *English Studies in Canada* 7 (Spring 1981): 81–92.

55.   Sagar, *Art of Ted Hughes*, 186–225.

56.   Ekbert Faas, *Ted Hughes: The Unaccommodated Universe* (Santa Barbara: Black Sparrow Press, 1980), 121–40; Scigaj, *Hughes: Form and Imagination*, 165–204.

57.   Eagleton, "New Poetry," *Stand* 19, no. 2 (1978): 76–80.

58.   Craig Robinson, *Ted Hughes as Shepherd of Being* (New York: St. Martin's Press, 1989), 86–94.

59.   Richard Tobias, "Verse," *World Literature Today* 53 (Autumn 1979): 683. Those who complained of the lack of a narrative or found the poems lacking in a unifying scheme were Peter Porter, "Judgment of the Birds," *Observer*, 1 October 1978, 34; Desmond Graham, "The Evidence of Poetry," *Stand* 20, no. 4 (1978): 75–80; Julian Symons, "Grigson: A Long Look Back," *Sunday Times*, 26 November 1978, 40; Alan Brownjohn, "Heads, Tongues & Spirits," *Encounter* 51 (November 1978): 63–65; Christopher Reid, "Flapping and other motions," *The New Review* 5 (Autumn 1978): 106–107.

60.   Robert Nye, "Poetry," *Times*, 7 September 1978, 14; Bedient, "New Confessions," *Sewanee Review* 88 (Summer 1980): 474–88. See note 59 for Reid.

61.   Craig Raine, "Promises, Premises," *New Statesman*, 5 January 1979, 19–20; Martin Booth, "Cosmic symbols, creation myths," *Tribune*, 13 October 1978, 8–9; Richard Murphy, "Last Exit to Nature," *New York Review of Books*, 10 June 1982, 38–40.

62.   Terry Gifford & Neil Roberts, *Ted Hughes: A Critical Study* (London & Boston: Faber & Faber, 1981), 199–231; Stuart Hirschberg, *Myth in the Poetry of Ted Hughes* (Dublin: Wolfhound Press, 1981), 152–177.

63.   Glyn Hughes, "Myth in a Landscape," *Guardian*, 24 May 1979, 16; Murphy, "Last Exit to Nature," 38–40.

64.   Carol Bere, "Remains of Elmet," *Concerning Poetry* 14 (Spring 1981): 17–26; Patricia Boyle Haberstroh, "Historical Landscape in Ted Hughes's *Remains of Elmet*," *Clio* 14 (Winter 1985): 137–54.

65.   No unity or tension: Brownjohn, "A Change of Landscape," *Encounter* 53 (August 1979): 45–51; David Rogers, untitled, *World Literature Today* 54 (Summer 1980): 434–35. Ordinary language, pathetic fallacy: Peter Porter, "Landscape with poems," *Observer*, 15 July 1979), 37; Geoffrey Grigson, "Ragged letters?", *Listener*, 26 July 1979, 125; Humphrey and Janet Clucas, "Ted Hughes and Fay Godwin," *Agenda* 19 (Summer–Autumn 1981): 107–13.

66.   Andrew Motion, "Flogged," *New Statesman*, 8 June 1979, 833. For Porter and Grigson, see note 65.

67.   Dana Gioia, "Poetry Chronicle," *Hudson Review* 33 (Winter 1980–81): 611–27; John Harvey, "One poet, two men," *Listener*, 17 April 1980, 510–11.

68.   Eric Homburger, "Critics playing spot-the-ball," *Times Higher Education Supple-

ment, 29 February 1980, 13; Peter Scupham, "The demon-farmer's carnival," *Times Literary Supplement*, 4 January 1980, 6; Eagleton, "Recent Poetry," *Stand* 21, no. 3 (1980): 76–80.

69. Christopher Ricks, "Cruelty Expert," *New York Times Book Review*, 20 July 1980, 13, 18; Ted Hughes, "Moortown," *BBC Radio 3*, prod. Fraser Steel, recorded 6 February 1980, 2.

70. Bayley, "Facts and Makings," 14–15; Dick Davis, "Perceiving What Is," *PN Review 15* 7, no. 1 (1980): 60–61.

71. Martin Booth, "Environment inner and outer," *Tribune*, 30 November 1979, 6–7; John Carey, "Grunts and groans," *Sunday Times*, 9 December 1979, 51; Joseph Parisi, "Poetry Bookshelf," *Chicago Tribune*, 22 February 1981, section 7, 4; Morrison, "Yous & Is & Doths & Thees," *New Statesman*, 4 January 1980, 22–23; P. F. Robinson, untitled, *Poetry Wales* 15 (Spring 1980): 67–71.

72. Carol Bere, " 'How Precisely the Job Can Be Done': Ted Hughes's *Moortown*," *Literary Review* 24 (Spring 1981): 427–34.

73. Scigaj, *Ted Hughes* (Boston: G. K. Hall, 1991), 22–26.

74. Robinson, *Hughes as Shepherd*, 147–95.

75. Scigaj, *Hughes: Form and Imagination*, 257–86.

76. Mary Kinzie, "Idiom and Error," *American Poetry Review* 13 (September–October 1984): 38–47; Davis, "Country Codes," *Listener*, 12 January 1984, 23.

77. Elizabeth Maslin, "Counterpoint: collaborations between Ted Hughes and three visual artists," *Word and Image* 2 (January–March 1986): 33–44.

78. Glyn Hughes, "Waters deeper still," *Guardian*, 25 September 1983, 21; Martin Booth, "Poetry in English," *British Book News*, February 1984, 112–13.

79. Ron Smith, "River," *San Francisco Review of Books*, 11 (Spring 1986): 15; Peter Redgrove, "Windings and Conchings," *Times Literary Supplement*, 11 November 1981, 1238; Scigaj, *Hughes: Form and Imagination*, 287–315; Scigaj, *Hughes*, 133–44.

80. Bedient, "Ted Hughes's Fearful Greening," *Parnassus* 14, no. 1 (1987): 150–63.

81. Helen Vendler, "Raptures and Rendings," *New Yorker*, 31 December 1984, 66–68, 70.

82. J. D. McClatchy, "The Return of Ted Hughes," *New Republic*, 3 September 1984, 39–41. Derek Walcott, "Medusa face," *Weekend Telegraph*, 21 October 1989.

83. Linda Wagner-Martin published her Plath biography with Simon & Schuster in 1987. At both the 1986 and 1987 MLA conventions, she gave papers highly critical of Hughes. Paul Alexander published his Plath biography with Viking in 1991. He was accorded a presentation highly critical of Hughes at a 1991 MLA special session entitled "Sylvia Plath and Ted Hughes: Chapters in a Mythology," with Diane Middlebrook, the Sexton biographer, as a respondent. Though Hughes appeared in the title of the session, not one Hughes scholar appeared on Professor Timothy Materer's program. In a letter to this author, Materer stated that Marjorie Perloff was in part responsible for the speakers and organization of his session.

For two years after my first (1986) book on Hughes, I advertised for papers and submitted special session requests on "Ted Hughes: Violence and the Feminine." In each case the request failed. After the second (1988) rebuff I requested a rationale for the refusal, and received a purely statistical statement about the hundreds of requests, acceptances, and rejections. The MLA has never offered a special session on Hughes; to the best of my knowledge not a single paper solely on Hughes's poetry has ever been read at a December MLA convention. I gave one on Hughes's early poetry at the 1982 SAMLA convention.

84. Bo Gustavsson, "Ted Hughes' Quest for a Hierophany: A Reading of *River*," *Studia Neophilologica* 59, no. 2 (1987), 209–16.

85. Denis Donoghue, untitled review of *The Art of Ted Hughes*, by Keith Sagar, *New Republic*, 31 January 1976, 30–31; Graham Martin, "Poet as myth-maker?", *New Statesman*, 26 June 1981, 18–19; Roger Garfitt, "Desolation and Development," *Times Literary Supplement*, 24 July 1981, 849–50.

86. Jo Shapcott, "Five father figures," *New Statesman*, 27 October 1989, 38.

87. Unsigned review, "Crow turns kind," *Economist*, 23 September 1989.

88. Carol Ann Duffy, "Poetry," *Guardian*, 19 October 1989.

89. Bernard McGinley, "Empathy with animals," *Financial Times*, 23 September 1989; Forbes, "If he could talk to the animals," *Independent*, 23 September 1989; James Aitchison, "Back to the hawk," *Glasgow Herald*, 23 September 1989; Mick Imiah, "Not with a bang but a hum," *Observer*, 17 September 1989, 46; Edna Longley, "What the Doctor Said," *London Review of Books*, 22 March 1990, 22–23; Dannie Abse, "More Cries from the Mammal House," *Listener*, 9 November 1989, 30.

90. Scigaj, *Hughes*, 133–57.

HUGHES AS LAUREATE

◆

Medusa Face

Derek Walcott

Ted Hughes's reputation may be enduring an eclipse of fashion because the preference now is for a verse that is detailed, actual, for elegiac sociology, the ordinary ordinarily recorded. His poetry is lonely and remote. Towers and hieratic stones are out of fashion; mist and ragged moors, Hardy-esque stoicism seem far too fabulous for contemporary verse's long season of common sense and urban light. Its mineral strength is condemned or ignored as a posturing, but one might as well accuse Stonehenge of having a stance.

The poetry is surveyed as a tour of primordial ruins, but the power of Hughes's work is that it preserves its own archaicness, that it shows us an England besieged by a rising sea of trash. It sometimes snarls back at us like a hounded, embayed beast, cornered and bleeding. Its width is massive, its ecology desperate.

Nature, in English poetry before Hughes, was a decent panacea. One went towards it, entered it like a roofless cathedral. It was a place of contemplation, not terror. It was the benign shrine of the pathetic fallacy. Sheep might softly graze there without blood and droppings. It often went no deeper than the surface of a shiny calendar, or the tender pieties of a child's book. Preceding Hughes, Lawrence demythologised all this. The myth of the Sabine farm with the farm-shit, the deaths and squealings that nobody wants to hear about or hear, Blake's little lamb strangled in a birth-caul.

But if Hughes's poetry were simply a matter of antithesis to pastoral, of showing the scabs and welts, the wounds of a long-suffering but enduring landscape without figures, without the Wordsworthian narcissism of contemplating imagination by its reflection in lakes made sacred by piety, then the pitch of his natural observations would be simply that of a school bully dangling a dead frog in the reader's face. And that is what they think; those who turn away from the page as a girl might from a dead frog.

Well, it was about time that a language which did not distance itself from nature by botanical pastoral catalogues thrust its vision through a cloud of flies and examined carcases with the disturbing casualness, the long, guttural off-hand phrases in Hughes's rythmn, of an abrupt farmer. Because the carcase was English poetry as well, not only that of a rotting sheep.

Reprinted from *Weekend Telegraph*, 21 October 1989, by permission of Farrar, Strause, & Giroux and the newspaper.

An interior decay may still be gnawing away at that carcase, and if Hughes's vision may be the bones of that poetry picked clean by crows, of bare ridges with a few memorial rocks, then it only carries, in its wide-ranging view, not apocalyptic fury, not a rage to frighten, but that barrenness that is there in the great Hebrew poets, Isaiah, Jeremiah, Job—the bare Yorkshire moors in stony light. Because the earth is going. Its topsoil is spinning away in dust. Because the sea is foul. Because the air is poison. Because the streams are sick.

But this is not the poetry of our day-to-day lives. These truths are too big and we believe they will go away if we concentrate on small, consoling things. So, naturally, we wish Hughes would go away. We wish he'd go and keep on practising to be a monolith. A monodic monolith. We can't stand his tone.

Hughes brought to poetry a toughness that was unbearable, a medusa-face that paralysed the high chatter that passes for criticism of the craft. In Sylvia Plath the toughness cracks apart into a hysteria that is almost clinical. Once the poetry of breakdown became popular Hughes had to become increasingly passé, because its strength was not personal, and therefore its endurance seemed pitiless and cruel. Yet the difference between Hughes and a poet like Robinson Jeffers, or even Lawrence, is that he does not carve his own visage from stone.

There isn't any Ted Hughes in Hughes's poetry of landscape. The "I" when it is there, is not taller than its surroundings. He is a poet of terror, not of the insomniac terrors of Plath, the muse of aspirin, but in the immense sense of terror, the Greek example of awe. The tragedy of white stones, not white pills, of the sudden asterisk of blood on the stones, of what Auden calls "libation and sacrifice." Would that it were all an act! But the mask is in the face. They say of marriage that man and wife eventually resemble each other. Poets come to look like their poetry. The page is a mirror, a pool. Hughes's face emerges through the pane of paper in its weathered openness as both friendly and honest. It speaks trust. The way a stone appears to speak about itself.

It is time to give up the image of the old blood-and-guts Hughes, the Patton of modern poetry, the bayed wolf always and only snarling back from its corner of England, and time to be touched by the tenderness it conceals behind the furious vocabulary, because it is a precious and common tenderness, as wet-eyed as the eternal dewiness of Edward Thomas's vision. Its rage is concern, not a prehistoric, macho blustering, and its genius is feminine, that of the female we call Mother Earth.

That exterior roughage, that nap of the furred hide rubbed backwards, not letting the line be smoothed and petted by our agreeing, that condition of always being rubbed the wrong way, isn't the same as saying that every panther is a pussycat at heart, and yet, in its eyes there is a mortal tenderness. That is wolf-watching. That is the *sunt lacrimae rerum* that glitters in the eyes even of beasts. Our own eyes are harder than those of beasts. We are the real predators. *For this is the Black Rhino, who vanishes as he approaches / Every second there is less and less of him / By the time he reaches you nothing will remain, maybe but the horn.*

The poem is itself predatory. It eats its subject, and the beautiful and terrifying honesty of Hughes's poetry is that it does not distance our ambiguity through moral outrage. Every poem of Hughes is its own elegy, yet the tone is never simply elegiac, never "If I should die," or "When I have fears that I may cease to be"; its brutal ecology is that even the most sensitive "I" degenerates into biodegradable rubbish, that even poetry, along with the rhino, is continually threatened with extinction. His "Thrushes" are fierce, stabbing machines, not by his own antithesis, but by Nature's. But they are beautiful, and the poem that closes in on their beaks becomes clear and beautiful because there is no such thing as irony in Nature.

The poetry of Hughes has brought us, in the most exact sense, closer to nature, its complete workings, than any English poet we can think of, including Clare and Hardy. Not because it is brutal, but because it is brutal and bright, otherwise all we would have would be a morose accuracy, the diary of a depressed naturalist. It is a poetry of exultation. It is behind its threshing furore as quiet as his "Dove" (*Now staying / Coiled on a bough / Bubbling molten, wobbling top-heavy / Into one and many*) [or "Sparrow Hawk"] (*Slips from your eye-corner—overtaking / Your first thought. / Through your mulling gaze over haphazard earth. . . . / Laser the lark-shaped hole / In the lark's song*).

Hughes's metre, for all the length of its lines, is not really Lawrentian or Whitmanesque, by which is usually meant that it is delivered from formal constraints, expansive and recent; instead, it is ancestral, rooted in Middle English, its phrases divided by a heavy caesura that often has the depth of a geological fissure, an abyss into which we are afraid to look.

The heredity in Hughes's metre requires considerable devotion to poetry. The history of it works the field with the rigour and metre of ancient tillage. It works it in the ugliest weather, and even though it may upheave and charge through our ideas of pastoral with the blunt power of a tractor, behind its belligerent growl there is a distant, older rhythm of poetry as work that goes as far back and as deep as Langland.

What else could it celebrate but force? What else can it believe in but an endurance beyond itself, and without the tiring buoyancy of Whitman, the moral evangelism of Lawrence, the modest botany of the Georgians? It seems to long for the whirlwind of anonymity, for the cold severity of pebbles as primal nouns. For terror, but for the terror of the great Greek tragic-poets. The moors revert to arenas of sacrifice. The gods are bloodied figures. The cheapest evasion is to call this myth-making.

Sometimes to read a Hughes poem is like trying to go out in bad weather, unaccommodated. The alternative is comfortable. To sit indoors and sip poems written for indoors. But great tragic poets require moral bravery from us, and that ancient virtue, of responsibility as awe, appears to be threatened with extinction like everything else. We do not want to hear this. We leave prophets to their job of prophesying, and prefer the domesticated, consoling mutter of contemporary verse, the metre of decent conversation, believing that poetry, as prophecy, is part of a very distant past. Often the stony light of Hughes's poetry seems to come as far back as the primal, tribal dawn of England.

It has a hallowing width, a spreading power, a tireless compassion like sunrise. It is Caedmon with old car-tyres and cold tractors in the morning. It shakes us awake and we read it for what it is, hard work. Its weather comes off the cold page with bracing, exhilarating realness. It is to be cherished any way we like, but, most naturally, with that irascible affection the English have always had for their climate.

It is, in every phrase, as pious as a bead of dew or the droppings of a sheep. It is so in Hughes's eyes, bless them. *Take telegraph wires, a lonely moor, / And fit them together. The thing comes alive / in your ear. / Towns whisper to towns over the heather* . . . and not his eyes only, but bless the pricked, sharp attention of his world-watching ears.

The New Poet Laureate

Seamus Heaney

Before the name of the Poet Laureate was announced, the bookies were offering 5 to 1 on Ted Hughes, which tells you more about the general attitude to the laureateship than it tells you about Ted Hughes. The office, after all, is a national English institution and there has been something institutional about many of the previous incumbents. Betjeman, Masefield, Robert Bridges, Tennyson—they seemed to imply a civic function for the poet, each of them could be easily enough imagined in the front pew of Westminster Abbey or in a morning coat at a palace garden party.

Somewhere behind the intonation of their poetry you could sense either the suasions of the Anglican pulpit or the muted strains of "Land of Hope and Glory." They stood for a kind of Englishness to which Philip Larkin, favourite for the laureateship last year, seemed the natural heir, for although Larkin's ironical, saddened poetry can hardly be described as public or civic, the sensibility that produced it is obviously patriotic, at one with the customs and institutions of the nation. It was hard to imagine Larkin, who had written so acutely about children as irritants, applying his strict, self-deprecating intelligence to the composition of an ode for a new wee prince, but it was nevertheless easy to conceive of him and his work as a ratification of equable, high-street Englishness. Easy to imagine a crowd watching a royal procession being watched by this benign, balding flat-dweller at his high window.

You could never imagine him, however, talking about the English as a tribe or talking, as Ted Hughes did in that brief interview on the day of his appointment, of the crown as an image of the tribe's unity and spiritual resource. That kind of idiom is at once analytical and sacral, gesturing towards the scientific language of anthropology and at the same time favouring old ways of feeling and knowing which anthropology inspects with curiosity. All that is at odds with the mainstream, secular, positivist British way of responding to experience. You have only to think of the jibe at the proletarian ordinariness of Ted Hughes's name made by the likes of Kingsley Amis, to realise what the Laureate is up against.

Hughes's appointment breaks the mould. Even though he is immensely popular, he is regarded as slightly beyond, and other than, the usual literary

Reprinted from *Belfast Review* 10 (March/May 1985), by permission of the author.

animal. As a student, he appeared to one of his Cambridge contemporaries as "a big hay-seedy guy" and to another as "part of the Celtic fringe." As a poet in his fifties, he still stalks the margins, finding his poetic territory in the northern milltowns and moors of Yorkshire; in the southern rivers and farmlands of Devon and Cornwall. The England he physically inhabits and the one he imaginatively embraces is old, the land of King Harold and King Alfred and King Arthur. In that time scale, the Windsors are runners-in usurpers of a dream realm still alive in Shakespeare's history plays and Malory's romances.

Hughes's trust in the efficacy of this mythic England has been vindicated by the very fact of his appointment at this time. Britain today is a country apparently obsessed with its fatigued class war and its self-wounding industrial crises, a country whose destiny is debated in terms of economics; whose official church is almost embarrassed by the mention of God; whose universities falter in their trust in the traditional humanist disciplines. That such a country should turn to a poet with an essentially religious vision, without a word to say on contemporary politics but with a strong trust in the pre-industrial realities of the natural world, is remarkable. In fact, it is a vivid demonstration of the truth of the implied message of Hughes's poetry that the instinctual, intuitive side of man's, and in particular the Englishman's, nature has been starved and occluded and is in need of refreshment.

I once attended a performance of Yeats's play *The Countess Cathleen*—the one about the countess who sells her soul in order to save the lives of the starving country people—at the Abbey Theatre, in Ted's company. He thought it impressive that a play about the selling of a soul should still draw capacity audiences in the national theatre, and contrasted the Abbey situation favourably with the situation in London's West End. This was symptomatic of his whole outlook, which is continuous with Yeats's vision of renewal through a retrieval of older spiritual resources; and Yeats's other hope, for an Irish literature which would link the people to their land as feelingly and mythically as the literature of Greece, is parallelled by Hughes's endeavour to achieve a body of poetry that once again puts the English audience in vital, imaginative contact with the geological, botanical, historical and legendary reality of England itself.

His first publication as Laureate, therefore, was both true to his own best creative processes and deeply bardic and public. On one level, it was about the immense rich surge of life that came over the fields and rivers of Devon and Cornwall during a sudden downpour of rain, a natural Hughes subject stirring him to a fine excess. But at another level it was an aspect of one of the most ancient rites of Indo-European kingship, the betrothal of the King to his physical territory. By dedicating the poem to the young Prince Henry and by drenching the royal domain, the Duchy of Cornwall, in a shower of benediction, Hughes not only made a graceful gesture but reaffirmed an ancient tradition and re-established, without sanctimoniousness, a sacerdotal function for the poet in the realm.

STYLE AND POETICS

◆

Beasts/Shamans/Baskin: The Contemporary Aesthetics of Ted Hughes

DAVID PORTER

As he lay in a doorway and watched the bullets lifting the cobbles out of the street beside him, so Ted Hughes has written of the Polish poet Czeslaw Milosz, "he realized that most poetry is not equipped for life in a world where people actually do die." But some is, Hughes added. The new poetics of Ted Hughes, the British poet, accordingly conceives poems as hard and predatory, like killer sharks "alert and shapely," instinctively about the business of managing the practical difficulties of survival. This radical conception means two basic things: poems inhabit the same world as assassinations and must not allow themselves to be made trivial by comparison; poems make the essential thing happen, they rescue us from inanition. This is their totemic value as the main regenerative acts of the human psyche.[1]

Hughes's own poetic mode is no sweet new style, but rather wily, elementary, and attacking like an animal. It is not the twitches and rustles of "confessional" poets out of university writing classes. Least of all is it like that of his generation of writers in England, whose poems someone has called mournful mouthings over pints of beer, soiled sheets, and garden implements. Hughes's style is conglomerate, ravenous, drawing in everything from Old English to shamanism to pop. His imagined poet is a scavenger over all the mishmash of the global junkyard, hardly the archetypal figure James Joyce saw as the God of creation, indifferent, paring his fingernails.

The deep shift from the familiar in Hughes's poetics explains why he is thought to have barbarized the vocation of poet, to have forsaken his humanistic obligations, and to be, in the *TLS* expression of Ian Hamilton, the English poet and critic, *mistaken*. Yet no poet writing today is more deeply endowed by the English literary inheritance than Hughes. The field of forces that constitutes his individual reality is, like the animals he depicts, complex and intricately balanced. As we shall see, it centers on a shamanistic seeking of experience pared of its surfaces. Shamanism is no trendy venture with Hughes. It is his radical analogue for the poetic event.

Reprinted from *Boston University Journal* 22 (Fall 1974): 13–25, by permission of the author and the journal. Graphic art by permission of Leonard Baskin.

Not surprisingly, violence and predatory motives in his poems provoke the hostility of readers because the images are uncompromising. The poem "Hawk Roosting" (*Lupercal*), is singled out by antagonists to illustrate Hughes's supposed obsessive regard for the brutish: "no falsifying dream / Between my hooked head and hooked feet"; "My manners are tearing off heads." The poem ends with savage presumption:

> The sun is behind me.
> Nothing has changed since I began.
> My eye has permitted no change.
> I am going to keep things like this.

But of course it is not the poet speaking. The primal urge of the natural world declaims here, a sort of soliloquy of the root force. Its sounding reveals Hughes's impatience to grasp antecedent issues by his selection of the hawk rather than the blowing daisy. Of the poem, so often misinterpreted, Hughes says, "actually what I had in mind was that in this hawk Nature is thinking. Simply Nature."[2] This force that also holds man erect enables him to survive, even to make heroic assertions against the destructive elements within and without. It is an ambiguous double-dealing power:

> What humbles these hills has raised
> The arrogance of blood and bone,
> And thrown the hawk upon the wind,
> And lit the fox in the dripping ground.
> —*Lupercal*, 14

Letting loose words after those hidden centers of energy which men share with the beasts involves violence, but we should not mistake Hughes's blunt means for the attitude one reader calls "glowering pessimism."[3] Hughes's vision, no matter how stark, reflects not a worship of the claw but an abiding humanism. Even the mayhem he promotes in his recent folk cycle *Crow* (1970) stands as the primary measure of man's stature. His judgment of the Yugoslav poet Vasko Popa reflects the core of his own sympathies. Popa's world, he writes, is "mysteriously active and dreadful but his affection for our life is closer than ever. The infinite terrible circumstances that seem to destroy man's importance, appear as the very terms of his importance."[4]

Like his learned friend Leonard Baskin, the American sculptor and print-maker, Hughes has been thought to purvey unrelieved desperation. A. Alvarez said in a review of *Crow* that "as a poet Ted Hughes has never shown much faith in human beings."[5] Daniel Hoffman describes Hughes's concerns as narrow, holding no healthy view of sensuousness, joy or love, to say nothing of immortality. He locates Hughes at the very extremity of human isolation as his "response to the conditions of contemporary life."[6] Stephen Spender has said that in *Crow* "everything in the world that is loaded against life is brought to play against chances of fulfillment and happiness."[7] But such views angle along the surface. Hughes's chosen philosophical adversary is Samuel Beckett. In the Popa essay, Hughes says the world of the East European poets (he mentions Holub and Herbert also) is "as horrible as Beckett's but they do not despair of it to the point of surrendering consciousness and responsibility to their animal cells. Their poetic themes revolve around the living suffering spirit, capable of happiness, much deluded, too frail, with doubtful and provisional senses, so undefinable as to be almost silly, but palpably existing, and wanting to go on existing—and this is not, as in Beckett's world, absurd."[8] In this description, let us mark well, we find Crow the poet, Hughes having fashioned that figure from folk tales into an aesthetic statement on the condition of the poet in a world set with entrapments and tyrannized by the anti-imagination.

Hughes asks of man what he asks of the poet and what he finds in the model of Vasko Popa, the integrity of sympathies intact: "He never loses his deeply ingrained humour and irony: that is his way of hanging on to his human wholeness."[9]

Characterizations of Hughes are as misleading as similarly gross assessments of Baskin. Baskin's dead men sculptures are regarded by some as grisly caricatures, bodies reduced to insults, lumps deprived of their features, shapeless in their nudity. Yet what Baskin accomplishes in this extreme effacement, cutting away the cosmetic details, is to reveal the ineradicable residue of man wherein still are managed gestures of courage, patience, and grace. Bronze makes the gesture of spirit, and though these figures lie or hang, they display the strength and beauty in man that are separate from his carnal existence, constituting the shared dignity of us all, unkillable.

The birds of both Hughes and Baskin also declare, however indirectly, the same regard for man. Baskin's birds have been described as belonging to "a bestiary of malevolent creatures," essentially a "condensation of sinister forces."[10] Some of the Crow poems compel a similar view of Hughes's creatures. In "Crow Tyrannosaurus," the poet-hero, though his brain conceives bright alternatives, is first of all a single efficient instrument of survival:

> Crow thought "Alas
> Alas ought I
> To stop eating
> And try to become the light?"

> But his eye saw a grub. And his head, trapsprung, stabbed.

And he listened
And he heard
Weeping

Grubs grubs He stabbed he stabbed
Weeping
Weeping

Weeping he walked and stabbed

Thus came the eye's
　　　　　roundness
　　　　　　　　the ear's
　　　　　　　　　　deafness.
　　　　　　　　—*Crow*, p. 13

Crow's rumination on the light trails after the falsely elegant archaism "Alas!" whereas the real business of survival sounds the rough rhythms of the alley. The language itself is trapsprung to catch the reality of clawed nature intermittently entertaining the beauty of intellectual forms, though such designs hardly promise to fit one for survival.

Crow enacts the human consciousness: he watches, handles pain, asks questions. But Crow is also an underprinciple, the irreducible wanting to go on existing. He is the outcast, the man in the black skin, all men facing the civilized emasculations. Baskin knows this. When a scholar referred to his bird as the "ignoble crow," Baskin replied: "Crows are hardly ignoble, which is why they interest me. Crows are bright, cunning, noisy, indefatigable, voracious, prodigal. The sort that would be excluded from a modern aviary, with 18 hole golf course, and official length swimming pool!!"[11] And, one adds by inference, the sort who sculpture or write poetry, those the system attempts to exclude from the precincts of authority. The crow provides both men with a basic dislocation of perspective from the familiar into the beast fable, inducing an acute alienation that makes our limitations and our possibilities visible again. The crow figure deprives us of the familiar rationalizations into which we have heaped our experiences.

The crow also conveys extraordinary ambiguity. In Baskin's standing crow sculpture (1960), as in some of the bronze reliefs, we encounter crow heroic, monumentally planted, broad chested, the very posture of the great man, a parody at the same time it captures the heroic essence in erect and solid gesture. The ambiguities multiply in Baskin's treatment. Elsewhere, his crow simultaneously suggests the bird-man, the Icarus soarer, a winged man-angel, the bird of peace, and the nightmare of the angel of death. All of these elements sit latent in that basic homely figure. It can be monumental, powerful, and terrifying; at other times it is beautiful in complexity and texture, a profession of possibility, yet also a frenzy in angry flight (as in

"Homage to Un-American Activities Committee," 1959). Baskin's dead crows are like his dead men and like Hughes's poems of the dead: they are the caught wonderment and possibilities of life that still photographs and carcasses cannot hold.

Hughes's crow moreover has qualities that Baskin's rarely suggest, less weighty and heroic attributes which expand the suggestiveness of this figure that now inhabits contemporary poetry. They are the aspects of crow-god-man-poet that are crass and trivial, the lesser addictions caricatured in the inanities of TV animated cartoons. Hughes's crow is all of these, the best heroics men can manage despite the flaws. Crow is like the man in "The Hawk in the Rain," bloodily-grabbed and dazed, caught in the ankle-sucking mud of the earth, but capable also of weightless moments of mastery symbolized by the hawk hanging in the sky.

Hughes's animals lead us into the constitution not only of his beliefs but of his poetic strategies. As a boy, he hunted animals and modeled them as well. At the age of fifteen, he tells young readers, his attitude to animals changed, and he "began to look at them from their own point of view." This identification carries directly to the poetry: "There are all sorts of ways of capturing animals and birds and fish. I spent most of my time, up to the age of fifteen or so, trying out many of these ways and when my enthusiasm began to wane, as it did gradually, I started to write poems. You mightn't think that the two interests, capturing animals and writing poems, have much in common. But the more I think back, the more sure I am that with me the two interests have been one interest."[12]

Animals and fish and birds have come to represent for Hughes intricate aesthetic shapes, life-giving sources to counter the sterility of contemporary life and, quite specifically, analogues of the poem, alert and shapely, and of the poet as well, attempting to survive in hazardous times.

"Maybe my concern," says Hughes, "has been to capture not animals particularly and not poems, but simply things which have a vivid life of their own, outside mine."[13] Like Baskin's men-creatures, strange beings existing in their own space, Hughes's figures also have a powerful individual reality. Yet they are always significant beyond their achievement as image. They locate for us our beginnings, the irreducible being, and the stubbornness of life. The hawk, the fox, the otter, the pike, and the crow are part of what we are when the hamburger bars, snowmobiles, plastic wrap, and debutante cotillions are subtracted. Basically, Hughes's animals, like Baskin's, are an act of radical subtraction, the paring away of the rubbishy accretions to reveal interior precincts of power and dignity. Mr. Alvarez has described Hughes's earliest animals with insight: "However violent and unforgiving he made them seem, they had their own special perfection; they falsified nothing and were true to their own blind and predatory laws. So though their lives were alien, they were still redeemed by a certain instinctive grace."[14] Hughes's famous pike is life, less all the irrelevancies:

> The jaws' hooked clamp and fangs
> Not to be changed at this date;
> A life subdued to its instrument.
> —*Lupercal*, 56

The hard aesthetic in these lines implies a poetry reduced to its instrumentality, possessing strength to survive (to mean) in the real world.

His animals also have a totemic significance. In visitations, they are the experienced dream of the life urge. They reify the power and cunning that only haunt our wakefulness. They are the tomcat: "Nightly over the round world of men, / Over the roofs go his eyes and outcry." They are the thought-fox

> that now
> And again now, and now, and now
>
> Sets neat prints into the snow
> Between trees, and warily a lame
> Shadow lags by stump and in hollow
> Of a body that is bold to come
>
> Across clearings, an eye,
> A widening deepening greenness,
> Brilliantly, concentratedly,
> Coming about its own business
>
> Till, with a sudden sharp hot stink of fox
> It enters the dark hole of the head.
> —*Hawk*, 14

Hughes has described the shamanistic experience in these words: "The shaman is 'chosen' in a number of ways. In some regions, commonly among the North American Indians, the aspirant inflicts on himself extraordinary solitary ordeals of fasting and self-mutilation, until a spirit, usually some animal, arrives, and becomes henceforth his liaison with the spirit world."[15] That trafficking with the underrealm obviously represents to Hughes's mind his primal act as a poet, as if the world under the world were the pooled language of the unconscious, the animals its extracted sentences, and Hughes their grammarian. As syntagms of that demonic language, these animals possess unhuman efficiency, demon's beauty, and speak how foreign that nether region is.

Hughes discovers deep human realities in his visions of animals. The poem "November" (*Lupercal*) and the stories "Sunday" and "The Rain Horse" (*Wodwo*) draw from the dissolving zone between man and animal where both share indistinguishably the same life-force. The dead birds at the end of

Leonard Baskin

Private collection

"November" are, like the tramps in the ditch, left-over containers when the life is gone elsewhere. Human-creature identifications, coming together in Hughes's live bull, delight us, move us toward the mystery:

> the warm weight of his breathing,
> The ammoniac reek of his litter, the hotly-tongued
> Mash of his cud, steamed against me.
> Then slowly, as onto the mind's eye—
> The brow like masonry, the deep-keeled neck:
> Something come up there onto the brink of the gulf,
> Hadn't heard of the world, too deep in itself to be called to,
> Stood in sleep.
>
> —*Lupercal*, 37

Here, now, out for his walk, is the retired Colonel who

> Came, face pulped scarlet with kept rage,
> For air past our gate.
> Barked at his dog knout and whipcrack
> And cowerings of India: five or six wars
> Stiffened in his reddened neck;
> Brow bull-down for the stroke.
>
> —*Lupercal*, 42

In the same way that we come upon ourselves in Hughes's animals, we come upon ourselves in the crow. But beyond this mirror function, Hughes's animals possess, as we have seen, a complex aesthetic meaning as well. They are allegories of the coherent life language can hold in balance against the life-stunning realities of existence. "How can a poem . . . about a walk in the rain be like an animal?" Hughes asks in his poetry primer, *Poetry Is*. "Well, perhaps it cannot look much like a giraffe or an emu or an octopus, or anything you might find in a menagerie. It is better to call it an assembly of living parts moved by a single spirit."[16] Of his jaguar poems, Hughes says he prefers to think of them "as first, descriptions of a jaguar, second . . . invocations of the Goddess, third . . . invocations of a jaguar-like body of elemental force, demonic force."[17] The particular jaguar in *The Hawk in the Rain*, his first book of poems, is a visitation from that force-field. The crowd "stands, mesmerized, / As a child at a dream." The jaguar is also a transfiguration of the poet holding the angry energy for which there is no release from the cage of language: "a jaguar hurrying enraged / Through prison darkness after the drills of his eyes / On a short fierce fuse." This is restless stalking survival force. Like the poet crouched in the doorway, the jaguar is concentrated fury against his entrapment. He is also the demonic counter-force to all the dreary lives of those childlike zoo-goers in search of their wild dreams. The poet arranges these visitations. It is the showman-poet who kills his prey, like the little man Billy Red in the story "Sunday," who, for spectators in the country pub yard, between pints of bitter, kills caged rats with his teeth. There is fierce pleasure in the contest between brute life and what destroys it. Animals serve that motif in Hughes, and they are not least of all a part of his definition of the poet in the contemporary world. As Thom Gunn wrote: "the harder a living thing resists the opposition of the elements, of other living things, or of death, the finer the quality of its existence. There is in fact a very clear-cut antithesis set up in Mr. Hughes's poetry: the pure unthinking energy of life against whatever opposed it."[18] As survival aesthetics, the significance is this: though you skin the poet, his sucking truth will weasel up somewhere else:

> They nailed to a door
>
> The stoat with the sun in its belly,
> But its red unmanageable life
> Has licked the stylist out of their skulls,
> Has sucked that age like an egg and gone off
>
> Along ditches where flies and leaves
> Overpower our tongues, got into some
>   grave—
> Not a dog to follow it down—
> Emerges, thirsting, in far Asia, in Brixton.
>   —*Lupercal*, 16

A deeply positioned balance is the primary structure and source of integrity in Hughes's poetic consciousness. This equation defines the fundamental task of the poet as he conceives it: "poetry is nothing if not . . . the record of just how the forces of the Universe try to redress some balance disturbed by human error." What upsets the balance is the over-mentalizing of our lives: "the psychological stupidity, the ineptitude, of the rigidly rationalist outlook—it's a form of hubris, and we're paying the traditional price. If you refuse the energy, you are living a kind of death. . . . [One must] accept the energy, and find methods of turning it to good, of keeping it under control."[19] Like Robert Graves, Hughes makes a very large claim for poetry in our age, nothing less than the keeping of the primal energy. This crucial axis in Hughes's mind involves less a to-ing and fro-ing between the hammerings of the blood on the one hand and the abstract dictations of the moralizing mind on the other, than a life-and-beauty-giving exertion between graceful order and demonic freedom, high principles and muscle. Thus, we are not surprised to learn that John Crowe Ransom, the poet of "The Equilibrists," is one of Hughes's acknowledged early models.

Equilibrium is imaged forth incessantly in the poetry. The water lily—

like a man's head, like a *poem*—holds its face upward to light while the under part roots deep in the bottom slime where:

> Prehistoric bedragonned times
> Crawl that darkness with Latin names.
> —*Lupercal*, 29

The long-necked lily links two worlds. The otter runs between earth and water. Confrontations erupt at the meeting-point between our decorous lives and the screaming savageness of clawed nature, as when the little miss triggers the caged macaw:

> All day he stares at his furnace
> With eyes red-raw, but when she comes they close.
> "Polly. Pretty Poll," she cajoles, and rocks him gently.
> She caresses, whispers kisses. The blue lids stay shut.
> She strikes the cage in a tantrum and swirls out:
> > Instantly beak, wings, talons crash
> > The bars in conflagration and frenzy,
> > And his shriek shakes the house.
> —*Hawk*, 13

The balance holds in doppelganger themes in the tales, as Daniel Hoffman has remarked, where protagonists are divided between human and bestial or mythological shape. The poems work less schematically, seeking the vast novelty of the dark world under the world, and taking momentary grips on its mystery, as the otter (to use an image of Hughes's) takes a stolen hold on the bitch otter in the field. The second book of poetry, *Lupercal*, like its name, is a summoning of the bestial forces to vivify life, to make the women fertile, and to have the demons out of their holes again. Poems stalk that experience:

> These feet, deprived,
> Disdaining all that are caged, or storied, or pictured,
> Through and throughout the true world search
> For their vanished head, for the world
>
> Vanished with the head, the teeth, the quick
> > eyes—.
> —*Lupercal*, 13

Hughes's obsession with sheer force is inseparable from his courting of conditions of equipoise. Repeatedly in the poems the imagination hauls upwards, following the hawk, to reach "the master-fulcrum of violence" as Hughes calls the point of balance in "The Hawk in the Rain." That is the

Leonard Baskin   *Nasrudin Gallery, Boston*

intersection of intense forces—whether in a life or in a poem—the point between what raises up and what destroys. Each poem is a position along the bar on that fulcrum, separate occasions marking the force of intense opposition. As in the hawk poem, that high risk leads to the laboriously, violently even, attained place of equal counterforces. At the point of that balance, in unfamiliar space, rests the life principle, "the diamond point of will."

Always, from that soaring feat, a fall is imagined or experienced. For that is the failed task, the fool's overreach, or the error in the universal structure that must then again be redressed. The poise unbalances, the weather turns, the soaring hawk

> suffers the air, hurled upside down,
> Fall from his eye, the ponderous shires crash on him,
> The horizon trap him; the round angelic eye
> Smashed, mix the heart's blood with the mire
> of the land.
>
> —*Hawk*, 11

The *fall* that occurs repeatedly in Hughes's work is parodied by exaggerated cartoon destructions in *Crow*. It is the inevitable plunge attending the chattering mindless high-flying in "Skylarks" or in "Wings," the imagined plunge of philosophical desperation in Sartre (whose "wings" are hideous and compared to skates' wings) or in Kafka (whose wings are broken), or transfigured into the filth of flies. We perceive that the soar-fall structure is the inward shape in many poems. In "Dick Straightup," it takes the form of the tumble from pub stool to gutter.

The core figure of balance structures Hughes's extraordinary essay on the central fable in Shakespeare, whose poetry he sees as a microcosm of the momentous counterforces warring within Queen Elizabeth and in her times between satanic necessities and heavenly aspirations. The balance rests in sexual terms, and finally, as Hughes reads Shakespeare, the central fable engages the mystery of integrating man's psychic wholeness. A similar balance between the rational and dark sides constitutes Hughes's own central uroboric fable.

His hawk in the rain balances sinew and air current against the down-bringing gravity, which is nature's version of bullets raising the cobbles. For a deadened culture, balance must be restored by primitive recoveries in the imagination. For the poet, balance comes from the deep, energy-giving worlds whose power can be summoned along the path of language. Poems alert to those root-sounds force openings back and down to our beginnings, to primal sources of brute being uncrippled by mentalizing. Language is one of the principal instruments of penetration. In his adaptation of Seneca's *Oedipus*, Hughes attempted to fashion language capable of that incision. He sought there, he says, "to make a text that would release whatever inner force this situation [of Oedipus] has, with the minimum interference from surface detail in word, plot, or movement."[20] Thus readers confront choppy, beauty-less rhythms in search of experience pared of its surfaces. Like the hawk in "The Hawk in the Rain," the poet seeks a high risk performance, self-sustained. Yet pure nature, functioning through its efficient instrumentality, as witnessed in "Thrushes," is a killing machine. With men it can be otherwise. Their acts can be reaches of imagination which for a moment transcend the necessities of brute survival and become the gestures of art. These are the boundaries of the vision; at their intersection, the undeflected instinct of the shark's mouth differs only in purpose from Mozart's brain. Grub-stabbing thrushes, Hughes's poem asks,

> Is it their single-mind-sized skulls, or a trained
> Body, or genius, or a nestful of brats
> Gives their days this bullet and automatic
> Purpose? Mozart's brain had it, and the shark's
> mouth
> That hungers down the blood-smell even to a
> leak of its own
> Side and devouring of itself: efficiency which
> Strikes too streamlined for any doubt to pluck
> at it
> Or obstruction deflect.
>
> —*Lupercal*, 52

Raising the deep specters is immeasurably different from a private act of therapy for Hughes. We remain oblivious to his originality, or at best diminish it, if we see simply another confessional poet having his nightmares in public. Alvarez has said of Hughes's maturation from the early work to *Crow* that he has "learned to control his private horrors and make them public by subjecting them to arbitrary rules, as a psychotic child repeats and controls his terrors by turning them into play."[21] The observation captures Hughes's (and Popa's) game strategies of surrealist poetry. But with Hughes, the stakes are different. His goal is to release the deep animations of the culture rather than to contain his private agonies (though they intersect at times); not so much to domesticate reality's depredations by word manipulation, but to put his readers, like the crowd before the jaguar's cage, into the presence of the demons themselves. This is the poet's task as he conceives it; demon is another word for both the poem and the poet.

The primary analogue of Hughes's enterprise is shamanism. It is a basic allegory, the dream of two worlds that anthropological study has supplied this contemporary poet. "What am I?" Hughes begins the poem "Wodwo," the title an Old English word he translates as "a sort of half-man half-animal spirit."[22] Defining a man's whole nature, the enigma Hughes describes as

the powerhouse at the center of Shakespeare's mind, is his also. It is the
sphinx's riddle, and inspection of the vast lower realms is thus thrust upon
the poet, as upon the shaman. Hughes's selections from Shakespeare, extracted from their contexts, reveal that central fable: the confrontation between Venus and Adonis, that is, between the hidden and the rational. In
that selection, Hughes says, "We see quite new things . . . , a new teeming
of possibilities, as we look through them into our own darkness."[23] The dark
revelation re-enacts the shamanistic adventure. All that energy and violence
in Hughes's first book of poetry seem now in this light to have been an
instinctive ambush for the demons of life. In the poem "Wind," the visitation
of a storm occupies the entire house of the mind and shakes its underpinnings.
There are lesser visitations: the meeting of a fop and a black goat in the hills,
for example (*Hawk*, 39). But the nether world in its merged beauty and
terror occupies fully the poem "Pike." The pond into which the poet-fisher
casts his line reaches "legendary depth," in imagination it is "as deep as
England. It held / Pike too immense to stir." The activity is all in the mind,
a shamanistic visitation as the fisherman-poet summons up to his mind's eye
the dark shapes from the tribal unconscious, returning them as totemic
powers for the revitalizing of the culture and to save the soul of England.
For a moment, two hundred ninety-eight words in a certain order have
explored the boundaries of language, and consequently of consciousness, and
shown them to be further out than we had imagined, ready for "what might
move, for what eye might move":

> The still splashes on the dark pond,
>
> Owls hushing the floating woods
> Frail on my ear against the dream
> Darkness beneath night's darkness had freed,
> That rose slowly towards me, watching.
> —*Lupercal*, 57

The shamanic experience lurks in all the images of the hunter, the caged
animals, and the other creature-confrontations. It is anything but a faddish
primitivism on Hughes's part. Rather, shamanism provides him with a
model for the original poetic act. It also explains the family relationship
between his poetry, folk-epic, plays and his children's verse and stories.
Hughes wrote in 1964: "The initiation dreams, the general schema of the
shamanic flight, and the figures and adventures they encounter, are not a
shaman monopoly: they are, in fact, the basic experience of the poetic
temperament we call 'romantic.' " In a shamanizing society, he continued,
" 'Venus and Adonis,' some of Keats's longer poems, 'The Wandering of
Oisin,' 'Ash Wednesday,' would all qualify their authors for the magic drum
[of the shaman]; while the actual flight lies perceptibly behind many of the

best fairy tales, and behind myths such as those of Orpheus and Herakles, and behind the epics of Gilgamesh and Odysseus. It is the outline, in fact, of the Heroic Quest. The shamans seem to undergo, at will and at phenomenal intensity, and with practical results, one of the main regenerating dramas of the human psyche: the fundamental poetic event."[24] We must note particularly the idea of practicality. For Hughes is not a mystic, but rather a man making the most practical sort of claims for poetry. "Shamanism," he said, "is not a religion, but a technique for moving in a state of ecstasy among the various spiritual realms, and for generally dealing with souls and spirits, in a practical way, in some practical crisis." This is a shamanism of useful transport, treating real delusions.

Hughes had his own practical crisis early, according to W. S. Merwin, whose account of it puts flesh on this mystical passage. Merwin, in 1959 or 1960, had sent his poem "Lemuel's Blessing" to Hughes to read. Eight years later, Merwin wrote:

> When I'd finished the poem . . . I showed it to Ted Hughes. It was the last winter that he and Sylvia were living around the corner from us in London. He told me a story. At Cambridge he set out to study English literature. Hated it. Groaned having to write those essays. Felt he was dying of it in some essential place. Sweated late at night over the paper on Dr. Johnson et al.—things he didn't want to read. One night, very late, very tired, he went to sleep. Saw the door open and someone like himself come in with a fox's head. The visitor went over to his desk, where an unfinished essay was lying, and put his paw on the papers, leaving a bloody mark; then he came over to the bed, looked down at Ted and said, "You're killing us," and went out the door.[25]

Hughes switched to anthropology at Cambridge! The account, whether or not reliable, records an early working out of Hughes's compulsion, no doubt with suggestive connections to Jung's experience. Hughes obviously meant to walk further in the place of demons all the while knowing the hazards. (For his version of the risks of hallucination, see the terrifying poem "Crow's Account of St. George.") We need not take up the drum ourselves to recognize that Hughes has associated in his poetics the shaman's visitation with the dream of the poet. The most common form of election to shamanhood, Hughes has written, comes "from the spirits themselves: they approach the man in a dream. At the simplest, these dreams are no more than vision of an eagle, as among the Buryats, or a beautiful woman (who marries them), as among the Goldi. But at the other extreme, the dreams are long and complicated, and dramatize in full the whole psychological transformation that any shaman, no matter how he has been initially chosen, must undergo."[26] The career is binding, its hold unbreakable. The true practitioner, primitive or modern day Yorkshire-Cambridge-London-Devonshire shaman, is totally committed: "One main circumstance in becoming a shaman, in the first place," says Hughes, "is that once you've been chosen by the spirits, and dreamed the dreams, there is no other life for you, you must shamanize or die: this belief seems almost universal." The false shaman-poet, like Billy Red the rat-biter in the story, catches not free spirits but caged ones, the clichés, and shakes what life there is from them for a free pint and the momentary titillation of the pub crowd.

Hughes has written on Shakespeare, Emily Dickinson, Yeats, Keith Douglas, Dylan Thomas, and Sylvia Plath, locating in each the deep-diving, conjuring, soul-restoring shamanic power. He finds them all wooers of the goddess. Of Sylvia Plath, he has said, she "had free and controlled access to depths formerly reserved to the primitive ecstatic priests, shamans and Holy men, and more recently flung open to tourists with the passport of such hallucinogens as LSD."[27] Dylan Thomas's death of alcohol poisoning in New York, Hughes interprets as a final shamanist summoning by Thomas of the central life out of his own brain stem. "What he was really waiting for, and coaxing with alcohol," wrote Hughes, "was the delicate cerebral disaster that demolishes the old self for good, with all its crushing fortifications, and leaves the *atman* a clear field."[28]

Shakespeare stands in Hughes's mind pre-eminently as the poet enacting the shamanic excursion. Of Shakespeare's central obsession with the body-mind antagonism in "Venus and Adonis," Hughes says, "it is a perfect example of the ancient shamanistic dream of the call to the poetic or holy life. . . . It embodies the biological polarity of the life of the body and archaic nervous system and the life of the reflexive cortex. In more concrete form, the fable contains hints of atavistic memories from earlier times, resurfacings of rituals and symbols of which Shakespeare cannot have heard or read."[29] The passions bear witness to the inner fire, a godly version of which, according to Hughes, burned in Cromwell. Hughes's parody of the whole compulsion unfolds in his privately printed account of the preacher's assault on the whorehouse, *The Burning of the Brothel* (1966).

Gut fire or hallucination, the indwelling of the demon force gives the poet of Hughes's especial admiration access to the darkness beneath night's darkness. He isolated Emily Dickinson's experiences of this *Other*, her glimpses of horrible nothingness. Of such visitations from the void, Hughes writes: "At any moment she is likely to feel it ushering itself in, with electrical storms, exalted glimpses of objects, eerie openings of the cosmos— 'a wind that rose, though not a leaf / In any forest stirred.' " It stared, says Hughes, "out of every smallest thing and gave the world its awesome, pathetic importance," adding "she never seems to have known quite what to think of [that *other* experience]. It seems to have recurred to her as a physical state, almost a trance state. In this condition, there opened to her a vision—final reality, her own soul, the soul within the Universe—in all her descriptions of its nature, she never presumed to give it a name. It was her deepest, holiest experience: it was also the most terrible: timeless, deathly, vast, intense."[30]

Hughes sees parallels between the psychotic state and the shaman's plunge, both being suspensions of the familiar which lead into openings of terrifying disclosure. The poet's craft is to make words enact those disclosures. Such probes to the underworld must, in a post-literate culture, be fashioned from a vast field of cluttered and vernacular experience. To Hughes the contemporary poet is thus a serious scavenger. The litter of his world includes surreal experience: dreams, nightmares, madness, terror, bestiality, automatism. We come upon Hughes himself ransacking the movies, animated cartoons, birthday card greetings, folk songs, montage overloading, children's fables, whatever comes to the hand in a wasting culture where advertising has replaced literature as the image-pool for the imagination and TV talk-show hosts have become the models of the intellect. Hughes's scavenging of the languages of all these media produces a boggling mixture of tangent literary forms: heroic epic, folk epic, myth, cycles, lyrics, chants, incantations. His cartoons in *Crow* characteristically play out violent dream terrors while they simultaneously chronicle a comic *survival* amidst wildly destructive forces.

The coherent element in these techniques of the pop culture roots in the need of men to face *practical* crises, to make life manageable by clinging to the simple structures of it. The shaman's aesthetic penetrates to those brute simplicities and hauls them back to the surface. As in *Crow*, and at each stage on the way to it, Hughes's aim has been to say, by getting deeper than our familiar reality, what it is at this time to be inside our lives and not looking in from the outside. Crow's single, unequivocal, consummate attribute is a creaturely wanting to go on existing. The same is true of the poems in which Crow has his existence. This unself-conscious practicality, the aesthetic instinct that equips poetry for survival, is fashioned by an art of intricate means and enormous intensity.

To this end, the poet tries to get back to beginnings, seeking the raw dream in the indestructible fables, summoning shaman-like the dogs of energy up through the interstices in the civilized pavements. Poems, in Hughes's conception, are castings of words around those lost origins and submerged energies.

Notes

1. Hughes has published four major books of poetry: *The Hawk in the Rain* (1957), *Lupercal* (1960), *Wodwo* (1967), and *Crow* (1970). His stories, plays, criticism, and reviews are numerous. The Milosz quotation is from Hughes's essay "Vasko Popa," *Tri-Quarterly*, 9

(1967), 201. The shark image is from the poem "Logos" in *Recklings* (1966), a limited edition of poems.

2. From an interview with Ekbert Faas, "Ted Hughes and Crow," *London Magazine*, 10 (Jan., 1971), 8.

3. Calvin Bedient, "On Ted Hughes," *Critical Quarterly*, 14 (Summer, 1972), 103.

4. "Vasko Popa," 205.

5. "Black Bird," *The Observer* (Oct. 11, 1970), 33.

6. "Talking Beasts: The 'Single Adventure' in the Poems of Ted Hughes," *Shenandoah*, 19 (Summer, 1968), 68.

7. "The Last Ditch," *New York Review of Books* (July 22, 1971), 4.

8. "Vasko Popa," 202. See also my forthcoming essay on Hughes entitled "Poetry Equipped for Life."

9. "Vasko Popa," 202.

10. Julius S. Held, *Baskin Catalogue*, Bowdoin College Museum of Art, 1962.

11. *Leonard Baskin* (Washington: Smithsonian, 1970), 10.

12. "Capturing Animals," *Listener*, 78 (Oct. 19, 1967), 498.

13. "Capturing Animals," 498.

14. Alvarez, 33.

15. "Secret Ecstasies," *Listener*, 72 (Oct. 29, 1964), 677.

16. *Poetry Is* (New York: Doubleday, 1970), 11.

17. Faas interview, 8.

18. "Certain Traditions," *Poetry* 97 (January 1961), 268.

19. Faas interview, 7.

20. "The Oedipus of Seneca," *Arion*, 7 (Autumn, 1968), 325.

21. Alvarez, 33.

22. *Poetry Is*, 58.

23. *With Fairest Flowers While Summer Lasts* (New York: Doubleday, 1971), v.

24. "Secret Ecstasies," 677–678. The quotation which follows is from p. 677.

25. Paul Carroll, *The Poem in its Skin* (Chicago: Follett, 1968), 149–150. I am indebted to Jim McEuen for tracking this down.

26. "Secret Ecstasies," 677. The next quotation is also found here.

27. "Notes on the Chronological Order of Sylvia Plath's Poems," *Tri-Quarterly*, 7 (Fall, 1966), 81–82.

28. "Dylan Thomas's Letters," *New Statesman*, 72 (Nov. 25, 1966), 783.

29. *With Fairest Flowers*, xxii.

30. *A Choice of Emily Dickinson's Verse* (London: Faber & Faber, 1968), 13.

Wolf Masks: The Early Poetry of Ted Hughes[1]

Stan Smith

I

'It was a violent time'. Thom Gunn's description of the Elizabethan age ('A Mirror for Poets'[2]) could equally be applied to the 1950s. Again and again the poetry of this decade returned to the central theme of violence, yet, constantly, shrank back from engaging with it. Gunn's own poetry, replete with latent aggression, nevertheless strove to contain its smouldering energy in couplets and formal stanzas and histrionic poses ('Even in bed I pose'[3]) as impersonal and self-disciplining as those nazi uniforms and leather-jackets with which his poems abound. The motor-cyclists of 'On the Move'[4] seemed to offer an adequate parallel to his own poetic stance:

> In goggles, donned impersonality,
> In gleaming jackets trophied with the dust,
> They strap in doubt—by hiding it, robust—
> And almost hear a meaning in their noise.

Much of the writing of 'The Movement' tried to explore the barbarous hinterland which recent history had shown lay behind the genteel littoral of western civilisation, but most poems had an air of 'donned impersonality' which seemed to brand them as exercises rather than explorations. The doubt was too profound, the revelation of depravity too recent and too raw, to make total candour possible. For many poets, an ostensibly empirical interest in the quotidian became, in fact, a rationale for escapism. Philip Larkin's picturesque evocations of provincial melancholy, Charles Tomlinson's attempt to transmute Constable or Cézanne into verse—their shared concern with the superficies of topographical or social landscape—indicate a primary failure of nerve summed in the lame argument, in equally lame pentameters, of Donald Davie's apologia, 'Rejoinder to a Critic':

Reprinted from *New Blackfriars* 56 (September 1975): 414–26, by permission of the author and the journal.

You may be right: 'How can I dare to feel'?
May be the only question I can pose. . . .
'Alas, alas, who's injured by my love'?
And recent history answers: half Japan!
Not love, but hate? Well both are versions of
The 'feeling' that you dare me to. . . . Be dumb!
Appear concerned only to make it scan!
How dare we now be anything but numb?[5]

Robert Lowell christened the period 'the tranquillised fifties';[6] in a now famous article[7] A. Alvarez spoke of the besetting sin of the age as 'the gentility principle', while, in an essay of the same period,[8] Tomlinson himself criticised his contemporaries for squandering the heritage of Modernism and retreating into 'a self-congratulatory parochialism,' singling out Larkin as a special offender. But Tomlinson's early poetry[9] is itself a product of the same general ethos, for all its gestures towards 'the community of European values' and 'the three great post-symbolists', Eliot, Pound and Yeats. Of the poets of the fifties, only a handful dared to be anything more than numb; and of these, Ted Hughes is, perhaps, the most honest in his attempts to come to terms with the restless and uncomprehended violence that continued to fret beneath the surface of an apparently convalescent European sensibility.

What I wish to suggest here is that the characteristic structures of feeling of this anaesthetised poetry of the fifties are founded in the experience of a particular social universe; that, in an obscure, largely unintentional and mediated manner, they fulfilled an ideological function in that universe; and that, while Ted Hughes' poetry shares in the experience, it is pervaded by tensions and intensities which offer the first signs of an upheaval, which, with the political and cultural revolt of the last few years, has erupted into history.

This experience can best be encapsulated, in the phrase coined by Herbert Marcuse, as the experience of a *one-dimensional universe*. The geopolitical settlement, conceived at Yalta and Potsdam, brought to birth at Fulton, and confirmed in the Truman Doctrine, seemed to have created a social universe insulated from historical refutation, in which history itself had come to a stop. Nothing in the future, it appeared, could rescind the status quo established and consolidated by the Cold War. In the post-war era which is the subject of Marcuse's *One Dimensional Man*:

Technical progress, extended to a whole system of domination and co-ordination, created forms of life (and of power) which appear to reconcile the forces opposing the system and to defeat or refute all protest in the name of the historical prospects of freedom from toil and domination. Contemporary society seems to be capable of containing social change—qualitative change which would establish essentially different institutions, a new direction of the productive process, new modes of human existence. This containment of social change is perhaps the most singular achievement of advanced industrial society.

This closed political universe necessarily entailed, too, a closed emotional universe. Yet, within the contained present, 'new modes of human existence' were felt as pressing possibilities. Since these modes of being found no point of insertion into established reality, they lacked a language and a set of categories that would make sense of them. They manifested themselves, therefore, as a frustrated and aimless violence, without apparent cause or object, irrational incursions into the world of commonsense. In Ted Hughes' poetry this contradiction, between the established rationality of the status quo, and the nameless and undefined potentialities latent but deadlocked within it, finds its objective correlative in strange, atavistic fantasies of animal intensity. And these fantasies burn their way through the fabric of everyday experience with memories of an older and more terrifying existence. For, as Marcuse suggests:

> This ambiguous situation involves a still more fundamental ambiguity. [We] vacillate . . . between two contradictory hypotheses: (1) that advanced industrial society is capable of containing qualitative change for the foreseeable future; (2) that forces and tendencies exist which may break this containment and explode the society. . . .

Both tendencies are there, side by side—and even the one in the other. Both tendencies coexist in the poetry of Ted Hughes: it derives its underlying tensions from the explosive ambiguity of the contradiction, at that precise juncture in the evolution of post-war society; and, too, it records the first stages in the disintegration of that unstable equilibrium.

II

The universe of Hughes' 'Pibroch' (first collected in *The New Poetry* (1962)) is mindless and elemental, a barren landscape of sea and rock, endlessly swept by the wind. This is a meaningless world, locked in its own facticity:

> The sea cries with its meaningless voice,
> Treating alike its dead and its living,
> Probably bored with the appearance of heaven
> After so many millions of nights without sleep,
> Without purpose, without self-deception.

Heaven, the ideal, is simply an appearance, a frame of stars set forever beyond reach. The world remains imprisoned within itself, beyond surpassing, going nowhere:

> Stone likewise. A pebble is imprisoned
> Like nothing in the Universe.
> Created for black sleep. Or growing
> Conscious of the sun's red spot occasionally,
> Then dreaming it is the foetus of God.

The absurd delusion is clearly in some way a parody of human pretensions, as 'meaning' and 'purpose' in the first stanza are equated with self-deception—arbitrary human impositions on a vacuity which precedes rationalisation.

This is, explicitly, a personal vision of a specific landscape; but it aspires to the authority of a more ultimate kind of statement. What Hughes offers here is a *metaphysical* vision, of a *cosmic* order arrested in the perpetual moment, incapable of qualitative change. And yet this apparently metaphysical vision has a more immediate and relative, social significance.

The poem claims to make an inclusive statement on the human condition: but it is most significant in its omissions. Organic life is almost totally absent from this landscape, and that which intrudes is atypical in its sterile futility:

> Drinking the sea and eating the rock
>
> A tree struggles to make leaves—
> An old woman fallen from space
> Unprepared for these conditions.
> She hangs on, because her mind's gone completely.

Insofar as there is change, it is degeneration, the slow erosion of whatever life, and consciousness, remain stubbornly hanging on.

The exclusion of organic life is no accident. For to admit its presence would be to introduce a different conception of nature: of growth, exfoliation, fecundity, of a process in which the material world constantly transcends itself, moving beyond its always temporary present into new forms and futures. Time here is merely an inert perpetuation of the present. A historical, relative experience of social deadlock has been transposed into a mythic dimension beyond human agency. To conceive of the deadlock in such cosmic, and therefore apolitical, terms, is to acquiesce in its totality:

> Minute after minute, aeon after aeon,
> Nothing lets up or develops.
> And this is neither a bad variant or a tryout.
> This is where the staring angels go through.
> This is where all the stars bow down.

Any aspiration to grasp a destiny beyond the actual is dismissed as the ludicrous rebellion of obtuse stone or imbecilic tree. Yet a little life and consciousness persist, stirring feebly in the black sleep of a lobotomised reality.

The essentially totalitarian nature of this universe is communicated, in 'Hawk Roosting' (*L.*), through the figure of the arrogant and ruthless hawk which is a recurrent image in Hughes' poetry. The bird, like some prime mover, surveys a landscape which it sees as a mere extension of its own egocentric life. The bird's all-powerful and all-seeing eye establishes it as a type of the vigilant authoritarian State of Orwell's *1984*, which allows its members no privacy or autonomy. Yet the intensity of this vision suggests that it is a purgation, not of some future and imaginary society, but of that paranoia which is the normal condition of the bourgeois soul here and now, in our own apparently 'open' societies:

> I sit in the top of the wood, my eyes closed.
> Inaction, no falsifying dream
> Between my hooked head and hooked feet:
> Or in sleep rehearse perfect kills and eat.
>
> The convenience of the high trees!
> The air's buoyancy and the sun's ray
> Are of advantage to me;
> And the earth's face upward for my inspection.
>
> My feet are locked upon the rough bark.
> It took the whole of Creation
> To produce my foot, my each feather:
> Now I hold Creation in my foot
>
> Or fly up, and revolve it all slowly—
> I kill where I please because it is all mine. . . .

This, the ultimate heir of Creation, in whom Creation has come to rest, is the epitome of simple, unreflective power, confident in its own supremacy and confirmed in its confidence, it seems, by the whole weight of an amoral, meritocratic universe which acknowledges the logic of success alone:

> No arguments assert my right:
>
> The sun is behind me.
> Nothing has changed since I began.
> My eye has permitted no change.
> I am going to keep things like this.

Here the perpetuation of the status quo is explicitly identified as an act of will, vindicated by force. But, again, the incarnation of this deadlock in the

figure of the hawk takes it beyond the realm of relative human events into
that of an inexorable nature. The bird's 'natural right' is, it seems, ratified
by the sun itself, which is behind it both literally and figuratively. By
converting conjunctural history into the absolute 'Creation' the poem precludes the possibility of refutation.

There seems to be a fundamental contradiction between the function of
the hawk image here and its role in the title poem of Hughes' first collection
of verse, *The Hawk in the Rain*. Whereas in 'Hawk Roosting' the mastery of
the bird lies in its identification with the rapacious reality which it embodies,
in 'The Hawk in the Rain' the bird seems set in opposition to this reality,
as an image of transcending freedom. The poem is structured around a
polarity of images, of eye and mouth, which focuses the central contradiction
of Hughes' emotional universe. While the 'earth's mouth' seeks to reabsorb
him back into the empiric present, the floundering individual strains after
the freedom symbolised by the apparently effortless achievement of the hawk:

> I drown in the drumming ploughland, I drag up
> Heel after heel from the swallowing of the earth's mouth,
> From clay that clutches my each step to the ankle
> With the habit of the dogged grave, but the hawk
>
> Effortlessly at height hangs his still eye.

The self struggles to break free from its corporal involution in a one-dimensional reality for which the glutinous physicality of the mud is an adequate
symbol. Each moment of action is bought dearly with every ounce of strength
from a material reality which spells extinction to the spirit, has the dogged
persistence of death itself, and will one day succeed in reappropriating (in
the devouring grave) the spirit's futile rebellion.

But now, though this hawk too is said to 'hold all creation', the 'still
eye' of the bird seems to suggest the spirit's possible independence from the
devouring earth, in its capacity to contain and totalise in vision the landscape
from which it has abstracted itself. The transcending eye encompasses its
object without consuming it: and, through distance, it insulates itself from
engulfment by the universe of which it is an object. Vision and detachment
seem to be power, an achieved mastery of stillness in the heart of the flux.

To the self below, incapable of a vision which sees life steady and sees
it whole, a 'morsel in the earth's mouth', such poise can seem mere illusion.
For, at ground level, the eye is caught up in the immediate violence of a
wind that tolerates no bystanding, and is felt with a kinetic, physical urgency:

> His wings hold all creation in a weightless quiet,
> Steady as a hallucination in the streaming air.
> While banging wind kills these stubborn hedges,

Thumbs my eyes, throws my breath, tackles my heart,
And rain hacks my head to the bone, the hawk hangs
The diamond point of will that polestars
The sea drowner's endurance: and I

Bloodily grabbed dazed last-moment-counting
Morsel in the earth's mouth, strain towards the master-
Fulcrum of violence where the hawk hangs still.

There is an ironic dimension to 'Hawk Roosting' lacking in 'The Hawk in the Rain'. The bird's implicit hubris in the former suggests the unacknowledged, untested limits of its power, limits which are confirmed in the last stanza of 'The Hawk in the Rain'. For the latter is no more really detached from the violence and oppression of the given than the despotic hawk of the former poem. The mastery of 'Hawk Roosting' resides in its eye; we see it exercised only in fantasy (lines 4 and 13). So, for 'The Hawk in the Rain', freedom is purely contemplative, a momentary and delusory abstraction soon to be destroyed by the loss of inner power and the pull of gravity:

That may be in his own time meets the weather
Coming the wrong way, suffers the air, hurled upside down
Fall from his eye, the ponderous shires crash on him,

The horizon trap him; the round angelic eye
Smashed, mix his heart's blood with the mire of the land.

Both hawks assume the freedom of total mastery. But they are free only to identify with the given, the achieved order of things. Though its naive solipsism leads 'The Hawk in the Rain' to see the whole world arranged around itself (so that it's the weather that is 'coming the wrong way', the air which 'falls from his eye', the shires that 'crash on him'), the bird's 'suffering' is not that of a tolerant but masterful martyr but that of a helpless victim. The eyes closed in self-satisfaction in 'Hawk Roosting' are really shut in ignorance—a solipsistic blindness revealed in the bird's readiness to assume that the objective rotation of the planet is a product of its subjective thought:

Or fly up, and revolve it all slowly.

Each is equally dependent on that Creation it believes it controls. The 'feet locked on the rough bark' may suggest the despot's grasp but in fact disclose the slave's chains. The meritocratic free spirit is the more securely enslaved by its ignorance of its dependence.

One of the few poems by Hughes which has an explicit political reference seems to justify this interpretation. In 'A Woman Unconscious' (L.), history is stalemated, unable to move forward, before the prospect of nuclear holocaust which has eliminated the very possibility of qualitative social change:

> Russia and America circle each other;
> Threats nudge an act that were without doubt
> A melting of the mould in the mother,
> Stones melting about the root. . . .

> Yet flitting thought . . .

> Shies from the world-cancelling black
> Of its playing shadow: it has learned
> That there's no trusting (trusting to luck)
> Dates when the world's due to be burned;

> That the future's no calamitous change
> But a malingering of now,
> Histories, towns, faces that no
> Malice or accident much derange.

In its transformation into a mere 'malingering of now' history fragments into innumerable private 'histories', particularised towns and faces that, for all their surface bustle, remain fundamentally unchanged by whatever succession of accidents befalls them. Human agency is stalemated: the self is no more than a 'flitting thought' across the face of an alien and reified society. Russia and America in all their swarming human plenitude, are reduced to the falsely concrete and diminished image of two animals in a fight. History again crystallises to instinct. And yet the 'world-cancelling black' is itself the product of human agency, the 'playing shadow' cast by that ephemeral consciousness which flits across the face of history. In this separation of instrument from will lies an alienation whose grotesque disproportion is revealed in that offhand parenthesis, '(trusting to luck)' and in the very ability to ask the rhetorical question with which the poem concludes:

> And though bomb be matched against bomb,
> Though all mankind wince out and nothing endure—
> Earth gone in an instant flare—
> Did a lesser death come

> Onto the white hospital bed
> Where one, numb beyond her last of sense,
> Closed her eyes on the world's evidence
> And into pillows sank her head.

What is out there, in the meaningless devalued world, haunted by the disabling prospect of its own annihilation, is unimaginable and illusory, compared with the felt intensity of personal life. Within this precarious and always potentially catastrophic stalemate, perspective shifts, necessarily, from the global to the personal, for it is only in personal terms, now, that time itself can unfold. And so the real, individual death is more meaningful, more tragic, than the possibility of a collective death forever deferred into a hypothetical and merely fantastic future. Reality is focussed here, in the immediate moment of joy and pain. And yet it is here too, in the immediacy of personal suffering, that the consequences of this impasse are most harrowing, in Hughes' poetry, and, ultimately, most destructive.

Hughes' poems reach out repeatedly to ambiguous images of the tension between boundless inner potency and an external limitation. The first two stanzas of 'The Jaguar' (*H.R.*) describe a zoo in which time itself seems incarcerated, where animal vitality has rotted in its own inertia. The animals are all, in a sense, redundant—like the boa-constrictor 'coiled like a fossil'—merely decorative appendages to a human world, stripped of the self-defining authenticity of instinct. They have become creatures in a bestiary, for

> It might be painted on a nursery wall.

But the spectators, too, share in the futility of the beasts: there is no basic distinction between the strutting parrots and the strolling crowds from whom, 'like cheap tarts', they solicit nuts, or between the apes adoring their fleas and the spectators equally seeking distraction in the admiration of the trivial. One creature alone haunts the vacuous present with a lost and alien intensity:

> . . . the crowd stands, stares, mesmerised,
> As a child at a dream, at a jaguar hurrying enraged
> Through prison darkness after the drills of his eyes
> On a short fierce fuse. Not in boredom—
> The eye satisfied to be blind in fire,
> By the bang of the blood in the brain deaf the ear—
> He spins from the bars, but there's no cage to him
>
> More than to the visionary his cell:
> His stride is wildernesses of freedom:
> The world rolls under the long thrust of his heel,
> Over the cage floor the horizons come.

III

There is, for the jaguar, no gulf between intention and act: all meaning is incarnate here and now, in the living moment. For the crowd, transcendence is only the inner wilderness of daydream. But the animal's instinctual unity of being acknowledges no gap between inner and outer: its very stride is 'wildernesses of freedom' (in contrast to the restless, forever dissatisfied running of the crowd after new distractions). Yet the paradox of the last line catches the ambivalence of this freedom which depends, for its validity, on the blunting of discrimination brought about by the intensity of the energy released. Instinct is deaf and blind, intoxicated by its own magnificence. And this intensity is in some way potentially self-destructive: the eyes burn like fuses to a powder-keg.

'Macaw and Little Miss' (*H.R.*) makes transparent the symbolic function of caged animals in Hughes' poetry. The poem shudders with a suppressed smouldering energy like that of the bird it describes. The language itself is dense, clustered and stubborn; unfolding slowly and painfully, as if reluctant or incapable of reaching any clear consummation, and with a stifling inertia which duplicates the suffocation of the bird which can only endure but not realise its own diabolical intensity:

> In a cage of wire-ribs
> The size of a man's head, the macaw bristles in a staring
> Combustion, suffers the stoking devils of his eyes.

A sentence whose main verb ('hangs') occurs within a line of its beginning nevertheless drags out through the rest of this and another stanza, in a seemingly endless crescendo of grotesque hyperbolic similes which clashes absurdly with the fading gentility of the setting ('the old lady's parlour'), and reaches its consummation in a spectacle of some weird cosmic convulsion which is itself subverted by the final diminishing image of puerile sadism:

> . . . he hangs as in clear flames,
> Like a torturer's iron instrument preparing
> With dense slow shuddering of greens, yellows, blues,
> Crimsoning into the barbs:
>
> Or like the smouldering head that hung
> In Killdevil's brass kitchen, in irons, who had been
> Volcano swearing to vomit the world away in black ash.
> And would, one day; or a fugitive aristocrat
> From some thunderous mythological hierarchy, caught
> By a little boy with a crust and a bent pin
> Or snare of horsehair set for a song-thrush,
> And put in a cage to sing.

The act of petty vindictiveness which rounds off the whole cycle is not gratuitous. It finds a parallel in the teasing cruelty of the old woman's granddaughter, in a way which explains the apparently excessive emotion with which the analogies invest the macaw. The girl is herself possessed by 'stoking devils' whose incinerating passions, finding no legitimate outlet, turn back upon her in concupiscent fantasies of violation totally at odds with her genteel context and innocent demeanour. She is haunted by visions of a desired yet terrifying catharsis which would be at once release and punishment:

> . . . The girl calls him 'Poor Polly', pokes fun.
> 'Jolly Mop'. But lies under every full moon,
> The spun glass of her body bared and so gleaming-still
> Her brimming eyes do not tremble or spill
>   The dream where the warrior comes, lightning and iron,
>   Smashing and burning and rending towards her loin:
>   Deep into her pillow her silence pleads.

The cajoling tenderness of her play with the macaw has a latent sexual ferocity. She caresses the bird only to frustrate its needs, as hers, too, are baffled:

> . . . she cajoles, and rocks him gently.
> She caresses, whispers kisses. The blue lids stay shut.
> She strikes the cage in a tantrum and swirls out:
>   Instantly beak, wings, talons crash
>   The bars in conflagration and frenzy,
>   And his shriek shakes the house.

Identity is a carefully sustained equilibrium of inner and outer pressures (the unspilled brimming), in which the self learns to accommodate its boundless possibilities to externally imposed norms and denials. Yet it is an equilibrium achieved only at great and inhuman cost in repression and sublimation. And should that precarious balance be upset, the whole house can be shaken in the conflagration. The pathological yearnings of the girl are the inner consequences of that one-dimensionality whose suffocating sterility (even the aspidistra 'succumbs/To the musk of faded velvet') turns the unfulfilled instincts back upon themselves, in an orgy of imagined self-chastisement. Yet, in such a universe, spontaneity would open the way to a new apocalypse, threatening the house of order and civilisation with a return of that chaos spoken of in 'Famous Poet' (H.R.) where 'half the world still burned'. What Hughes embodies, here, is the lived acknowledgement of that impasse Davie defined abstractly: 'How dare we now be anything but numb?'

IV

Hughes' poems seem intensely personal in their febrile energy; yet, on examination, they exhibit a striking impersonality. Repeatedly, an inner urgency is mediated through analogues of animal life which distance the speaker from too intimate an involvement in the experience he portrays. In many of the poems, the speaker seems hardly to have an existence separate from his articulation: often he seems to be speaking out of the very awareness of the creature he depicts, and the language has the harsh, tactile immediacy, the muscular density, of the animal it defines. Yet these bestiaries are never merely means of contrasting animal spontaneity with human apathy. His animals are not usually simple expressions of unalloyed instinctual joie-de-vivre. Most of them are in fact deeply ambiguous creatures, poised between two worlds: voracious carnivores in suburban zoos, or, like 'Esther's Tomcat' (L.), moving from the everyday, domestic world into a night which is as old as time, and as dark. And, recurrently, the retreat into instinct is associated by Hughes with a return to a feudal ethos of cruelty, superstition, and half-barbarous grandeur in speech and gesture.

'An Otter' (L.) is one such creature, whose amphibious nature ('neither fish nor beast') expresses a deep ambivalence in the self. Here, too, the world of primary instinctual awareness is endowed with an atavistic mystery: the otter

> Brings the legend of himself
> From before wars or burials. . . .

Yet it is a creature that belongs nowhere, 'Crying without answer' in the night, and its return to the water, fleeing the humans who fear and persecute it, is also a search for a lost world of being:

> Of neither water nor land. Seeking
> Some world lost when first he dived, that he cannot come at since.

So that the animal itself, as so frequently in Hughes' poems, is invested with the nostalgia that it symbolises. Indeed, it's this which seems the cause of its persecutions. It is feared because it is the symbol of a lost and elusive human identity, forever hounded by the guardians of consciousness, of the super-ego, who would reduce it to 'nothing at all,/To this long pelt over the back of a chair', and evading pursuit by reimmersing itself in the dark stream:

> The air
> Circling the globe, tainted and necessary,
>
> Mingling tobacco-smoke, hounds and parsley,
> Comes carefully to the sunk lungs.
> So the self under the eye lies,
> Attendant and withdrawn.

This recurrent association of animal instinct with nostalgia for a *historically* lost human world, whether feudal or primordial, suggests the glimmering recognition that the dispossession of the self is not a metaphysical condition. These creatures, in their ambivalence, reflect back to man his own ambiguity, poised, the becalmed master-fulcrum of violence, between two dimensions of being, as the plant in 'To Paint a Water-Lily' (*L.*), lies at the intersection of air and water, 'The two minds of this lady', 'still/As a painting' yet 'nudged [at] her root' by the 'Prehistoric bedragonned times'. 'Pike' (*L.*) is another such image of the ahistoric unconscious waiting its moment to return from the 'Stilled legendary depths' of a pond 'as deep as England':

> It held
> Pike too immense to stir, so immense and old
> That past nightfall I dared not cast
>
> But silently cast and fished
> With the hair frozen on my head
> For what might move, for what eye might move.
> The still splashes on the dark pond,
>
> Owls hushing the floating woods
> Frail on my ear against the dream
> Darkness beneath night's darkness had freed,
> That rose slowly towards me, watching.

This is no ordinary fish, but, clearly, a symbol of some archaic modality of being 'so immense and old' the rational self shrinks back from inviting it into vision, into contemplation. And yet, at the same time, the murderous fascination is irresistible. What's more, it is, ultimately, the watcher, not the watched.

When Hughes attempts to deal with human violence directly, he seems impelled to distance himself by writing of fictional or legendary or historically symbolic others, 'Fallgrief', 'The Reverend Skinner', 'A Misanthrope', 'The Ancient Heroes and the Bomber Pilot', 'The Martyrdom of Bishop Farrar' (*H.R.*). When a personal relationship is involved, it is almost always mediated, as if direct confrontation might invite the collapse of the self's carefully nurtured stability. In 'Six Young Men' (*H.R.*), even the faded photograph of six war-victims, their smiles 'Forty years rotting into soil', has the capacity to unnerve the speaker with an emotion which can hardly be borne, and which rises from depths beyond history:

> That man's not more alive whom you confront
> And shake by the hand, see hale, hear speak aloud,
> Than any of these six celluloid smiles are,
> Nor prehistoric or fabulous beast more dead;

> No thought so vivid as their smoking blood:
> To regard this photograph might well dement,
> Such contradictory permanent horrors here
> Smile from the single exposure and shoulder out
> One's own body from its instant and heat.

The intuition of 'some universal cataclysm' revealed in particular casualties, like those bodies piled into graves in 'Griefs for Dead Soldiers' (H.R.), is a 'Moment that could annihilate a watcher'. It is for this reason that Hughes so rarely writes directly of personal relationships. Any outgoing of the self to others simultaneously exposes it and adds new and unknown factors to its precarious equipoise. For 'The Dove Breeder' (H.R.) 'Love struck into his life/Like a hawk into a dovecote'. 'Parlour Piece' (L.) admits this, and the very admission has to be itself doubly distanced: by the arch title, and by the use of the third person plural which endows it with a specious objectivity. It is because love is so dangerous that it can be defined only by the conventional imagery of fire and flood, and must be deliberately constrained ('chaperoned') by the banality of its setting. For the personal collapse would seem to have immediately apocalyptic consequences. Emotion is anti-social, anarchic:

> With love so like fire they dared not
> Let it out into strawy small talk;
> With love so like a flood they dared not
> Let out a trickle lest the whole crack,
>
> These two sat speechlessly:
> Pale cool tea in tea-cups chaperoned
> Stillness, silence, the eyes
> Where fire and flood strained.

Hughes is certainly obsessed by violence, but his concern seems to be to propitiate, rather than celebrate it. And yet, simultaneously, he is attracted to the ferocity he abhors: it strikes a responsive chord in the self. In 'February' (L.) the ambivalence at the core of Hughes' work is acknowledged. An unidentified 'he', clearly the poet, seeks desperately to evade the persecuting fantasies aroused by a remembered photograph of 'the hairless, knuckled feet/ Of the last wolf killed in Britain':

> These feet, deprived
> Disdaining all that are caged, or storied, or pictured
> Through and throughout the true world search
> For the vanished head, for the world
>
> Vanished with the head, the teeth, the quick eyes—
> Now, lest they choose his head,

Under severe moons he sits making
Wolf-masks, mouths clamped well onto the world.

Hughes' own poems are wolf-masks, with which he seeks to placate the avenging spirit, denied fulfilment in a world which preserves its memory only as photographic trophies. The title of his second book of poems, *Lupercal*, alludes to the Roman ceremony, in February, which sought to ensure the fertility of the flocks by making placatory sacrifices to the wolf, to win him over to protection rather than pillage. Ironically, the poet is pursued because he himself first started to search after a lost vision, for the 'vanished head, for the world/Vanished with the head'. His own nostalgia has summoned up these greedy revenants. Ultimately, it is a nostalgia for the future, not the past.

Notes

1.   This article confines itself, by and large, to the two volumes of Hughes' poetry written in the 1950s—*The Hawk in the Rain* (1957) and *Lupercal* (1960), hereafter *H.R.* and *L.*

2.   *Fighting Terms* (1954).

3.   'Carnal Knowledge', *op. cit.*

4.   *The Sense of Movement* (1957).

5.   The same tone is displayed, but often with greater subtlety, throughout *Brides of Reason* (1955) and *A Winter Talent* (1957).

6.   *Life Studies* (1959).

7.   *Beyond the Gentility Principle* (printed as the Introduction to the anthology *The New Poetry* (1962).

8.   'Poetry Today', in *The Modern Age* (1961).

9.   *Seeing is Believing* (1960).

So what we need, evidently, is a faculty . . . which keeps faith, as Goethe says, with the world of things and the world of spirits equally.

   This really is imagination. This is the faculty we mean when we talk about the imagination of the great artists. The character of great works is exactly this: that in them the full presence of the inner world combines with and is reconciled to the full presence of the outer world. And in them we see that the laws of these two worlds are not contradictory at all . . . We recognize these works because we are all struggling to find those laws, as a man on a tightrope struggles for balance, because they are the formula that reconciles everything, and balances every imbalance.

(76,M,91–2)

Yes, I met Jung early, and though I think I have read all the translated volumes, I've avoided knowing them too well, which no doubt frees me to use them all the more.[1]

Poetics

EKBERT FAAS

Looking back over Hughes' career since 1957, one finds little in the young poet's surroundings that might have inspired the startling new vision he developed within little over a decade. The results have obvious analogues in today's avant-garde art. Yet what to the American poets of the late fifties, for instance, had already turned into a common quest within several clearly defined movements was a solitary path of singlehanded experimentation to an English poet of the same decade. As if to add to this task, Hughes, while addressing an audience recently trained on the civilized sensibility of Robert Conquest's *New Lines* poets, had been inspired to write his first poems of adulthood by an anthology of American poets dominated by the New Critical school of Richard Wilbur and John Crowe Ransom.[2] The impact of a style largely derivative of Eliot's metaphysical period is apparent in the grimly backhanded wit, the elaborate conceits and contorted syntax of early poems such as "A Modest Proposal" or "The Decay of Vanity."

Reprinted from *Ted Hughes: The Unaccommodated Universe* (Santa Barbara: Black Sparrow Press, 1980), 37–51, by permission of Black Sparrow Press and the author.

Ironically, this indebtedness may have helped the poet gain his first acceptances in predominantly American magazines, and win a contest sponsored by the New York YMHA, giving *The Hawk in the Rain* immediate publication by Harper. What the influence meant to his development is obvious from its almost total disappearance in *Lupercal* (1960). Yet even this second volume, which by a careful pruning of previous stylistic excesses established Hughes as "a poet of the first importance" (A. Alvarez),[3] gave small indication of what was ahead.

Analogously, Hughes' comments on poetry before 1962 sound more or less conventional. In a *Poetry Book Society Bulletin* statement of 1957 he introduced himself as dealing with the "war between vitality and death" and celebrating "the exploits of the warriors of either side" (57,H). Despite its rebellious invectives against "the soots and verdigris and corrosive deposits of our poetry industry," his 1962 essay on Keith Douglas strikes a similarly conservative note. A general understanding of poetry as in one sense "the eternal's view of the temporal" and the qualities to be admired in Douglas's work—an "aggressive nimbleness of mind," an "obsession to get the facts down clear and straight," the "thoroughness of his artistic conscience" refining a "style that combines a colloquial prose readiness and variety with a poetic breadth" (62,D,1069–70)—are documented by poems as strongly influenced by a Donne or Marvell as several in *The Hawk in the Rain*. Except for a brief description of Douglas' later poems as loose "constellation[s] of statements" (63,D,47)—a phrase characteristically added to the essay in '63 before it became the introduction to Douglas' *Selected Poems* (1964)—there is little here to reflect Hughes' ongoing change from an empathetic miniaturist of plants, animals and men into a visionary spellmaker of polyhistoric dimensions and sweeping vatic gestures. What the essay praises "is not a mind trained in philosophy, or privileged by visions" but "common life, recounting what it has had to undergo" (62,D,1069). Ironically, it was this very privilege of vision which the poet was secretly searching out in his deeper self.

1. "FLASH VISION" CREATIVITY

The critical acclaim that Hughes, hardly turned thirty, enjoyed after the publication of *Lupercal* might have been enough to make him end, like other poets before him, in either lifelong poet laureate self-complacency or dead-end suicidal inability to resurrect the early achievement. As if alive to these dangers, we find Hughes, early in 1962, pondering the fate of some of his predecessors. Yeats, for instance, being alert to his true genius, went on "developing as a poet" and "pursuing those adventures, mental, spiritual and physical . . . that his gift want[ed]." By contrast, Wordsworth at first trusted his gift, "producing the real thing," but subsequently became "absorbed by the impersonal dead lumber of matters in which his gift ha[d] no interest." Yet as Hughes was well aware, chance plays an important role in such destinies, and his obsessive concern with the elusiveness of inspiration reveals some of his own fears at the time—"it visits [the poet] when he is only half suspecting it, and he is not sure it has visited him until some days or months afterwards and perhaps he never can be sure." No craft, education, professional dedication and experimental ingenuity, not even the most thorough artistic conscience, will produce great poetry in default of this inspiration.

What emerged from such fears was a new poetic credo setting the parameters for Hughes' future creativity. Here also, the poet begins to join a new multicultural aesthetics shared by a number of his contemporaries in both America and Europe. The poet, Hughes concludes,

> can study his art, experiment, and apply his mind and live as he pleases. But the moment of writing is too late for further improvements or adjustments. Certain memories, images, sounds, feelings, thoughts, and relationships between these, have for some reason become luminous at the core of his mind: it is in his attempt to bring them out, without impairment, into a comparatively dark world that he makes poems. At the moment of writing, the poetry is a combination, or a resultant, of all that he is, unimpeachable evidence of itself and, indirectly, of himself, and for the time of writing he can do nothing but accept it. If he doesn't approve of what is appearing, there are always plenty of ways to falsify and "improve" it, there are always plenty of fashions as to how it should look, how it can be made more acceptable, more "interesting," his other faculties are only too ready to load it with their business, whereon he ceases to be a poet producing what poetry he can and becomes a cheat producing confusion.
>
> (62,C,44–5)

Artistic creativity should spring with unimpeded spontaneity from the deepest core of the human mind, and no revision should be allowed to falsify this primal impulse. Such notions are shared not only by Hughes' twentieth century peers and such isolated forerunners as Blake, Keats, Whitman or Rimbaud but by numerous artist literati from non-Western cultures. The poet, according to Chinese æsthetician Lu Chi (ca. 300 A.D.), for instance, simply has to accept the volcanic uncontrollable outbursts of his imagination—

> When it comes, it cannot be checked;
> When it goes, it cannot be stopped.[4]

According to Arthur Rimbaud, he should give free expression to the collective soul ("l'âme universelle") in which he immerses himself—"if what he brings back from *down there* has form, he gives form; if it is formless, he gives formlessness."[5] For whatever forms the poem will assume organically as an expression of this impulse, must, as Tung Yu wrote, emerge "like the unfolding and blooming of leaves and flowers."[6] Or if poetry, in Keats' words, "comes not as naturally as the Leaves to a tree it had better not come at all."[7] Rather than plan and revise, the poet should catch the sudden "flash of insight," as Bashō says, and "put it into words before it fades away in [his] mind."

> Composition of a poem must be done in an instant, like a woodcutter felling a huge tree or a swordsman leaping at a dangerous enemy. It is also like cutting a ripe watermelon with a sharp knife or like taking a large bite at a pear.[8]

This concept of a "first flash vision" (71,O), "a single 1,000-volt shock, that [lights] up everything" (P,120), as the true source of great poetry, has become more and more prominent in Hughes' poetics. Without it, he wrote in his 1971 *Orghast* commentary, a man might write "a heart-searching book of poems every two or three years for thirty years without setting down one live or true word" about his "real life." His "huge suffering lump of vital shut-away truths," the "luminous spirit" or "crowd of spirits" in which our individual selves find their real homeground through self-annihilation, remain incommunicado (71,O). Only by an infinite alertness to this flash vision will the poet's words, so classical Chinese æstheticians put it in a crucial formula, turn into a "resonance or vibration of the vitalizing spirit and movement of life" (*ch'i-yün shêng-tung*),[9] or as D. H. Lawrence wrote, be like "life surging itself into utterance at its very well-head."[10]

Yet, what are the concrete strategies by which such visions can find embodiment in words and hence be transferred to the reader? The psychophysiological model which Hughes, like others of his contemporaries, proposes as an answer, again finds crucial analogues among the classical writings of Eastern artist literati rather than among the predominantly ideational art theories of the West. Thus Bashō advised his disciples to learn "about pines from pines, and about bamboos from bamboos," meaning that they should immerse themselves "within an object . . . perceive its delicate life and feel its feeling, out of which a poem forms itself."[11] Hughes seems to emulate such Zen Buddhist empathy when he claims that the poet, before writing about something, should imaginatively "touch it, smell it, listen to it, turn [himself] into it" (P,18).

Though such notions have become predominantly associated with the name of Charles Olson in modern Anglo-American poetics, Hughes' life ironically provides a better illustration of them than the writing desk habits of the American poet. Long before Olson's 1950 "Projective Verse" essay could have taught the younger poet how to "cause the thing he makes to try to take its place alongside the things of nature,"[12] Hughes' childhood hunting around Mytholmroyd and Mexborough taught him a more natural lesson. Thus, beginning to write poems at about fifteen was "partly a continuation of [this] earlier pursuit":

> The special kind of excitement, the slightly mesmerized and quite involuntary concentration with which you make out the stirrings of a new poem in your mind, then the outline, the mass and colour and clean final form of it, the unique living reality of it in the midst of the general lifelessness, all that is too familiar to mistake. This is hunting and the poem is a new species of creature, a new specimen of the life outside your own.
>
> (P, 17)

The way Hughes talks about the poem itself or its impact on the reader has remained equally indebted to this early impulse. The images, rhythms and words of a poem should be an "assembly of living parts ruled by a single spirit," all "jump[ing] to life as you read them." And just as poetry ought to be made "out of experiences which change our bodies, and spirits," so the words employed in it should belong directly to one or several of the five senses. For words can be like little goblins, "as if each one had eyes, ears and tongue, or ears and fingers and a body to move with." And if the poet knows how to control them, they "can so affect you that delicate instruments can easily detect the changes in your skin perspiration, the rate of your pulse and so on" (P, 17–18, 32).

2. EXERCISES IN MEDITATION AND INVOCATION

Apparently unfamiliar with similar creeds held by American poets, Sylvia Plath for a time became the disciple of her husband. Her letters abound with praise of all the things she learned in this all-absorbing working partnership: how she sharpened her impressionistic perceptions according to Hughes' photographic vision, how she enriched her imagination by reading not only novels and poems but "books on folklore, fiddler crabs and meteorites," or how she learned to break through a writing block by just pouring out "a few pages of drivel until the juice came back." Yet the major impact on her poetic development derived from the psychic powers of her "hypnotizing husband," a subject which, as early as July 1956, she had planned to explore in a short story of that title. Ted would often hypnotize Sylvia to sleep, a practice which also, as he recalls, made her focus and concentrate on work in certain ways. One of the possible results, as recorded in a letter of June 1958, was that Sylvia decided to dispense with the conscious use of "symbols, irony, archetypal images and all that" as favored by the climate of the New Criticism. We will try, she wrote, "to get along without such conscious and contrived machinery. We write and wake up with symbols on our pages, but do not begin with them."[13] In late 1959, while staying in a lonely artists' colony at Yaddo, Ted and Sylvia devised "exercises of meditation and invocation" (66,P,85) which Hughes, aided by handbooks of Cabalistic and Hermetic magic, had been pursuing for some time. The main technique was to invoke and hold composite images with the aim of unlocking hidden sources of imaginative energy. Franz Bardon's *Initiation into Hermetics* describes a more advanced form of such "Concentration of thoughts with two or three senses at once" by imagining, say, a gong

> of which you must hear not only the sound but also see the person sounding it . . . If you have reached this degree of concentration, try to do the same exercises, with your eyes open, whether fixing your look at one definite point, or staring into vacancy. The physical surroundings, then, must no longer exist for you, and the imagery you chose is to appear before your eyes floating in the air like a fata-morgana.[14]

The aim of these exercises of meditation and invocation was "to break down the tyranny, the fixed focus and public persona which descriptive or discursive poems take as a norm" (66,P,85). With similar intent Sylvia devised "a deliberate exercise in experimental improvisation on set themes" which, as Hughes recalls, allowed her "to let herself drop, rather than inch over bridges of concepts." Her final, most accomplished work, starting with "Tulips," composed in hospital during March 1961, was the fulfilment of this magically liberated imagination. As Hughes recalls, she wrote "Tulips" "without her usual studies over the Thesaurus, and at top speed, as one might write an urgent letter. From then on, all her poems were written in this way" (66,P,85–6).

Hughes' own development along similar lines was gradually reinforced by modern depth psychology and its analogues in Eastern thought. As early as 1960, the poet had had ample opportunity to explore this connection in trying to turn Evans-Wentz' translation of the *Bardo Thödol*, complete with Carl Jung's "Psychological Commentary," into an oratorio for his Chinese friend from Yaddo. Yet there is more than the evidence of such direct influence that points to the deep affinity existing between basic concepts of Hughes' post-1962 poetics and those of the East as seen through the eyes of Jung.

Post-Freudian psychiatry has tried to carry its searchlights into the ghost-ridden psychic realms of what Buddhists call the huge memory store-house of the "universal Mind" in which "discriminations, desires, attachments and deeds" have been collecting "since beginningless time" and which "like a magician . . . causes phantom things and people to appear and move about."[15] Partly with the help of such insights, Carl Jung managed to render a detailed account of these realms. A major step along this way was his 1938

introduction to *The Tibetan Book of the Dead*. What the *Bardo Thödol* describes
as the dead man's journey through mystical enlightenment (*dharma-kāya*),
the phantasmagoria of the "Universal Mind" (*sambhoga-kāya*), and the ego-
inspired fantasies of the personal "mind-system" (*nirmāna-kāya*) back through
the "Womb Door" into reincarnation, serves Jung as an inverse model for
our ongoing reinitiation into the collective unconscious.[16] By 1954 the same
Sanskrit terminology had come to provide him with the central concepts for
describing the human psyche.

> The unconscious is the root of all experience of oneness (*dharma-kāya*), the
> matrix of all archetypes or structural patterns (*sambhoga-kāya*), and the *conditio
> sine qua non* of the phenomenal world (*nirmāna-kāya*).[17]

Jung's model of the human psyche, as Sino-Japanese scholars are ready
to acknowledge before our own,[18] opens a badly needed new access to the
basic notions of Eastern æsthetics, and by extension, to their present-day
analogues in the West. For long before Romantics and Surrealists began to
explore their troubled egos, or isolated mystics managed to safeguard their
visions from religious persecutors and doctrinaire rationalists, Eastern artists
had ranged freely through the entire human psyche, from the personal mind,
through the collective unconscious, towards mystical enlightenment. Traditional translators, much like the early missionaries who emasculated primitive literature, are to be blamed for the one-sided image we still have, for
instance, of Chinese poetry as abounding with self-complacent serenity and
pathetic fallacies. More recent renderings such as A. C. Graham's of Late
T'ang poetry or Gary Snyder's of Han-shan's afford us glimpses both of the
unrelentingly de-anthropomorphized vision of Eastern mystics and a world
of nightmare phantasmagoria beside which most surrealist art looks like the
horror chamber of a charmingly obsolete country fair.

Theoretical treatises, again brought to light by more recent scholarship,
fill in the picture. In classical Chinese æsthetics, for instance, it is an assumption so common as to go almost without saying that art springs from an
immersion into the innermost core of the mind. Yet enough artists have left
hair-raisingly firsthand accounts of what it means to follow their two most
basic precepts of creativity, that poetry, for instance, should be "a vehicle of
the Way" (*wen yi tsai Tao*) by "express[ing] in words the intent of the . . .
mind" (*shih yen chih*).[19] After nine years of meditative exercise, one of them
writes, his self "both within and without, has been transformed . . . My eye
becomes my ear, my ear becomes my nose, my nose my mouth."[20] Prescribing
an immersion into the subconscious through "Meditation before Writing,"
Lu Chi, down to the very images he employs, anticipates Hughes' similar
plea from *Poetry in the Making* by over one and a half millennia: "All external
vision and sound are suspended." And the mind is "as a diver into a secret
world, lost in subterranean currents. Hence,/Arduously sought expressions,

hitherto evasive, hidden,/Will be like stray fishes out of the ocean bottom to emerge on the angler's hook."[21] Or as Hughes puts it:

> There is the inner life, which is the world of final reality, the world of memory, emotion, imagination, intelligence, and natural common sense, and which goes on all the time, consciously or unconsciously, like the heart beat. There is also the thinking process by which we break into that inner life and capture answers and evidence to support the answers out of it. That process of raid, or persuasion, or ambush, or dogged hunting, or surrender, is the kind of thinking we have to learn and if we do not somehow learn it, then our minds lie in us like the fish in the pond of a man who cannot fish.
>
> (P,57–8)

Although familiar with Eastern thought practices, Hughes, with his natural antipathy against today's mail-order Buddhism, is an unlikely person to have borrowed these notions from such sources. Instead, an entirely natural impulse, prior even to his interest in Hermetic and Cabalistic magic, had opened an access to the meditation and concentration rituals of Eastern sages. Just as hunting led him to write poetry at fifteen and from there to evolve a whole new body poetics of the neo-*"primitive-abstract*,"[22] so another childhood passion taught him the "trick or skill" to "catch those elusive or shadowy thoughts, . . . and [to] hold them still so [he could] get a really good look at them." Certainly, none of this was learnt at school. Here, on the contrary, he was often unable to articulate what might be no more than a "numb blank feeling" although it seemed so much more fascinating than the ideas he was made to write about in essays. The "mental exercise in concentration on a small point" which finally revealed some of these hidden interior treasures was acquired while fishing. Despite Hughes' disclaimers about trying to turn "English lessons into Yoga sessions," his account of this childhood pursuit, as given in *Poetry in the Making*, is close enough to what one might find in a Buddhist primer of meditation:

> I fished in still water, with a float. As you know, all a fisherman does is stare at his float for hours on end. I have spent hundreds and hundreds of hours staring at a float—a dot of red or yellow the size of a lentil, ten yards away . . . All the little nagging impulses, that are normally distracting your mind, dissolve . . . If they do not, then you cannot settle down: you get bored and pack up in a bad temper. But once they have dissolved, you enter one of the orders of bliss.
>
> (P,57–8,60–3)

3. CONCEPT OF LANGUAGE

But how can such insight into "the world of final reality" be embodied in human language, a medium so much of conscious reasoning and purpose-oriented communication? A deep distrust of its cognitive potential, which is as old as the teachings of Lao Tzu, the Buddha or the Upanishads, has protected the East from what Wittgenstein called the over two thousand year long "bewitchment of our intelligence by means of language."[23] Metaphysical claims for language as a secret code of the Absolute, which have haunted poets and philosophers since the days of Socrates, are as alien to their Eastern peers as our present-day despair over language. In all areas of mental activity, language was considered no more than a means to those ends which are ultimately inaccessible to any form of human communication. As Chuang Tzu's often repeated parable from the third century B.C. puts it:

> The fishing net is used to catch fish. Let us take the fish and forget the net . . . The word is used to convey ideas. When ideas are apprehended, let us forget the words. How delightful to be able to talk with such a man, who has forgotten the words![24]

The schoolboy poet's classroom experience of being unable to articulate the tantalizing stirrings of his innermost self, implanted a similar scepticism in Hughes. Hence his later conviction that "the meaning of our experience is finally unfathomable," and language a mere tool, an indicator or general directive towards it. Words, "learned late and laboriously and easily forgotten . . . are unnatural, in a way, and far from . . . ideal for their job" (P,119). Such insight, like Chuang Tzu's, is at once more radical and hopeful than the despair of many poets who like Hugo von Hofmannsthal have felt words disintegrate in their mouths like "mouldy mushrooms,"[25] and have been driven to creative or real suicide by this language crisis. Against the critics who in their wake have been announcing the death of literature or a new æsthetics of silence, Hughes seems to propose a future poetry beyond silence which at the same time may be man's oldest,—a poetry of "truly primitive speech, a medicine bag of provisional magic and rough improvisations—childlike, playful, bizarre, in a perpetual restless state of dissolution and re-invention."[26] To Hughes, the strategies developed by East European poets like Popa, Holub or Herbert "of making audible meanings without disturbing the silence" (67,P,202) are the best refutation of Adorno's famous dictum that writing poetry has become impossible under the shadow of the death camps. It may be true that such memories have totally devalued an already debased currency of ideational and humanitarian concepts to which Western languages have been subjected for so long. As Hughes himself is prepared to admit:

> The silence of artistic integrity "after Auschwitz" is a real thing. The mass of the human evidence of the camps, and of similar situations since, has screwed up the price of "truth" and "reality" and "understanding" beyond what common words seem able to pay.

Yet though poets may now want to write "as if [they] had remained silent," their task of making this silence audible, even if by no more than "a seasoned despair, a minimal, much-examined hope, a special irony" (76,P,10), is a more challenging one than ever. All the less justifiable seems to be the real silence of those who, like Laura Riding, gave up poetry by despairing over language as such. For to "respect words more than the truths which are perpetually trying to find and correct words is the death of poetry."[27] Behind such respect is no more than the unwarrantable claim with which language has been charged by post-Platonic ideational philosophy or by the Biblical creed that all creation is ruled by an underlying "Logos."

Hughes' 1966 poem of that title, which also marks the beginning of his mythopoeic period, is the first to reveal in what esteem the poet holds such philosophizing. In ways that are typical for many poems from then on it reverses the biblical doctrine:

> Creation convulses in nightmare. And awaking
> Suddenly tastes the nightmare moving
> Still in its mouth
> And spits it kicking out, with a swinish cry—
> which is God's first cry.
>
> Like that cry within the sea,
> A mumbling over and over
> Of ancient law, the phrasing falling to pieces
> Garbled among shell-shards and gravels,
> the truths falling to pieces.
>
> (W,34)

Numerous poems since "Logos" in which the emergence, destructiveness and recent collapse of language are the central concerns of a sociohistorical critique are more than obvious and have been amply discussed.[28] More innovative than their negative message, is Hughes' search for man's original language uncorrupted by our Judaeo-Christian and Greek ways of thinking. There were others before him who were dissatisfied with the reason-, time- and space-dominated patterns of Standard Average European when compared, say, with the situational immediacy of Hopi (B. L. Whorf),[29] or who have speculated about non-or pre-Western languages as resembling "vivid short-hand pictures of actions and processes in nature" (E. Fenollosa)[30] or expressing an archaic form of "rotary image-thought" (D. H. Lawrence).[31] Olson, by way of illustrating his conviction that the original "phonetic and ideographic" potential is "still present and available for use as impetus and explosion in our alphabetic speech,"[32] uses examples (in their turn derived from Fenollosa) closely resembling those of Hughes. Where the latter discovered a relationship between HOAN, his Orghast word for "light," and the forms of the verb "to be" ("You can't say 'is' without saying 'light,' " Hughes observed),[33] Olson found that our abstract "is," for instance, "comes from the Aryan root, *as*, to breathe," just as "be" is from "*bhu*, to grow."[34] Yet despite such similar pursuits in theory, there is little to parallel Hughes' attempts towards their realization in practise. Whatever else they might suggest, lines like

clun alclun hoandaclun	closed all closed heaven closed
urdboltabullorgaclun	clayrockdarkness closed
deyool omclun	worse woman closed[35]

certainly bear out the author's belief that the actors in true poetic drama should speak in anything but discursive language. Instead they should use "every muscle, every inflection, every position," their utterances consisting of mere "tones and sounds, without specific conceptual or perceptual meaning" and the whole spectacle turning into a luminous sound image of the poet's "flash vision" that "makes the spirits listen" (71,O). Again, the basic concept is hardly a new one. As early as 1933 the author of "Le théâtre de la cruauté" had demanded that words, if the theatre is to allow them at all, should first be reattached "to the physical movements which gave them birth, so that the logical and discursive aspect of language may disappear under its physical and affective one."[36] Yet only after 1971, when Peter Brook commissioned Hughes to provide his actors with a "subtext for improvisation" for a play to be performed at the Fifth Arts Festival of Shiraz, were such speculations ever put into practice. It has been amply documented how Hughes discarded an early attempt to write the script in his own language ("English was hopeless. It could never have come near it"),[37] and then worked his way from early Orghast, a rigidly hieroglyphic language threatened with premature ossification, towards the final version, a free sound sequence retaining hieroglyphic elements but at the same time resembling "an electro-cardiogram and encephalogram combined."[38] Although Hughes holds that similar experiments remain meaningless in poetry,[39] their final result recalls Ginsberg's attempts to explore the relations "between poetry and mantra chanting by means of the yoga of breath."[40] "The ideal Orghast," Hughes concluded after the work was done, "would be a language with a fairly fixed system that opened it to a magical, mantra way of speaking it."[41]

4. MYTH, PARAPSYCHOLOGY AND THE POETIC IMAGINATION

Of course, an "animal" instead of a "mantra" way of speaking would be the more appropriate formula for what Hughes has in mind here. For to him, the supreme gift of flash vision is not so much as it is, say, to Bashō, a matter of human spiritual enlightenment, but of an experience which on its deepest level is shared by all living beings.

It is human, of course, but it is also everything else that lives . . . Some animals and birds express [it] pure and without effort, and then you hear the whole desolate, final actuality of existence in a voice, a tone . . . Far beyond human words. And the startling quality of this "truth" is that it is terrible. It is for some reason harrowing, as well as being the utterly beautiful thing.

A little anecdote related in the same context vividly illustrates Hughes' belief that the imagination should be at home amongst the "crowd of spirits" surrounding us:

Once when his spirits were dictating poetic material to Yeats, an owl cried outside the house, and the spirits paused. After a while one said: "We like that sort of sound." And that is it: "That sort of sound" makes the spirits listen. It opens our deepest and innermost ghost to sudden attention. It is a spirit, and it speaks to spirit.

(71,O)

Via immediate predecessors like Yeats, Goethe or Blake, this concept of the imagination, like his pre-creative exercises of meditation and invocation, places Hughes in the mainstream of the Hermetic tradition. Just as Hughes, echoing Goethe, believes that the imagination should keep faith "with the world of things and the world of spirits equally" (76, M, 92), so Pico della Mirandola claimed that the poet should have "familiarity with the race of demons, knowing that he is issued from the same origin," or Giordano Bruno that the imagination is "the sole gate to all internal affections and the link of links."[42] Also like his Hermetic predecessors, Hughes believes in the concrete reality of myths. To him they are more than idle fantasies from mankind's adolescence, secret subliminal scripts recording man's civilized discontents, or archetypal projections of a collective unconscious.

It is true that Jung's 1912 discovery of this ancestral memory with its common traces in ancient religious scrolls as well as modern schizophrenics' dossiers, meant a major breakthrough in the ongoing rehabilitation of myth. Its basic model, however, remains that of a slide-projector in which the actual presence of the mythic numen (or image on the screen) remains an illusion, always ready to vanish with the repository of archetypes in the individual's unconscious (or the carousel of slides in the projector). Although most parapsychologists embrace the same model, their evidence seems to speak against it. For what are we to make of psychic feats performed by men like Raudive and Ted Serios, for instance, who under conditions of strictest scientific supervision are able to conjure up voices and images so that they register on Polaroid cameras and tape recorders?[43] Are their brains the store-house projectors of these images and voices or do they simply relay them in the way that television sets register and transmit images and sounds floating through space? Perhaps it is time to recognize that this dichotomy should be solved not by one of Western logic's customary "either or" verdicts but by the "both and" acceptance of a duality such as modern nuclear physics has had to acknowledge in comparable issues. One such "lesson of atomic theory" resulted in Niels Bohr's "law of complementarity." As the physicist points out, this law tries to resolve a problem already confronted by thinkers like the Buddha and Lao Tzu "when trying to harmonize our position as spectators and actors in the great drama of existence."[44]

In the light of similar considerations, Hughes asserts that myth is both real and imaginary, just as the imagination is at once spiritual and concretely physical. The two are connected not by a one-way system of projective or receptive dependence but by interchangeable correlations. In one of his typical sweeps of polyhistoric eclecticism Hughes points out how physicists have verified supernatural phenomena while at the same time reinstating "the wild Heraclitean/Buddhist notion that the entire Universe is basically made of fire." Thus

> they've landed themselves, and us, in a delicately balanced, purely electrical Creation, at the backdoor of the house of activities formerly called "supernatural." For a purely electrical Creation is one without walls, where everything, being an electrical power, can have an electrical effect on every other thing, and where electrical effects are vital effects.
>
> (64,M,500)

As early as 1958, Hughes made light of "our science" and "small psychology" which try to debunk the supernatural as mere dream fantasies while unable to escape its thrall.

> Did they dream it?
> Oh, our science says they did.
> It was all wishfully dreamed in bed.
> Small psychology would unseam it.
>
> Bitches still sulk, rosebuds blow,
> And we are devilled. And though these weep
> Over our harms, who's to know
> Where their feet dance while their heads sleep?
>
> (L,48)

His 1964 review of T. C. Lethbridge's *Ghost and Divining-rod* allowed the poet to present these versified convictions in a more explicit manner. Besides apparitions which are indeed mere projections of a diseased imagination there are, Hughes points out, "ghosts or 'presences' which haunt one spot, where different people, and animals, react to them." To be sure, even Lethbridge's explanation—a ghost being an electrical field created by "some individual in a state of intense emotion," stored in the "Ge-field of the earth" and finally discharged into or registered by the awareness of another individual in a low state of electrical potential—leaves much to be answered. Yet to Hughes there is proof enough that such things are evidently part of the logic of the earth and may soon be verified "by some spectacular development of sensitive recording equipment." His own response to such speculations makes no secret of the world the poet feels most at home in:

> What an entertaining place the world would become again! What a chaos! The only respectable sanities to survive undiscredited in all that would be physics and art.
>
> (64,M,500)

In other words, what physics' scientific credentials have recently managed to rehabilitate, art has—or at least ought to have—treated as its domain throughout history. How then can the imagination be a mere projector of repressed subliminal fantasies or archetypal images? Even Shakespeare's notion that it gives a local habitation and a name to airy nothing hardly describes the concrete magical potential which Hughes attributes to the human mind. With the possible exception of Jerome Rothenberg, none of his contemporaries seems to come closer than Hughes to rejoining the primitive shamanistic belief that it is possible to acquire the "technique for moving in a state of ecstasy among the various spiritual realms, and for generally dealing with souls and spirits, in a practical way, in some practical crisis." Whether primitive shaman or modern mythographer poet, the experiences and techniques are common ones pointing to "something closer to biological inevitability [rather] than to any merely cultural tradition" (64,E,677). In modern society these are also shared by the depth psychiatrist, and Hughes, by way of introducing such notions, is fond of quoting the anecdote from Jung's autobiography in which the Swiss doctor, while trying to illustrate some general point in conversation with a patient, gave a "detailed circumstantial account of that man's own private life" (P,122,cf.64,M,500).

To Hughes, such feats as well as the psychometrist's gift to conjure up, from the sight of a "weapon or tool used in a crime" (P,12), an image of the criminal, are potentials dormant in all of us. And modern parapsychologists seem to agree with him in acknowledging some kind of negative or positive psychic power in everybody. Where the two tend to disagree is as to how such phenomena should be explained. In the same way that ghosts are presences to Hughes, while to most parapsychologists they are psychic projections, so the imagination to him is a concrete physiological or magical power while to the majority of scientists its potential is limited to an ill defined realm of the psychological. In sum, the poet considers both as "common propert[ies] of life's electrical constitution" (64,M,500). The imagination is "simply one of the characteristics of being alive in these mysterious electrical bodies of ours, and the difficult thing is not to pick up the information but to recognize it—to accept it into our consciousness" (P, 123).

As this pedagogical afterthought for the school readership of *Poetry in the Making* may suggest, Hughes, after all is said, is far from being a poet of the occult. His insistence on ghosts or on the imagination's conjuring powers is the natural reaction of a poet exasperated by our customary rejection of entire realms of psychic and mythic experience simply "because they inhabit a gulf where our careful civilisation would disintegrate" (64,M,500). Apart from that, there is little in a piece such as the recent "Myth and Education" that a man as worldly-wise as Goethe might not have agreed with. And it is in the German poet's demand for an imagination which keeps faith "with the world of things and the world of spirits equally" (76,M,92), that Hughes finds his own ideal formula for man's greatest spiritual potential. If the two poets differ, it is over a fact which Goethe may have foreseen, though hardly to its full extent: that is to say, the sudden outbursts of violence and destructiveness called upon us by the same puritanical rationalism which, since the very beginnings of Western culture, has made us repress or minimize man's potential for evil. In Hughes' words, such repression has turned our whole inner world into a "place of demons" which finally erupted in a spectacle that left the world stage littered with millions of tortured and massacred human bodies in little over fifty years. Ironically, we more than ever refuse to own up to what we see when we catch a glimpse of our inner selves. "[We] recognize it with horror—it is an animal crawling and decomposing in a hell." Yet, as never before, our only hope lies in an acceptance of this inner world.

> Down there, mixed up among all the madness, is everything that once made life worth living. All the lost awareness and powers and allegiances of our biological and spiritual being. The attempt to re-enter that lost inheritance takes many forms, but it is the chief business of the swarming cults.
>
> (76,M,90–1)

It is also the business of Hughes' more recent poetry. But a discussion of how the poet approaches it through a new kind of psychological rather than moralistic didacticism belongs to a later chapter.

Notes

1. From a letter to the author received on August 23, 1977.
2. See Fass, "Ted Hughes and Crow. An Interview with Ekbert Faas." *London Magazine* 10, 10 (January 1971), 14.
3. *Observer*, March 27, 1960.

4. See J. J. Y. Liu, *Chinese Theories of Literature* (Chicago: University of Chicago Press, 1975), p. 73. For the following see also Faas, *New American Poetics*, pp. 9ff.

5. *Complete Works: Selected Letters (English and French)*, ed. W. Fowlie (Chicago: University of Chicago Press, 1966), pp. 303–309.

6. See S. Bush, *The Chinese Literati on Painting. Su Shih (1037–1101) to Tung Ch'i-Ch'ang (1555–1636)*: Harvard-Yenching Institute Studies XXVII (Cambridge, Mass.: Harvard University Press, 1971), p. 56.

7. *The Letters*, ed. M. B. Forman (London: Oxford University Press, 1952), p. 107.

8. See Makoto Ueda, *Zeami, Basho, Yeats, Pound. A Study in Japanese and English Poetics*. Studies in General and Comparative Literature, vol. I (The Hague: Mouton, 1965), pp. 39, 52–53.

9. See O. Sirén, *The Chinese on the Art of Painting* (New York: Schocken Books, 1971), pp. 21–22.

10. *Selected Literary Criticism*, ed. A. Beal (New York: Viking Press, 1956), p. 87.

11. Ueda, *Zeami, Bashō, Yeats, Pound*, p. 38.

12. See *Selected Writings*, ed. R. Creeley (New York: New Directions, 1966), p. 25.

13. See Sylvia Plath, *Letters Home, Correspondence 1950–63*, ed. Aurelia Schober Plath (New York: Bantam Books, 1977), pp. 302, 303, 352, 394.

14. *A Course of Instruction of Magic Theory and Practise* (Wuppertal: Dieter Ruggeberg, 1971), pp. 76, 77, 291.

15. *Lankāvatāra-sūtra*, A Buddhist Bible, ed. D. Goddard (Boston: Beacon Press, 1970), p. 300.

16. See *The Tibetan Book of the Dead*, ed. W. Y. Evans-Wentz. With Psychological Commentary by C. G. Jung (London: Oxford University Press, 1960), p. xlix.

17. *The Tibetan Book of the Great Liberation*, ed. W. Y. Evans-Wentz. With Psychological Commentary by Dr. C. G. Jung (London: Oxford University Press, 1972), p. 1.

18. See, for instance, Ueda, *Zeami, Basho, Yeats, Pound*, p. 25, or Chang Chung-yuan, *Creativity and Taoism. A Study of Chinese Philosophy, Art, and Poetry* (New York: Harper & Row, 1970), p. 16.

19. See Liu, *Chinese Theories of Literature*, pp. 69, 114.

20. Chang Chung-yuan, *Creativity and Taoism*, p. 87.

21. See *Anthology of Chinese Literature*, ed. C. Birch (New York: Grove Press, 1967), pp. 205–6

22. Olson, *Selected Writings*, p. 28.

23. *Philosophical Investigations* (New York: Macmillan, 1968), p. 47e.

24. See Chang Chung-yuan, *Creativity and Taoism*, pp. 43–4.

25. *Prosa*, 4 vols. (Frankfurt am Main: S. Fischer, 1952–9), 11, 12.

26. "Laura Riding," see above, chapter I, note 1.

27. Ibid.

28. See, for instance, Keith Sagar, *The Art of Ted Hughes* (Cambridge: Cambridge University Press, 1975), pp. 123ff.

29. *Language, Thought, and Reality. Selected Writings*, ed. J. B. Carrol (Cambridge, Mass.: Massachusetts Institute of Technology Press, 1964), passim.

30. *The Chinese Written Character as a Medium for Poetry*, ed. E. Pound (San Francisco: City Lights Books, 1968), p. 21.

31. *Apocalypse* (London: Heinemann, 1972), p. 45.

32. *Human Universe and Other Essays*, ed. D. Allen (New York: Grove Press, 1967), p. 18.

33. See Smith, *Orghast*, p. 51.

34. *Selected Writings*, p. 18; also see Fenollosa, *Chinese Written Character*, p. 15.

35. See Geoffrey Reeves, "The Persepolis Follies of 1971," *Performance* I (December 1971), pp. 47–71, 64.

36. *Le théâtre*, pp. 181–2.
37. See Smith, *Orghast*, pp. 42, 180.
38. See Reeves, "The Persepolis Follies," p. 66.
39. See Smith, *Orghast*, p. 43.
40. "Interview," *Spectrum*, 21, 34 (20 November 1970), p. 12.
41. See Smith, *Orghast*, p. 210.
42. See Frances A. Yates, *Giordano Bruno and the Hermetic Tradition* (New York: Random House, 1969), pp. 28, 266.
43. See H. C. Berendt, *Parapsychologie* (Stuttgart: W. Kohlhammer, 1972), pp. 77ff.
44. See Fritjof Capra, *The Tao of Physics* (Bungay, Suffolk: Fontana, 1976), p. 16.

KEY TO ABBREVIATED REFERENCES

I. BOOKS (in alphabetical order)

L   *Lupercal*. London: Faber and Faber, 1960.

P   *Poetry in the Making*. London: Faber and Faber, 1967.

W   *Wodwo*. London: Faber and Faber, 1967.

II. CRITICAL ESSAYS, INTERVIEWS, REVIEWS etc.
(in chronological order)

57,H   "Ted Hughes Writes." *Poetry Book Society Bulletin*, 15 (September 1957).

62,C   "Context." *London Magazine*, 1, 11 (February 1962), pp. 44–45.

62,D   "The Poetry of Keith Douglas." *Listener*, 67 (21 June 1962), pp. 1069–71.

63,D   "The Poetry of Keith Douglas." *Critical Quarterly*, 5 (1963), pp. 43–48.

64,E   Review of Mircea Eliade. *Shamanism*. *Listener*, 72 (29 October 1964), pp. 677–678.

64,M   Review of Louis MacNeice. *Astrology*. etc., *New Statesman*, 68 (2 October 1964), p. 500.

66,P   "Notes on the Chronological Order of Sylvia Plath's Poems." *Tri-Quarterly*, 7 (Fall 1966), pp. 81–88.

67,P   "Vasko Popa." *Tri-Quarterly*, 9 (Spring 1967), pp. 201–205.

71,O   "Orghast: Talking Without Words." *Vogue* (December 1971).

76,M   "Myth and Education." *Writers, Critics, and Children*, ed. Geoff Fox etc., New York: Agathon Press, 1976, pp. 77–94.

76,P   Introduction János Pilinszky. *Selected Poems*. Translated by Ted Hughes & János Csokits. Manchester: Carcanet New Press, 1977.

"The Poetry Does Not Matter"

KEITH SAGAR

The first lines of the first poem in Hughes's first book *The Hawk in the Rain* plunge us into a world which is soon to become familiar:

> I drown in the drumming ploughland, I drag up
> Heel after heel from the swallowing of the earth's mouth,
> From clay that clutches my each step to the ankle
> With the habit of the dogged grave. . . .
> —"The Hawk in the Rain"

"The Hawk in the Rain" pitches us into the thick of the battle between vitality and death, which Hughes claimed was his only subject. It is, in this poem as in many, a one-sided battle. Three of the four elements seem to be in alliance with death. Earth, even the earth of ploughland, is not fertile but a mass grave. Water drowns. Rain falls not to engender new life but to convert earth to down-dragging mud and to hack to the bone any head that presumes to raise itself. Air manifests itself only as wind that kills any stubborn attempts at life. The very language is a series of blows pounding life down. What hope amid all this for the fire of vitality or spirit? It is located only in the eye[1] of the hawk, which seems effortlessly, by an act of will, to master it all, to be the exact center, the eye of the storm, the "master-Fulcrum of violence." The hawk is as close to the inviolability of an angel as a living creature can be, but he too is doomed at last to "mix his heart's blood with the mire of the land." Yet the effect of the poem on the reader is far from depressing. If the man trying to cross a ploughed field in a cloudburst cannot be the "master-Fulcrum of violence," the same man later sitting at his desk making a poem of the experience can: "I turn every combatant into a bit of music, then resolve the whole uproar into as formal and balanced a figure of melody and rhythm as I can. When all the words are hearing each other clearly, and every stress is feeling every other stress, and all are contented—the poem is finished."[2] Art is bringing resolution to what without it would remain uproar.

This is true of even the best poems in *The Hawk in the Rain* such as "Wind." Here Hughes brilliantly mimes the distorting and leveling power

---

This essay was written specifically for this volume and appears here for the first time.

of a gale, seeking to find a language, like that of the ballads, which "cannot be outflanked by experience." His wind is real enough, and carries much the same larger meaning as the wind Castaneda's Don Juan calls the "nagual," a wind that threatens to obliterate the "tonal"—"everything we know and do as men" (or in Hughes's words "book, thought, or each other"):

> As long as his *tonal* is unchallenged and his eyes are tuned only for the *tonal's* world, the warrior is on the safe side of the fence. He's on familiar ground and knows all the rules. But when his *tonal* shrinks, he is on the windy side, and that opening must be shut tight immediately, or he would be swept away. And this is not just a way of talking. Beyond the gate of the *tonal's* eyes the wind rages. I mean a real wind. No metaphor. A wind that can blow one's life away. In fact, that is the wind that blows all living things on this earth.[3]

But the language of "Wind" is not quite that of the ballads. The very skill Hughes exhibits in the manipulation of language reinforces the *tonal* and keeps the wind out. The man who "cannot entertain book, thought, / Or each other," can still write a magnificent poem, with such finely crafted lines as:

> The wind flung a magpie away and a black—
> Back gull bent like an iron bar slowly.

The later Hughes will no longer erect such verbal barricades:

> Tumbling worlds
> Open my way
>
> And you cling.
>
> And we go
>
> Into the wind. The flame-wind—a red wind
> And a black wind. The red wind comes
> To empty you. And the black wind, the longest wind
> The headwind
>
> To scour you.
>
> —"The guide"

Given the landscape of mud and blood, the vast no-man's-land, that is the world of Hughes's early poems, it is not easy for him to say how men should try to live in such a world. It is easier to say how they should not. What Hughes pours his most vehement scorn on is the egg-head's pride and "braggart-browed complacency in most calm / Collusion with his own /

Dewdrop frailty"; his spurning of the earth as "muck under / His foot-clutch"; his willingness to oppose his own eye to "the whelm of the sun" ("Egg-Head"). Pride and complacency are man's commonest defenses against receiving the full impact of the otherness and endlessness of the natural world, for example "the whaled monstered sea-bottom." What Hughes is trying to say in this poem is, I take it, that the egg-head is resisting birth, which requires the breaking of the ego-shell, because the wisdom that would then flood in would be accounted madness in our world of single vision. In *Moby Dick*, when the negro boy Pip fell overboard, thought he had been abandoned, and was then rescued, he went about an idiot:

> The sea had jeeringly kept his finite body up, but drowned the infinite of his soul. Not drowned entirely, though. Rather carried down alive to wondrous depths, where strange shapes of the unwarped primal world glided to and fro before his passive eyes; and the miser-merman, Wisdom, revealed his hoarded heaps; Pip saw the multitudinous, God-omnipresent, coral insects, that out of the firmament of waters heaved the colossal orbs. He saw God's foot upon the treadle of the loom, and spoke it; and therefore his shipmates called him mad. So man's insanity is heaven's sense; and wandering from all mortal reason, man comes at last to that celestial thought, which, to reason, is absurd and frantic; and weal or woe, feels then uncompromised, indifferent as his God.

"Egg-head," however, is at the opposite pole from any divine indifference. The superiority of the speaker manifests itself with just as much fervency and trumpeting as the egg-head is accused of. The style is confident and masculine and aggressive to the point of "braggart-browed complacency."

In *Lupercal* there is again some discrepancy between style and content. The style has all the necessary weight and strength to mime the pressure of the huge forces of the natural world upon the living organism. But the energies are invoked (often in the form of predatory beasts) with a sometimes over-weening masculine confidence that they can be controlled by the imposed form of the poem itself—the artistry of the poem working in much the same way as ritual worked in the ancient world (as in the Roman Lupercalia). Were the poems really, as he thought at the time, containing the energies, or were they shutting out by their tightly closed forms "wandering elemen-tals" that, had they come in, would have overwhelmed all pretense at art?

The style of *Lupercal* is confident of its ability both to evoke and control the energies, to plug in to the "elemental power-circuit of the universe." Hughes's imagination, purged of the poetic cult of beauty and the Words-worthian sentimentalities, becomes a great intestine rejecting nothing:

> This mute eater, biting through the mind's
> Nursery floor, with eel and hyena and vulture,

> With creepy-crawly and the root,
> With the sea-worm, entering its birthright.
> —"Mayday on Holderness"

Thus the poet can clamp himself well onto the world like a wolf-mask, and speak with the voice of the glutted crow, the stoat, the expressionless leopard, the sleeping anaconda, the frenzied shrew, the roosting hawk—which is "Nature herself speaking." Yet again there is some discrepancy. We are told that the stoat "bit through grammar and corset," that its "red unmanageable life . . . licked the stylist out of [the] skulls" of Walpole and his set ("Strawberry Hill"). But the poem that tells us so is a triumph of intelligence and style, in a volume of great stylistic achievement, orthodox grammar, and corseted stanzaic and even rhyming verse.

This discrepancy is also apparent in "To Paint a Water Lily," with its elegant rhyming couplets. The poem is a verse exemplum of Carlyle's observations on Nature in "Characteristics":

> Boundless as is the domain of man, it is but a small fractional proportion of it that he rules with Consciousness and Forethought: what he can contrive, nay, what he can altogether know and comprehend, is essentially the mechanical, small; the great is ever, in one sense or other, the vital; it is essentially the mysterious, and only the surface of it can be understood. But Nature, it might seem, strives, like a kind mother, to hide from us even this, that she is a mystery. . . . Under all Nature's works, chiefly under her noblest work, Life, lies a basis of Darkness, which she benignantly conceals; in Life, too, the roots and inward circulations which stretch down fearfully to the regions of Death and Night, shall not hint of their existence, and only the fair stem with its leaves and flowers, shone on by the sun, shall disclose itself and joyfully grow.

Hughes's example is the water lily, whose leaves are simultaneously the floor of the sunny, conscious world, accessible (visually) to any Sunday painter, and the roof of another, less colorful and "aesthetic" world, the unconscious, inaccessible to all the senses, accessible only to the imagination. Hughes refuses merely to praise the rainbow colors of nature (for which the painterly style of the poem is well suited), but strives to escape the tyranny of the eye and listen rather to the inaudible "battle-shouts / And death-cries everywhere hereabouts." He refuses to paint only the dragonfly alighting on the water lily if his imagination can see into the life of the pond and the horror nudging her root. However, in this poem at least, it can only gesture in that direction.

> Prehistoric bedragonned times
> Crawl that darkness with Latin names

is a nursery picture, fancy rather than imagination, and "jaws for heads" is mere Hammer horror. The underwater world, the unconscious mind, is a closed book to the poet. There is no hint of the wisdom of Pip, of the shamanic journey into the "regions of Death and Night" that Hughes's poems are later to become.[4]

"Pike" is a much better poem, moving from the descriptive and narrative modes of total authorial command in the first nine stanzas into a more open dramatic mode, where what is being dramatized is precisely the fear arising from the speaker's ignorance of what is rising toward him out of the "Darkness beneath night's darkness." As Gaston Bachelard writes (not in relation to this poem): "Night alone would give a less physical fear. Water alone would give clearer obsessions. Water at night gives a penetrating fear. . . . If the fear that comes at night beside a pond is a special fear, it is because it is a fear that enjoys a certain range. It is very different from the fear experienced in a grotto or a forest. It is not so near, so concentrated, or so localized; it is more flowing. Shadows that fall on water are more mobile than shadows on earth."[5] It is also the fear that what is rising toward him might be too monstrous, too alien, too ego-destroying for the poetry he is yet able to write to deal with. Fishing in deep water at night is the perfect image for the kind of poetry Hughes really wants to write, poetry that projects the most naked and unconditional part of the self into the nightmare darkness, not with the intention of bringing back trophies into the daylight world, but of confronting, being, if necessary, supplanted by, whatever happens to be out there. The poems about fishing and water tend to be those in which this is to be most fully achieved, culminating in "Go Fishing":

> Join water, wade in underbeing
> Let brain mist into moist earth
> Ghost loosen away downstream
> Gulp river and gravity
>
> Lose words
> Cease
> Be assumed into the womb of lymph
> As if creation were a wound
> As if this flow were all plasm healing
>
> Be supplanted by mud and leaves and pebbles
> By sudden rainbow monster-structures
> That materialise in suspension gulping
> And dematerialise under pressure of the eye
>
> Be cleft by the sliding prow
> Displaced by the hull of light and shadow
> Dissolved in earth-wave, the soft sun-shock,
> Dismembered in sun-melt

Become translucent—one untangling drift
Of water-mesh, and a weight of earth-taste light
Mangled by wing-shadows
Everything circling and flowing and hover-still ·

Crawl out over roots, new and nameless
Search for face, harden into limbs

Let the world come back, like a white hospital
Busy with emergency words

Try to speak and nearly succeed
Heal into time and other people

Here, as Nicholas Bishop points out, "the personal pronoun is absolutely eliminated from the poem as the protagonist becomes 'translucent' to the processes of both the entire surrounding river-scape and those of the explored inner world."[6]

The early sixties was a period of intense experimentation in search of a poetry able to grope its way through that darkness without the map-grid of imposed form or the flash-light of rationality which would have scared away all its creatures. The most significant breakthrough at this time was "Wodwo," first published in 1961. The success of the poem depends partly on the choice of persona, a "little larval being" that might have just emerged from an egg or chrysalis, with human intelligence and curiosity, the human temptation to simply appropriate whatever it encounters, yet still naked and open, exposed and tentative,[7] but mainly on finding the right voice for such a creature.

Grammar and corset, rhymes, stanzas, "poetic" effects of all kinds, rhetoric, have gone. And with them has gone the imposition of personality that those techniques had largely served. What we are left with is a very free verse, close to colloquial prose, flexible, responsive at every moment to the demands of the sense and to nothing else. It is a totally unforced utterance, a world away from the bludgeoning verse of "The Hawk in the Rain." The wodwo is no "diamond point of will": his "I suppose I am the exact centre / but there's all this what is it . . . very queer but I'll go on looking" denies the desirability of being a "master-Fulcrum of violence" and at the same time the desirability of using the formal elements of poetry, its melody and rhythm, as a means of resolving the uproar, thereby sealing off the poem from the real world. No possible pattern is final or definitive or at the "exact centre." How can it be when "there's all this"?

The language is reduced to a functional minimum from which, like the wodwo itself, it is now free to move out into new forms of expression: "The nearest we can come to rational thinking is to stand respectfully, hat in hand, before this Creation, exceedingly alert for a new word" (Faas, 172).

This freedom seems to be related to a more inclusive vision. "Still Life," for example, begins as uncompromisingly as "Pibroch," but we gradually realize that the bleak vision is not this time that of the poet himself, but that of "outcrop rock" taking itself to be the exact center, the one permanent exclusive reality. The poet stands to one side, saying "but there's all this." The less insistent style allows for a play of humor undercutting the claims of outcrop stone to be all there is, "being ignorant of this other, this harebell"

> That trembles, as under threats of death,
> In the summer turf's heat-rise,
> And in which—filling veins
> And known name of blue would bruise
> Out of existence—sleeps, recovering,
> The maker of the sea.

And in "Full Moon and Little Frieda" we have balance instead of intolerable pressure, fullness instead of lack, unspilled milk instead of spilled blood, and a human being, albeit a child, in a reciprocal and rewarding relationship with a human world and a natural world at one with each other. The poetry here does not impose the momentary resolution, but mirrors it while remaining itself transparent, like water in a brimming pail.

The tragic events of February 1963 put an abrupt end to this atonement. Hughes was thrown back at a stroke into a much more deeply felt despair than ever before. It was as though he had seen the face of the goddess, who had blighted him and struck him dumb. Before his three-year silence descended he wrote, however, "The Howling of Wolves" and "Song of a Rat." The style here has gone very cold, metallic, each line the sharp tooth of a steel trap. The diction is a succession of blank monosyllables forced between teeth:

> The eyes that never learn how it has come about
> That they must live like this,
>
> That they must live

or "The rat is in the trap, it is in the trap." To dress such testimony up as "poetry" (with the association of that word with "pleasure" relentlessly insisted on by the BBC), would clearly be absurd, almost obscene. Great poetry is truth-telling, and the truth must be in the telling as much as in the authenticity of the vision. Pain, which otherwise is condemned to express itself in silence or inarticulate cries, has, in poetry, its only speech.

That speech will not be the speech of ordinary rational discourse. It searches for the buried world under the world, and for a speech beneath words. The poet opens himself to be "pierced afresh by the tree's cry":

> And the incomprehensible cry
> From the boughs, in the wind
> Sets us listening for below words,
> Meanings that will not part from the rock.
> —"A Wind Flashes the Grass"

Meanings emerge from silence, from the blank unprinted page, sparely, one syllable for a line, in a voice that is not the commanding voice of the poet, but the faceless voice that issues the imperatives of living and dying to tree, gnat, skylark, and man alike:

> A towered bird, shot through the crested head
> With the command, Not die
>
> But climb
>
> Climb
>
> Sing
>
> Obedient as to death a dead thing.
> —"Skylarks"

The style or non-style of *Crow* is another new departure. At the end of his 1970 interview, Ekbert Faas asked Hughes why he had "abandoned such formal devices as rhyme, metre and stanza." Hughes conceded that "formal patterning of the actual movement of verse somehow includes a mathematical and musically deeper world than free verse can easily hope to enter. . . . But it only works . . . if the writer has a perfectly pure grasp of his real feeling . . . and the very sound of metre calls up the ghosts of the past and it is difficult to sing one's own tune against that choir. It is easier to speak a language that raises no ghosts" (Faas, 208). What he did not say, and may not yet have become conscious of in theory, though it is clear enough in his practice, as Nicholas Bishop has shown, is that the mathematical and musical accomplishments of formal verse might actually prevent the poet's language becoming "totally alive and pure," and deny him access to the deepest levels of his own psyche. Hughes went on:

> The first idea of *Crow* was really an idea of a style. In folktales the prince going on the adventure comes to the stable full of beautiful horses and he needs a horse for the next stage and the king's daughter advises him to take none of the beautiful horses that he'll be offered but to choose the dirty, scabby little foal. I throw out the eagles and choose the Crow. The idea was originally just to write his songs, the songs that a Crow would sing. In other words, songs

with no music whatsoever, in a super-simple and a super-ugly language which would in a way shed everything except just what he wanted to say without any other consideration and that's the basis of the style of the whole thing.

But Hughes does not explain what, in the folktale, is the advantage of choosing "the dirty, scabby little foal," the advantage of crows over eagles, or of super-ugly language over the beautiful musical language of our poetic tradition. In a letter to me Hughes expanded a little: "I tried to shed everything that the average Pavlovian critic knows how to respond to. It was quite an effort to get there—as much of an effort to stay there—every day I had to find it again. My idea was to reduce my style to the simplest clear cell—then regrow a wholeness and richness organically from that point. I didn't get that far." But again Hughes does not explain the need for this stylistic asceticism. For that explanation we must turn to his writings on the Eastern European poets, who seemed to Hughes to have discovered a universal poetic language, independent of surface sound and texture and therefore translatable, an ABC of what counts. In his 1969 essay on Popa he had written:

> No poetry could carry less luggage than his, or be freer of predisposition and preconception. No poetry is more difficult to outflank, yet it is in no sense defensive. His poems are tying to find out what does exist, and what the conditions really are. The movement of his verse is part of his method of investigating something fearfully apprehended, fearfully discovered, but he will not be frightened into awe. He never loses his deeply ingrained humor and irony: that is his way of hanging on to his human wholeness. And he never loses his intense absorption in what he is talking about, either. His words test their way forward, sensitive to their own errors, dramatically and intimately alive, like the antennae of some rock-shore creature feeling out the presence of the sea and the huge powers in it. This analogy is not so random. There is a primitive pre-creation atmosphere about his work, as if he were present where all the dynamisms and formulae were ready and charged, but nothing created—or only a few fragments. . . . [There is an] air of trial and error exploration, of an improvised language, the attempt to get near something for which he is almost having to invent the words in a total disregard for poetry or the normal conventions of discourse.[8]

What first attracted Hughes to Pilinszky's poems was, he says, "their air of simple, helpless accuracy." Pilinszky described his own poetic language as "a sort of linguistic poverty." He takes "the most naked and helpless of all confrontations" and asks "what speech is adequate for this moment?" His vision is desolate; his language as close as he can get to silence: "We come to this Truth only on the simplest terms: through what has been suffered, what is being suffered, and the objects that participate in the suffering."[9]

The more affirmative, the more radiant with meaning, a work is going to be, the more essential that its starting point is Nothing, the silence of Cordelia, so that it cannot be said that the affirmative meanings have been smuggled in with the loaded language, that anything has been left unquestioned, that the negatives have not been fully acknowledged. Pilinszky has taken the route Hughes started out on in *Crow*:

> Though the Christian culture has been stripped off so brutally, and the true condition of the animal exposed in its ugliness, and words have lost their meaning—yet out of that rise the poems, whose words are manifestly crammed with meaning. Something has been said which belies neither the reality nor the silence. More than that, the reality has been redeemed. The very symbols of the horror are the very things he has redeemed.
> They are not redeemed in any religious sense. They are redeemed, precariously, in some all-too-human sense, somewhere in the pulsing mammalian nervous-system, by a feat of human consecration: a provisional, last-ditch "miracle" which we recognize, here, as poetic.
>
> —Pilinszky, 12

Hughes did not get that far in *Crow*, but he did in the sequel *Cave Birds*, in the *Gaudete* epilogue, and in the best poems in every subsequent book.

Notes

1. On the significance of the eye in Hughes, see Keith Sagar, *The Art of Ted Hughes* (Cambridge: Cambridge University Press, 1975), 16–17.

2. Ekbert Faas, *Ted Hughes: The Unaccommodated Universe* (Santa Barbara: Black Sparrow Press, 1980), 163; hereafter cited as Faas.

3. Carlos Castaneda, *Tales of Power* (London: Hodder & Stoughton, 1974), 176.

4. Compare the later poem "Chiasmadon" (collected in *Moortown* as "Photostomias"). This primitive deep-sea fish is also known as the dragon-fish, and could well be described as having jaws for head. "Photostomias" is a fine example of Hughes' mature imagination at full stretch. See Leonard M. Scigaj, *The Poetry of Ted Hughes: Form and Imagination* (Iowa City: University of Iowa Press, 1986), 276–77.

5. Gaston Bachelard, *Water and Dreams*, trans. Edith R. Farrell (Dallas: Instructional Publications, 1983), 101–102.

6. Nick Bishop, *Re-Making Poetry: Ted Hughes and a New Critical Psychology* (Hempstead: Harvester Wheatsheaf, 1991), 248. See also Bishop's fuller analysis of this poem in Sagar, ed., *The Challenge of Ted Hughes*, under consideration at a British press. I am heavily indebted to Bishop's work throughout this essay.

7. As Hughes wrote of children: "Preoccupations are already pressing, but they have not yet closed down, like a space helmet, over the entire head and face, with the proved, established adjustments of security." *Children as Writers 2* (London: Heinemann, 1975), v.

8. Vasco Popa, *Selected Poems*, trans. Anne Pennington (Harmondsworth: Penguin, 1969), 11–12, 15.

9. Janos Pilinszky, *Selected Poems*, trans. Ted Hughes and Janos Czokits (Manchester: Carcanet, 1977), 11; hereafter cited as Pilinszky.

Animal Music: Ted Hughes's Progress in Speech and Song

Don McKay

In the blighted landscape of *Crow*, scarred with the repeated failures of genesis, it is startling to come across "Glimpse" close to the end of the book:

> "O leaves," Crow sang, trembling, "O leaves—"
>
> The touch of a leaf's edge at his throat
> Guillotined further comment.
> > Nevertheless
> Speechless he continued to stare at the leaves
> Through the god's head instantly substituted.[1]

Crow, bred out of God's abortive efforts to create, surviving on carrion and garbage, reveals this surprising capacity for awe, and attempts to sing in the manner of a romantic ode. This gesture toward lyric flight, "O leaves," is tossed up and shelved there, a striking exception to the book's policy of using words as stones or sandpaper for their cumulative weight or abrasive action. "O leaves" does preface another of the many failures documented in *Crow*, but it is a failure of a different order from, to take an example, the inability of the protagonist in "A Bedtime Story" to write his autobiography:

> But somehow his arms had become just bits of stick
> Somehow his guts were an old watch-chain
> Somehow his feet were two old postcards
> Somehow his head was a broken windowpane
>
> "I give up," he said. He gave up.
>
> Creation had failed again.
>
> —*Crow*, p. 60

Reprinted from *English Studies in Canada* 7 (Spring 1981): 81–92, by permission of the author and the journal.

Unlike this routine silence of destitution, the silence of "Glimpse" is due to the presence of an overwhelming power in the leaves, a newly apprehended divinity.

Commenting on the prevailing anti-lyricism of *Crow*, Ted Hughes draws an analogy from folklore:

> The first idea of *Crow* was really an idea of a style. In folktales the prince going on an adventure comes to a stable full of beautiful horses and he needs a horse for the next stage and the king's daughter advises him to take none of the beautiful horses that he'll be offered but to choose the dirty, scabby little foal. You see, I throw out the eagles and choose the Crow. The idea was originally just to write his songs, the songs that a Crow would sing. In other words, songs with no music whatsoever, in a super-simple, and a super-ugly language which would in a way shed everything except just what he wanted to say without any other considerations.[2]

The prince has learned to distrust pleasant appearances, and to tap the power of ugliness instead. But his end is not cynical despair or absurdist philosophy, and neither is Hughes's. Both act in the faith that the route to achieving a greater beauty and stronger magic lies in the paradox of the negative way.

Along that route Hughes exposes and indicts the God of Christian humanism and rationalism, the God who is known through his logos, and whose failures are reflected in the corresponding corruption of human speech. The bankruptcy of the logos is narratively related in "A Disaster," where the word, "all mouth" is seen digesting man and his products, "sucking the cities/Like the nipples of a sow," absorbing civilization into itself. When it attempts to digest the earth, however, its efforts weaken and it shrinks "Like a collapsing mushroom."

> Its era was over.
> All that remained of it a brittle desert
> Dazzling with the bones of earth's people
> Where Crow walked and mused.
> —*Crow*, p. 21

Crow's wasteland was produced, it seems, not by biblical or nuclear holocaust but by exhaustion, the senescence of a world view. What remains after the era of logos comes to an end is the host of physical and oral gestures which fill the pages of *Crow*: grins, smiles, frowns, laughter, screams, and

> A cry
> Wordless
> As the newborn baby's grieving
> On the steely scales.
> —*Crow*, p. 48

Song is the union of speech, which identifies us as human beings existing in a culture, and music, which for Hughes connects us to nature. Besides their rational cargo, Hughes believes, our voices are capable of a primal animal music, which has magical properties.

This animal music is very different, of course, from the conventionally "musical voice." The real virtuosi in this line are certain animals and birds—though their ranges are pretty limited. When they speak the spirits listen. Not many human voices can make the spirits listen.[3]

It is one measure of Hughes's poetics that the condition of music does not mean a lofty or abstract perfection but a state of communion with natural forces. In the poems at the end of *Gaudete* which address the nature goddess, music is construed as "the maneater / On your leash,"[4] which eats people and transfixes them.

Such music is only a ghostly presence in *Crow*, a desire, for Crow is unable to fit his corrupted speech to the music of earth, which has been "over-sold like detergents." In "Crow Tries the Media," he yearns toward song, but finds that his tongue moves "like a poisoned estuary" (*Crow*, p. 35), an image which does connect speech with earth through mutual pollution. But the yearning itself, here as in other poems of absence like Eliot's "Ash Wednesday" or Olson's "In Cold Hell, In Thicket," signals the possibility of change and breaks the grip of stasis, like the first grudging movement of an intractable bolt. The progress from *Crow* to *Gaudete* may be seen as the poet's struggle to fashion speech worthy of the goddess, to complete Crow's lyric gesture somehow, and write love poems to the earth.

Toward this end Hughes then turned away from the speech of rational consciousness altogether and immersed himself in animal music. "Orghast" is the name of an extraordinary play directed by Peter Brook and of the language Ted Hughes invented/discovered for it. To do this Hughes descended a linguistic well, attempting to reach the level at which all men, regardless of native tongues, would instinctively understand. (Appropriately, it remains unpublished and so purely oral, although both the language and the workshops in which the play took shape have been chronicled and discussed.[5]) Hughes sees Orghast as a language of the body, untainted by abstractions. In Orghast, he points out, it is impossible to say "is" without saying "light," and in many cases the meaning resides in the sound: KR means devour; ULL swallow; MAMA—a sound derived from the shape made by the lips taking the breast. Orghast appeals to Hughes for some of the same reasons the Chinese written character appealed to Pound and Fenollosa as a medium for poetry, as a grounding of language in sense, with the emphasis on aural rather than visual immediacy. Hughes takes up a physiological argument in somewhat the same spirit as D. H. Lawrence in *Fantasia of the Unconscious*, to dramatize the efficacy of aural over visual stimuli.

The deeper into language one goes, the less visual/conceptual its imagery, and the more audial/visceral/muscular its system of tensions. This accords with the biological fact that the visual nerves connect with the modern human brain, while the audial nerves connect with the cerebellum, the primal animal brain and nervous system, direct. In other words, the deeper into language one goes, the more dominated it becomes by purely musical modes, and the more dramatic it becomes—the more unified with total states of being and with the expressiveness of physical action.[6]

To draw the inference: if Crow wishes to recover a sense of music he must descend lower into language and the nervous system, abandoning the human surface for the animal depths. Crow, as a humanoid animal, has himself been de-natured by God and moral strictures; he stabs grubs and eats them instinctively while worrying whether he ought to stop eating "And try to become the light" (*Crow*, p. 12). And out of this double bind, Hughes affirms, comes the ascendancy of visual over auditory modes of knowing.

> Grubs   grubs   He stabbed   he stabbed
> Weeping
> Weeping
>
> Weeping he walked and stabbed
>
> Thus came the eye's
>   roundness
>   the ear's
>   deafness.
>   —*Crow*, p. 13

The story immersed in the prespeech of "Orghast" is the governing myth of Hughes's work. It is, as Hughes sums it up, "the story of the crime against material nature, the Creatress, source of life and light, by the Violater, the mental tyrant Holdfast, and her revenge."[7] Hughes's debt to Robert Graves's visionary poetics in *The White Goddess* is large, although he clearly digests and reconstructs the doctrine in his own way. Roughly speaking, it may be observed that *Crow* deals with the first part of this myth, the crime against nature, while *Gaudete* recounts one version of her revenge. But it should also be noted that the substance of the myth has underlain Hughes's writing from the outset, and lies implicitly in the concentrated acts of perception focussed on animals, plants, and landscape in *The Hawk in the Rain, Lupercal*, and *Wodwo*. It is, after all, a narrative formulation of Hughes's belief that poetry is a "depiction of the Universe redeeming a disturbed balance."[8] In "Logos," a poem in *Wodwo*, the myth surfaces in a form which reveals its repercussions for language, in anticipation of "Orghast." Here, as in *The White Goddess*, it is God's insistence on absolute control and hoarding of all life unto himself that constitutes his crime and error[9]—a situation reminiscent of the autocracy of Urizen in Blake's mythology. But this mental tyrant cannot hold the whole together by the strength of his will; creation "convulses in nightmare," as the sea pulls everything to pieces "except its killers, alert and shapely."[10] The grandiloquence of the opening line, "God gives the blinding pentagram of his power," is cancelled by a casual dismissal in the last one, its sensational news of a matriarch presented as a piece of small talk in a trifling conversation about some well-intentioned bumbler: "God's a good fellow, but his mother's against him." While the logos disintegrates in the grinding of the sea, Hughes hears and transmits a descent towards prespeech, like the muttering of an old man approaching baby talk.

> A mumbling over and over
> Of ancient law, the phrasing falling to pieces
> Garbled among shell-shards and gravels,
>   the truth falling to pieces

Perhaps the poetry of Dylan Thomas is also a conditioning factor, especially in the third line just quoted, as the poet pushes logos toward babble. Hughes does voice his admiration for Thomas in a review of his letters, seeing him as a visionary poet aware, like Hughes, of an "infinitely mothering creation."[11] And Hughes is able to exploit images and aural patterns like Thomas's without falling prey to his manner or rhetorical stance.

Between "Orghast" and *Gaudete*, Hughes published *Season Songs*, a cycle of poems on the seasonal pattern. Formally regular and thematically affirmative, these seem, when placed beside Hughes's other work, to be songs of innocence, and it is interesting to note that the book is listed on the dust jacket of *Gaudete* among his works for children. *Season Songs* speaks out of a rural context, where nature and man meet harmoniously, rather than out of the denatured landscape of *Crow*. Hughes lets his voice spread, leaving aside shamanistic urgency for the more regular, recurrent wisdom of the folk, while he focusses on domestic farm animals rather than shapely predators. Often these poems are cousins of ballads or pieces of lore preserved in nursery rhymes. "Leaves" borrows its form from "Who Killed Cock Robin," while "The Golden Boy" is the mythic tale of the wheat which is buried, cultivated, slain, and eaten told in many folk songs and ballads like Burns's "John Barleycorn." The "Golden Boy" presents a version of Mary which adds the elements of fertility to the conventional religious figure, and equates love with the natural processes of growth. She might be taken as the presiding deity of *Season Songs*, mediating between the logos-God of *Crow* and the enraged nature goddess of *Gaudete*, exemplifying the "infinitely mothering creation" that Hughes associates with the vision of Dylan Thomas.

> But the Lord's mother
> Full of her love
> Found him underground
> And wrapped him with love
> As if he were her baby
> Her own born love
> And nursed him with miracles
> And starry love
> And he began to live
> And to thrive on her love[12]

These lines are simpler than most in *Season Songs*, but they do illustrate the prevailing metaphorical and rhythmic strategies of satisfying and reinforcing expectations, as opposed to Hughes's usual strategy of forcing the pace with adventurous metaphors. The repetitions of diction, rhythm, and structure reinforce the underlying assurance of renewed fertility in *Season Songs*, whereas the recurrent phrasings and formulae of *Crow* work as reminders of the grinding stasis of the wasteland.

Gaudete is a rich, ungainly combination of literary forms, including surrealistic sequences, psychological realism, a short narrative in the manner of a folk tale, and tightly controlled love poetry. And this reflects the book's concentration on metamorphosis. Whereas *Crow* and *Season Songs* depict the stable circumstances of the wasteland and pastoral, *Gaudete* takes place when, as Hughes observed earlier in "Childbirth," "There was not looking at table or chair,"[13] when repressed primal forces seek expression in the sphere of ordinary reality. The writing in the prologue and main body of the book is a protean medium shifting from long poetic lines into prose paragraphs, then back into verse, as the narrative proceeds. This passage from the main body of the narrative relates the torment of Mrs. Westlake, whose barren life has been thrown into relief by new passions she can't cope with:

She feels the finality of it all, and the nearness and greatness of death.
Sea-burned, sandy cartilege, draughty stars, gull-cries from beyond the world's edge. She feels the moment of killing herself grow sweet and ripe, close and perfect.

The walls wait. The senseless picture frame.
Eyes half closed
She sits stupidly, like something cancelled. Forcing
        the seconds to pass.

                              —*Gaudete*, p. 39

The writing has an attentive quality, as though it were tuning and re-tuning itself to the tenor of events and the turbulent emotions of the characters.

The love poems in the epilogue are, then, a stylistic resolution which provides some of the satisfaction accompanying the emergence of a definite key, as well as a measure of their author's devotion to the goddess.

But as narrative, *Gaudete* is explicit, focussing centripetally, driving the point home. In this respect it contrasts with *Crow*, which suggests the existence of a core story or myth without divulging it, and coheres around the character of Crow himself. The full title, *From the Life and Songs of the Crow* informs us that the printed poems are but a selection, that the book could go on and on, reinforcing the overall impression of interminable time. Hughes consciously chose this form for his book, for he did have a mythic narrative about Crow in mind but decided against using it.[14] The result is a book which both activates and denies our expectations of mythological coherence, brooding over version after version of botched genesis, suggesting a coreless culture too exhausted to hold itself to a centre. In *Gaudete* the earth spirits, no longer powerless to be born, hold creation in their grip, and the narrative takes on analogous insistence, both in the conclusive structure of plot and the procedures of style. Hughes frequently sets aside his talent for concision in favor of a writing heavy with description, laden with adjectives and exploratory phrases. He often stops the action and examines the scene before him (the book began as a film scenario) physically and psychologically, creating a sense of very dense, pregnant moments piling on top of one another until the climax breaks with their accumulated weight. In this passage Commander Estridge senses the gathering horror in the Beethoven sonata his daughter plays on the piano, built up with vague and ponderous latinate phrases like Conrad's in *Heart of Darkness*:

> The music she plays bewilders the old man.
> He cannot interpret those atmospherics
> And soundings and cries.
> It is shouting something impossible, incomprehensible,
>   monstrous.

> The dutiful hands of his daughters
> Which control his days
> With routine breakfast egg and toast, with coffee,
> With crisply ironed clothes, and warmed bed—
> They are tearing him to pieces, elated
> Under those sickly, sulphurous blooms
> And the hellish upset of music.

> In the dark hall, walled with stuffed wild life,
> He listens. And he hears
> Something final approaching.
> Some truly gloomy horror is pushing.

> Something that makes nothing of names, or affection,
> or loyalty, or consideration.
> —*Gaudete*, p. 42

This is the music of natural energy perceived from the vantage point of ordinary life, an unknown predatory power which is later revealed in the epilogue as the man-eating predator on the goddess's leash.

The central paradox of *Gaudete* is that the goddess's revenge is also her gift or blessing, as the title, meaning "rejoice," implies. A survey of its content does little justice to *Gaudete*'s richness in incident, but does elicit this prevailing doubleness, the situation of dialectical conflict aggravated to the point where only an apocalyptic conclusion is possible. In *Crow* the opposites, like the instinctive stabbing of grubs and moral guilt, cancel one another into ironic stalemate; here the conflict between natural energy and social forms explodes/flowers into tragically-shaped myth. Reverend Lumb (L'homme), and Anglican minister, is abducted by earth spirits and "duplicated" in a rite which involves tying him to an oak and lashing the two of them, until the oak becomes another Lumb (Limb). The Argument tells us that the changeling is returned to earth to act in the minister's role, but the narrative presents us with a realistic version—a divided man who must now act as nature's agent but also wishes to be an ordinary man, free of these compulsions. He has, we learn, turned the Women's Institute into a fertility cult and secretly makes love to each of its members in the hope of procreating a dionysian savior. The main body of the work consists of cinematic scenes from the last day of Lumb's ministry, in which we observe him, often through the eyes of another observer, going about his sexual mission, and villagers experiencing its repercussions. At the same time Lumb intends to escape, at the day's end, with Felicity, the girl he loves as an ordinary man. As his extremely busy day progresses, Lumb, moving with the speed and ardour of a doctor in an epidemic, is found out by both worlds. The men of the village obtain evidence of his sexual activities when a snooping poacher snaps a damning, hastily developed photograph, and Maud, Lumb's voiceless housekeeper and high priestess, uncovers his plan to run off with Felicity with the use of a crystal ball. Here, in camera and crystal ball, we have the two instruments of the book's vision, providing clear, satirically edged portraits and primal visions respectively. At the climax of the evening's rite Maud kills Felicity (whom Lumb, dressed as a stag, has just mounted ceremonially) and denounces the minister, breaking her silence with a "throat-gouging scream" (*Gaudete*, p. 147). The women, clad in animal skins, drugged, frenzied as Maenads, turn upon him and Lumb barely escapes—only to be hounded down and finally shot by the men, whose rage has been gathering momentum and direction at the pub. This portion of the book ends with the burning of all the bodies—Lumb's, Felicity's, and Maud's (she has committed suicide)—and the church which contains them.

Lumb has been the conductor of an energy which radiates to all the citizens, sharpening their lives into acuity. Each receives smaller doses of the vision/pain which afflicts him. As well as the examples of Mrs. Westlake and Commander Estridge cited previously, one might single out Dunworth, a weak executive who catches Lumb and his wife in the act and is unable to pull the trigger on his gun, suddenly overwhelmed by her beauty.

> Dunworth gazes back at his wife
> Almost forgetting where he is or what he is doing.
> He is helplessly in love.
> He stands there, in his child's helplessness,
> As if he had searched everywhere and at last somehow
> he had found her.
> An irresponsible joy chatters to be heard, somewhere
> in the back of his head, as he gazes at her,
> Feeling all his nerves dazzle, with waftings of vertigo,
> As if he were gazing into an open furnace.
>
> —*Gaudete*, p. 87

But it is in Lumb's poems in the epilogue that the paradox of impossible pain and irresponsible joy emerges most clearly, where the vision of Lumb is made accessible, ironically, by its distancing into art. A short, straightforward story, rather like a folktale ("In a straggly village on the West Coast of Ireland, on a morning in May") explains the provenance of the manuscript. Three girls tell the village priest about a strange tramp—the original Lumb, returned to earth "but changed," as the Argument laconically declares—who performed a miracle for them by drawing an otter out of the sea-lough with a kind of animal music.

> He pursed his lips against the back of his hand. The girls waited. Suddenly their nerves seemed to shrivel, like a hair held in fire. An uncanny noise was coming from the back of the man's hand. A peculiar, warbling thin sound. It was like a tiny gentle screaming. A wavering, wringing, awful sound, that caught hold of their heads and was nearly painful. It was like a fine bloody thread being pulled through their hearts.
>
> —*Gaudete*, pp. 173–74

The priest is much moved by the story, and responds in a way that indicates Lumb's vision has reverberated inside.

> 'If that is a miracle,' he said finally, 'To bring an otter up out of the lough, then what must that poor man think of the great world itself, this giant, shining beauty that God whistled up out of the waters of chaos?'
> And as he spoke the priest was suddenly carried away by his words. His thoughts flew up into a great fiery space, and who knows what spark had

jumped on to him from the flushed faces of the three girls? He seemed to be flying into an endless, blazing sunrise, and he described the first coming of Creation, as it rose from the abyss, an infinite creature of miracles, made of miracles and teeming miracles.

—*Gaudete*, p. 175

This portion of the epilogue should not be overlooked, or hastily relegated to a transitional role, for it functions in *Gaudete* as *Season Songs* does in the stretch of Hughes's corpus to the present: the place where the energy of natural forces is accepted into human life, contained and ritualized by poetic forms and traditional beliefs. The priest, at a safe remove from its destructive force, is able to introduce the energy into the conventional framework of his belief, enlivening the body of Christianity without burning the church, in somewhat the same way that "The Golden Boy" brings fertility myth and the mother of God together in *Season Songs*. Hughes has always been aware of the need to domesticate the divine energy, and speaks of this in a theoretical way which is germane to the cases of Lumb and the priest. This is a facet of Hughes's art we sometimes overlook when we write or think of him as a celebrator of violence.

If you refuse the energy, you are living a kind of death. If you accept the energy, it destroys you. What is the alternative? To accept the energy, and find methods of turning it to good, of keeping it under control—rituals, the machinery of religion. The old method is the only one.[15]

In the poems Lumb is a visionary casualty, another of the uncanny peasants, common in the celtic tradition, who have been broken into vision. His poems are seldom lyrical in the conventional sense, but spare and taut, filled with silences caught between lines or groupings of lines, as though spaces were left, as Dylan Thomas puts it, for whatever is not in the poem to "creep, crawl, flash, or thunder in."[16] Speech itself is seen as a corruption and construction of animal music (which Lumb is able to perform in a literal sense, as his miracle demonstrates), an imprisoning of the cries of birds and the "awkward gullets of beasts" that "will not chill into syntax."

Words buckle the voice in tighter, closer
Under the midriff
Till the cry rots, and speech

Is a fistula

Eking and deferring
Like a stupid or a crafty doctor.
—*Gaudete*, p. 176

When the poems do approach song, they catch the after-echoes of the goddess's predatory music and find a voice that is ancient and impersonal, reaching deeply into tradition. At times, as in the poem which follows, they resemble the celtic riddle poems, like Taliesin's "Hanes" and the "Song of Amergin," upon which Graves roosts and pecks in *The White Goddess*:

> She rides the earth
> On an ass, on a lion.
> She rides the heavens
> On a great white bull.
>
> She is an apple.
> Whoever plucks her
> Nails his heart
> To the leafless tree.
> —*Gaudete*, p. 184

The poem announces her symbols, and sums up the ordeal of her worship. But the very fact of a multiplicity of symbols, coupled with the ease with which we are slipped from ass to lion to bull, pleads for their subservience to the energy beyond them. The poetic act is humble, pointing to manifestations of the goddess without claiming to exhaust them or drawing attention to itself. It is a wiser and sadder poetry than the unsung poem beginning with Crow's "O leaves" promises to be, looking back to the moment of intense vision as *Crow* looks forward to it. Where Crow failed to accomplish the pure music of nature in speech, Lumb knows that the attempt is, in a sense, blasphemous, an encounter with tabu, and restricts words to being accurate reporters, rather than riders, of that energy.

> Trying to be a leaf
> In your kingdom
> For a moment I am a leaf
> And your fulness comes
>
> And I reel back
> Into my face and hands
>
> Like the electrocuted man
> Banged from his burst straps
> —*Gaudete*, p. 180

Notes

1. Ted Hughes, *Crow* (New York, 1971), p. 80. Further references are incorporated in the text.

2. Ted Hughes, interviewed by Ekbert Faas in the *London Magazine* (January 1971), p. 20.

3. Ted Hughes, interviewed by Tom Stoppard in "Orghast," *TLS* 1 October 1971, p. 1174.

4. Ted Hughes, *Gaudete* (London, 1977), p. 182. Further references are incorporated in the text.

5. See A. C. H. Smith, *Orghast at Persepolis* (London, 1972).

6. Ted Hughes, in Smith, p. 45.

7. Ted Hughes, in Smith, p. 132.

8. *London Magazine*, p. 8.

9. Robert Graves, *The White Goddess* (New York, 1948), p. 527.

10. Ted Hughes, *Wodwo* (London, 1967), p. 34.

11. Ted Hughes, "Dylan Thomas's Letters," *New Statesman*, 26 November 1966, p. 783.

12. Ted Hughes, *Season Songs* (New York, 1975), p. 38.

13. Ted Hughes, "Childbirth," *The Hawk in the Rain* (London, 1957), p. 45.

14. See Keith Sagar, *The Art of Ted Hughes* (Cambridge, 1975), p. 110.

15. *London Magazine*, p. 10.

16. Dylan Thomas, "Notes on the Art of Poetry," in Gary Geddes, ed. *Twentieth Century Poetry and Poetics* (Toronto, 1973), p. 595.

MAJOR POETRY VOLUMES

◆

Ted Hughes

A. E. Dyson

. . . 'the demeanour of a mouse—Yet is he monster'. Despite Ted Hughes's description of a 'famous poet' in these terms, there is little mouse-like about his own work; and if he is 'monster', he sounds an oddly creative one. Born in 1930, at Cambridge in the early '50s, and now resident in the U.S.A., he has become widely known through poems in various journals, and especially through *The Hawk In The Rain*. This volume was published by Faber and Faber in 1957, and won the First Publication Award in an Anglo-American contest sponsored by the New York City Poetry Center and judged by W. H. Auden, Stephen Spender and Marianne Moore. It is, to my mind, the most distinguished volume of verse by a poet of Mr. Hughes's generation to have appeared, and it notably escapes the various poetic labels that the last ten years have thrown up. The style is neither 'Movement' nor 'Maverick', and no traces can be found of the Neo-Augustanism at present supposed to be in fashion. The most obvious immediate influences are Hopkins and Dylan Thomas, possibly because like these poets Ted Hughes is concerned to recreate and participate in experience, not to reflect upon it from a distance. But the tone and mood are too distinctive to be derivative. The deeper influences are Donne, Webster and the early seventeenth century writers generally. Ted Hughes's values are much nearer to those of this period than they are to either Hopkins or Dylan Thomas; reading him, one is aware of closer affinities with the seventeenth century than even the poets of the twenties and thirties, with their rediscovered admiration of the Jacobeans, offered.

The major theme in the poems is power; and power thought of not morally, or in time, but absolutely—in a present which is often violent and self-destructive, but isolated from motive or consequence, and so unmodified by the irony which time confers. For Ted Hughes power and violence go together: his own dark gods are makers of the tiger, not the lamb. He is fascinated by violence of all kinds, in love and in hatred, in the jungle and the arena, in battle, murder and sudden death. Violence, for him, is the occasion not for reflection, but for *being*; it is a guarantee of energy, of life, and most so, paradoxically, when it knows itself in moments of captivity,

Reprinted from *Critical Quarterly* 1 (Autumn 1959): 219–26, by permission of the author and the journal.

pain or death. He looks at the caged jaguar, as it hurries 'enraged Through prison darkness after the drills of its eyes', and finds victory in its untamed will

> there's no cage to him
> More than to the visionary his cell.
> His stride is wildernesses of freedom

Beast and visionary are linked in the triumph of will over circumstance; in *The Martyrdom Of Bishop Farrar* he goes further, and finds triumph in a moment of martyrdom. The flame 'shrivels sinew and chars bone', but the spirit rises superior to suffering. The bishop's victory is one of pure stoicism, creating in the flames a timeless moment of glory, which is the currency of heroism, and so good coin long after his own flesh is consumed

> His body's cold-kept miserdom of shrieks
> He gave uncounted, while out of his eyes
> Out of his mouth, fire like a glory broke,
> And smoke burned his sermons into the skies.

One is reminded here, and often in the other poems, of Yeats's *Easter 1916*. Essentially ordinary men are taken, by one act of heroism consummated in death, out of the humdrum world 'where motley is worn' into the lasting world of symbols. The cause they died for may be unnecessary, it may fail, but this matters little, since the heroic exists neither in its motives nor its consequences, but in itself

> All is changed, changed utterly,
> A terrible beauty is born.

So in Ted Hughes's poems, there is a constant striving towards moments of significance; moments of greatness which will last, as symbols if not as facts; ideal events more enduring than their agents, whose death, indeed, is their own occasion to be. Love, like death is valued for its power of providing such moments. First, there is the violence of encounter, restless, compulsive, pitiless

> There is no better way to know us
> Than as two wolves, come separately to a wood.
> Now neither's able to sleep . . .

but after, the lovers break through to a moment of glory; they duck and peep,

> And there rides by
> The great lord from hunting . . .

Ted Hughes values such moments for their intensity; but he has to isolate them from past and future, cause and effect, reflection and evaluation before he can savour them to the full. Hence the absence of compassion, anger, humility, nostalgia, disgust and the other attitudes belonging to the perspectives of time. His intelligence is often wholly absorbed in the battle to embody moments of power in words: it is the purity of intoxication, not the complexities of hang-over, that engage him. The poem *September* is about the timeless sense of union which desire can bring.

> When kisses are repeated and the arms hold
> There is no telling where time is . . .

Incompatibilities is about the no less timeless disunion which can come from the same impulse

> Desire's a vicious separator in spite
> Of its twisting women round men . . .

The Song, 'O lady, when the tipped cup of the moon blessed you', explores the tenderness and romance of love, *The Decay Of Vanity* explores its transience and hollowness.

Instead of the opposites coming together, and generating the complexities which modify them in sober reflection, they are resolutely segregated, and so kept pure and strong. In this way, the poems recreate the intensity, the absolute quality of each state—union and disunion, romanticism and cynicism—treating experience not as parable or text but as sacrament. Articulation itself becomes a mode of participation, at least for the moment when feeling is being grasped.

All of this, of course, is exactly similar to Donne. And as in Donne, one finds explosiveness of utterance; imagery which is developed intellectually, but assimilated at every point to the central emotional experience; vividness and even grotesqueness of phrase and metaphor; metre which twists and turns in its wrestling with meaning

> Love you I do not say I do or might either.
> I come to you enforcedly . . .

and a general sense of being at the white-hot moment of experience: directly involved, so that the experience of the words is inseparable from the insight with which they grapple, and is, indeed, the high point of awareness itself.

When this is said, one can see the poems dividing into two groups;

those in which the poet seems wholly identified with some moment of power and violence, and vicariously elated; and those in which he realizes such a moment fully, but remains a human and time-bound intelligence outside the experience, aware of the unbridgeable gulf between symbol and fact, eternity and time. In the former group, one can mention the very fine poem *Hawk Roosting* which appeared in the last *Critical Quarterly*. The hawk's victorious moment of triumph—might without mercy, conquest without effort, privilege without responsibility, energy without consciousness of end—is explored in vividly memorable phrases (the words and statements suggesting animal consciousness deeper than either words or statements); and remains, without any specific comment from the poet, but unanswerably, the embodiment of one possible mode of being

> I kill where I please because it is all mine.
> There is no sophistry in my body:
> My manners are tearing off heads—
>
> The allotment of death.

This is at one pole: other poems, as one would expect, hold such a moment of triumph, ruthless and timeless, in balance against a more human sense of time, with the knowledge both of complexity, and of limitation, which this brings. In the other fine hawk poem, the title poem of *The Hawk In The Rain*, the poet also enters imaginatively into the hawk's victory, this time as it rides 'Effortlessly at height' above the storm. But here, he remains conscious, also, of the 'habit of the dogged grave' which keeps him earth-bound, and which in the end will smash the bird, too—though in the hawk's 'own time', a choice that enables the bird to submit to its fate, and so snatch a martyr's triumph even in destruction

> . . . maybe in his own time meets the weather
> Coming the wrong way, suffers the air, hurled upside down,
> Fall from his eye, the ponderous shires crash on him,
> The horizon trap him; the round angelic eye
> Smashed, mix his heart's blood with the mire of the land.

In this poem, the striving towards the 'master-Fulcrum of violence where the hawk hangs still' is balanced by awareness of time: the hawk's holding of 'all creation in a weightless quiet' is 'steady as a hallucination', and the word 'hallucination' pinpoints the ambivalence which a human intelligence cannot help feeling about the reality of such moments. The poem *Six Young Men* confronts this ambivalence directly. The poem is about a photograph of six young men who went to the war and were all killed. Because of their death, the photograph becomes in one sense eternal. The dead men, as heroes, remain living symbols, 'mightier-than-a-man dead bulk and weight'. Yet the photograph itself is already 'faded and ochre-tinged', the clothes that the dead men wear in it are now unfashionable. The intense guarantee of life that is felt in their death has to be balanced against 'Forty years rotting into soil' and the other erosions of time. So the poem's final statement is a paradox—similar in content to that of Keats's *Ode To A Grecian Urn*, even though tone and mood could scarcely be further removed

> That man's not more alive whom you confront
> And shake by the hand, see hale, hear speak loud,
> Than any of these six celluloid smiles are,
> Nor prehistoric or fabulous beast more dead;
> No thought so vivid as their smoking blood:
> To regard this photograph might well dement,
> Such contradictory permanent horrors here
> Smile from the single exposure and shoulder out
> One's own body from its instant and heat.

Grief For Dead Soldiers, a poem equally fine, avoids the ambivalence by separating three 'griefs' about death in action, and exploring each in isolation. The 'secretest' grief, which is that of the widow, is one thing:

> Closer than thinking
> The dead man hangs around her neck, but never
> Close enough to be touched, or thanked even,
> For being all that remains in a world smashed . . .

the 'truest' grief, which is that of the calm craftsmen digging graves for the unburied dead as they wait 'like brides to surrender their limbs' is another. But apart from these, unmodified by them, and 'mightiest', is the public grief at the cenotaph. Here, the deaths are ideally celebrated. The dead become symbols, as enduring as the marble of the cenotaph itself; pure heroism, protected from the irony which the other two more human griefs would undoubtedly generate if allowed to mix, is celebrated as enduring magnificence

> their souls
> Scrolled and supporting the sky, and the national sorrow,
> Over the crowds that know of no other wound,
> Permanent stupendous victory.

In almost any other post world-war-II poet one can think of, these lines could scarcely be anything other than ironic; and the 'griefs' of the widow, and of the agents of oblivion, would be among the stuff of irony. Ted Hughes alone manages to isolate the heroic—not denying the other facts, but denying their power to negate the quality of heroism itself. Perhaps it is no surprise that he should write of the first rather than the second world war, and be obsessed by such types of warfare (bayonet charges, trench fighting) as belong to the pre-hydrogen age, when personal heroism was still of merit in the scheme of things. The quality of violence he writes of, however, is sufficiently up-to-date; one cannot write off his achievement as mere nostalgia for the good old days of meaningful slaughter.

The Casualty illustrates as well as any the themes that have been discussed. At the start, the doomed airman is caught into the loneliness of violent death. His burning aircraft removes him from the company of the indifferent living, who watch from below, into the company of the more meaningful dead. In falling 'out of the air alive' he becomes of unique interest. The price is immediate death, the breaking of his body beyond repair ('Now that he has No spine, against heaped leaves they prop him up'). Yet it is the living, confronted by his death, who stand 'helpless as ghosts', and the dead man, by virtue of his sudden death, who 'Bulks closer greater flesh and blood than their own'. The word 'alive', with its serious, non-ironic application to the dead man falling, is pivotal, enabling death to take on its full ambivalence as an event both terrible and glorious:

> A snake in the gloom of the brambles or a rare flower.

This 'either/or' in the fact of death is the dichotomy which Ted Hughes takes care never to resolve. It is by segregating the two possibilities, and stopping them from meeting, that he is enabled to enter into both as he does: exploring the 'rare flower', in particular, undiverted by that ironic no-man's-land between the 'either/or' where most of his contemporaries are to be found.

It is of interest that the onlookers, in this poem, should be seeking to enter into the airman's experience

> Greedy to share all that is undergone,
> Grimace, gasp, gesture of death

but that their 'sympathies' should be described in terms of greed, and the parasitic. In *Famous Poet*, Ted Hughes describes the poet as one who, like these onlookers, tries to 'concoct The old heroic bang' from the deeds of others—but who is himself 'wrecked' in the attempt, and ends, not united with his object, but exhausted and diminished, 'like a badly hurt man, half life-size'. Perhaps, we may feel, the irony which Ted Hughes resolutely keeps out of heroic events he cannot wholly exclude from heroic people. Events partake of eternity, as poems do; but people, and poets, can never be free of the doom of a turning world.

Hence he celebrates, in his own poems, the frozen moments of great-ness—the photograph, the cenotaph, the martyr burning, the hawk riding the storm, the jaguar free in his cage, the lover at the moment of consumma-tion. To remember these things can give meaning to birth and life, and incite to vigour and endurance. To some degree it can put magic back in life, and also meaning; but no human can stay on such heights for long.

What, then, can be a provisional judgment on these poems? (provi-sional, because Ted Hughes has only begun to write, and these first works will attract much more critical attention before any definitive placing is likely). There is a temptation (for a radical, at any rate), to make easily adverse judgment upon them—as, for example, that the pre-occupation with violent death is adolescent, or sadistic; or that there is something sinister about a creative intelligence which can devote itself to the recreation and celebration of violence rather than to critical reflections upon it. Such objec-tions may have some point, but they are less relevant in considering poetry than they would be (say) in drama or the novel. For one thing, Ted Hughes's control of words and metre in his best poems is profoundly mature already: the style is clearly the expression of a serious and adult intelligence, and a guarantee of validity in itself. Then again, poetry need not always evaluate experience. Sometimes its main function is to extend awareness, creating new areas which the reader can assimilate into his own total morality later, as he will. Ted Hughes, more than any recent poet I can think of, has the skill to do this. The quality of violence, which many of our finest novelists (Angus Wilson, William Golding and others) explore as moralists, is pre-sented *in* Ted Hughes's poems in a manner which makes us more alive to what certain forces in modern politics and life really are.

His own obvious values are not unimportant—the quest for resilience and endurance, the response to birth as miracle, the sense that being able to ask 'Why?' may still be more important than hearing answers. But beyond these, he offers us the *feel* of power, as something inescapably to do with life, however we may feel its deadly qualities too. The God of the tiger must be known today, whether we choose to worship or not. Also, refusal to worship might, we are reminded, be itself another kind of death.

Ted Hughes's present achievement is within fairly narrow limits, but there are hints of various developments that make the prospect of his next poems exciting. In *Griefs For Dead Soldiers*, for example, the widow, unlike the crowd at the cenotaph, 'cannot build her sorrow into a monument and walk away from it'. Is this an *en-passant* felicity, or might we hear more, in future poems, of the monumental, and heroic, as evasion? There is no knowing, since the critic has no crystal to see the future at this level. The theme of violence, and power, offer rich possibilities, however; especially to a poet as sensitively alive as Mr. Hughes.

Summing-up will have to be personal. Though for my own part I dislike violence, and even more the acceptance of it as a norm, I find in these poems something powerful and compelling. The tone is strong and honest, individual and unmistakeable. Ted Hughes's voice is the most distinctive we have heard in poetry since Dylan Thomas and this, in itself, marks him out—especially since he is swimming against the prevailing currents of detachment, irony, urbanity and Neo-Augustan influences generally. Our present literary scene is full of very *good* poets, who offer varied and deep pleasures: poetry is flourishing these days as seldom before. But Ted Hughes is more than very good. I don't doubt that, hydrogen bombs and his own ethos of violence permitting, he will be one of the select few to be read a hundred years from now.

Thinking Animal: Ted Hughes

FREDERICK GRUBB

There is a wagtail sitting on the gate-post. I see how sweet and swift heaven is. But hell is slow and . . . viscous and insect-teeming: as is this Europe, now, this England.

—D. H. Lawrence: *To Ottoline Morrell*

Ted Hughes was born in 1930—again, the generation of Gunn and Porter. He is not interrogating a comfortable era or defining his apartness by taking tests. He prefers to go beneath and beyond society. A Yorkshireman born and bred, he is like D. H. Lawrence aware of a conflict between townee smartness and rural strength. He is not a seeker: he embraces the given. He has plunged into the abundance of his background and become a richer Douanier Rousseau, a case of the well-trained primitive.

In his first volume, *The Hawk in the Rain* (1957), there is a vehement expressionism which sometimes bawls itself out—the merciless amassment of hectoring physical images either batters us into insensibility or wins our dazed assent; we feel like a punch-drunk boxer, conceding victory to Mr Hughes. Poems like *The Hawk in the Rain, Egghead, Wind*, and *Phaetons* deliver blows like 'rain hacks my head to the bone', 'bloodily grabbed dazed last-moment-counting', 'wind that dented the balls of my eyes', and 'drags him on fire / Among the monsters of the zodiac'. Hughes is *talking the energy out*; when the full range and depth of a situation is available, when all sophistries of response are banished we find our true bearings in it. And the fine meticulous image, provided it is deeply felt, is vital to the whole. A 'glass half full of wine' left out 'to the dark heaven all night' dreams 'a premonition / of ice across its eye', and this is 'a skin, delicately here / Restraining a ripple from the air'. Later 'Mammoth and Sabre-tooth celebrate reunion'. The minuscule takes its rightful place in the ancientness and vastness of this world. The exuberance of *Roarers in a Ring*, about farmers roistering in a pub, refers to 'faces sweating like hams' yet 'the air new as a razor'. In *September*, Hughes holds disparate natural facts in equipoise. He withdraws from the foreground into the middle distance. But the vision remains rooted:

Reprinted from *A Vision of Reality: A Study of Liberalism in Twentieth-Century Poetry* (New York: Barnes & Noble; London: Chatto & Windus, 1965), 214–25, by permission of Random Century Group.

> *It is midsummer: the leaves hang big and still:*
> *Behind the eye a star,*
> *Under the silk of the wrist a sea, tell*
> *Time is nowhere.*

Hughes can be as subtle as the reader, and is not averse to sensitives. What he demands is that emotion should be complete, that it should never exclude, withhold, prevaricate. Animals, the weather, landscape, gregariousness ('company' is a favourite word) are felt in their most provocative and dangerous moments. Nature advances on the poet: she is not solicited, and is treated with all the objectivity and deference of a person. The intelligence lies in the way Hughes goes out to meet nature, struggles with it, arranges it in his mind, enriching his imagination. When he compares the nocturnal movements of the fox to his own creative process (*The Thought-Fox*) the word 'compares' is a critic's falsification of what is happening: the fox is 'coming about its own business', the poet is equally going about his. The word 'like' is redundant, for the fox is out there; its instinctiveness and finesse is at one with the mind in creation; it becomes actor and inspiration:

> *Till, with a sudden sharp hot stink of fox*
> *It enters the dark hole of the head.*
> *The window is starless still; the clock ticks,*
> *The page is printed.*

Hughes's animus is against the intellectual who has disabled the improvement of feeling by selecting and systematizing the facts:

> *A leaf's otherness,*
> *The whaled monstered sea-bottom, eagled peaks*
> *And stars that hang over hurtling endlessness,*
> *With manslaughtering shocks*
> *Are let in on his sense . . .*
> *   —Egghead*

It is not a case of one impulse from a vernal wood being worth more than the egghead's wisdom. The poet insists only that when phases of enhanced imagining come they should be welcomed, allowed to cleanse the mind. In *Famous Poet* Hughes has produced a kind of anti-manifesto: the monstrous 'famous poet', the 'near-finished variety artist' who 'slumps in his chair / like a badly hurt man, half life-size' is a scapegoat for the banishing of one of Hughes's temptations. If the poet ever expressed 'the vital fire . . . that puts the gloss on a normal hearty male' this has ossified into a formula—'Repeat that!' still they cry. The poet is a caricature of his essence, a 'Stegosaur' echoing a time when 'half the world still burned'. Emotion, more than reason, because it looks 'easier' may degenerate into a convention.

Because Ted Hughes gives himself utterly to the given, his art is generous. The moment of vision, the eruption of feeling, is treated as seriously as Empson would treat a concept or Auden an event: and, since vision and feeling are often an excuse for dropping seriousness of any kind—they are, in fact, treated with contempt—Hughes has made a great leap forward. Ideas are guided towards ends through the motor of feeling, and the health and quality of the feeling, resulting in action, bears a relation to the chances of arriving on target. *The Horses* describes how the poet watches horses grazing on the moors under a foggy sunrise. The unrhymed couplets welcome as much interplay of syntactical and metrical variation as is possible within the form. Full of enthusiastic information which the poet could have withheld for technical reasons or through fear of appearing sentimental, the occasion is offered in a hesitant, antithetical idiom, which shows respect for its intrinsic force; we are put right in the picture, but in no exhibitionist or vainglorious spirit:

> *Slowly detail leafed from the darkness. Then the sun*
> *Orange, red, red erupted*
>
> *Silently, and splitting to its core tore and flung cloud,*
> *Shook the gulf open, showed blue,*
>
> *And the big planets hanging—*
> *I turned*

The poem ends with a request which, in the current state of cynicism, is risky:

> *In din of the crowded streets, going among the years, the faces,*
> *May I still meet my memory in so lonely a place*
>
> *Between the streams and the red clouds, hearing curlews,*
> *Hearing the horizons endure.*

There it is, impregnated with the poet's personality: no taking advantage. One hopes that his request will be granted and one's trust that it will be proves that the poem has communicated, has become partly our own. Hughes applies his generosity to people. Love is 'so like a fire' that it must not be 'let out into strawy small talk', so like a flood that a trickle would make the whole crack. The lovers regard each other speechlessly, relishing the plenitude. (In Thom Gunn the reserve would be a defence against giving oneself away.) A circumspect girl secretary, apparently rejecting sex, has the instinctive innocence, the commitment to domestic obligations which seems an enhancement of sex. 'All / Day like a starling under the bellies of bulls / She hurries among men, ducking, peeping.'

Is man, as an intelligence opposed to nature, kept out of these poems? Hughes has the reverence for the historical continuum that we noticed in Thom Gunn, for whom the chosen act begs the same questions whenever it occurs; Gunn is inward with the Jacobean legend—ambition, poses, calculated ends, the ins and outs of intrigue, simulated emotion. Hughes harks back to a mediaeval world: the baleful naturalism of the Border Ballads, the rude, vivid communality of Chaucer and Langland, the aristocratic virulence of Shakespeare's History Plays; and he points forward to the loamy richness of the eighteenth-and nineteenth-century country parish, the habitats of Crabbe, Cowper, and Tennyson and still a living thing today.* *Soliloquy of a Misanthrope* yields 'when I am got under my gravestone', 'praise God heartily', 'old acquaintance', 'the smirk of every man', 'every mouth confessing its crude shire'. I am not suggesting that Mr Hughes is the village idiot; he projects tried and known and rich imagery in enacting contexts because, in fact *or analogue*, these contexts have always existed and reach their full strength in that way. *The Decay of Vanity, The Hag, A Modest Proposal, Vampire, Fallgrief's Girl Friends, Two Wise Generals,* and *Invitation to the Dance* infer a cocktail party, the sex war, puritanism, diplomacy and atrocities and all employ archaistic and historical images. Because the generals compromise, don't say what they feel, they 'find their sleeping armies massacred'. The condemned prisoner, persecuted by an 'inquisitor', still despises 'the shy and idle'; his private courage augurs well for the future of human courage— witness the tremendous line which should stand as an epitaph on all the victims of oppression—'the light of his death's dawn put the dark out'. A possessive mother and her college daughter are 'a cajoling hag' and a 'pretty princess'. A party gate-crasher is a 'vampire', giving nothing, only taking. Voracious lovers, fighting like wolves in a forest, are quieted when 'the great lord from hunting' appears; one thinks of Donne's 'else a great Prince in prison lies'; a vivid tableau, as from an Uccello, follows and symbolizes the glory of requited desire:

> *His embroidered*
> *Cloak floats, the tail of his horse pours,*
> *And at his stirrup the two great-eyed greyhounds*
> *That day after day bring down the towering stag*

---

*'. . . England is perishing, and he was English. He was not British or enlightened or far-sighted or adaptable. He was English, and most so when he forgot his nationality and took a country walk.' E.M. Forster wrote this of Cowper in 1932.

Leap like one, making delighted sounds.

In *The Decay of Vanity* the woman is the 'Queen' who crowns the poet King; he embalms her remains 'heart-brokenly', then forgets. Years later another man 'looms up' and, 'by the majesty in his stride', 'dreams he sweeps some great queen towards his bed'. The man's conceit is a confession of inferiority, for the woman is still beautiful—'a royal trophy'—and in 'a world of pride' this makes the man the poet's scavenger. The weighing of personality, the apportionment of justice, in this poem is magisterial. The woman being beautiful, all the characters are in the right. But it is unequivo- cally a contest: the best man wins. Pride of this order is disapproved of today, so the royal analogy gives an unfamiliar value some historical colour. The 'disfocusing of contemporaneity' in these poems vindicates unpopular sources of strength by exposing their roots.

Hughes's vivacity owes little to the Lawrentine 'lapsing out' into blood consciousness. He greets the intellect as in league with, though not subordi- nate to, nature, and his poems are often models of the ordering of experience. Hughes's poems are reared on the objective. This is clear in *The Casualty*. Farmers and housewives 'wait with interest for the evening news' before rushing out to find the crashed, burning airman. We see the victim react on his environment and become a new creature—'a snake in the gloom of the brambles or a rare flower'. Despite the terror which all share, there is reticence in the poet's approach. He does not make the man speak, nor does he mention the pain he must be feeling; the man is a natural object, doing what everybody will have to do in a particularly dramatic way; the watchers are rightly 'greedy to share all that is undergone'. Individuality is irrelevant for the watchers, for what is pain to the man is recharged reality to them, yet his humanity is crowned at the moment it returns to the general. The victim is set apart, honoured, for this. In a poem called *Bayonet Charge* a recruit sees a hare die violently; this wipes out vague idealism and he sees himself as mature amid 'the cold clockwork of the stars and the nations'.

Griefs for Dead Soldiers isolates three griefs: mightiest, that of the Ceno- taph; secretest, that of the mother who 'cannot build her sorrow into a monument / And walk away from it'; and truest, that of the burial party. Mr C. B. Cox has asserted that Hughes separates the griefs to avoid irony about the public grief. I take the poem as an *ironical commendation* of future public grief—for the 'mightiest grief' is in the future tense, presented apoca- lyptically; and the 'crowds' who constitute 'the national sorrow' *know of no other wound*. By contrast, the 'secretest' grief is movingly sensitive, the 'truest' is grimly realistic. The thing is a fact of nature; this realism has been, therefore it is, and to complacent generations it will not be an excuse for vulgar nationalism but an almost supernatural reminder of the lost meaning of tragedy. Wilfred Owen might have written poetry like this had he lived.

Six Young Men is about soldiers photographed against a landscape which the poet knows well—'I know / That bilberried bank . . .'

> *From where these sit*
> *You hear the water of seven streams fall*
> *To the roarer in the bottom, and through all*
> *The leafy valley a rumouring of air go.*
> *Pictured here, their expressions listen yet,*
> *And still that valley has not changed its sound*
> *Though their faces are four decades under the ground.*

Then he tells us about the deaths. The man 'you confront', 'see hale', is not 'more alive', nor is 'fabulous beast' more dead than these soldiers, since the intensity of life recorded in the photograph continues in nature; it is the human expression of that life which is tragically (he leaves us in no doubt about that) superannuated. In another poem a push-buttoner, agent of cold-blooded, administration ridden war, hears the 'heart-beat' of an ancient warrior in his room. Time vanishes; war at least becomes a matter of spectacular risk. 'When archaeologists dig their remainder out / Bits of bone, rust / The grandeur of their wars humbles my thought'.

In Hughes's second book, *Lupercal* (1960), animals outnumber men. This is deceptive, for Hughes's intelligence refines the poems about animals, while the men gain by having their animality appraised intelligently. Hughes has been taunted with hiring animals as gangsters to indulge his primitive drives. Does he disgorge human impulses at a subhuman level? Disgorge sounds bad because we are trained to sublimate, to lose in pretension what we gain in refinement. Yet there remains an automatism of naturalism as dangerous as the automatism of material progress; and Hughes is not guiltless of the former, though he could teach a few things to the latter. (Mr Vernon Scannell upbraided Hughes's 'anthropomorphic fallacy' in *Encounter*, in a skit called *Ruminant*, where a particularly bovine cow is caught in the act of 'composing a long poem about Ted Hughes'.) First, it is arguable that a modern poet's obsession with nature is needed to compensate for indifference, and this in a country which is notoriously sentimental about animals provided they are tame or comical and do not read a lecture to humans (how many animal addicts care about natural conservation?), and second, I think the poems are more objective, more complex, than the Vernon Scannells allow. Take *View of a Pig*, where the animal is dead; any attempt by the poet to 'work out' his aggression would be lunatic. He is intensely preoccupied with the deadness—'too dead now to pity'—of the pig as a quality worth exploring; the distinction between man and beast is riveting—'I stared at it a long time'; the enacting life is his remembered life, 'once I ran at a fair in the noise . . .' Now beasts alive are very wicked, they affirm themselves; their rejection as literary pets makes these poems as original as Lawrence's. The tension he feels between the otherness, and the nearness, of the beasts makes this poet realize his own strength. The violence of a frustrated era is attracted away from cruel, destructive outlets and returned to source, where it can be appreciated and, energizing us, put out to graze.

In *Hawk Roosting* the animal is alive, it alone speaks, but in two voices: a descriptive voice, telling the reader what he sees—'my feet are locked upon the rough bark'—and the instructive voice of the poet which utters what is seen at the same time that it cross-examines the reader by implication. It claims that 'there is no sophistry in my body / My manners are tearing off heads', 'no arguments assert my right', 'I am going to keep things like this'. Quotes from Hitler? Hughes has not raved violent nonsense through a microphone; he has written about a hawk; by engaging our interest, he exposes our fear of instinct, our bent for apologia, our postponement of choice—the 'falsifying dream'. If our kinship with the hawk is demonstrated, it is because we share—or should share—its adjustment as both expression and controller of its environment—'It took the whole of Creation / To produce my foot, my each feather / Now I hold Creation in my foot.' Less emblematic, more puzzling, is the Otter—versatile, endearing, 'neither fish nor beast'—an English eccentric, apt to give the hunt the slip. His affinities with man are of the order of imaginative simile (he crosses the sea in three nights 'like a king in hiding. Crying to the old shape of the starlit land') or of half satirical inference ('the self under the eye lies / Attendant and with-drawn'). *Pike* is physically and sensually triumphant, a marvel of visual images communicated aurally, the menace of the tactile lurking in the incisive splendour of the language. The pike—'a life subdued to its instru-ment'—is clearly other than we, the gauleiter of a police state:

> Or move, stunned by their own grandeur,
> Over a bed of emerald, silhouette
> Of submarine delicacy and horror.
> A hundred feet long in their world.

When the poet comes on the scene, he participates as enemy—'silently cast and fished'—and victim 'with the hair frozen on my head'; he is the object of aggression. It is an aggression which does him good. *Bullfrog*, also concerned with effects, divides man from beast through technical mastery; Hughes abandons quatrain in favor of a flexible form. The bullfrog, at first sight alarming, is an engaging character, worthy of affection, and the delighted poet wants to talk about, and to, the bullfrog at the moment when it is in action. The result is a lively example of what syncopated rhythm can do to harmonize events through the controlled diversification of texture:

> With their lithe long strong legs
> Some frogs are able

> *To thump upon double-*
> *Bass string though pond-water deadens and clogs.*
> *But you, bullfrog, you pump out*
> *Whole fogs full of horn—a threat*
> *As of a liner looming. True*
> *That, first hearing you*
> *Disgorging your gouts of darkness like a wounded god . . .*

We find there is no assault on our emotion nor any attempt to abdicate from consciousness into merging. Nature is distanced, as in Shakespeare, precisely *through* intense intricate response (see *Bullfrog*) to the point where it throws into relief the tragic isolation and irrevocableness of articulate being:

> *The deeps are cold:*
> *In that darkness camaraderie does not hold:*
> *Nothing touches, but clutching, devours.*
> *   —Relic*

Because we feel the pity and terror as repugnant we remain outside; because we apprehend its truth and revolt against it, the assertion of free will is born. 'Time in the sea eats its tail', mindless, repetitive, and casts back upon the shores from which they came 'the spars of purposes'. Ted Hughes knows an alternative: neither to exclude the tragic, nor to frustrate the will. Just as the Pike was 'subdued to its instrument', and the Hawk expressed and controlled creation, the Intelligence is not asked to grovel, it is urged to admit and exercise its kinship with nature. *Thrushes* opens with a breathtaking dynamic insight into birds pecking on a lawn; that domestic familiar, the thrush, metamorphoses into a monster of instinctive efficiency, all 'bounce and stab', 'a ravening second', overtaking 'the instant' and inimical to 'procrastinations', 'yawning stares', 'sighs', and 'head-scratchings'. In an aside, we are told that 'Mozart's brain' had this power of purpose; but most men are content with sitting at a desk, 'outstripping' their diaries. Emphasis is on intelligence—he singles out 'Mozart's brain'—and on kinship (not plaything of nature).

The feeling of brotherhood brings charity and amused understanding. The tramp, asleep in 'the let of the ditch' (when was that term last incarnated in English?), is adrift in the rain-sodden November countryside, yet he is the reverse of alienated, for he too is 'subdued to his instrument'. 'I thought what strong trust / Slept in him.' The hermit, believing that he can commune with God better from a position of security, abandons his exile to be greeted by a bourgeois chorus of 'I'd be delighted', 'Yours sincerely', and 'Thank you very much indeed'. In this poem we mark the disfocusing of contemporaneity again; in *The Retired Colonel* we are reminded of the historical continuum.

That diehard of defunct Empire who caused Macspaunday such distress in the 1930's is treated with the amused charity of a *specimen*: to reverse Mr E. M. Forster, he retains the 'glory of the animal' even if he has given up 'the tail coat and a couple of ideas'. Unnecessary to judge his fall; he is a man; he is a trophy:

> *And what if his sort should vanish?*
> *The rabble starlings roar upon*
> *Trafalgar. The man-eating British lion*
> *By a pimply age brought down.*
> *Here's his head mounted, though only in rhymes,*
> *Beside the head of the last English*
> *Wolf (those starved gloomy times!)*
> *And the last sturgeon of Thames.*

Dick Straightup, the Yorkshire villager, 'eighty winters on the windy ridge / Of England' shames other specimens—the 'scholar' and the 'thin clerks' who exercise in their bed-sitters at midnight. Just by 'surviving among hills' he has rooted himself so deeply in his environment that he sits 'full of legend and life'; he baffles reporters (we can imagine) for the continuity he represents is 'bigger and deeper than the village'. His old age, being a natural event, is as glorious as youth; his death is consummation.

Reverence for the historical continuum, the sense of interaction, free from merging, between intelligence and nature, and the fact that animals are World Citizens means that Hughes is far from being a regional poet. Mr R. S. Thomas has taught us that regional poetry may vivify the rudiments on which national tradition is founded; it may also be the alibi of fugitives from justice. Democratism, I have implied, is Hughes's habitat, and within democratism, England. For the first time since Kipling, an English poet names his country straightforwardly, without partisanship, disarming ridicule. *Nicholas Ferrer* inherits complex overtones—Anglicanism, our Civil War, Eliot's later poetry—but its mood, atmosphere, and imagery are in simple English; as in Gaunt's deathbed speech, essence transcends association. When the poems have announced locales—*Pennines in April, Mayday on Holderness*—nothing is put in to make the poem sentimental; their enthusiasm includes general reminiscence along with regional observation; it is a far-sighted world of 'measuring the miles of silence / Your eye takes the strain'. In the 1930's they made inventories out of social abuses ('smokeless chimneys, damaged bridges, rotting wharves and choked canals' . . .) *Mayday on Holderness*, absolved of that, puts the clock back: towards complexity and roots:

> *From Hull's sunset smudge*
> *Humber is melting eastward, my south skyline:*

> *A loaded single vein, it drains*
> *The effort of the inert North—Sheffield's ores,*
> *Bog pools, drags of toadstools, tributary*
> *Graves, dunghills, kitchens, hospitals.*
> *The unkillable North Sea swallows it all.*
> *Insects, drunken, drop out of the air.*

Infected by the 'motherly summer' rather than the slump, confidence and love unfold as inventory, image added to image until 'the stars make pietas. The owl announces its sanity' and the scene travels beyond Yorkshire, beyond the recall of war (' "Mother, Mother!" cries the pierced helmet. Cordite oozings of Gallipoli') to vanish in the jungle.

Hughes's technique is original, his attitudes are instructive—the reader is intended to learn, to admire (or condemn) and do otherwise (or likewise). The poems give us the emotional jolt we need, yet leave an area between evidence and reaction which we may bridge by taking thought. Adverse criticism must fasten on the zones where Hughes seems to be faking the evidence. In certain poems and in riot spots within poems there is technical delinquency, as if Hughes, taken aback by abatement of inspiration, was trying to foment it by roughening the texture with the aid of muscle-flexing, grotesquerie, and the gnomic. This malpractice is not so much offensive as irrelevant—we know and like him, he ought to relax! Or the inspiration works at such pressure that it transmutes into vision. We define vision as feeling operating so intensely that it expels all the normal compromises and reticences, reveals the entire point: the interest of the vision depending on the extent to which it includes in a single unit—vision—a multitude of affairs normally apprehended apart. In *Crow Hill, Crag Jack's Apostasy, The Perfect Forms*, and others there is an absoluteness of feeling which is visionary. In *Crow Hill* it is robust, serious, simple—'what humbles these hills has raised / The arrogance of blood and bone'. In *Crag Jack, Forms*, and some uncollected verse there is a touch of obsession, of goggling not inclusion, of too earnest *grand guignol*, of the primitive exalted over meaning—'the undying tail-swinging / Stupidity of the donkey / That carries Christ', and 'pray / That I may see more than your eyes / In an animal's dreamed head'. There is no denying the strength of the verse, but the impact is of sterile frightfulness and morbid impasse. In hypnotic episodes this poet seems to be bewitched by the vortex in a sinister sense.

Praise of animal as example becomes obsession with animal as tyrant in *The Bull Moses*. True, nothing human is imputed to the bull's intentions, but there is a comically prudent deference in the poet's approach; we are no longer captivated by the way the poet treats the theme. (A Latin poet—Lorca for example—would intellectualize the bull, treat it as at once challenge and transcendent symbol.) *Witches, Strawberry Hill*, and *Fourth of July* make the mistake of abandoning precept and evidence for admonishment. 'Small psychology would unseam it', 'has licked the stylist out of their skulls', '. . . the few jaws / Piranha and jaguar' are eloquent but the case is presented too brazenly; the instinct of witches, stoats, and the fauna and flora of the Amazon are not allowed to correct, yet are a bizarre alternative to, scientific research, Augustan polish, and the plight of wage-slaves who 'lean over headlines, taking nothing in'—not that one fails to see Mr Hughes's point. This 'take it or leave it' strain in Mr Hughes is at variance with his argumentative mood.

As Ted Hughes has plumbed the maelstrom to the point of hysteria, as he knows in his flesh with what intimacy our creative and destructive impulses are allied, he is able, in a panic, to write a compassionate poetry of knowledge. This is why his H Bomb poem is one of the few which will survive nuclear disarmament. Sense-impregnated *knowledge*, unifying a complex statement, rather than juridical intelligence 'containing' crisis, pervades *A Woman Unconscious*. The threat to man embraces the whole of nature ('the toil of all our ages a loss / With leaf and insect') but the fact that 'Russia and America circle each other' does not diminish individual being; destruction would be 'a melting of the mould in the mother' (the stress on kinship) and man is central. Thought 'shies' away from the dreadful 'playing shadow', knowing that the menace is not unique, but 'a malingering of now': the *timor mortis conturbat me* that horrified men always. The death of a woman— explicitly cited as 'one'—is not a 'lesser death' than the death of all mankind. Her 'last of sense' divorces her, not from herself, but from 'the world's evidence'. To bring intimate ('one') and compressed ('last of sense') and far-flung ('the world's evidence') data into such fruitful proximity, to honour the need of life for all through the death of one, to resist the temptation to localize the panic and to distil calm by setting it in the perspective of time, and to outlaw complacency, is a feat of honour.

As in 'a slumber did my spirit seal . . . earth's diurnal course / With rocks, and stones, and trees' this is an art of life-ennobling fear.* At worst the threat *reminds* us of 'the mould in the mother', 'the quick of the earth', 'the toil of all our ages', 'leaf and insect'. Thought, provoked, *suggests* that 'malingering of now' is better than 'calamitous change', and calms us. We *feel* the 'lesser death' to be greater than the threat. 'One', gathering into itself 'the mould in the mother', could be a near relative, or any stranger, or the unity of mankind invoked against 'all mankind wince out'. The 'malingering' *is* now 'the world's evidence', all we have, pregnant with value, and the 'last

---

*The element of a tragic practical joke is comparable to the satiric practical joke in *William Empson at Aldermaston* by Alan Brownjohn, where the colourful gaiety of the fortress, a parody of life, is answered by the eccentric gaiety of the marchers, and the point is clinched with a relevant quotation from an unlikely poem—'That deep blankness / Was the real thing strange'—by the man with the Chinese beard.

of sense' is a tragic loss. The reader has been guided, by the poet, to make the vital responses himself. For philosophic integrity sweetened by imaginative strangeness, for the acceptance of fate lightened by future hope, this poem may be ranked not too far below Wordsworth's Lucy Saga. As always with excellence, it is the life in the poems, however grim their context, which makes the life outside the poems also worth preserving.

Talking Beasts: The "Single Adventure" in the Poems of Ted Hughes

Daniel Hoffman

All right, what's a wodwo? With the title of Ted Hughes's [*Wodwo*] we may well begin; it comes from the epigraph, and that is an untranslated quotation from *Sir Gawaine and the Green Knight*:

> Sumwhyle wyth wormez he warrez, and wyth wolves als,
> Sumwhyle wyth wodwos, that woned in the knarrez . . .

Riffling through the glossary in my Tolkien and Gordon edition, I piece it out like this—

> Sometimes against dragons he battled, and wolves also,
> Sometimes with wild men (or trolls) that lived on the crags . . .

The next couple of lines add to Sir Gawaine's adversaries bulls, bears, boars, and giants that harassed him on the high rocks.

Ted Hughes is famous as a poet of violence, for certain poems in his first book, *The Hawk in the Rain* (1957), and its successor, *Lupercal* (1960), brought into English verse an animal ferocity unknown since the death of Lawrence. So it is perhaps legitimate to wonder whether the voice in this new collection is that of Sir Gawaine or of the wodwo. Certainly here are many terrifying poems (also stories and a play—more of these later), in some of which it is as if the feral spirits lurking inside the skins of beasts themselves speak, or are spoken for:

> The wind sweeps through and the hunched wolf shivers.
> It howls you cannot say whether out of agony or joy.
>
> The earth is under its tongue.
> A dead weight of darkness, trying to see through its eyes.
> The wolf is living for the earth . . .

Reprinted in condensed form from *Shenandoah* 19 (Summer 1968): 49–68, by permission of the author and the journal.

The voice, or the thing described—the thing into which the poet's sensibility has entered so thoroughly that it has become that thing and reveals its nature—may even be a plant. It's typical of Hughes to choose the most intractable character in the vegetable world for his first poem in *Wodwo*:

> Against the rubber tongues of cows and the hoeing
> hands of men
> Thistles spike the summer air . . .

Let's see what can be inferred about Hughes's work from the epigraph and this first poem. Quoting the lines from *Sir Gawaine* in the original dialect is itself a clue to something. This is the vanished, archaic language of Hughes's native Yorkshire. The poem from which it comes is not only the most shapely of Arthurian Romances, but a quest poem in which the hero passes from this world into a world seeming as real though limned by magic and enchantment; a world in which nature is hostile to human needs, where physical courage is meaningless unless the expression of moral courage, where mortal combat is the test of a man's character, and his Quest is an obligation gratuitously assumed.

From the opening lines of "Thistles" it is evident, too, that Ted Hughes is a poet with a rural sensibility (not that this is the only way to describe it). He knows, as Frost said in another context, "the need of being versed in country things." The agricultural life may not seem to count for much in modern Britain, but perhaps Hughes finds it appealing exactly because it is so little like the depersonalized existence of urban man. A countryman at least is in touch with brute realities, and turns real clods of actual earth with his hoe. Thistles, he tells us, are "Every one a revengeful burst/Of resurrection, a grasped fistful/Of splintered weapons and Icelandic frost thrust up/ From the underground stain of a decayed Viking." The rural life, like the archaic dialects that linger in remote crofts, is attuned to savage sources, ancient truths, instinctual behests. Of the thistles, Hughes concludes,

> Then they grow grey, like men.
> Mown down, it is a feud. Their sons appear,
> Stiff with weapons, fighting back over the same ground.

The tongue of the wild man or troll in the crags is Hughes's idiom. It is the harsh utterance of a Romantic Primitive with an unremitting view of natural determinism. Hughes's idiom defines some of the stations in the adventure of a quest hero, though not, to be sure, Sir Gawaine.

The introduction into a poem on thistles of the imagery of "splintered weapons," of Vikings and "Icelandic frosts" suggests some lines of thematic continuity in Hughes's work. Clustered together here, like thistles in a clump, are bristling images of brute nature, of warfare, and of the archaic human past. These comprise three of his constant themes. If *Wodwo* is Hughes's most powerful book thus far, the trajectory of his career—unlike that of the best American poets who, like him, started out in the fifties— is marked by the consistent intensification of his original position, rather than by sharp discontinuities. Hughes's style is much more flexible now than in his first book, he has all but abandoned the conventions of stanzaic and rational structure with which he began, yet the imaginative thrust of his work is toward a similar conception of experience.

There is a variety of forms in *Wodwo* which may be initially confusing. Interspersed, as I've said, between an opening and a concluding set of poems are half a dozen short stories and a long play for voices. Compared to the fairly obvious connection between Lowell's poems and the autobiographical fragment in *Life Studies*, the congruence between Hughes's prose and verse is not so evident. Yet he insists on the unity of his book, saying that the prose "may be read as notes, appendix and unversified episodes behind the poems, or as chapters of a single adventure to which the poems are commentary and amplification." I don't propose that *Wodwo* is a code to be cracked, but it does take some doing on the reader's part to grasp its implicit unification. The "adventure" is revealed by sharp thrusts of consciousness, sudden gulps of knowledge wrested painfully from intractable experiences. The process begins with *The Hawk in the Rain*, for the "single adventure" in Hughes's work is a continuous one.

That first book has an intensity lacking in most English poetry of the 1950's. In the year when it appeared, thanks to Hughes's winning the Poetry Center Introductions contest in New York, Robert Conquest's *New Lines* laid down in London the principles by which English poetry was to redeem itself from the preceding decade of decay. Dylan Thomas and the New Apocalypse poets just after war had replaced intellect in poetry with the babbling of the Id, and the corruption of public taste ensued. Conquest defined the necessary new poetry as "free from both mystical and logical compulsions," "empirical in its attitude to all that comes," showing "reverence for the real person or event." Technically, it demonstrates "the refusal to abandon a rational structure and comprehensible language, even when the verse is most highly charged with sensuous or emotional intent." In their dictional and rational conservatism, in their pragmatic attention to the actual, the New Lines poets (or The Movement, as they were soon known) reflected a realistic sense of life in contemporary Britain. The romantic afflatus of poetry in the war years struck a swollen music distinctly false in the shrinking empire and straitened economy of the post-war period. Their poetry—Philip Larkin's is the most consistent and accomplished—accurately caught the wry tone of diminished possibilities, the retrenchment of their country as a world power, the circum- scribed life that seemed the Englishman's lot. But Ted Hughes's work is based on quite other notions of the language and the unavoidable themes which a contemporary poet must use, although in some technical respects his early work seems not to contradict Conquest's manifesto.

The Movement poets were urbane and sophisticated; they dealt with ennui and trivia, the office job, the domestic muse, eschewing, for honesty's sake, the grandiloquence of myth. But a few years later, Hughes, reviewing a book by E. O. G. Turville-Petrie on *Mythology of the North*, made these observations about the pertinence to the contemporary sensibility of Scandinavian and Anglo-Saxon paganism:

> This particular mythology is much deeper in us, and truer to us, than the Greek-Roman pantheons that came in with Christianity, and again with the Renaissance, severing us with the completeness of a political interdict from these other deities of our instinct and ancestral memory. It is as if we were to lose Macbeth and King Lear, and have to live on Timon and Coriolanus . . . there's no doubt which of these two belongs in our blood. . . . It's false to say these gods and heroes are obsolete: they are the better part of our patrimony still locked up.
>
> —*The Listener*, 19 March 1964

Such a passage casts the glare of its smoky torch upon the Icelandic frost and dead Vikings in "Thistles," as well as on the source of Hughes's title, *Wodwo*. Here is a poet determinedly atavistic—yet, by a paradox which readers of poetry will not find incomprehensible, the more resolutely he delves into "our instinct and ancestral memory," into what he feels deepest, truest, and most locked up, the more accurately he defines his situation as a modern man, and a part of ours.

Yet Ted Hughes does not write overtly of myths. Indeed, he becomes more a myth-poet in *Wodwo* than he was in *The Hawk in the Rain*, though still not overtly so. The reason for this is that Hughes is not concerned to retell old myths in new clothes, or to mythologize contemporary life. His concern is to treat certain experiences as though for the first time, as though he, their first experiencer, were their first poet, the maker of their myths. Therefore his myths do not ordinarily invoke old names from vanished pantheons, but reveal intrinsic patterns of actions, of realization, which the old myths, too, expressed. This process of mythologizing experience comes clear in *Wodwo*. . . .

At a time when his contemporaries in The Movement and their successors in The Group (see E. Lucie-Smith and Philip Hobsbaum, *A Group Anthology*, Oxford, 1963) demanded a rational poetry, Hughes dug deeper into his nature and his culture to discover an irrational poetry that would with integrity express the inextinguishable savagery of man. What he found was a way of dealing in terms of a personal sensibility and an individual's experience with those monstrous facts of life which the mind cannot express rationally, because it must deny them or cease to be rational.

The irrational part of human nature is of course that part which is found also in nature untrammelled by the human mind. Ted Hughes has explored it in the beasts, the thistles, and the birds. The early poems about animals seem to be exploring the reciprocal possibilities between a nonhuman and a human persona. . . . Creatures in Hughes's later poems appear simply as themselves, acting out their creature-natures.

*   *   *

Wodwo is both a continuation and an intensification of the main themes in the earlier work. Once more, as in *Lupercal*, the personae of the poems are frequently creatures. In the five stories, Hughes returns to the doppelgänger theme prominent in his first book. The protagonist is divided in the tales between a human and a bestial or mythological shape. In the first story, a man, like the farmer in "The Hawk in the Rain," stands transfixed on a rainy moor, while a beast—this time a horse, one come to life from the group that stood "Megalith-still" in the early poem—menacingly bears down on him, hooves flashing. The man flings stones at his adversary, they threaten one another. Another tale, "Sunday," takes place not in church but at a country pub where the locals have expectantly assembled. A scrummy little beggar, one Billy Red the rat-catcher, comes in. The landlord has some rats in a wire cage. These he sets free one by one. Billy Red, quicker than the eye, lunges for each rat. He seizes it, in his teeth. The eager crowd set up his drinks. This is a fable that won't go away after you've read it: the rat-catcher taking the shape of his prey, the laughing farmers (so like the countrymen in the early poem, "Roarers in a Ring") implicated in the brutality of Billy Red's transformation. In another story, "The Harvesting," Hughes's epigraph is that snatch of song, "And I shall go into a hare/With sorrow and sigh and mickle care," taken from Robert Graves's reconstruction of the chant of the Allansford witch-coven. The story grimly tells of Mr. Grooby's hunting a hare, and how his dogs destroy Mr. Grooby instead. Again the hunter has become the hunted creature. Madness throbs in the air.

Just such a reversal of roles is what happens in war, where the killer may become the killed, where the enemy and the self may be interchangeable, where the dead may be the living and the living be the dead. Ted Hughes's long radio play, "The Wound," seems a natural elaboration of the tales in which the hunter becomes the hunted. When "The Wound" was produced by the BBC in 1962, with spooky music by Alexander Goehr, it seemed an overlong Gothic horror play, a combination of Andreyev's *The Red Laugh* with a decor out of "The Fall of the House of Usher." Perhaps the text has since been rewritten; reading it now, six years later, without the obtrusive soundtrack, I find "The Wound" really *scary*; the terror is not that of its Gothic conventions but, as Poe said, "of the soul."

The play takes place in the streaming consciousness of Private Ripley as the accompanies his sergeant on a long, painful trek across no man's land, searching for a chateau. Once there they find a ghastly banquet going on, the hall filled with screeching beldames. It is the house of the dead. Ripley's journey is away from consciousness, reason, life, through a rain (probably of blood; it is often raining in the country of Hughes's mind), toward the castle of spectres. These female figures—harridans, seductresses, a frenzied pack of whorehounds—feed the sergeant meat which proves to be the flesh of his comrades. But he has already eaten it, in the trenches. Ripley is lured away from the table by a wench whose attentions are ambiguous. The scene coalesces nightmare figures with witchcraft rituals—Tam Lin in the old ballad may have sat at such a table. The surreal texture pierces the walls of consciousness, by stabs and slashes forcing Ripley's unwitting acknowledgment of what really happened: Ripley's comrades and their sergeant were killed horribly in the trenches, before his eyes. Ripley, terribly wounded, is momentarily among them. Somehow he staggers from that place of blood where the beldames are devouring their guests while the sun, "trying to rise," is "your life, working at the hole in your head." Ripley falls into a friendly trench, his head bleeding.

Both its length and its position make "The Wound" the central episode in that "single adventure" of which Hughes speaks in his prefatory note to *Wodwo*. We can spell out the rest of that adventure in the poems, but before trying to do so we may be guided by another review Hughes wrote for *The Listener*. Discussing Mircea Eliade's study, *Shamanism*, in that weekly (29 October 1964), Hughes was struck by its description of "not a religion, but a technique for moving in a state of ecstasy among the various spiritual realms, and for generally dealing with souls and spirits, in a practical way, in some practical crisis." Reflecting on the varieties of shamanism, Hughes finds in the Tibetan Book of the Dead that "the main business of the work as a whole . . . is to guide a dead soul to its place of death, or back into life—together with the principal terrific events, and the flying accompaniment of descriptive songs, exhortations to the soul, threats, and the rest. . . ." This seems tellingly close to describing the theme and action in "The Wound," although that play was written at least three years before Hughes read Eliade's book. Still, some of the material synopsized in *Shamanism* was doubtless already familiar to Hughes, who had read anthropology while at Cambridge.

The main outline of the shamanistic experience consists in the shaman's being chosen by a spirit—"usually some animal"—which arrives, often in a dream, and "becomes henceforth his liaison with the spirit world." However chosen, the shaman must undergo a "psychological transformation." The spirit realm into which he is initiated traditionally consists of "familiar figures . . . the freezing river, the clashing rocks, the dog in the cave entrance, the queen of animals, the holy mountain. . . . The results, when the shaman returns to the living, are some display of healing power, or a clairvoyant piece of information." Of course this landscape, this process of transformation, this contact with figures from the spirit world, and the consequent return, enriched, to the living world, comprise the adventures, among the wodwos on the high rocks, in *Sir Gawaine and the Green Knight.* It is also the central adventure in all of Ted Hughes's work, whether or not he was himself consciously aware from the first that this is so. Now we can infer that the creatures in his poems—the fierce thrush, the menacing pike, the dreamlike horses and rapacious hawk—are totem beasts, messengers from the spirit world who bring the protagonist a "clairvoyant piece of information" or "some display of healing power."

Hughes in fact regards the shaman's experience not as a function of any particular religion (according to Eliade it "flourishes alongside and within the prevailing religion") but rather as "something closer to biological inevitability than to any merely cultural tradition." The process is a root fact of being, therefore worldwide, universal through time, instinct with human nature and, in our faithless age, more likely expressed in poetry than in religious observance:

> The initiation dreams, the general schema of the shamanic flight, and the figures and adventures they encounter . . . are, in fact, the basic experience of the poetic temperament we call "romantic." In a shamanizing society, "Venus and Adonis," some of Keats's longer poems, "The Wanderings of Oisin," "Ash Wednesday," would all qualify their authors for the magic drum, while the actual flight lies behind many of the best fairy tales, and behind myths such as those of Orpheus and Herakles, and behind the epics of Gilgamesh and Odysseus. It is the outline, in fact, of the Heroic Quest. The shamans seem to undergo, at will and at phenomenal intensity, and with practical results, one of the main regenerating dramas of the human psyche.

This may be as close as Hughes has come to a discursive statement of his deepest convictions. The similarity to Robert Graves's view of poetry is striking—in the same review, Hughes quotes approvingly Graves's foreword to *The Sufis* by Idries Shah; yet if one compares the passage cited above to Graves's twenty-fourth chapter, "The Single Poetic Theme," in *The White Goddess*, the differences in their positions are as evident as the resemblances. Graves's theme, the one he finds in some of the same poems and legends cited by Hughes, is of course the celebration of the love goddess in her triple aspect as Mother, Muse, and bringer of death along with ecstasy. Hughes's definition of shamanism may include that theme but the psychological energy is not drawn, as Graves's is, into a love-knot. For Hughes it leads toward the Quest, the psychological transformation of the soul approaching and returning from its place of death. Hughes has not published a single poem Graves would recognize as a celebration of love.

Looking again at the structure of *Wodwo*, we find "The Wound" at the center, preceded by the tales in which the perpetrator of violence against an animal becomes the victim of his own design. Surrounding these (the play and stories together comprise Part II) are poems. Immediately preceding and following Part II are poems on the nature of God, e.g., "Reveille" in Part I: "No, the serpent was not/One of God's ordinary creatures . . ."

> The black, thickening river of his body
> Glittered in giant loops
> Around desert mountains and away
> Over the ashes of the future.

And, in Part III, "Theology":

> Adam ate the apple.
> Eve ate Adam.
> The serpent ate Eve.
> This is the dark intestine.

Parts I and III present also poems of war, the manifestation in human affairs of the irreducible beast who may be a sacred totem. In Part I, "Boom": "More More More/Meaning Air Water Life/Cry the mouths/That are filling with ashes"; in Part III, "Out," a longer poem, "My father sat in his chair recovering/From the four-year mastication by gunfire and mud"—here the suffering and the imagery re-imagine Ripley's initiation into the feast of the dead in "The Wound." The animal poems echo the war poems and resurrect some of the totem beasts already met. "Skylarks" arise "Like a warning/As if the globe were uneasy," their "barbed" flight reminiscent of the poem "Thrushes" in *Lupercal*. "The Howling of Wolves," "Gnat Song" and "Ghost Crabs" augment the experiences recorded in "Pike" and "Hawk Roosting." In "Song of a Rat," the relationship between man and rat in the story, "Sunday," is reversed; there the man became ratlike, here what the rat experiences is human:

> The rat is in the trap, it is in the trap,
> And attacking heaven and earth with a mouthful of screeches
>   like torn tin,
> . . . .
> When it stops screeching, it pants
>
> And cannot think
> "This has no face, it must be God" or
>
> "No answer is also an answer."

The intensity, consistency, and rigor of Hughes's work demand that we measure it by the highest standards. What he has written is as true as he can make it to what he most deeply feels. In the making of his style he has, as he said of Keith Douglas, broken free from "the terrible, suffocating, maternal octopus of ancient English poetic tradition." His diction is piercingly direct, his forms entirely functional. He abandons stanzaic and metrical conventions for line-breaks and the spacing of bursts of lines which try to capture the shape of the experience, rather than impose any arbitrary pattern upon it. The movement of this verse, like its spare language, is designed to render the energy of the mind in its moments of most significant thought, its deepest awareness.

Yet Hughes's consistencies are achieved at a heavy price, for the universe imagined in these poems—the experiences available in them, the particular journey of the protagonist, the necessitous direction of his Quest—excludes many of the possibilities of life. The dream which calls this shamanizing poet is a dream of suffering and a dream of death. The brute instinct in his blood is the destructive element. In a group of six poems published after *Wodwo*, we see still more clearly the role of a totem creature bringing a clairvoyant message from the spirit world. This time, in "Crow Lore" (*The Listener*, 29 January 1968), the totem is directly in touch with God, for all the good it does him, as in "Crow's First Lesson":

> God tried to teach Crow how to talk.
> 'Love,' said God. 'Say, Love.'
> Crow gaped, and the white shark crashed into the sea
> And went rolling downwards, discovering his own depth.
>
> 'No, no,' said God, 'say Love. Now try it. LOVE . . .'
> . . . .
> And Crow retched again, before God could stop him.
> And woman's vulva dropped over man's neck and
> tightened.
> The two struggled together on the grass.
> God struggled to part them, cursed, wept—
>
> Crow flew guiltily off.

In the world from which Ted Hughes's totem spirits speak, Love is possible only for God, if there is a God. In "Crow Lore" the cruel epiphanies brought by the totem are spelled out in fables as filled with energy as with despair. It is as though the pained iconoclasm of an earlier fabulist, Stephen Crane, had found the most effective means to reveal a counter-Gospel. As the poems in "Crow Lore" make clear, for Hughes our bodies are part of the machinery of the trap in which we are caught like rats and against which none of our screechings can prevail. All this suggests that Hughes's sensibility is caught, like "The Warriors of the North" in *Wodwo*, in "the gruelling relapse and prolonguer of their blood/Into the iron arteries of Calvin."

The shamanic experience is indeed "one of the main regenerative dramas of the human psyche," but what Hughes has thus far rendered of it by no means expresses the entire message that his beasts might bring. If we compare the route of his "single adventure" with the itineraries travelled by the Quest Heroes in the poems he mentions by Keats, Eliot, Yeats, or, perhaps more pertinently, Sir Gawaine, the narrow concentration of Hughes's poems is clear. Unlike the heroes of these earlier and greater poems, his protagonist hears nothing from his totems of human immortality. He never celebrates sensuous experience but in fearful fascination of death by violence. Neither joy nor love partakes of his sacred feast, nor does Nature offer any consolatory unification of experience. Further, the hero who is vouchsafed the bleak truths of his spirit-creatures seems to have come from, and returns to, no tribe. Unlike Sir Gawaine, he represents the court and civil code of no community; he has no social context and belongs to our world of families, class structure, and politics, only by implication. In Hughes's poems a sensibility of extreme aloneness confronts the ultimate abstractions—Life, Energy, Instinct, Death—in the discrete concretions by which they may be known. Yet whatever the private wounds which may have imposed it upon him, the very extremity of his isolation represents a valid response to the conditions of contemporary life.

Ted Hughes has tremendous gifts, and if a further range of experience than he has already charted is not given him, he is still—as "Crow Lore" attests—discovering how nearer to approach that freedom of style he defined in Douglas: a style that is "able to deal poetically with whatever it comes up against" in "a language for the whole mind." Should his Crow at last exhaust his fury against the rat-trap of existence, Hughes may return from his shamanic visions bearing not only the "clairvoyant information" of our instinctual violence, but also a "healing power." As he has written, "Once you've been chosen by the spirits, and dreamed the dreams, there is no other life for you, you must shamanize or die." Whatever comes next from him is sure to be written down in new poems that will be wonderful and wild.

Crow: A Mythology of the Demonic

CHARLES V. FERNANDEZ

I

Ted Hughes was interviewed by Ekbert Faas in the January, 1973 *London Magazine*. In reply to a statement by Faas that his two jaguar poems, like "Hawk Roosting," are interpreted as celebrations of violence Hughes commented: "I prefer to think of them as first, descriptions of a jaguar, second . . . invocations of the Goddess [Nature or Isis, Mother of the Gods], third . . . invocations of a jaguar-like body of elemental force, demonic force."[1] Hughes takes up this demonic force again in *Crow*. As he himself states: "We go on writing poems because one poem never gets the whole account right. There is always something missed" (Faas p. 15). But what exactly is this demonic force? Let us attempt to examine the demonic itself and try to define its basic characteristics more concretely.

The word "demonic" or "daimonic" comes from the Greek *"daimon."* Socrates, in the *Symposium* of Plato, repeats a conversation he had with Diotima of Mantineia, his instructress in the art of love. He says, among other things, that: "He [Love] is a great spirit (daimon), and like all spirits he is intermediate between the divine and the mortal . . . He interprets . . . between gods and men . . . he is the mediator who spans the chasm which divides them, and therefore in him all is bound together . . . For God mingles not with man; but through Love all the intercourse and converse of God with man, whether awake or asleep, is carried on. The wisdom which understands this is spiritual; all other wisdom, such as that of arts and handicrafts, is mean and vulgar" (vv. 202–203). The demonic in *Crow*, as we shall see, is similar, but not so closely associated with the spirit Love.

The demonic of Hughes has five major characteristics. It is first of all irrational; in the sense that it is unknowable by rational thought processes and does not act according to rational principles. It is emotion not reason. It is experienced not thought. Second, it is a type of violence. It is a violence not to be confused with "The ordinary violence of our psychotic democracy . . . our materialist, non-organic democracy which is trying to stand up with

Reprinted from *Modern Poetry Studies* 6 (Autumn 1975): 144–56, by permission of the author.

a bookish theory instead of a skeleton" (Faas p. 6). It is "the bigger energy, the elemental power circuit of the Universe" (Faas p. 9). Third, the demonic, in contrast to the "materialist, non-organic democracy," is of organic importance but not material in essence. It is intrinsic, like a skeleton, not extrinsic like theories. Fourth, the demonic has a definite creative potential when used correctly. It is the creative inspiration of the artist, the procreative drive of male and female sexuality, and the recreative energy of dance, games, dreams, and nightmares. And fifth, the demonic can be destructive. Energies of this type "once invoked will destroy an impure nature and serve a pure one" (Faas pp. 8–9).

The demonic, Hughes believes, is becoming increasingly more destructive because of man's increasing inability to control it through religious rituals and myth and technological formulae. The trouble, as Hughes sees it, is that: "When the wise men know how to create rituals and dogma, the energy can be contained. When the old rituals and dogma have lost credit and disintegrated, and no new ones have been formed, the energy cannot be contained, and so its effect is destructive—and that is the position with us . . . In the old world God and divine power were invoked at any cost—life seemed worthless without them. In the present world we dare not invoke them—we wouldn't know how to use them or stop them destroying us" (Faas p. 10).

Christianity then, as well as technology, has become for Hughes "just another provisional myth of man's relationship with the creator."[2] Crow, in this circumstance, serves a threefold purpose. By the reinterpretation of religious myth, using Crow as a representative of the demonic, Hughes attempts to show the vital part the demonic plays, not only in creation, but in the continuation of creation, procreation. He also shows the failures of Christianity and technology to contain the demonic force. And finally, by reinterpreting the religious myth, he attempts to control the demonic by sketching out, in Crow, a new myth. "The whole myth is to be told as an epic folk-tale in prose with songs by and about Crow interspersed" (Sagar p. 29).

II

The basis for this myth is the Eskimo legend that "tells that in the beginning the raven was the only creature and the world was, like him, black" (Sagar p. 29). This is the legend contained in the first of the Crow poems "Two Legends." There are several other Eskimo legends dealing with the origin of Crow. Sagar, in his monograph on Hughes, paraphrases one as:

God, having created the world, has a recurring nightmare. . . . Meanwhile man sits at the gates of heaven waiting for God to grant him an audience. He has come to ask God to take life back. God is furious and sends him packing. The nightmare appears to be independent of creation, and God cannot understand it. The nightmare is full of mockery of the creation, especially of man. God challenges the nightmare to do better. This is just what the nightmare has been waiting for. It plunges down into matter and creates Crow. God tests Crow by putting him through a series of trials and ordeals which sometimes result in Crow being dismembered, transformed or obliterated, but Crow survives them all, little changed. Meanwhile Crow interferes in God's activities, sometimes trying to learn or help, sometimes in mischief, sometimes in open rebellion. It is, perhaps, his ambition to become a man, but he never quite makes it.

—Sagar p. 29

That this legend is the origin of the *Crow* myth is confirmed by Hughes who says that his Crow is "created by God's nightmare's attempt to improve on man" (Faas p. 18).

We are now in a position to appreciate the aptness of the title "Crow's Song of Himself" for a poem which deals with just such a series of trials and ordeals as the Eskimo legend describes. We can also recognize this poem as the center of the *Crow* mythology. Crow, the product of the demonic force which is God's nightmare, produces other demonic forces. The demonic force of excessive greed, for instance, is symbolized by money. Alcohol is demonic in that it makes man drunk, irrational, and liberates him from inhibitions, while fruit is a product of the demonic force of procreation. Man is a mixture of earth and the demonic spark of life, and woman, his other half, is united to him in the demonic force of sexuality. When God acknowledges that His nightmare has improved on man He realizes His creation is imperfect and needs a Redeemer to redeem it from its faults.

If Crow's origin is deep in Eskimo myth his life and activities are deep in Christian myth. Hughes, through the mythology of *Crow*, places the demonic forces at the center of Christianity's three principal myths: the Beginning, the Creation of Man, and the Redemption. "Lineage" deals with Beginning. Its first three words echo both the *Old Testament* (Genesis 1:1) and the *New Testament* (Revelation 1:1). The genealogy of the next fourteen lines is similar to the genealogies of Genesis (5:1–32) and Matthew (1:1–16). But the similarity ends there for, according to the *Crow* myth, in the Beginning was not "the Word" but "Scream." Scream is the origin of all things. It is the violent exhale of the "bowel-emptying" birth cry in "A Kill." In contrast to the rational word it is irrational. It is the demonic force which set creation in motion by begetting "Blood," the symbol of life. It is from Scream that Adam, man, and Mary, woman, come. It is they who beget God, religion, to control the demonic. And it is god, or more correctly the frantic sounding "Never Never Never / Never" of his nightmare, from which Crow arises. Crow, to complete the cycle, is "Screaming for Blood," the demonic lust for life.

Hughes deals with the Creation of Man in "A Childish Prank." The basis for this poem is again legend; this time from Jewish tradition:

> In a Talmudic version of the creation, God, having made man and woman of the clay of the earth, tries for hundreds of years to lure into these inert bodies the free souls which fly through space. But the souls value their liberty, and will be neither cajoled nor tricked into bodies. Crow steps in and invents sexuality.
>
> —Sagar p. 32

Although God has already created them "Man's and woman's bodies lay without souls, / Dully gaping, foolishly staring, inert." God falls asleep pondering the problem of how to instill in them the spark of life, the "soul." But once asleep the demonic force of His nightmare is freed from the constraints of His rational thought.

It is this demonic element which is missing in the bodies. Crow, a creation of the demonic, remedies the situation by giving man and woman sexuality. The "Worm" is "God's only son" because, according to many myths, it is a symbol of regeneration, the "being born again" of the Christian Redemption. Thus, according to the *Crow* myth, the real "Redeemer" is the demonic force which "redeems" man by instilling in him the ability to regenerate himself through sex. This force, to create, or procreate as the case may be, peers through Eve's eyes. We may now see that Crow, walking through "A black doorway: / The eye's pupil" in "The Door," is a symbol of man's creativity. The two halves of the Worm seeking to become one again through the sexual intercourse of man and woman, like Crow being chopped in two in "Crow's Song of Himself" to produce man and woman, is very similar to the story Aristophanes tells in Plato's *Symposium*. The story goes that "Primeval man was round, his back and sides forming a circle; and he had four hands and four feet, one head with two faces, looking opposite ways, set on a round neck and precisely alike; also four ears, two privy members, and the remainder to correspond" (vv. 189–190).

Aristophanes' primeval man also had three sexes: male, female, and androgynous. As a punishment for insolence Zeus halved these early men and moved their sex organs from their backs to their fronts. Each half then went through life searching for its other half and trying to become one with it again through sexual intercourse. That demonic love, in the *Crow* mythology, is indeed this sexual love of Aristophanes and Jewish tradition, as opposed to the spiritual love of Socrates, is confirmed in "Crow's First Lesson." Here God tries to teach Crow the rational word "Love." But Crow

> retched again, before God could stop him.
> And woman's vulva dropped over man's neck and
> tightened.
> The two struggled together on the grass.

The only love Crow knows, that is, is the demonic kind. It is neither rational nor spiritual, but irrational and physical.

As we have seen, in "Crow's Song of Himself" and "A Childish Prank," the demonic plays an important role in the Christian Redemption. "Crow Blacker Than Ever" deals specifically with this theme. According to the *Crow* mythology when:

> Things looked like falling apart . . .
> Crow nailed them together,
> Nailing heaven and earth together—

The demonic, that is, saves creation from destruction by binding it together. This idea of the demonic "binding" heaven and earth, God and man, we will remember from Socrates' conversation with Diotima quoted earlier. In the demonic "all is bound together." It is "the mediator who spans the chasm" between God and man. This clarifies the relationship of Hughes's demonic to that of Plato. Hughes's demonic is physical, sexual love, not spiritual or Platonic. In this sense it is like the love of Aristophanes as opposed to that of Socrates. But Hughes's demonic not only binds man to woman but also man to God. In this sense it is more like what Socrates describes. Thus Hughes's demonic is a compound of both.

Crow's calling this "joint" "my Creation" (capital "C") leads us to believe that, in the *Crow* myth, the demonic is integral, not only to the Beginning and Creation, but to the continued existence of that creation as well. Since, according to this myth, Creation is completed by the bestowal of sexuality on mankind we must assume that its continued existence is due to this same bestowal. "Snake Hymn" confirms this assumption. The snake, as we have seen, is not God in *Crow*, but rather the demonic force of regeneration. According to the poem, then, the snake "was the gliding / And push of Adam's blood." The fact that this blood, or this snake, then "slid into Eve" is symbolic of both her coming to life and the sexuality which is its spark. This blood then "slid from her womb" as the Christian Redeemer "knotted on the cross." In other words, it is through the demonic force of sexuality that man is regenerated, the race continued, and the Redeemer born. Through procreation there is the possibility of the evolution of a better species of man, thus, in some way, "redeeming" the original race.

III

But the demonic of the *Crow* myth, as seen in "Snake Hymn," is not to be confused with the Redeemer of the Christian myth. Neither is the demonic's part in the Christian Redemption to be confused with a physical body and its death. The body that is the Redeemer is just the "skin of agony" shed by the demonic, as a snake sheds its skin, "To hang, an empty husk." Indeed, according to the *Crow* myth, there is no "Redemption," as Christianity conceives of it, and it is a failure of Christianity to believe in one. The Redeemer, in "Crow Blacker Than Ever," is only a physical "joint" between heaven and earth which ultimately "became gangrenous and stank— / A horror beyond redemption." The death of Christ and the resurrection of His body, which Christianity holds as the culmination of man's redemption, is nothing more than the annual shedding by a snake of its skin. The failure of Christianity is in viewing the death of Christ as a "final act of redemption" instead of the demonic as a continuing process of creation. The body of Christ, the Eucharist of the Christian myth, is, in "Crow Communes," a not readily intelligible "cipher." It is the "first jest" of Christianity that this cipher will "divulge itself to digestion / Under hearing beyond understanding."

Yet, although the Eucharist, according to the *Crow* myth, does not have the mystical powers of spiritual sustenance as originally intended, it does make Crow feel "much stronger" because it gives the physical sustenance of tearing and eating flesh. It is for this reason that God, in "Crow's Song of Himself," goes off in despair. This God, like Christianity, has become impotent according to Hughes. It is He who, in "Lineage," "begat Nothing." In "A Childish Prank," He is unable to give life to His creations and, overwhelmed by this problem, falls asleep. His "great carcase" is again asleep, "exhausted with Creation," in "Crow Communes." In "Crow's First Lesson," He can neither teach spiritual love nor prevent physical love. "Apple Tragedy" shows Him as an "interloper" capable only of sham magical tricks like the Quasi-transubstantiation of " 'You see this apple? / I squeeze it and look—cider.' "

In its effort to rid itself of the demonic, Christianity also uses such sham magic. In "Conjuring in Heaven," it tries the now-you-see-it-now-you-don't approach of theologians who try "to prove it didn't exist." The opposite approach is that of "Apple Tragedy." Here Christianity admits the presence of the demonic only so that it can project its own guilt onto the demonic by telling man the half-truths of a sham morality based on innate "sin." Thus the demonic becomes the evil "demon" and sexuality becomes guilt-ridden and "sinful." Thus woman, in order to explain the "wild time," must cry " 'Rape! Rape!' " and man, in order to keep his honor, must "hang himself" for shame. Christianity, instead of formulating a ritual to contain the demonic, makes a Redeemer to atone for it. The end result, needless to say, is that "everything goes to hell."

"Crow's Song of Himself" may be read as another failure of Christianity to deal with the demonic, this time by obliterating it through torture. The fate of heretics and witches, those tragic victims of the Inquisition and other forms of religious intolerance, is well known and need not to be gotten into here. But even as Christianity "hammered" and "roasted" and "crushed" and "tore" at them it was doomed to "despair." It could not destroy the demonic by destroying a physical "husk."

The failure of Christianity to contain the demonic was, of course, preceded by the failures of other myths and religions. "Crow's Playmates" and "Crowego" contain their accounts. "Crow's Playmates" shows the result of religions which tried to contain the demonic by the enchantment of natural forces like the "mountain god" and the "river-god." But one by one, "god" after "god," the emphasis shifted from a recognition of the demonic, through the worship of natural forces, to a worship of the natural objects associated with those forces. With this shift came the progressive alienation of these religions from the demonic and hence their failure. "Crowego" shows the most powerful of the mythical heroes not containing the demonic, but rather contained by it. These myths, like the early religions, are now just the ineffective "quag of the past."

IV

Technology replaced Christianity as the container of the demonic. So awesome is the power of technology's atom bomb, the "serpent . . . from the hatched atom," in "A Horrible Religious Error," that "God's grimace writhed, a leaf in the furnace" and mankind willingly submits to it with the words, " 'Your will is our peace.' " Its "alibi self twisted around it" refers to the sophistic reasoning that such technological "advances" as the atom bomb are "for the good of all mankind." The replacement of religion by technology and the reasoning behind it is indeed a horrible religious error. In "Notes for a Little Play" God is not even invited to the post-atomic-explosion marriage of two "Mutations—at home in the nuclear glare."

Inspite of this show of strength of technology, the demonic Crow remains unimpressed. Indeed, his reaction to the atomic serpent of "A Horrible Religious Error" is to "Beat the hell out of it" and eat it. The demonic, that is, remains supreme; its power undiminished and uninfluenced by atomic power. Thus it is that in "Notes for a Little Play" where "the flame fills all space. / The demolition is total" the only two survivors "fasten together" in marriage and the process of creation continues inspite of the devastation. The final conclusion of Crow in regard to technology and religion is contained in "Crow's Theology":

> Crow realized there were two Gods—
> One of them bigger than the other
> Loving his enemies
> And having all the weapons.

Obviously this "bigger" god, he that "loved the shot-pellets" and "spoke the silence of lead," is technology, the "god" of modern man who loves his enemies to death for their own benefit.

It is through technology that super-rational modern man tries, not so much to contain the demonic, as to examine it out of existence. "Crow's Account of St. George" is the account of the technological knight's attempt to vanquish the demonic dragon. His weapons are "tweezers of numbers," a "knife-edge of numbers," and a "ceremonial Japanese decapitator" and he uses each in turn as he approaches closer to the "nest of numbers" he thinks is the center of life. But it is just here that he finds that the heart of life is not a rational mathematical formula but "A bird-head, / Bald, lizard-eyed, the size of a football, on two staggering bird-legs;" that is, the demonic, symbolized by Crow. The result of man's technological battle with the demonic is the destruction of his connection to the demonic through sexuality, his "wife and children."

St. George, seeking to explain the demonic, does not recognize it when he finds it. His scientific principles are useless to him when, through the fear engendered by its confrontation, he attempts to exert the ultimate form of control by destroying it. But what he does with the Japanese decapitator is, in a sense, to destroy himself by alienating himself more than ever from the demonic. This assumption is reinforced in "Revenge Fable." Here Hughes shows the alienation of technological man. He seeks to "get rid of his mother," the demonic, as he:

> pounded and hacked at her
> With numbers and equations and laws
> Which he invented and called truth. . . . .
> Going for her with a knife,
> Obliterating her with disgusts
> Bulldozers and detergents
> Requisitions and central heating
> Rifles and whisky and bored sleep.

The result is not figurative but literal decapitation as "His head fell off like a leaf." When man invokes the demonic but has no rituals suitable to contain it he is himself destroyed.

Man cannot contain the demonic with a life style based on the technology of the atom, detergents, and central heating. Neither can he control it through the verbal rationale of such a life style. In "The Battle of Osfrontalis" Crow refuses to become involved with the various types of words which seek to contain him. He does this by refusing to take them seriously. His reaction to these words half way through the poem is to "whistle"; a series of sounds containing no words. When the words realize their seriousness is ineffective they take refuge in "the skull of a dead jester." But the demonic cannot be contained either by a serious view of a meaningful existence or by an absurdist view of its meaninglessness. Crow "yawned—long ago / He had picked that skull empty."

"A Disaster" is about one word in particular, the "progress" of technology. Technological progress is a pig:

> sucking the cities
> Like the nipples of a sow
> Drinking out all the people
> Till there were none left,
> All digested inside the word.

But although it can digest rational man in its body of empirical facts, it cannot stomach the irrational demonic of the natural earth. The progress of technology ends in the "collapsing mushroom" of the atom bomb, in total destruction, "Its era was over."

"The Contender" provides the best summary of technology's relation to the demonic. Technology is the "contender," the "strongest of the strong." Yet with this strength it ignores the demonic of sexuality, "All the women in the world could not move him." Although its pose is that of an extrovert, attempting to unify all existence, it is in reality an introvert, attempting to explain existence as a self-contained, rationally ordered physical phenomenon. "In his face-upwards body he lay face downwards." It is for this reason that "All the men in the world could not move him" and the importance of their lives and their creative potential are just "shadows and little sounds." "The Contender" presents technology as a Promethean character who, like Christ, is "crucified" in an attempt to save man. But, according to the *Crow* myth, technology, like Christ and Christianity, is only engaged in a "senseless trial of strength." Its failure both to understand and to contain the demonic leads Crow, in "Crow Alights," to realize the "horror of Creation."

V

Hughes attempts in *Crow* to sketch out a new mythology, one which will adequately contain the demonic. This paper is, in effect, a sketch of that sketch. It traces three themes: the centrality of the demonic, the failure of Christianity to contain it, and the failure of technology to do the same. For all its length it leaves out much more than it includes, but nevertheless enough has been stated and implied to draw a few conclusions. If we accept the demonic as a reality, as did the Eskimos, various religions, and philosophers like Plato, we must recognize in it the inspiration to create, procreate, and recreate. We must also realize that existence is not a static phenomenon, but a continual process of regeneration.

That the demonic, as Hughes attempts to show, is central to the three chief events of the Christian myth should not surprise us. The ritual beliefs of the Beginning, the Creation of Man, and the Redemption were formulated expressly in an attempt to contain it. Technology is the "god" of modern man. It too is an attempt to explain the inexplicable. Both efforts have failed. Christianity, when it recognizes the demonic, sees in it only the "demon." Christian morality emphasizes, not the demonic as the vital force which sustains life, but rather the innate sinfulness of the sexuality with which that life is sustained. Technology tries to contain the demonic within the rational walls of its scientific theories. It assumes that all things, even the demonic, may be understood and explained logically. Thus, when confronted with the irrational demonic, the technological knight cannot recognize it for what it is and, in seeking to destroy its threat to his universe of equations, ultimately destroys himself. The demonic cannot be defined, destroyed, examined, or explained.

The failures of Christianity and technology leave us with no myth, ritual, dogma, or formula to contain the demonic. Neither can we destroy it for, as we have seen, we will ultimately be destroying ourselves. What, then, is left? Must we face a vision of reality so horrible that suicide (as in "That Moment") or insanity (as in "Criminal Ballad") are the only alternatives? No. There is one other way: to reformulate and revitalize, as Hughes attempts in *Crow*, a mythology of the demonic.

Notes

1.   Ekbert Faas, "Ted Hughes and Crow," *London Magazine*, 10, No. 10 (January, 1973), p. 8.
2.   Keith Sagar, "Ted Hughes," *Writers and Their Works*, No. 227 (1972), p. 32.

Genetic Memory and the
Three Traditions of *Crow*

Leonard M. Scigaj

In *Creative Mythology* Joseph Campbell adopts the Old Germanic term *wyrd* to specify what he considers to be the central tradition of Western literature after the breakdown of God-centered medieval Catholicism. For Campbell *wyrd* describes the hero's compulsion toward goal-oriented adventures, in time and historical experience, in order to realize a secular Eros-Amor. The love throes of Tristan, the *erstrîten* of Parzival, the *Steigerung* of Faust, and even the Nighttown misadventures of Stephen Daedalus and Leopold Bloom—all such action in Western literature signifies for Campbell "that sense of yearning and striving toward an unknown end, so characteristic of the Western living of life—so alien to the Oriental," which comprises *wyrd*. After adventures involving psychological rounds of love and death, the hero wins the transfiguring experience of Eros as Kosmogonos, a cosmos-creating, consciousness-enlarging power of love within the self that one can afterward find in all things, all events.[1]

Another tradition in Western literature, a comic inversion of the adventure hero, is that of the trickster and his modern counterpart, the picaro. From primitive folklore to contemporary novels, comic heroes such as Coyote, Raven, Don Quixote, and Benny Profane appear as carefree rogues whose amorality or haphazard, episodic actions satirize social conventions. They afford the reader, as John Greenway says of trickster heroes, the pleasure of censuring the rogue's transgressions through ridicule. In this tradition we laugh at their misdeeds without fear of harming the social fabric, for rogue heroes are unchanging inferiors who develop no transfiguring inwardness.[2]

Ted Hughes's *Crow* occupies an ambivalent position between the two traditions. When Leonard Baskin visited Hughes three weeks after Sylvia Plath's death of 11 February 1963, he found Hughes "in a great depressed state" and tried to rally him "from despair into activity" by commissioning him to write a modest poem, "The Anatomy of Crow," to be based upon Baskin's crow engravings, and to be printed by him at the Gehenna Press. Yet nothing came of the project until five years later, when suddenly the plot of a group of *Crow* poems assumed epic proportions quite beyond Baskin's

Reprinted from *Perspectives on Contemporary Literature* 9 (1983): 83–91, by permission of the author.

intent.[3] The *Crow* poems, the first of which were published in July of 1967,[4] are certainly far from Baskin's original suggestion, but much closer to Hughes's readings in the traditions of the adventure hero and the trickster, during the first three years immediately after Plath's death.

In a 1964 review of Mircea Eliade's *Shamanism*, Hughes conflated the shamanic journey of magical death and dismemberment, with the epic and romantic tradition of the heroic adventure.[5] For almost a decade prior to this review Hughes had consciously adopted Robert Graves's position that union with the White Goddess, the "poet's enchantress," was "the only theme of his songs."[6] Hughes also reviewed John Greenway's *Literature Among the Primitives* and *The Primitive Reader* for the *New York Review of Books* in December of 1965, just eighteen months before the first *Crow* poems reached print.[7] Each of the Greenway volumes contains a chapter on the trickster figure. When Hughes gave readings of his *Crow* poems soon after publication, he referred to both traditions. In the 1973 Claddagh Records recording of *Crow*, Hughes linked Crow with the heroic adventurer by stating that "Crow's whole quest aims to locate and release his own creator, God's nameless hidden prisoner, whom he encounters repeatedly but always in some unrecognizable form."[8] Earlier, during a 1970 BBC radio reading, Hughes indicated Crow's affinity with the trickster by declaring that, though Crow's "ambition is to become a man," he really "never quite manages."[9]

Hughes's use of both the adventure hero tradition and the trickster tradition in *Crow* poses two important questions. If Crow is an adventure hero *manqué*, what impedes his development? And, if Crow originates as a trickster, what, exactly, is Hughes satirizing? *Crow* is not simply a facile satire of Western man's tendency towards violence; *Wodwo* (1967) already contained numerous surrealistic poems about the violence of world wars. A common denominator of the two traditions, however, is the Western compulsion to act, whether deliberately or irresponsibly. Crow consciously tries to realize his vision of Eros in "Crow Tries the Media" and "Crow's Undersong"; in numerous other poems Hughes satirizes Western mythology, science, religion, and mass media. In "A Kill" we learn that Crow's genetic heritage predisposes him toward violence, and in other poems we view Crow becoming acculturated to a pervasive violence in his environment. The answer to the two questions perhaps lies in the realization that both the impediment to Crow's becoming an adventure hero, and the object of the satire in the trickster poems of *Crow*, derive from a criticism of yet a third tradition, Western empiricism, which applies directly to the God of *Crow*, and to the landscape of the poems—the universe created by this God.

In essays and in an interview published during the *Crow* period, Hughes reiterates that post-Renaissance Western science—especially its inert laboratory analysis, its refusal to consider subjective states, and its utilitarian attitude toward the environment—and Western religion's repression of sexuality and relegation of the natural world to the devil, have caused a divorce of man from nature and a tendency to rely only upon abstract thinking, quantifiable fact and material success.[10] Here Hughes also employs Jung's use of Heraclitian *enantiodromia* to account for twentieth century violence. Jung reasoned that an overemphasis upon rationalism in our Western culture causes a repression of instinctual life and, ultimately, a reversion to its opposite—an explosive, enraged energy.[11] The God of *Crow* is the bored *deus absconditus* of a post-Renaissance mechanical universe which seethes with enraged energy due to an enforced instinctual depravation in man. Hughes intended the God of *Crow* to be "the man-created, broken down, corrupt despot of a ramshackle religion, who . . . accompanies Crow through the world in many guises, mis-teaching, deluding, tempting, opposing and at every point trying to discourage or destroy him."[12]

Crow fails to rise from trickster to adventure hero, to realize Campbell's transfiguring vision of Eros Kosmogonos, because the spiritless scientific materialism and repressed sexuality in Western culture impede him. In 1970, at the time Hughes collected his Crow poems into a volume, he wrote that

> The subtly apotheosized misogyny of Reformed Christianity is proportionate to the fanatic rejection of Nature, and the result has been to exile man from Mother Nature—from both inner and outer nature. The story of the mind exiled from Nature is the story of Western Man. It is the story of his progressively more desperate search for mechanical and rational and symbolic securities, which will substitute for the spirit-confidence of the Nature he has lost.[13]

Crow, the stunted everyman of a deprived culture, is born with Western man's hyperactive urge for action and adventure encoded upon his genetic memory, and is weaned in a landscape which magnifies any expenditure of energy exponentially. In infancy Crow's every movement, instead of accommodating him to the maternal care of the natural world ("Crow and Mama"), alienates him from it; his cries, laughs, first steps, and tantrums have the effect of scorching his mother's ear, bloodying her breasts, and filling her face with scars and gashes. When she attempts retaliation, Crow knows he must "get going." He finds refuge in a car, a plane, and a rocket. Crow finally lands on the Moon, but only to find himself "Under his mother's buttocks."[14] In cartoon form Hughes satirizes twentieth century technology, from the invention of the automobile to the Apollo expeditions, as a crazed, neurotic flight into "mechanical and rational and symbolic securities."

What Hughes considers to be the enraged instinctual depravation of Western empiricism is assimilated into Crow's genetic heritage. Hughes often brooded over Freud's concept of phylogenetic inheritance, of a genetic residue of violence passed on from the primal horde to each subsequent generation.[15] Crow's foetal development ("A Kill") occurs in terms of strangling, clubbing, and stabbing, exaggerations which yet insist that the genetic memory of a violence-prone heritage is encoded into the very embryonic development of Crow. The growth of Crow's legs in the womb of his culture flogs him lame; the development of his eyes shoots him blind.

Crow's blindness or myopic vision is especially important. Hughes is conversant with modern theories of general semantics and phenomenological studies of the intentionality of perception (Korzybski and Merleau-Ponty, for instance), which indicate that perception is an active process, that the mind organizes what it sees through principles developed in part from cultural values and assumptions, and that even language itself carries built-in assumptions about the nature of reality. Crow views the world entirely through the objectivity of his neutral camera eye; his perceptions are strongly influenced by our Western culture's long-standing connection with a rational, empirical tradition that dissociates scientific laws and factual evidence from the subjective responses of the beholder, through the logic of Cartesian dualism ("Crow Alights"). In "Crow's Account of the Battle," scientific laws and the linear logic of rational progress operate "as planned," but *enantiodromically* heap destruction along the way, and leave memory traces of violence even in hair and teeth:

> The cartridges were banging off, as planned,
> The fingers were keeping things going
> According to excitement and orders.
> The unhurt eyes were full of deadliness.
> The bullets pursued their courses
> Through clods of stone, earth and skin,
> Through intestines, pocket-books, brains, hair, teeth
> According to Universal laws
> And mouths cried "Mamma"
> From sudden traps of calculus,
> Theorems wrenched men in two,
>
> . . .
>
> Reality was giving its lesson,
> Its mishmash of scripture and physics,
> With here, brains in hands, for example,
> And there, legs in a treetop.

Creation viewed through Crow's empirical eye becomes "a cortege / Of mourning and lament" ("Crow Tyrannosaurus") which impels his head into "trapsprung," frenetic action. While eagles soar and swallows swoop, Crow comprehends none of their freedom; he is compelled to stand "spraddled head-down in the beach-garbage, guzzling a dropped ice-cream" ("Crow and the Birds"). Experience is devoured according to compulsive action, but with none of the inner illumination that Campbell describes. The empirical tradition discounts the subjective, prizing only goal-seeking, analytic behavior. Somewhere behind the cauterized landscape of *Crow* lies Locke's dismissal of secondary qualities—those subjective considerations inadmissible of quantification, calibration or assimilation into inert factual data. Crow's empirical eye perceives even a little stream as "an auxiliary motor" fastened onto the "infinite engine" of a Newtonian mechanical universe ("Crow Hears Fate Knock at the Door").

When Crow interprets the St. George and the Dragon myth ("Crow's Account of St. George"), he creates a universe that operates according to linear logic, and depicts St. George as an adventure hero in the empirical tradition. Here "everything in the universe / Is a track of numbers racing towards an answer," and St. George "rides those racing tracks," producing silence with refrigeration machinery, and genetic engineering with the "tweezers of number." As the pace of St. George's inventing quickens to joyous delirium, nature becomes *enantiodromically* demonized in his eyes, and he stabs at it with ever-increasing fury, as the deluded Ajax once hacked at sheep. The result is a repeat performance of the empirical "primal crime" in our phylogenetic heritage: the dragon of all-nature, like Tiamat in the Babylonian *Enuma Elish*, is slain in psychotic frenzy, and St. George, the mad scientist, finally awakens to find his wife and children bathed in their blood.

When Crow approaches God for help, the paternalistic author of this "mishmash of scripture and physics" is revealed as bored, snoring away while his clockwork juggernaut hums ("Crow Communes"; "A Childish Prank"), or violent, opposing Crow's every attempt at self-realization ("Crow's Song of Himself"). Crow is either left to his egocentric devouring, or he is browbeaten with abstract concepts, which only result in repressing his instinctual life into demonized libidinal energy within his unconscious ("Crow's First Lesson"):

> God tried to teach Crow how to talk.
> "Love," said God. "Say, Love."
> Crow gaped, and the white shark crashed into the sea
> And went rolling downwards, discovering its own depth.
>
> "No, no," said God, "Say Love. Now try it. LOVE."
> Crow gaped, and a bluefly, a tsetse, a mosquito
> Zoomed out and down
> To their sundry flesh-pots.

Soon Crow's perceptions are so poisoned with scientific rationalism that every attempt to comprehend his world becomes a struggle with the Proteus of Western empiricism ("Truth Kills Everybody"). The consequences are disastrous: once again Crow plugs into a universe of repressed destructive energy, where Proteus becomes "a naked powerline, 2000 volts," or "The earth, shrunk to the size of a hand grenade." Even Crow's thoughts become poisoned with the inheritance of repressed violence; in "Magical Dangers" Crow's thoughts of palaces, fast cars, and wages recoil upon him, plucking out his spine, choking him, blindfolding him. Crow's attempts to raise himself from trickster to culture hero ("Crow Improvises"; "Crow Blacker Than Ever") only release more violent energy, create more agony. In such a universe Crow becomes acculturated to apprehending his God as the one who has "all the weapons" ("Crow's Theology").

Crow tries to attain a vision of Eros Kosmogonos, but his path is blocked. The God of his Western culture has created a very restrictive landscape. The empirical tradition places no cultural value upon the anima, or inwardness. In "Crow's Undersong" the only possible vision of Eros is that of a sad account of a diminished, frightened, easily bruised lover. Though "She has come amorous it is all she has come for," she seems distracted, out of sorts, and incompetent in the strictures of a materialist world. When "Crow Tries the Media" to sing very simply and clearly about her, he learns that "this tank had been parked on his voice," and that "Manhattan weighed on his eyelid." Crow has little chance of rising to the status of an adventure hero in Hughes's macabre scenario of cultural constriction.

Hughes interjects many Buddhist and pre-Buddhist tags into *Crow* as foils for his protagonist's obsessive striving and objective analysis, and as clues toward a way of perceiving that may gain Crow his freedom. But the adventure hero *manqué* is incapable of comprehending their import. In "Examination at the Womb Door," Crow rationalizes with egocentric bravado to gain admittance to temporality, when he should recognize that *karmic* rebirth into a decaying phenomenal world of desire, the *Sidpa Bardo*, is the only result of passing through the Womb Door.[16] Crow might achieve the "nothing" state of Buddhist *śūnyatā*, of a liberating self-identification with all of reality, and free himself of egotism and dualistic thinking,[17] but in "Crow Frowns" authorial irony intervenes to tell the reader what Crow himself cannot discern:

> He is the long waiting for something
> To use him for some everything
> Having so carefully made him
>
> Of nothing.

If Crow could recognize that obsessive striving for goals or answers outside the self is *avidyā* or ignorance, he could begin to perceive the universe from the starting point of his own unique subjectivity. Then he could learn the *Átman* doctrine of the *Upanishads* (*Chāndogya Upanishad*, 6:8–16)—that he himself is the creator and interpreter of his own universe ("Robin Song"). But nothing in his inherited Cartesian perceptions teaches him to value inwardness. Crow is condemned by his culture to act impulsively upon a supposed external reality ("Crow's Fall"; "A Horrible Religious Error"), and perpetually to view his problems as things existing outside himself, in some Black Beast or outside irritant ("The Black Beast"; "Crow on the Beach"). Crow's faith in his cerebral cortex remains inviolate; whereas Hughes intrudes with dramatic irony to declare that "He was what his brain could make nothing of" ("Crow's Playmates"). The double entendre within "make nothing of" contains a potentially liberating clue. Crow's brain cannot comprehend ("make nothing of") the fact that he *can* reunite himself with his gods by discarding dualistic thinking and instead cultivating *śūnyatā*, the oneness ("nothing" as no one thing) of all that is perceived. Crow could benefit immeasurably from the *Bardo* doctrine that his fears are self-created, for when he strikes out at the environment he really strikes at himself ("Crow Sickened"):

> Decided to get death, but whatever
> Walked into his ambush
> Was always his own body.
>
> Where is this somebody who has me under?

Similarly, Crow fails to recognize that his accusations are self-reflexive: "Crow sat in its chair, telling loud lies against the Black Beast."

The Buddha depicted compulsive cravings and attachments to this world as the unrelieved torment of burning desire in his "Fire Sermon," but Crow cannot comprehend this wisdom. In "Crow's Last Stand" he prefers, like General Custer, to be trapped one final time by the bravura of his own empirical eye:

> Burning
>   burning
>   burning
>   there was finally something
> The sun could not burn, that it had rendered
> Everything down to—a final obstacle
> Against which it raged and charred
>
> And rages and chars
>
> Limpid among the glaring furnace clinkers
> The pulsing blue tongues and the red and the yellow
> The green lickings of the conflagration
>
> Limpid and black
> Crow's eye pupil, in the tower of its scorched fort.

Hughes is not a believer in Buddhist orthodoxy; he places many Buddhist tenets in *Crow* to offer one of many possible ways of achieving inwardness in the history of human culture, and to provide a foil and an antidote to the compulsive striving and rationalism of our post-Renaissance empirical tradition. Crow may be the indestructible trickster figure of folklore who attests to man's indomitability and energy, but the failure of his attempt to achieve a consciousness of selfhood in our technologically advanced culture must give us pause. At the time of the publication of *Crow*, Hughes wrote in an essay that our neurotic civilization "is the direct result of the prohibition of imagination, the breakdown of all negotiations between our scientific mental attitude and our inner life."[18] In *Crow* Hughes affirms that the longer our culture is permeated with the empirical tradition, the longer our inherited memories of inert objectivity will narrow our perceptions, inhibit our psychological development, and cause periodic explosions of repressed libidinal energy. The more our culture fails to value inwardness, the more our brains will devolve into file cabinets of fact, and the more our psyches will atrophy into swarms of petty neurotic ailments. In this landscape Eros Kosmogonos and the adventure hero tradition will vanish.

Notes

1. Joseph Campbell, *The Masks of God: Creative Mythology* (New York: Viking Press, 1970), pp. 553, 636, 647.
2. See John Greenway, *The Primitive Reader* (Hatboro, Pennsylvania: Folklore Associates, 1965), pp. 57–62; Greenway, *Literature Among the Primitives* (Hatboro, Pennsylvania: Folklore Associates, 1964), pp. 89–90.
3. Correspondence from Leonard Baskin to this writer, dated 11 March 1977.
4. See the poem publication dates in the first edition of Keith Sagar, *The Art of Ted Hughes* (London: Cambridge Univ. Press, 1975), p. 188.
5. Ted Hughes, "Secret Ecstasies," *The Listener*, 72 (29 Oct. 1964), 677–78.
6. The quote is Graves's, from *The White Goddess*, 2nd ed. (1966; rpt. New York: Farrar, Straus and Giroux, 1975), p. 388. For Hughes's early use of *The White Goddess* see Sagar, pp. 11, 14.
7. Hughes, "Tricksters and Tarbabies," *New York Review of Books*, 5 (9 Dec. 1965), 33–35.
8. Claddagh Records, CCT 9–10; rpt. Sagar, p. 118.
9. Reprinted in *The Listener*, 84 (30 July 1970), 149. Hughes was also familiar, as he states in the Greenway review (see note # 7), with Paul Radin's *The Trickster*.
10. For Hughes's observations on Western science and religion, see especially the Ekbert Faas interview with Hughes, entitled, "Ted Hughes and Crow," *London Magazine*, 10 (Jan. 1971), 5–20; and two different essays written by Hughes with the same title: "Myth and Education," *Children's Literature in Education*, 1 (1970), 55–70; "Myth and Education," in *Writers, Critics and Children*, ed. Geoff Fox et al. (New York: Agathon Press, 1976), pp. 77–94.
11. In a letter to Ekbert Faas, dated 23 August 1977, Hughes stated that he has read "all the translated volumes" of Jung. See Ekbert Faas, *Ted Hughes: The Unaccommodated Universe* (Santa Barbara, Calif.: Black Sparrow Press, 1980), p. 37. Jung's clearest statement on Heraclitus' *enantiodromia*, though he utilizes the concept frequently in his writings, occurs in

the definitions section in *Psychological Types*, trans. H.G. Baynes, rev. R.F.C. Hull (Princeton: Princeton University Press, 1971), pp. 425–26:

ENANTIODROMIA means a "running counter to." In the philosophy of Heraclitus it is used to designate the play of opposites in the course of events—the view that everything that exists turns into its opposite.

I use the term *enantiodromia* for the emergence of the unconscious opposite in the course of time. This characteristic phenomenon practically always occurs when an extreme, one-sided tendency dominates conscious life; in time an equally powerful counter-position is built up, which first inhibits the conscious performance and subsequently breaks through the conscious control.

A use of *enantiodromia* to explain the outpouring of evil in WW II as an extreme "running counter to" caused by the banishment of darker instinctual forces in our progress-oriented rationalistic culture, is found in *Civilization in Transition*, trans. R.F.C. Hull (New York: Pantheon Books, 1964), pp. 80–83.

12. Claddagh Records, cited above.

13. Hughes, "The Environmental Revolution," *Your Environment*, 1 (Summer 1970), 81–83.

14. Hughes, *Crow* (New York: Harper & Row, 1971), p. 5. Subsequent quotations from Hughes's *Crow* are as found in this edition.

15. See the Hughes poem "Out" in *Wodwo* (New York: Harper & Row, 1967), pp. 156–58, and passing comments about Freud's concept of inherited genetic memory in two of Hughes's reviews of this period: "Superstitions," *New Statesman*, 68 (2 Oct. 1964), 500; "Dylan Thomas's Letters," *New Statesman*, 72 (25 Nov. 1966), 733. For a concise summary of Freud's writing on "archaic heritage" and "phylogenetic inheritance," see Liliane Frey-Rohn, *From Freud to Jung*, trans. F. G. Engreen & E. K. Engreen (New York: G. P. Putnam's Sons, 1974), pp. 126–32.

16. W. Y. Evans-Wentz, ed., *The Tibetan Book of the Dead*, trans. Lama Kazi Dawa-Samdup, 3rd ed. (1957; rpt. New York: Oxford Univ. Press, 1960), pp. 175 ff. For Hughes's conscious use of the *Bardo Thödol* see Scigaj, "Oriental Mythology in *Wodwo*," in *The Achievement of Ted Hughes*, ed. Keith Sagar (Athens: Univ. of Georgia Press, 1983), pp. 126–53, esp. p. 141. See also Faas, "Ted Hughes and Crow," pp. 16–17; Sylvia Plath, *Letters Home*, ed. Aurelia Schober Plath (New York: Harper & Row, 1975), pp. 354, 371, 399.

17. See D.T. Suzuki, *Mysticism: Christian and Buddhist* (New York: Harper & Brothers, 1957), pp. 16, 28, 30.

18. Hughes, "Myth and Education," *Children's Literature in Education, p. 60.*

The Economy of Flesh in
Ted Hughes's *Gaudete*

RAND BRANDES

Ted Hughes's *Gaudete* (1977) falls squarely between the nuclear holocaust nightmares of *Crow* (1971) and the shamanistic quest for "wholeness" in *Cave Birds* (1978). *Crow* reflects the poet's lack of faith in the ability of established Western institutions to produce real social and religious, and by extension political, change in the world. Social institutions such as Christianity (primarily Protestantism), educational programs, and the institutionalization of science and technology are depicted in *Crow* as inherently destructive, particularly because they rely almost exclusively on the unemotive intellect. Like the dispossessed punk rockers and Rastafarians of the seventies in England, *Crow* embodies an apocalyptic longing for the end of the world, the end of Babylon, so that it can start over, from scratch in Crow's case.[1] On the other hand, *Cave Birds* transforms the disappointed search for social change into the provisionally successful quest for individual transcendence and wholeness through psychic suffering. If the society cannot change, according to Hughes, then at least the individual, through spiritual discipline and cosmic awareness, can heal one wound between humanity and the Otherness of the Great Mother.

Gaudete is partitioned into four major sections: an "Argument," "Prologue," "central narrative," and "Epilogue." The central narrative of *Gaudete*, which was originally devised as a script for a movie in 1964, obliquely parodies the utopian impulses and promises of the numerous "false" Messiahs of the 1960s and 1970s. In place of the book's destined-to-fail protagonist Lumb, one could insert Timothy Leary, Allen Ginsberg, The Who's "Tommy," or even Charles Manson, who anticipated Jim Jones. These charismatic figures' calls to turn on and tune out, to use sex and drugs not simply as forms of rebellion but also to open the doors of perception, had the double appeal of social *and* individual transformation. Of course, the insidious megalomania of these characters was often at the center of their "movements," whose ideologies, in the end, simply reproduced the diseases and psychoses of the patriarchal political body.

While *Gaudete*'s "Argument" and "Prologue" underwrite the basic pa-

This essay was written specifically for this volume and appears here for the first time.

triarchal ideologies of the central narrative, the "Epilogue" attempts to deconstruct these ideologies by offering a subjective, fluid, open, and decentered text informed by a matriarchal mythopoetics. The success of this project depends upon how one reads the "Epilogue" itself, whether one accepts Hughes's counter-perspective to the central narrative, and finally if one believes that the "Epilogue" has rescued the entire *Gaudete* text from Hughes's depiction of women. The first section of this essay addresses the pre-"Epilogue" *Gaudete* text, while the second addresses the "Epilogue" and the inclusive text. This division itself suggests *Gaudete*'s problematic design and its resistance to monologic readings and critical appropriations.

Much of what will be said here (particularly regarding the central narrative) not only contradicts almost everything Hughes has said about his metaphysics and ideologies, but also argues against the preoccupations of the vast majority of Hughes scholars.[2] I am not offering this reading of *Gaudete* as typical or neutral; some of Hughes's best neo-pastoral writing and truly imaginative similes appear in this book. Still, in many ways this is Hughes's most problematic book, even more so than *Crow*—not only in its construction, but also in its reception. Ironically, the poet's degrading depiction of women and his objectification of the female body in all of his works are the direct results of his desire to reconnect with the White Goddess and the feminine self. His cosmic vision may be matriarchal, but his political vision remains patriarchal. Even in the "Epilogue" Hughes does not (with one notable exception) write about real, complicated women who are culturally conscripted; he instead offers a cosmic feminine principle—the apotheosized disembodied woman: "An unearthly woman wading shorewards" (183).[3] *Gaudete*, including the "Epilogue," is more than the story of "A lecherous priest and a gaggle of spoofed women. Hysterical bored country wives. Credulous unfortunate females" (128). It is the story of the modern world's inability or refusal to give women back their bodies, their spiritual and political bodies.

Most critics agree that "*Gaudete* is about man's divorce from his own life."[4] However (and this cannot be said strongly enough), although all persons in the modern world, male and female, may be cut off from their inner lives and divided against themselves, the consequences are different for men than for women; men still control the power, the power over the (female) body in this world. Although there are various degrees of victimization as played out in *Gaudete*'s economy of flesh, some forms are more destructive than others.

The foregrounding of the body in *Gaudete* emphasizes not only the "absurd helplessness"[5] of the characters or their need for "rebirth" and "revitalization,"[6] but also and most importantly that our body is ultimately all we have; it is the final site of all struggles and transformations. The words "body" or "bodies" are mentioned over seventy times in the book, and in his interview with Faas, Hughes concludes with a statement about the body:

"All the forms of natural life are emissaries [from the underworld]. The actual bodies of the people are emissaries."[7] Most critics have discussed these struggles and transformations in *Gaudete* from mythological or anthropological perspectives.[8] They cite Graves, Jung, Campbell, Castaneda, or Eliade while mentioning shamans, doppelgängers, "the shadow," the White Goddess, Hercules, fertility gods, and scapegoats. These are all illuminating and helpful references and are certainly close to Hughes's conscious intentions. However, it is dangerous to follow the poet into the hinterlands of the Collective Unconscious, especially since there is a substantial element of "irony" in *Gaudete*. If one does not "buy" the mythic subtext, all that is left is the body of the text and the text of the body (or "bodily thickness," as Hughes says)—bodies tragically empty and brutally abused.[9] In *Gaudete*, the body, particularly the female body, pays the price for all our mistakes and paradoxically all our attempts at perfection.

I

In *Gaudete*, the Reverend Lumb attempts to "heal" not the souls of his parishioners, but their bodies. The reason for this is that the Lumb of the main narrative is a changeling made from an oak tree who has "interpret[ed] the job of ministering the Gospel of love in his own log-like way" (9). Lumb forms a love cult among the women of the village to supposedly produce a new Messiah. This Messiah could represent the desire for social change, a desire for a new leader and a new gospel, as one character claims: "The church began with women. . . . The Roman Empire was converted by a woman. / And now the whole thing's worn back down to its women. / It's like a herd of deer, he [Smayle] says, why is it always led by a hind?" (65). The cruel irony of this passage is clear, based on the exploitation, objectification, and transformation of women into animals as worked out in the narrative. The women (or at least their bodies), which are the "medium" for social change, will not be the benefactors of this change. They appear powerless before Lumb and remain powerless. They cannot control their own bodies when with Lumb nor their destinies with their husbands, or male "superiors."

Lumb fails in his task not only to produce the new Messiah, but also to change the status quo. He has not been able to get outside of the society itself; he has simply reproduced its fundamental hierarchies. Symbolically, the failure of Lumb is the failure of the central narrative to get beyond the body, to deconstruct the basic binary codes of male-female, body-soul, relationships that marginalize the latter concepts of each pair. Ultimately, as another critic has mentioned, the failure of the central narrative (and perhaps the entire *Gaudete* text) is that while it celebrates the feminine principle and the White Goddess, it cannot accommodate real, complicated people.[10] While the imaginative center of the entire text may be "psychological" or "mythic" as some argue, the significant conflict is in the marginalized ideological struggle over the body—a struggle foregrounded in the central narrative.

From the opening epigrams and "Argument" through the "Prologue" and main narrative to the highly acclaimed poems of the "Epilogue," the body "means" something: the body can "know," thus it is an epistemological site; it can be read, thus it is a (rhetorical) text; it can be exchanged for something, thus it is a currency/commodity; it can be subjugated or killed, thus it is a thing. The body can also be divided against itself and therefore not be "itself," as the epigram taken from Parzival suggests: "These two, however, were one, 'my brother and I' is one body, like a good man and good wife. Contending here from loyalty of heart, one flesh, one blood, was doing itself much harm" (8). The divided body requires "healing"; the source of this healing is presented in the first epigram regarding Dionysus. The body is not healed through discipline in the text, but through indulgence, through the Dionysian carnival of flesh. In *Gaudete* there are two Lumbs— the original and the changeling. These Lumbs actually fight each other in the main narrative. However, for the majority of the poem there is only one Lumb; this Lumb, though not conclusively "whole," experiences moments when he appears to be fully integrated and in touch with the elemental Dionysian energies of the flesh. Thus, the disease (the divided self) and the cure (the embodiment of elemental energies) are encapsulated in the two epigrams and are consubstantial in the two Lumbs.

The poem's "Argument" informs us of Lumb's call to the underworld and the appearance of the double, his motives, mission, eventual fate and his reappearance "in the West of Ireland, where he roams about composing hymns and psalms to a nameless female deity" (9). From the beginning of the book the reader is encouraged to think in mythic terms, to look through the narrative's surface and to focus upon Lumb's psychic quest and not to read the poem (especially the central narrative) as a novel, particularly a novel based on social realism.[11] This may be the result of Hughes's decision to strip down the narrative, which was "much more complicated in detail and had many more characters and irrelevant novelistic digressions" (Faas, 214). (These absent "digressions" are the absent ["real"] lives of *Gaudete*'s characters.) But as Terry Eagleton has mentioned, *Gaudete* is closer to "traditional realism than it would superficially seem" even though the content is "clearly non-realistic."[12] Although Eagleton argues that this is the case because Hughes "mirrors" with his language instead of "constructing" with it, it appears that even the content is "realistic" in its reproduction of traditional hierarchical discourses—discourses that the text attempts mythically to mask. This masking informs the treatment of the body in the poem's bloody prologue.

The "Prologue" begins with Rev. Lumb wandering aimlessly through the streets of a village in Northern England. He suddenly stumbles upon "dead bodies . . . piled in heaps and strewn in tangles everywhere between the heaps" (11). This vision of carnage obviously originated in Hughes's work with *Seneca's Oedipus*. Unlike Oedipus', however, Lumb's riddle is not that of the Sphinx, but of the bodies themselves. Lumb "looks for wounds"; he tries to read the bodies, but there is an excess of meaning. The bodies mean more than he can understand. The "mass-graves" are beyond his comprehension; it is a question not of "quality"—death—but of quantity—"piles." The piles of bodies anticipate the tons of bulls' flesh and guts that are part of the ceremonial production of his changeling. But first he encounters the "woman entangled in the skins of wolves" (14) whom he has apparently been called to heal. Lumb's comment that "He is not a doctor. He can only pray" introduces the significant thematic and imagistic thread of the doctor, healing, and the medicalization of discourses on the body that run throughout *Gaudete*. Apparently, the real Lumb cannot help the woman because he is not in touch with his own body's inner life; he has sacrificed the body to the spirituality of the soul. Lumb is the inversion of Dr. Westlake, who appears in the main narrative and is unable to work in any other realms—such as the emotional or spiritual—than that of the physical.

Since the original Lumb has sacrificed his body to the soul, the "naked body" (17) must be reborn under the fertile and powerful flesh of the sacrificed bulls. Again it is the sheer quantity of blood and guts required for the ritual that is significant. The quantity of flesh used corresponds to the spiritual resistance encountered. The laws of physics are at work: for every action there is an equal, opposite reaction. This spectacle of disembowelment is equivalent to Lumb's rebirth: "He looks down at his blood-varnished body, crusting black, already flaking, and trembling with shock and bewilderment" (19–20). The "Prologue" has established an economy of flesh in the text in which everything of importance, everything capable of producing change, must buy into this economy, must measure its successes or failures in relation to the body.

From the very first words of the main narrative we, the readers, become watchers of bodies and implicated in the soft-porn voyeurism of the narrator's main characters, such as Major Hagen: "Binoculars / Powerful, age-thickened hands" (23). We have been thrown into the profane world of the body just as Lumb was thrown into the sacred mythical world. In Lumb's world the bull was a ritual animal capable of giving new life; ironically, in Hagen's world this regenerative energy, the "sperm of bulls" is for sale. Critics have pointed out that Hagen is anticipated in the figure of "The Retired Colonel" (*Lupercal*), and that the characters in *Gaudete* are stereotypes and caricatures. As mentioned, this flatness is partially the result of the absence of History in the book and a lack of concern for the characters' pasts.[13] But it is also a by-product of the emotional distance between characters, a distance manifested in Hagen's lens. As Hagen watches his wife, Pauline, with Lumb, we watch, trying to read the scene, to decode their gestures. Hagen's gaze gives him some control over the situation, but it also suggests his impotence. His subsequent killing of the dove is a compensatory action designed to re-establish his manliness. He speaks in sign language and gives the dead dove to Lumb as a fetish charged with his hate.

Joe Garten, another voyeur and the "inverted child equivalent of Hagen" (Faas, 215), extends the theme of the gaze and its ramifications. Like Hagen watching his wife, Garten, a "petty poacher and the scrounger," watches Mrs. Westlake, the doctor's wife, waiting in her car on a back road. His gaze locks onto the woman: "he fastens himself to her" (30). Mrs. Westlake is described as having a "fox-fine profile" and "china cheek bone" (30)—the play on "fox" and the allusion to the classical image of beauty "china" brings the text in line with those discourses that objectify the woman in order to possess her. This is a rite-of-initiation for Garten into manhood; it is similar to looking into a girlie magazine for the first time. But this "innocent" gaze foreshadows and makes possible Garten's later photographing of Mrs. Evans with Lumb—the event that brings the action to a crisis. Far from innocent, the gaze is destructive, not because it can merely "witness" (and is therefore evidence) but because it can possess.

The action returns to Pauline Hagen, who is now alone and suffering the aftershock of the confrontation. She is powerless and wants to scream; her silence here reflects the silence of the whole book. (*Gaudete* would be a "silent" movie; there is no dialogue, just oneiric *reportage*.) No one, but especially the women, has a voice in the poem. The women cannot enter normal discourse; they are literally seen and not heard. Pauline closes her eyes and feels how Lumb's "presence stray[s] all over her body" (31). As with the piles of bodies in the "Prologue," the significant word is "all." Lumb's power is registered in the amount of flesh he can cover, and the degree of her feelings corresponds to this amount. If one removes the "all," the emotional impact is lessened exponentially. The same is true in the following scene where Pauline anoints her face with leaf-mould, though she really "wants to rub her whole body with it" (32). Again the intensity of the feelings corresponds to the surface area of flesh covered.

The "anointing" scene is often cited as one of the most positive scenes in the book, since Pauline "lets herself go" and momentarily merges with the elemental forces of nature.[14] However, like Major Hagen's compensatory killing of the dove, Pauline's spontaneous ritual is essentially meaningless in everyday commerce. Alone and in silence, her presence and worth are not autonomous or guaranteed but dependent on Lumb, whose "glance keeps glimpsing through her body" (32). She only exists if she can imagine herself being watched. Instead of wholeness, she is divided, projecting a vision of herself as an object. Like Lumb she is divided against herself even when supposedly at one with Nature.

A few poems later, Mrs. Westlake experiences sensations similar in intensity to Pauline's, but of a different nature. After her fight with Lumb,

Mrs. Westlake feels "All over her body the nerves of her skin smoulder" (38), and she metaphorically plunges into "a winter" scouring "her whole body's length with writhings. Sweat prickles her brow, she exclaims at the mirrors" (38). The parallels with Pauline's ritual are clear in their inversions. Instead of anointing herself, she "scours" herself. Instead of feeling good about Lumb all over her body, she "smoulders." She must look into the mirror, "trapped in a mirror . . . driven inward, obsessively studying self-images as if seeking a viable self."[15] As John Berger suggests in relation to paintings, "The mirror was often used as a symbol of the vanity of woman. . . . The real function of the mirror was otherwise. It was to make the woman connive in treating herself as first, and foremost, a sight."[16] She must see herself seeing herself. This "doubling" continues to the end of the poem, where she imagines "She is watching herself now, with richer satisfaction, in Lumb's bedroom, tugging a knife through her throat" (Berger, 40).

This schizophrenic position is enhanced by Mrs. Westlake's meditations on the body as text. In the midst of her agony she feels as if she is in a "doctor's waiting room," and figuratively she is, since she is in her husband's medical reference library. She looks at the books "to numb" herself. (Numbness is a central theme in the book and signifies the physical equivalent to the Joycean spiritual paralysis.) The following passage is significant so I will quote at length: "The volumes are swollen with the details of Lumb's body. . . . The glistening tissues, the sweating gasping life of division and multiplication, the shoving baby urgency of cells. . . . She is gripped by the weird pathos of bio-chemistry, the hot silken frailties, the giant, gristled power, the archaic sea-fruit inside her" (39). The imaginative intensity of this passage approaches that of the much acclaimed lines of Lumb's "prayer" (52–53). Ironically, however, in her attempt to escape Lumb she re-creates him; the tragic irony of the passage is that she is pregnant by Lumb and is contemplating suicide. What is growing inside her is her death wish, which foreshadows Janet's suicide in the subsequent poems. The "swollen" volumes are the textualized body, a body that excites her as well as brings her to grief.

Mrs. Westlake's emotional swings here could be related to her "hysteria," which affects our reading of the later scene when the drunken Dr. Westlake hears "the crying of his wife at some bodily extreme" and believes that "her writhing and cries are actually sexual spasm" and that Lumb is "actually copulating with her . . . through that hand on her ankle / In some devilish spiritual way" (75). Even though the elemental life imagined in the "swollen" texts is exactly that life which she "needs," it ironically destroys her—not because she cannot accomodate it, but because she doesn't "want" to be pregnant by Lumb. As Mrs. Evans confesses, later, "It has nothing to do with loving the vicar. . . . She doesn't even like him" (114). The Little Lumb inside her is killing her; she is literally possessed by Lumb. The Little Lumb in Janet, Estridge's daughter, actually kills her or she kills it.

Critics agree that the "reason" that Lumb establishes his love cult, excluding the new Messiah of the "Argument," is to reconnect the villagers and society with their elemental energies. Hughes has confirmed and encouraged this conclusion. After commenting that Maud, Lumb's housekeeper, is the Goddess's "Doppelganger" and therefore "in a way has control over Lumb to bring about this renovation of women and therefore of life in general in this world," Hughes says that "whole situation" is "impossibly crystallized in the immovable dead end forms of society and physical life" (Faas, 215). To say that this is a loaded passage would be an understatement. Beside the fact that one "renovates" rooms, why start with the "women"? Why give up on both "society" and the "physical life"? If one ignores these concerns, then the concept of "elemental energies" is plausible in regard to the main "adult" characters who are certainly entrenched; clearly their lives have dried up. However, Lumb's impregnation of the young girl Janet and his wooing of Jennifer raises other issues. In fact, Lumb's future wife, Felicity, is only eighteen. Felicity's youth may be explained away; she needs to be young and "innocent" in terms of the plot, and Janet's "innocent" dead body is needed to incite the men into action. Still, the reader is encouraged to see her body first as a sexual object. Though Janet may have been sacrificed to the Goddess from a mythical perspective, her body is ultimately offered up to the readers' gaze; Janet's gazing at her own body precludes ours.

As with Mrs. Westlake, Janet looks in a mirror before she hangs herself, not only to confirm her pregnancy but to confirm herself and her decision: "Janet, / Is examining her body, / Her swollen stomach, delicate glossed as the flank of a minnow, / In a long pierglass" (44). She is posing for the reader; it is no surprise then that her face is described as "relaxed expressionless, as for a studio portrait" (44). The poet has painted the nude in such a way as to entice the reader not to sympathize with Janet, but to long/lust for her. Janet is not naked; she is nude: "To be naked is to be oneself. To be nude is to be seen naked by others and not to be recognized for oneself. A naked body has to be seen as an object in order to become a nude. (The sight of it as an object stimulates the use of it as an object)" (Berger, 54). Janet is significantly hairless: "Hair is associated with sexual power, with passion. The woman's sexual passion needs to be minimized so that the spectator may feel that he has the monopoly of such passion" (Berger, 55).

In contrast to Janet, two women in the text who are hair-covered, wield greater power. Not only is the woman Lumb encounters in the "Prologue" covered with hair ("animal mane") and therefore sexually powerful, but so also is the "baboon woman" Lumb metaphorically gives birth to in his dream. These representations of the Goddess have power; they are naked but not nude. Conversely, Janet's hairlessness and powerlessness are reflected in the mirror before our gaze.

Janet's sister, Jennifer, is the most obvious sex object in the book; her primary function is to arouse not only the repressed Dr. Westlake, but also the reader. Ironically, we never see her nude; it is only her voice "which flows so full of thrilling touches / And which sobs so nakedly in its narration" (57). The suggestiveness of the passage is obvious in addition to others, such as "The perfumed upheaval of all this ringing emotion and physical beauty / Is exciting him. . . . Her creamy satin blouse, stretching and flexing like a skin" (56). Even though we get a view of Jennifer's "dark-haired ankles," it is only a titillating "glimpse." The real gaze follows: "Westlake / Keeps losing Jennifer's words / As he gazes fascinated / Into the turbulence of her body and features" (57). Later in the book, when drunk, Westlake reconstructs Jennifer's body: "And her live sister is worse—all that loose, hot, tumbled softness, / Like freshly-killed game, with the dew still on it, / Its eyes still seeming alive, still strange with wild dawn, / Helpless underbody still hot" (72). The objectification of Jennifer's body into a helpless "it" is symptomatic of the entire male community's, including Lumb's, inability to interact with real women because to do so would require dealing with real emotions. Though a marginal character, Jennifer literally embodies the body on display. Like her sister, she is offered up to the male gaze.

Immediately after, or perhaps simultaneously with, Janet's death, when her body is powerless, Lumb ironically is at his peak of power, physical power. The juxtaposition of the dead female body and the virulent male body heightens the basic gender distinctions which run throughout the book. Lumb looks at the land and feels "As if his whole body were a hot engine" (49). As with the woman's body, the "whole body" signifies the intensity of the experience. His meditations take him from the landscape to the metaphysics of existence: "He sees in among them, / In among all the tiny millions of worlds of this world / Millions of yet other, alternative worlds. . . . Each waiting for him to escape into it, to explore it and possess it, / Each with a bed at the centre. A name. A pair of shoes. And a door" (50). And no body! That Lumb's universe rotates around a bed is no surprise, nor is the fact that he wants to possess it.

At the height of his power, over which he stands Atlas-like, the female body, the Other, is absent. Unlike the women who need to be seen "to be," Lumb does not need real women. He simply needs the Magna Mater, his mother. Hughes critics often cite these passages as the strongest in the book, and they are precisely because Lumb is at his strongest. Away from the women, alone, Lumb is free to bask in the glory of his elemental presence. But this is a heartless, empty Lumb who decides "To carry his body, with all its belongings, / Right to the end of its decision" (52). This is the Will speaking—the Will separate from the body. This separation mirrors the women's separation: their bodies are carried away, robbed of their power.

As Lumb's moment of revelation and transcendence is preceded by a woman's despair, so is it afterward when Mrs. Walsall steps outside herself to see herself: "She knows she is unacceptably ugly" (54). In contrast to Mrs. Westlake, who tried to "numb" herself by looking at the swollen volumes,

Mrs. Walsall tries "to let the water / Numb her body. She fixes her mind / Under the numbing water. / She stands at the sink, numbed" (55). Lumb's epiphany is framed by two women, one dead, one numb. Their bodies pay the price for his transcendence.

Women's bodies also exact the toll of Lumb's aggressive sexuality. Although a few of the women seem to initiate the sexual encounters, as when Mrs. Holroyd "sets Lumb's hands on her breast," Lumb primarily is the active participant. The women are not only silenced, but immobilized and objectified through the animalistic similes used to describe them. In the sex scene between Betty and Lumb in the quarry, Betty is represented as a frog: "The minister sprawls face downward, as if murdered, / Between slender white legs, which are spread like a dead frog" (61). The simile may come from the perspective of Garten, who "witnesses" the encounter. Whatever the perspective, Lumb is still on top with the "dead" animal beneath him. In Betty's later encounter with what must be Lumb, the animal trope is reversed. "Betty / Naked at her dresser mirror" suddenly discovers that "A bigger hot body nestles in beside her, / Overpowers her, muscular and hairy as a giant badger." They wrestle "in a ball of limbs" until "Her laughs try to smother her shrieks" (89). Even if this is Betty's "dream," the bestial element is disturbing; the literal presentation of Lumb as a "sexual animal" is problematic. The animal analogy also informs Lumb's encounter with the "vixen" Mrs. Davies: "they are flung / With more life than they can contain / Like young dogs / Unable to squirm free from their torturing infinite dogginess" (92–93).

The comparison of Lumb's "mating" to the mating of animals is elaborated upon in his coupling with Mrs. Walsall: "[Mr. Walsall's] wife is biting a stick. / Animal gurgles mangle in her throat / While her eyes, her whole face, toil / In the wake of a suffering. . . . Her head thrashes from side to side among the small ferns and periwinkles. . . . Lumb labours powerfully at her body" (96). Mrs. Walsall, who had previously "numbed" herself, is now at the mercy of Lumb. She is a prisoner, gagged and tortured—not a being but a body: "for the prisoner, the body and its pain are overwhelmingly present and voice, world, and self are absent; for the torturer, voice, world and self are overwhelmingly present and the body and pain are absent."[17] These are only a few of the numerous examples one could cite where the female body is transformed into either an animal or a silenced object.

What is at stake in the central narrative is not that Lumb, the superman, is "bad" or evil for oppressing women, or that the women are his "victims," but that "the fertility god" simply represents the hierarchies of the society at large. Lumb (the Changeling) reproduces the dominant culture's attitude towards women. Lumb does not fail at his task because of "mythic" forces, but because he has not gotten beyond the hegemony of the culture itself.[18] Still, it is important to remember that Lumb is both perpetrator and "victim." His body is both his and not his as the fight with his double, the "naked stranger," shows. Lumb's struggle with his double over Felicity (Lumb's bride-to-be) is the negative inversion of his harmonious tapping of cosmic energies in the "tree-prayer" passages. Lumb's battle is physical, not psychic. After a long and painful struggle in the lake (the portal to the underworld), Lumb rips off his adversary's hand. This highly charged archaic gesture provisionally "frees" Lumb from his double since his double no longer mirrors Lumb: he only has one hand. Lumb is his own victim.

Much has been said by others about the mythic and ritualistic aspects of the orgy in the cathedral that closes the central narrative, during which Maud, Lumb's occult assistant (really overseer), murders Felicity. Even though the orgy does not represent Hughes's best writing and relies on standard props of the "Black Mass" or "Voodoo," it is significant in the density of its physicality and reliance on the body as a controlling metaphor. At the opening of the ritual the music has entranced the women so that "They no longer feel their bodies" (139). Ironically, many of these women have not felt their bodies throughout the narrative; this mystical "numbness" simply mocks their everyday numbness and is an extension of it. Felicity's body, the central and most significant body, is not numb but alive: "Wings lift through her and go off. / A tiger / Is trying to adjust its maniac flame-barred strength to her body" (140). Like the animal imagery associated with the women earlier, Felicity loses her body at precisely the moment that she is supposed to be gaining it. Felicity feels "honey-burning sweetness . . . oozing out all over her body," which is "splitting all the leafy seams of her body" (140–41). This is not the fullness of life for Felicity; it is the emptiness that she is to sacrifice to "the love animal" (141). Young, powerless, and in love, Felicity is turned into a ritualistic instrument: "her body has given up trying to move," for "She knows she herself is to be the sacramental thing" (141).

Felicity, who has ironically always been a "thing" in the text—"she is the most exotic thing in the nursery" (91)—represents all of the village women who have been idealized and idolized not in order to give them power but to keep them under control. What appears from the outside to be a "blessing" is really a curse. The women's bodies suffer the diminution of the sacred when Felicity "knows" that "she and all these women are moving inside the body of an incandescent creature of love," and that "They are the cells in the glands of an inconceivably huge and urgent love-animal" (142). Devoid of their own bodies, they become an organism in a cosmic body. Bodiless, they assume the body of another. The metaphor returns to music in the next poem, set in the cathedral where "The music inside their bodies is doing what it wants at last" (146). The frenzied pace becomes too much for all the participants and "they all cry together / As if they were being torn out of their bodies" (146). This cry is one of fear and pain, not only the ritualistic pain but the long-repressed pain of the suffering victims. Maud stabs Felicity and tells the women (the first words spoken during the ritual) that Lumb has betrayed them and was going to run off with Felicity. While she talks, "Felicity's body lies still, no longer any part of what matters, / Twisted unhumanly, demonstrating her unimportance" (147). This is the body language of the dead.

Critics argue that the women receive real power from Lumb but are unable to manage it.[19] No one, male or female, could handle the spiritual power offered by Lumb and his cosmic counterparts: "If you refuse the [divine] energy, you are living a kind of death. If you accept the energy, it destroys you" (Faas, 200). Even if, as Hughes suggests, one uses "rituals, the machinery of religion," to control this power, women are still the machinery and its "fuel," not its operator nor its benefactor. The women are not offered real power—real domestic, political power. The men who burn the bodies of Lumb (who is killed in a lengthy chase scene), Maud (who kills herself), and Felicity in the cathedral are the real power brokers. Social change is impossible according to Hughes, so the only solution is to pursue individual spiritual transformation. This transformation is what the poet records in the "Epilogue" poems.

II

In the "Epilogue" Hughes offers a Heraclitian text that attempts to "objectify" the male body by incorporating it into the more encompassing global economy of biological and physical life. Hughes cannot "become" a woman, but he can write from the "woman" inside him, as some feminists have suggested: "Yet one can become woman without having a female body. Through writing some may elude the phallocentricism that imprisons others."[20] Like Hughes, Robert Bly has struggled with the difficulty of writing about the Goddess, "the mother consciousness," as a man: "A man's father consciousness cannot be eradicated. If he tries that, he will lose everything. All he can hope to do is to join his father consciousness and his mother consciousness so as to experience what is beyond the father veil."[21] In the "Epilogue" Hughes leaves the body behind (the word only appears three times), the body of the male gaze, by offering it up to the forces of life and death embodied in the "nameless goddess."

The forty-five poems collected in the "Epilogue" have been discussed at length by others, many of whom believe they are Hughes's best and most important works.[22] These poems are introduced by a brief narrative describing the reappearance of Lumb in the West of Ireland. Lumb returns to the world, but "Beyond the Pale," probably in north Connemara near Cleggan, where Hughes and Plath visited the poet Richard Murphy during the breakup of their marriage. Geopolitically, Lumb has moved beyond the borders of British imperialism and metaphysically beyond positivism. Lumb, whose life has ended with a "bang" and not a whimper, has learned his lesson; now he is a poet, a bard, composing hymns to the White Goddess. The verses amazingly appear out of the water, carried by an otter who is called by Lumb and who then gives them to three girls.

The priest who transcribes the verses is simply a modern scribe. His work parallels that of the medieval scribes who transcribed the ancient pagan myths of Ireland. One such myth, the *Buile Suibhne* (*Sweeney Astray*), contains a scene in which the cleric Ronan's "psalter" is thrown into a lake and miraculously returned by an otter that "rose out of the lake with the psalter and brought it to Ronan."[23] Critics claim that the "Epilogue" is as close as Hughes comes to being a "devotional poet" (Gifford and Roberts, 192)— that is, until *River*—but he is a devotional poet in the Druidic tradition— a tradition Hughes encountered in the translations from the *Carmina Gadelica*. The Irish influence upon the entire book and particularly the "Epilogue" poems cannot be overemphasized. Hughes knows that the ancient Irish not only worshiped the Gravesian "White Goddess," but also that many ancient Irish societies were matriarchal.

The "Epilogue" opens with a question: "What will you make of half a man / Half a face / A ripped edge . . ." (176). Unlike the "divided self" and mutilated body(ies) of the "Prologue," which appear in the imperative mode, the fragmented body, the male body, of the "Epilogue" appears in the interrogative mode; it tropically, literally, and grammatically becomes the object of the (antigrammatical) sentence. The question ends: "How will you correct / The veteran of negatives / And the survivor of cease?" (176). In a language and syntax that will dominate *Cave Birds*, the rhetoric of postmodern folk surrealism, the no longer skeptical speaker in the poem waits like Godot for "correction" and not "completion." As Irene Claremont De Castillego writes: "Waiting is I believe as essential part of feminine psychology today as it was for Penelope."[24] The significance of waiting, not passively but passionately, runs throughout the poems, suggesting a mode of (Eastern) consciousness and not simply a mode of static "being." "In a world where all is temporary / And must pass as its opposite," the speaker(s) confess: "I neglected to come to degree of nature / In the patience of things" (179). The entire "Epilogue" is a question waiting to be answered, never to be completely answered, where one must be satisfied with half-truths and intuitive provisional formulations.

In the "Epilogue" Hughes offers subjective questions as an alternative to objective answers as a source (and end?) for poetic discourse. This subjectivity appears in the poet's attempt to come to terms with Sylvia Plath's suicide, a death that can be read as a synecdoche for his attempt to come to terms with all that is "feminine" in society and the world.[25] Consequently, even though he does not represent culturally (dis)placed women in the "Epilogue" (they are still both creative and destructive goddesses), he does attempt to write about one real woman—Plath.[26]

It happened
You knocked the world off, like a flower-vase.

It was the third time. And it smashed.

I turned
I bowed
In the morgue I kissed
Your temple's refrigerated glazed
As rained-on graveyard marble

(186)

This is not the voyeuristic suicide of Jennifer in the central narrative. In fact, it is not Plath's body that we "see," that is presented for our gaze, but the body of the poet: "Defunct . . . In the glaring metropolis of cameras" (186). Nor is this the camera of Garten's pornographic gaze seducing us with promises of "possession." Ironically, the poet sees himself as being seen. This doubling, despite the obvious sarcasm, shifts the point of view; his body, his life, not Plath's, is momentarily exposed: "And for all rumours of me read obituary. / What there truly remains of me . . . Is that very thing— my absence" (187). In the "Epilogue," the male body is not powerfully present but vulnerably absent. All that remains of the body is the skin, the word/image that ends the "Epilogue."

In the final poem of the "Epilogue," the "glare" of the world and the goddess temporarily replace the objective "gaze" of the patriarchal society and poet.

Glare out of just crumpled grass—
Blinded, I blink.

Glare out of muddled clouds—
I go in.

Glare out of house-gloom—
I close my eyes.

And the darkness too is aflame.

So you have come and gone again
With my skin.

(200)

Unlike the "gaze" of the central narrative, which presents itself as the "source" of "reality" (the only reality) and which objectifies the body, symbolically killing it by dehumanizing it, the "glare" of the poem "reflects" an ever-changing, multifarious spiritual reality that forces the subject to see itself as simply an object among other objects—thus relinquishing its status as "creative" subject. Hughes deconstructs the social body of the main narrative by turning the gaze upon itself. In the "mirroring" world of the "Epilogue" the body learns a new language, a language attuned to the global politics of the (eco)feminists.

Hughes's experiments with language, form, and perspective in the "Epilogue" do not make him a feminist nor do they completely redeem the "spirit" of *Gaudete's* central narrative. What they do do, however, is to show us a much more socially progressive and self-consciously "articulated" dimension of Hughes's writing. Hughes does not (and probably will not) "play" with language as do many of his contemporaries, nor does he buy into "social realism" or postmodern skepticism. One regrets the absence of these elements and others in his work and wonders how far his resistant mythical method can take him. The body, and in particular the female body, suffers in the central narrative of *Gaudete*; whether the "Epilogue" has satisfactorily redeemed, if not politicized, this suffering is debatable. In his most recent work, *Wolfwatching* (1991), Hughes still foregrounds the mythical, but he also enters into dialogue with the political elements of social discourse. After his cynical reconstruction of social reform and political change in the central narrative of *Gaudete*, Hughes is slowly buying into a reality whose economy is the economy of flesh.

Notes

1. Dick Hebdige, *Subculture: The Meaning of Style* (London: Methuen, 1979), 27–29.
2. Critics merely allude to the "total victimization of the female" (Faas, *Unaccommo-dated* 122) in *Gaudete* or briefly mention "Lumb's sexual exploits" (Scigaj, *Ted Hughes* 91) which appear in the "comic episodes" as "erotic farce" (Gifford and Roberts, *A Critical Study* 162; for full citations, see notes 5–7 below). Even in an article with a promising title by Edward Larrissy, "Ted Hughes, the feminine and *Gaudete*," the author only discusses Lumb's ability to "fascinate and inflame women" (*Critical Quarterly*, ns. 25.2 [1983]:38).
3. Ted Hughes, *Gaudete* (New York: Harper and Row, 1977). Hereafter cited in text.
4. Peter R. King, *Nine Contemporary Poets: A Critical Introduction* (London: Methuen, 1979), 142.
5. Terry Gifford and Neil Roberts, *Ted Hughes: A Critical Study* (London: Faber and Faber, 1981), 155; hereafter cited as Gifford and Roberts.
6. Leonard M. Scigaj, *Ted Hughes* (Boston: Twayne, 1991), 86.
7. Ekbert Faas, *Ted Hughes: The Unaccommodated Universe* (Santa Barbara: Black Sparrow Press, 1980), 215; hereafter cited as Faas.
8. See any of the book-length studies with substantial sections on *Gaudete*, such as Sagar (see note 22), Gifford and Roberts, Scigaj, or Faas.
9. Terry Gifford and Neil Roberts, "Hughes and two contemporaries," in Keith Sagar, ed., *The Achievement of Ted Hughes* (Athens: University of Georgia Press, 1983), 96.

10. Gifford and Roberts argue that Hughes is not interested "in the continuity of the lives" of the characters in *Gaudete* (168), and that the book is "grossly reliant on caricature and the stereotypes of outdated popular fiction" (197).

11. "*Gaudete* suggests that Hughes could not write a novel," according to Gifford and Roberts, 168.

12. Terry Eagleton, "New Poetry," review of *Gaudete, Stand* 19 (1978), 78.

13. Terry Eagleton in "Myth and History in Recent Poetry" sees the absence of History not only as symptomatic of Hughes's work, but also of much contemporary "mythic" poetry: "Myth provides a measure of freedom, transcendence, representativeness, a sense of totality; and it seems no accident that it is serving these purposes in a society where those qualities are largely lacking." Michael Schmidt and Grevel Lindop, eds. *British Poetry Since 1960*, (Oxford: Carcanet Press, 1972), 239.

14. Although they qualify their enthusiasm for the entire "anointing" scene, Gifford and Roberts do see it in a potentially positive light: "Perhaps the description of Mrs. Holroyd . . . can be seen as a rather bold attempt to represent an organic unity with the natural environment. . . . It is significant that it is the women . . . who attempt to exercise their own 'control and decision' by contact with nature" (160).

15. Sandra M. Gilbert and Susan Gubar, *The Madwoman in the Attic* (New Haven: Yale University Press, 1979), 160.

16. John Berger, *Ways of Seeing* (London: Penguin, 1972), 51; hereafter cited as Berger.

17. Elaine Scarry, *The Body in Pain: The Making and Unmaking of the World* (Oxford: Oxford University Press, 1985), 46.

18. Craig Robison also observes that Lumb ironically reinforces those social values that he came to dismantle: *Ted Hughes as Shepherd of Being* (Cambridge: Cambridge University Press, 1978), 85. In addition, Lumb's inability to get beyond society has also been used as an excuse for Hughes's reproduction of oppressive hierarchies; Peter King claims: "If [Hughes's] expression of the unity of being that he desires is much less in evidence, it is because as a man and a poet he writes from within our divided nature." *Nine Contemporary Poets*, 151.

19. "Our own response is that a genuine power is unleashed, which the women are utterly unprepared to cope with." Gifford and Roberts, 185.

20. Jane Flax, *Thinking Fragments: Psychoanalysis, Feminism, and Postmodernism in the Contemporary West* (Berkeley: University of California Press, 1990), 215.

21. Robert Bly, *Sleepers Joining Hands* (New York: Farrar, Straus, Giroux, 1983), 48.

22. Keith Sagar, *The Art of Ted Hughes*, 2nd. ed. (Cambridge University Press, 1978), 209.

23. Seamus Heaney, *Sweeney Astray* (New York: Farrar, Straus, Giroux, 1983), 4.

24. Irene Claremont De Castillego, *Knowing Woman: A Feminine Psychology* (Boston: Shambhala, 1990), 178.

25. In fact, several critics interpret *Gaudete*, and especially the "Epilogue," as "signifying a reconciliation with the departed spirit of Sylvia Plath." Leonard M. Scigaj, *Hughes*, 95. See also Edward Larrissy, "Ted Hughes," 39.

26. In a letter to Leonard Scigaj, Hughes claims that the poem's subject is not Plath; this claim is certainly suspect for those familiar with the "vase" image in Plath's "Poem for a Birthday."

Cave Birds: Hughes's Progress of the Masculine Soul

NEIL ROBERTS AND TERRY GIFFORD

Cave Birds is, we believe, Hughes's finest book to date. It is certainly his most consistent—only a few of the twenty-eight poems are open to radical criticism—and several poems, certainly "The executioner", "The knight", "Bride and groom" and "The risen", are among Hughes's greatest achievements. The terror that is essential to its subject, the hero's transformation, is never far removed from a sense of splendour, and a promised or actual joy. Hughes permits himself a much greater richness of language than in Crow, yet the poems are more disciplined than many in the earlier sequence. The "living, suffering spirit, capable of happiness"[1] emerges from the reductive questioning of Crow as a subject of celebration, and the metaphysical discovery hinted at in Crow's final poems—the discovery of the universal in the self—is the basis of Cave Birds. The authenticity of this celebration is the fruit of the rigours of the earlier sequence.

Cave Birds was first presented to the public in a "performance" at the Ilkley Literature Festival in May 1975, shortly followed by a broadcast on BBC Radio 3. Ten of the poems, with accompanying drawings by Leonard Baskin, were published in an expensive limited edition at the same time, and most of the other poems appeared in various magazines, often with revisions, between 1974 and 1976. The text published by Faber in October 1978 contains two fewer poems than the broadcast version, and also lacks the brief narrative links that Hughes provided for the broadcast.[2] With one exception, each poem is accompanied by a Leonard Baskin drawing.

The Faber edition also informs the reader that Cave Birds is an "Alchemical Cave Drama". Each one of these words is likely to be puzzling to many readers. Hughes's use of the word "alchemy" refers to the aspect explored by C. G. Jung in his numerous writings on the subject: the mystical transformation, or rebirth, that occurred within the alchemist in the course of the outward operation. This idea of transformation is the most important link, though there are also more detailed correspondences with alchemical writings, such as the symbolic flaying ("A flayed crow in the hall of judgement")

Reprinted in condensed, definitive form from Ted Hughes: A Critical Study (London & Boston: Faber & Faber, 1981), Chapter 7. By permission of the authors.

and dismemberment ("The accused") and, most prominently, the symbolic marriage of body and soul.

The word "cave" is also likely to puzzle readers as it does not occur anywhere in the text. To us it suggests both the inwardness of the drama, its location in the "cave" of the protagonist's being, and the mysterious, frightening character of caves—the likelihood, perhaps, of encountering in them just such awesome mutations as we see in Baskin's drawings.

Thirdly, in what sense is a sequence of poems, however much written in character, a "drama"? It is perhaps helpful to remember that most of Hughes's plays have been written for radio, and that in his two published adult plays, "The Wound" and "Eat Crow", the suitability of the medium is evident, since almost the entire action takes place within the protagonists. *Cave Birds* is a drama of inner voices, not of action but of reaction, taking place as much between individual poems as within them.

Although at Ilkley the drawings were projected on to a screen during the performance, what is most difficult to reconcile with the dramatic character of the work is the vital relationship between the poems and drawings. Most of the drawings were done before the poems, and the poems originated as responses to the drawings. Dates are written on many of the drawings, and these help the reader to distinguish the earlier ones which inspired their accompanying poems from those which were done later as illustrations. These later drawings, we think, are inferior (the illustration to one of the finest poems, "Bride and groom", is particularly disappointing) but the earlier ones, such as "The summoner", "The interrogator", "The plaintiff", "The gatekeeper" and "The owl flower", are integral parts of the sequence. In some cases the poems cannot be understood without the drawings. Unless one recognises Baskin's interrogator as a vulture, for example, it is impossible to understand the sustained metaphor of the poem.

In the most extreme case, "The owl flower", the poem has to be seen, in the first place, as a poem *about* the drawing. This is perhaps the most magnificent of all the Baskins, and drawing and poem work as a single imaginative unit. Baskin's luminous figure suspended, off-center, in blackness, seems to be hurtling towards the looker from the depths of space: "Big terror descends." The poem, which in isolation would be an incomprehensible accumulation of arbitrary images, is in fact focussed unremittingly on this disturbingly ambiguous figure. It dramatizes the poet's response, its images suggesting his attempts to control the terror by fixing the figure with familiar natural images. Flames, blossom, plumes, a leaf, wounds, tongues: all these things can be seen in the figure but none suffices, and in the end their proliferation draws attention to the ambiguity. This attempt to control the power of the figure is most evident in the lines

> A leaf of the earth
> Applies to it, a cooling health.

It is of course the poet who is "applying" the outline of a leaf to the figure, and applying it also to his own heated and disturbed imagination.

This is not to say that the poem is just a series of notes in the margin of the drawing. The contradictory attributes that Hughes sees in the figure are those of nature itself: the creative and destructive heat of the sun, the coolness of a leaf, the softness of petals and the hardness of stone, the fruitfulness of sap and pollen, the deathliness of wounds. The figure seems at one moment comforting, the next frightening; it even seems to be scared itself by its own radiance. In the context of the "drama" (it is the penultimate poem) it is both the transformed protagonist and what, as a consequence of his transformation, he sees in the world.

We begin to see that the poems characteristically work at more than one level, and that these "levels" are linked. In most cases a reading begins by tracing the poet's response to the drawing, but one's final understanding is enhanced by the fact that this is also the experience of a persona who has undergone several stages of a transformation, in which changes in himself are paralleled by changes in his awareness of the nature of things. Other poems are simultaneously accounts of real experience—in particular, death and sexual love—and stages in a symbolic adventure.

The sequence begins with a kind of psychic trauma in which the hero's complacent view of the world and his place in it is shattered by the visitations of various terrifying bird-beings who confront him with the evidence of his material nature and mortality. His own ego is symbolized (in the drawing of "The accused") by a cockerel. He is taken on a journey into himself, the first stage of which is a classic process of death and rebirth. The death is both the destruction of the complacent ego and a full conscious realization of his own actual physical death. He is changed from a cockerel to a "flayed crow in the hall of judgement". After an interlude in which he is offered and rejects various illusory heavens he enters the second major stage, the symbolic marriage with a female who is both his hitherto imprisoned daimon or inner self and the spirit of material nature. The last poem, an apotheosis of the transformed hero as a falcon, is followed by a brief Finale which undermines any complacent sense of finality the reader may have about the process we have been taken through.

The sequence opens with a striking poem, "The scream," which immediately confirms that this book is an extension of the central concerns of Hughes's work. The tone of the opening lines suggests that the first-person voice of the poem is a persona:

> There was the sun on the wall—my childhood's
> Nursery picture. And there was my gravestone
> Which shared my dreams, and ate and drank with me
>   happily.

The tone catches a too-easy acceptance of the nature of things that amounts to glib complacency in its expression. The happy acceptance of the hero's own death is childishly expressed, indicating no distinction between his response to this and his response to what he sees as a world without tensions. What begins as naivety becomes callousness at the point when the hero's response to violent death is a self-satisfied cosmic generalisation:

> When I saw little rabbits with their heads crushed
> on roads
> I knew I rode the wheel of the galaxy.

His easy praise is prevented by the part of his nature that he has failed to take account of and which therefore appears to be autonomous:

> The scream
> Vomited itself.

What is released by the scream in this first poem is to be the evidence and the focus of the accusation in the trial which is heralded by the appearance of the summoner in the following poem. The confidence that Hughes has in this first poem, which we feel to be justified, is indicated by the omission of the narrative introduction to the broadcast of *Cave Birds*: "The hero's cockerel innocence, it turns out, becomes his guilt. His own self, finally, the innate nature of his flesh and blood, brings him to court."

The first six lines of "The summoner" are clearly a response to Baskin's drawing, although this is not to suggest that the images work only in a visual way:

> Spectral, gigantified,
> Protozoic, blood-eating.
>
> The carapace
> Of foreclosure.
>
> The cuticle
> Of final arrest.

When Hughes uses a technical word like "foreclosure" it is usually in a quite precise way. In this case it indicates the threat of dispossession, since a foreclosure is a barring of the right of mortgage redemption upon non-payment of dues. The threat has clear implications for the hero, whose complacency has been a non-payment of dues to the material world and to that part of his own material nature which surfaced in the scream. Thus the threat of the summoner has always been there, if only at the fringe of the hero's consciousness.

"The interrogator" is one of those poems which derive their wit from the image on the page opposite. When the reader sees that this bird is a vulture the wit of the title can be seen at work in the precision of the poem's images. In stripping a body the vulture is doing the sun's work of reduction ("The sun spies through her. Through her// He ransacks the camouflage of hunger"), and what is revealed is the material nature of humanity, "a dripping bagful of evidence." In the lines,

> Some righteous angered questions
> Agitate her craw

Hughes merges the animal and the human to typically sardonic effect, producing a sinisterly menacing image of an interrogator. It is the word "righteous" which makes the very literal insistence on the hero's mortality so powerfully suggestive. His response to the interrogator, however, in "She seemed so considerate", is a morbid obsession with the fact of death, although the only "fellow creature" he still cares for is his "pet fern." The fern is dead, evidence that, in the words of the interrogator, the protagonist's "world has died". These words have a double meaning. His illusion of reality (expressed in "The scream") has been destroyed, and for him the death that he formerly shrugged off has become a horrific, ever-present reality: "their heads sweated decay, like dead things I'd left in a bag / And had forgotten to get rid of." The "cancelling" of his world produces an apathy that incidentally foreshadows his own death and rebirth: "Whether dead or unborn, I did not care."

Obviously judgement is what the hero is now waiting for, and the judge is appropriately the next figure in the sequence. But who is to sit in judgement and what can the concept of judgement mean in the material universe? Hughes's meditation on Baskin's fine drawings sets up a dense maze of paradoxes.

> The pondering body of the law teeters across
> A web-glistening geometry.
>
> Lolling, he receives and transmits
> Cosmic equipoise.
>
> The garbage-sack of everything that is not
> The Absolute onto whose throne he lowers his
> > buttocks . . .

This poem must present something of a shock to the reader, in that the judge is clearly different from the other "legal" figures. This figure is an abstraction ("The pondering body of the law") who is at the same time a physical denial of abstractions. Previous figures have represented aspects of the natural world that demand fear and awe, but this parody appears to challenge the narrative. It is not until one recognises the voice of the hero from "The scream" that this poem's place in the narrative can be seen. This figure results from an attempt to reconcile two conceptions of nature. First there is the idea that a figure presiding over the universe is preserving equilibrium. The concept of pure balance lies behind the sort of expression the hero used in "The scream" ("I knew I rode the wheel of the galaxy"), just as it underlies "web-glistening geometry" and "cosmic equipoise." Against this conception is the voracious view of nature represented by the judge's gluttony. The judge seems to think that his fat buttocks will sit with dignity on the throne of the Absolute. The capital letter betrays the grand illusion at the centre of the parody.

The wit of the poem draws attention to the fact that these two conceptions of nature cannot be reconciled. A concise phrase like "A Nero of the unalterable" sums up the poem's parody of a presiding figure maintaining balance over what are in fact the unalterable workings of physical processes. In effect the poem is saying that there can be no judge since "judgement" is irrelevant to a description of material processes. The poem acts as a warning early in the sequence that the figures be seen, not as independent controlling forces but as representatives of the hero's own physical nature.

This is true of the figure who appears in the next poem, "The plaintiff", who is presented entirely through a sequence of precise and vital metaphors embodying a burning core of vitality:

> This bird
> Is the life-divining bush of your desert
>
> The heavy-fruited, burning tree
> Of your darkness.

Hitherto imprisoned in the darkness of the self unacknowledged by the protagonist, it has been roused by the trial:

> Your heart's winged flower
> Come to supplant you.

This creature is significantly female, anticipating a later stage in the hero's experience. The hero is aware that this process of supplanting or cancelling has started, since his next speech is begun in what he knows to be his "fading moments" and ends in a powerful image of his rejection by the world:

> The whole earth
> Had turned in its bed
> To the wall.

The hero's claims to be living a life that is the opposite of complacent ("How close I come to a flame / Just watching sticky flies play" etc.) are transparently desperate exaggerations that betray their own falsity. The special pleading of his claim to be an "imbecile innocent" only draws attention to his guilt. In fact the voice of the plaintiff seems to prevent the hero from saying these things because she is murmuring the evidence of his guilt from the depths of his inner life:

> Right from the start, my life
> Has been a cold business of mountains and their snow
> Of rivers and their mud.

Her metaphors indicate her unity with the material world and suggest that the warming moments of his outer life are no protection against inward processes. As in "The plaintiff" Hughes finds images that suggest many dimensions to the connection between the inner life of the hero's material reality and the processes at work in the natural world. The forces of the hero's material nature now cut through the "anaesthetic" of his own outer life, swell like the waters of "snow-melt," and close it. The pathos of this moment is beautifully caught in a reversal that presents his death from his own perspective. For him it is the natural world that has died and rejected him.

In "The executioner," which follows, the reader is invited and encouraged, step by step, to contemplate his/her own non-being. The poem has a rhetorical structure directed to this end, of which the incantatory effect produced by its repetitions is only the most obvious feature.

> *The executioner*
>
> Fills up
> Sun, moon, stars, he fills them up
>
> With his hemlock—
> They darken
>
> He fills up the evening and the morning, they darken
> He fills up the sea
>
> He comes in under the blind filled-up heaven
> Across the lightless filled-up face of water

The executioner begins by unravelling, or cancelling, the Biblical account of the first three days of Creation. All the images in these lines, apart from the hemlock, refer directly to Genesis 1:1–18 and draw from the force of its rhythm and imagery in reversing the process. But suddenly in a terrifying

implacable dream-world vision the poem moves closer to our intuitive awareness of the death that is part of us:

> The tap drips darkness darkness
> Sticks to the soles of your feet.

The final stage draws simultaneously on several levels of suggestion. The
mirror and the cup are domestic details with strong folklore resonances: the
shock (as in "Crow's Vanity") of no longer seeing one's own face in the
mirror; the poisoned chalice. What is movingly created from these lines
onwards is the feeling of the helpless drift into non-being: "You touch him".

In the context of the *Cave Birds* sequence it can be seen that the
overwhelming sense of non-being that the poem communicates in isolation
is balanced by the developing use of the word "filling" (with its hint of
fulfilling) towards the moment at which death is also rebirth: "It feels like
the world / Before your eyes ever opened." In context the significance of
these lines is heightened by the conclusion of the earlier poem, "She seemed
so considerate": "Whether dead or unborn, I did not care." It is, however,
only by so convincingly suggesting the experience of actual death that the
poem can work effectively as part of a symbolic drama of death and rebirth.

"First, the doubtful charts of skin" starts as a perfunctory journey
through the hero's body, parts of which seem deliberately obscure, but the
hero then moves into a landscape which recalls the archetypal landscape of
the folklore of quest, and specifically Eliot's use of it in *The Waste Land*:

> In this decayed hole among the mountains
> In the faint moonlight, the grass is singing
> Over the tumbled graves, about the chapel
> There is the empty chapel, only the wind's home.
> It has no windows, and the door swings,
> Dry bones can harm no one.
> Only a cock stood on the rooftree.

The cockerel-hero of *Cave Birds* enters, via his own body, a strikingly similar
place:

> I came to loose bones
> On a heathery moor, and a roofless church.
>
> Wild horses, with blowing tails and manes,
> Standing among graves.
>
> And a leaning menhir, with my name on it.
> And an epitaph, which read:
> "Under this rock, he found weapons."

This discovery, and the concept it represents, is central to the magnificent and pivotal poem, "The knight." If the hero's finding weapons in his own grave suggests that he must discover his own subjection to death and that this knowledge strengthens his life, it is the quality of that subjection and the completeness of that power which constitute the achievement of "The knight."

The discipline of the poem's central metaphor (Baskin's drawing tells us that the "knight" is a dead bird) permeates the tone of the poem so that complete submission to the process of death achieves a still knowledge of unity with the material universe:

> *The knight*
>
> Has conquered. He has surrendered everything.
>
> Now he kneels. He is offering up his victory
> And unlacing his steel.
>
> In front of him are the common wild stones of the
> earth—
>
> The first and last altar
> Onto which he lowers his spoils.

And that is right. He has conquered in earth's name. The "conquest" of the knight is without irony: the simple statement and its dignity of "rightness" expresses the achievement of accepting his own death as an actual contribution to the earth itself. The quiet celebration of his own body's physical decay is here the product of a discipline of consciousness. It is in this sense that the knight's bones are his weapons. In the final stanzas the implications of this achieved state of consciousness are indicated in the completeness of the self and the sense of oneness with the processes of the universe:

> the skull's beauty
>
> Wrapped in the rags of his banner.
> He is himself his banner and its rags.
>
> While hour by hour the sun
> Strengthens its revelation.

To the knight the sun's revelation is that he is unified with the material universe. In the alchemical sequence such a revelation will become embodied in a new persona for the hero. Perhaps this is what is glimpsed in the form of the eagle-hunter at the end of the next poem, "Something was happening".

In this poem a man passes "vacantly" through life, dismayed by the recurrence of spring, while a woman suffers:

> As I hung up my coat and went through into the
> kitchen
> And peeled a flake off the turkey's hulk, and stood
> vacantly munching
> Her sister got the call from the hospital
> And gasped out the screech.
>
> And all the time
> I was scrubbing at my nails and staring through the
> window
> She was burning.

In context, the poem asks to be read as a "naturalistic" version of the relationship between the protagonist and the female who haunts the narrative in one aspect as the interrogator, in another as the plaintiff, and who is most fully identified in "A riddle" in which, among other accusations, she says "As you saved yourself / I was lost." In fact this poem can be seen as the relationship of "A riddle" exemplified in an actual incident which is also a summary of the narrative so far. Having ignored the suffering of the female figure, the hero finds himself cancelled by the world: "The earth, right to its far rims, ignored me." The poem concludes:

> Only the eagle-hunter
> Beating himself to keep warm
> And bowing towards his trap
> Started singing
>
> (Two, three, four thousand years off key.)

The song of the eagle-hunter hints at the hero's transformation—finding the voice of the self that is in tune with the elements to which he is also subjected—his "bowing towards his trap" suggests a nature that is both reverent and practical. It is not until later in the sequence that the new form of that song can be discovered for the hero. At this stage it must remain archaic, in tune with the primeval dimension in which the resilient natural self of the eagle-hunter lives.

The process of rebirth, then, is begun in the poem "The gatekeeper" which repeats in a series of generalizations the points established in a less dogmatic way in earlier poems. In the next poem the hero is flayed, a transformation motif that Jung remarks on in his commentary on the visions of the alchemist Zosimos the Divine.[3] In the words of Lawrence's Birkin, the hero must "cease to be, for that which is perfectly [himself] to take place in [him]."[4] The opening of this poem, "A flayed crow in the hall of judgement," superbly re-creates the sensations suggested by Baskin's drawing:

> Darkness has all come together, making an egg.
> Darkness in which there is now nothing.
>
> A blot has knocked me down. It clogs me.
> A globe of blot, a drop of unbeing.
>
> Nothingness came close and breathed on me—a frost
> A shawl of annihilation has curled me up like a new
> foetus.

The complete integration of images of non-being with the spark of re-creation they contain is perfectly suggested by the womb-darkness, the bloodclot that is also the "globe" of life, the frost that curls leaves and creatures into a foetal shape, and the water-drop image of reduction and source. The questions which the hero then starts to ask develop the consciousness which is at the mercy of processes outside itself.

> Do purposeful cares incubate me?
> Am I the self of some spore?
>
> In this white of death blackness,
> This yoke of afterlife?
> What feathers shall I have? What is my weakness good
> for?

The final questions of the poem strongly recall Hamlet's famous speech:

> If it be now, 'tis not to come; if it be not to come, it will be now; if it be not now, yet it will come. The readiness is all. Since no man has aught of what he leaves, what is't to leave betimes? Let be.[5]

Hamlet's condition in the final act of the play is perhaps a useful analogue to this stage in the cockerel's transformation. If we can see the condition of Shakespeare's hero not as a paralysed fatalism but as a recovered and enlarged sense of self, deriving from an acknowledgement of his subjection to forces outside himself, it should be possible to respond similarly to the fatalistic implications of Hughes's sequence.

> I shall not fight
> Against whatever is allotted to me.
>
> My soul skinned, and the soul-skin laid out
> A mat for my judges.

The hero's rebirth is followed by a pair of poems in which a figure who claims to be his "guide" offers him a choice of illusory heavens which he experiences and rejects.

> Here is the heaven of the tree:
> Angels will come to collect you.
> And here are the heavens of the flowers:
> These are an everlasting bliss, a pulsing, a bliss
>   in sleep.
>
> And here is the heaven of the worm—
> A forgiving God.
> Little of you will be rejected—
> Which the angels of the flowers will gladly collect.
>   —"A green mother"

This is a paradisal vision that de-natures earth and blurs the distinction between the this-worldly and the other-worldly. The poem's irony is evident in a splendid example of Hughes's mordant wit:

> In none of these is the aftertaste of death
> Pronounced poor.

In the following poem the hero actually finds himself in one of these heavens, which is reminiscent of the *Songs of Innocence* and Shelley's visions of a regenerated earth in *Queen Mab* and *Prometheus Unbound*:

> They were so ecstatic
> I could go in among them, touch them, even break
>   pieces off them
> Pluck up flowers, without disturbing them in the
>   least.
> The birds simply flew wide, but were not for one
>   moment distracted
> From the performance of their feathers and eyes.
> And the animals the same, though they avoided me
> They did so with holy steps and never paused
> In the glow of fur which was their absolution in
>   sanctity.
>   —"As I came, I saw a wood"

This illusion offers as a redemption a return to the state of complacency with which he started. We are reminded of the repeated warnings in the *Tibetan Book of the Dead* that the various deities encountered in the Bardo state are illusions created out of the dead person's "thought-forms". What enables the hero of *Cave Birds* to recognize and turn away from the illusion is the remembrance of his own carnivorous nature:

> But a voice, a bell of cracked iron
> Jarred in my skull
>
> Summoning me to prayer
>
> To eat flesh and to drink blood.

These are perhaps the most straightforward of the *Cave Birds* poems. They serve as a warning that the transformation is not an abolition of nature's predatoriness and destructiveness. They form an interlude between the re-birth and the second stage of the transformation, which begins with "A riddle". The female who speaks here dominates the rest of the sequence. She is clearly identical to the plaintiff—"the life-divining bush of your desert"— who informed the hero that "Right from the start, my life / Has been a cold business of mountains and their snow / Of rivers and their mud." Here she appears both as accuser and as corrective to the illusions of the Green Mother: the world into which this mother will deliver the hero is "a changed, unchangeable world / Of wind and of sun, of rock and water", and he will be delivered into it "To cry" (whereas the Green Mother "has wiped her child's face clean / Of the bitumen of blood and the smoke of tears"). This world is changed only to the hero's perception, and what he perceives is, in fact, that it is unchangeable.

This figure who, for want of a precise word, we call the hero's daimon, is the compensatory sufferer for the triumphs of the conscious self: she is what pays the price for the hubristic claims of the ego ("As you chose your direction / I was torn up and dragged"). But since she is also nature itself she is indestructible, and always available to take over after such a process of ego-destruction as the hero has undergone. "A riddle" is the first of a group of four poems which, in the context of the sequence, celebrate a symbolic marriage between the hero's conscious self and a female who repre-sents the natural processes both within and outside him. To a certain extent this poem is dependent on the sequence, and some readers may think that, in isolation, the speaker's assertion that she is daughter, bride and mother to the protagonist is a pretentious pseudo-mystical paradox. These relation-ships can be articulated however. It is the hero's task to bring this being to conscious birth, but he is obviously dependent on her for his existence and, moreover, the birth of the daimon is for the hero himself a rebirth from which he emerges radically changed. The "marriage" between the two is the achievement of wholeness: both a union between the divided parts of himself and a sense of belonging in the world.

In the superb poem "Bride and groom lie hidden for three days" the lovers "bring each other to perfection": both a real act of love and an achievement of this twofold wholeness. In the union celebrated in this poem each creates the other, so that the marriage is a synthesis of the mother-son and daughter-father relationships. At the same time it is a self-sufficient love poem celebrating, in a delicate and original way, the sense of coming into possession of a new body through sexual union. The sustained mechanical metaphor that runs through it is not reductive, any more than Donne's famous lines, "If we be two we are two so / As stiff twin compasses are two"[6] or even the Song of Songs, "the joints of thy thighs are like jewels, the work of the hands of a cunning workman."[7] Hughes has found a fresh language with which to treat what might have been thought an overworked subject. He escapes the sentimental, quasi-religious, tired poetic effect of limiting the treatment of love to metaphors drawn from the organic world. He shows that it is possible to describe the human body as a machine and still find it a thing of wonder. He undermines, in short, the conventional habit of regarding machinery as something the very thought of which threatens one's most intimate experience. This language is also much more resonant than might be expected. It contributes to the simplicity and innocence of newly-created beings discovering themselves, and to the sense of the lovers as craftsmen surprised and delighted by their own skill.

In this group of poems (which also includes "His legs ran about" and "After there was nothing there was a woman") it is impossible and unnecessary to make a rigid distinction between the levels of meaning. Sexual union is a metaphor for wholeness of being and oneness with the world; it is also both a cause and a consequence of wholeness and unity. Interlocking, as it were, with this group is another group that deals directly, in individual terms, with the transformed nature of the protagonist. The reader's attention is made to alternate between these complementary groups so that the way one reads "The guide," for example, is influenced by the marriage group, and influences our reading of that group in turn. The poem was earlier titled "A true guide," emphasizing the contrast with the false guide of "A green mother."

> Where the snow glare blinded you
> I start.
> Where the snow mama cuddled you warm
> I fly up. I lift you. . . .
>
> I am the needle
>
> Magnetic

> A tremor
>
> The searcher
> The finder

This is the first of the bird-figures that has nothing terrifying, absurd or equivocal about it. Its straightforwardly beneficent nature indicates, of course, the change that has taken place in the hero. The guide seems to represent the achievement of an intuition, a sure instinct for living, that starts from subjection to the elements. We are reminded of the hero's delivery, by the speaker of "A riddle," into "a changed, unchangeable world / Of wind and of sun, of rock and water" and, from much earlier in the sequence, the plaintiff's words, "Right from the start, my life / Has been a cold business of mountains and their snow / Of rivers and their mud." This transformed condition is further expressed in "Walking bare":

> What is left is just what my life bought me
> The gem of myself.
> A bare certainty, without confection.
> Through this blowtorch light little enough
>
> But enough.

He is integrated into the world in the sense that he does not interrupt its processes; he is a channel for messages that have nothing to do with him; he no longer considers himself the privileged recipient of every sign:

> Hurrying worlds of voices, on other errands,
> Traffic through me, ignore me.

The sequence concludes with "The risen," one of the finest of the poems, whose effect depends on the most subtle relation between levels of meaning to be found anywhere in the sequence, yet whose success entails an ironic reflection on the way the sequence has seemed to develop. Like so many of the best poems, it starts out as a response to the Baskin, which is also one of the best in the book. A falcon stands on broad talons and trunk-like legs, its wings raised but not spread. Behind him, less broad than himself, is a black background, like a doorway that he seems to have come through. In isolation the poem's subject would seem to be simply the falcon, with a shift at the end to the question, whether the bird's splendour and control can ever be attained by a human being: "But when will he land / On a man's wrist." The poem captures, in an almost naturalistic way, the bird's speed, its sudden inexplicable disappearance and emergence somewhere else, and above all the electrifying alteration that takes place in everything within its range of vision, altering nature by simply being there.

> Under his sudden shadow, flames cry out among
> thickets.
> When he soars, his shape
>
> Is a cross, eaten by light,
> On the Creator's face.

"The risen" exemplifies a characteristic style and structure of several of the best poems in the sequence. It moves not so much by development as by accretion. Each couplet has a haiku-like compression and completeness, as if the poet were striving for his subject to be fully present at every point. Consider for example the lines:

> In the wind-fondled crucible of his splendour
> The dirt becomes God.

The density of suggestion, reaching back into the sequence, makes the word "splendour" more substantial than an admiring gesture. "Fondled" suggests that the falcon is the minion of nature's tenderness, but the agent of the tenderness is the wind that also "scours" and "empties" (in "The guide"). And the fondling cannot be separated from the implications of "crucible"— the subjection to the "burning unconsumed" of the bird's own nature, which in turn, of course, brings to mind the phoenix. "Crucible" also recalls the alchemical transformation, and the syntactical ambiguity suggests that the crucible is not merely the receptacle in which the splendour is created, but is the splendour itself. The bird achieves its divinity by being subjected to its divinity—just as the bird-beings to whose terrors the hero was subjected were all aspects of his own nature.

This reminds us that the falcon, too, is an apotheosis of the transformed hero. Or is it? Despite the pervasive bird imagery, the reader becomes accustomed to thinking of the hero as a man, and of the sequence's development as the transformation of a man. This being so, the final couplet

> But when will he land
> On a man's wrist

must come as a shock. It is clearly a challenge to the reader, as much an imperative as a question, a warning against any complacent assumption that reading or writing a poem is a substitute for reality. It is also perhaps a reminder to the poet himself of how natural it is for him to write a poem—

however great—about a bird as the culmination of a human drama. In the text "The risen" is immediately followed by a "Finale":

> At the end of the ritual
>> up comes a goblin

which one cannot help reading as a comment on that final couplet. Hughes has used these words before, in an interview with Ekbert Faas:

> We go on writing poems because one poem never gets the whole account right. There is always something missed. At the end of the ritual up comes a goblin. Anyway within a week the whole thing has changed, one needs a fresh bulletin. And works go dead, fishing has to be abandoned, the shoal has moved on. While we struggle with a fragmentary Orestes some complete Bacchae moves past too deep down to hear. We get news of it later . . . too late. In the end, one's poems are ragged dirty undated letters from remote battles and weddings and one thing and another.[8]

It is admirable that a writer should feel like that about a work as complete and ambitious as *Cave Birds*.

Notes

1.   Introduction to Vasko Popa: *Selected Poems*, Harmondsworth, Penguin, 1969, p10.

2.   These poems are printed in Keith Sagar, ed., *The Achievement of Ted Hughes*, Manchester University Press, 1983, as "The Advocate" (p346) and "Your Mother's Bones" (p348).

3.   See C.G. Jung, *Collected Works Vol. 13: Alchemical Studies*, London, Routlege and Kegan Paul, 1967.

4.   D.H. Lawrence: *Women in Love*, Harmondsworth, Penguin, 1982, p209.

5.   *Hamlet*, Act 5 scene 2.

6.   John Donne, "A Valediction Forbidding Mourning"

7.   The Song of Songs, Chapter 7, verse 1.

8.   Ekbert Faas, *Ted Hughes: the Unaccomodated Universe*, Santa Barbara, Black Sparrow, 1980, pp204–5.

Historical Landscape in Ted Hughes's
Remains of Elmet

PATRICIA BOYLE HABERSTROH

In *Remains of Elmet*, a volume of poems illustrated with photographs by Fay Godwin,[1] Ted Hughes turns to a Yorkshire landscape to create a racial history which places the recent decline of the Calder Valley in an inevitable cycle of natural process and human response to that process. Hughes's headnote describes the latest disaster in the valley in which he was raised:

> Throughout my lifetime, since 1930, I have watched the mills of the region and their attendant chapels die. Within the last fifteen years the end has come. They are now virtually dead, and the population of the valley and the hillsides, so rooted for so long, is changing rapidly.

While Hughes's note and Goodwin's photographs describe a contemporary landscape dotted with abandoned textile mills, the volume of poems suggests that this collapse is the latest version of the disaster highlighted by the book's title: the defeat of Elmet, the last British kingdom to fall to the Angles. By focusing on Elmet, Hughes places the present plight of the Calder Valley in a historical perspective where the modern collapse recapitulates the disaster which occurred as the marauding Angles destroyed the last vestige of Celtic culture.

Hughes makes almost no reference to the specific details of the fall of Elmet; in this case the historical event serves as a signpost for the direction English culture would take in the centuries that followed. Elmet, located in a South Yorkshire valley, was one of two Celtic kingdoms fighting to survive during the Anglian attacks of the sixth and early seventh centuries. These small kingdoms, remnants of the larger Celtic population which had gradually disappeared after the Romans conquered Britain, flourished in Yorkshire where Celtic settlements reappeared as Roman power began to wane. Since it divided northern and southern Britain, Elmet blocked the unification of the invading Angles. Eventually, however, Edwin, exiled brother-in-law of the Northumbrian leader Aethelfrith, seized power after Aethelfrith's death and began to bring together the confederation of lands which eventually

Reprinted from *Clio* 14 (Winter 1985): 137–54, by permission of the author and the journal.

became Anglo-Saxon England. Elmet, having long withstood the Northumbrian pressure, finally yielded when Edwin expelled the Celtic king Certic. Baptized at York in 627, Edwin became the first Christian king of Northumbria. Indeed Bede, who sees Edwin as a great hero who brought peace to the land, mentions a debate in the royal council which brought about the acceptance of the Christian God and the rejection of pagan deities.[2]

While the names of Edwin and Certic never appear in *Remains of Elmet*, readers familiar with Hughes's earlier poetry and prose could anticipate that he would come out on the side of the Celts against Bede's celebration of Edwin's victory. Hughes's inversion of Christian myth and ritual, particularly evident in *Crow* but obvious in much of his poetry, expresses attitudes revealed in a 1964 review of E.O.G. Turville-Petre's book, *Myth and Religion of the North*. Hughes argues that a pre-Christian mythology is part of a life "deeper" and "truer" in the English character "than the Greek-Roman pantheons that came in with Christianity, and again with the Renaissance, severing us with the completeness of a political interdict from these other deities of our instinct and ancestral memory." Of this pre-Christian mythology, Hughes writes: "It's false to say these gods and heroes are obsolete: they are the better part of our patrimony still locked up."[3]

In the imagery of *Remains of Elmet*, Hughes draws upon that ancient mythology. The nature spirits, preeminent in the Celtic culture finally wiped out at Elmet, still lie deep in the English psyche and are beginning to reveal themselves as the valley wrestles free from the domination of the Christian mind. If the fall of Elmet cleared the way for the creation of Anglo-Saxon England and marked the end of Celtic influence, then the present collapse of the valley signals the end of that Christian culture that rose upon the ashes of Elmet. And, as this civilization topples, Hughes pictures the land reawakening: nature exercising her rights to the valley as the mills and chapels crumble.

Hughes does not view himself as unique in his appreciation of pre-Christian culture, arguing that many modern writers "do not seem to belong spiritually to the Christian civilization at all. In their world Christianity is just another provisional myth of man's relationship with the creator and the world of spirit."[4] But like Lawrence, whom he acknowledges having read early in his life, Hughes maintains that English civilization lost its soul when it accepted Christianity's provisional myth. Partial blame for the present tragedy in the Calder Valley can be placed on the culture that superseded Elmet: one which denied fundamental natural instincts and refused to accept an equilibrium between the human and natural worlds which had been at the heart of Celtic culture. Lost with the Celts was a veneration of the power and energy of natural process.

Hughes finds proof for this lack of respect in the history of the Yorkshire landscape after the Celts disappeared. In the centuries following the collapse of Elmet, the invaders settled and shifted, abandoning the Calder Valley which in its decline became known as "The Waste." As Hughes explains in his headnote: "For centuries it was considered a more or less uninhabitable wilderness, a notorious refuge for criminals, a hide-out for refugees." When the valley was once again settled, the farming population gradually evolved into the nineteenth-century industrial society which exploited the land for natural resources needed to build and operate the textile mills. Once again the land was sacked, this time nature subordinated to the demands of technology. Hughes draws a direct line from the early Christian Angles to the nineteenth-century industrialists, seeing the beginning and end of a cycle, the technological abuse of nature a final consequence of the Anglian conversion to Christianity and the latest example of turning the landscape into a waste. For Hughes, however, the ruined mills reveal that that technological society is now doomed, like Elmet, to extinction. Agreeing with Yeats, under whose influence he was "spellbound" for six years,[5] Hughes opts for a cyclical view of history, projecting inevitable change and disruption, foreshadowed presently by the gradual diminishing of the influence of Christianity.

As Hughes focuses on the limitations and consequences of the Christian culture that displaced the Celtic, he suggests that the history of the Calder Valley is bound up in inevitabilities inherent in natural process, inevitabilities de-emphasised in Christian dogma and ritual. Christian civilization grew from a religion whose God's human incarnation, in the figure of Christ, visited earth briefly, but then vanished to preside with the Godhead in an otherworldly paradise. Focus then shifted from the earth to an abstract heaven and hell, and the human drama began to revolve around a life after death, the present often overshadowed by the glow from a future paradise. Soon nature acquired overtones of evil, and the powerful energy inherent in natural process, guaranteeing both life and death, fell under the control of a mysterious but judgmental God who governed the universe and meted out punishment and reward. Rejecting this view, Hughes draws attention back to nature and locates heaven and hell within the visible world. Birth and death, creation and destruction occur as nature and humanity interact in the continuation of process. The potential for loss and recovery resides for Hughes in the known world. Elmet, then, can symbolize both loss, the assimilation of Celtic culture into Anglo-Saxon England, and recovery, those pre-Christian gods waiting to be unlocked as Anglo-Saxon England dies out.

While Elmet can be viewed as the historical prototype of the inevitable collapse of civilizations which thrived in the Calder Valley, the Celtic kingdom, as well as Anglo-Saxon England, fits into a larger context which stretches beyond the borders of recorded history. Both of these civilizations rose and fell in the moraine of a glacier, the prehistoric natural disaster which formed the valley. Because the glacier carved the "last ditch" that Elmet and subsequent cultures flourished in, the moraine holds the remains of the people who lived and died in the valley and becomes the repository of the past history of Yorkshire. The threat of another disaster, symbolized in the poems as another glacier, always hangs over the valley. Historical change, then, illustrated in the rise and fall of Elmet or in the growth and collapse of the modern mills and chapels, is incorporated into a larger cycle of natural process which transcends the limits of recorded history.

Hughes thus creates a poetic history of the Calder Valley ultimately more important for him than a conventional listing of names and dates. In these poems he weaves personal, familial, and racial experiences within the setting of a particular Yorkshire landscape whose face has been transformed from wilderness to populated hillsides many times over. Revealing the causes and effects of these transformations seems to be a major impetus for the poems, one which links past, present, and future in a very particular but ultimately timeless landscape. Hughes's fellow poet Richard Murphy rightly judges that *Remains of Elmet* is neither autobiography nor history, but that it incorporates both.[6]

Autobiography influences to a great degree the emphasis on the inherent wilderness of Yorkshire, a wilderness that ultimately will not be subdued. The mills, so dominant in the landscape of Hughes's youth, are by-products of that rational mind exalted by Christian civilization at the expense of the natural and instinctive. Hughes's linking of mill and chapel symbolizes the fusion of technology and Calvinistic Protestantism which evolved within the Anglo-Saxon culture that replaced the Celtic. Giving priority to mind over instinct, to abstract idea over the "logic of the earth," the builders of these mills and chapels temporarily tamed the wilderness, but, in so doing, sowed the seeds of their own destruction, visible in the ruins now sprinkled across the valley.

Rising in the midst of these ruins, however, the ancient energy of nature reasserts itself, seen most obviously in poems which highlight the wild, natural beauty of the Yorkshire hills. Poem after poem in *Remains of Elmet* reveals "beauty spots" in a landscape Hughes knows well. Explaining his own fascination with such places, Hughes once described their enduring value and the ways in which they connect past with present:

> Usually these places are famous for one thing—they look wild. . . . These are the remains of what the world was once like all over. They carry us back to the surroundings our ancestors lived in for 150 million years. . . . It is only there that the ancient instincts and feelings in which most of our body lives can feel at home and on their own ground. . . . Those prehistoric feelings, satisfactions we are hardly aware of except as a sensation of pleasure—these are like a blood transfusion to us, and in wild surroundings they rise to the surface and refresh us, renew us.[7]

Written long before *Remains of Elmet*, the language of this passage—"remains," "ancient instincts," "rise to the surface"—anticipates both the imagery and theme of this volume and illustrates Hughes's belief that the world around us provides not only our link with the past but also our only hope for the future.

Autobiography also enhances the tone of *Remains of Elmet* as personal memories and experiences of the Calder Valley affect the poet's response. In describing the process at work in the valley, Hughes laments the loss but admires the gain, creating an ambivalence developed in tone, image, and structure. In the collapse of the mills and churches, the beauty and endurance of the natural wilderness are again revealed; but in that collapse a communal tragedy inheres, and for Hughes, by birth attached to that community, loss counterbalances gain. Sacrifice and salvation continually cancel each other out, creating a volume of poetry which succeeds because of the tension between the two. Hughes thus creates a unique poetic history of the valley, linking allusions to remote kingdoms like Elmet to images of the people who presently live in the valley. By choosing to set his poem in the "wildness" of the Yorkshire landscape, Hughes records both the suffering of those about to be swallowed up by the land, and the value of the beauty spots uncovered as the mills disappear, beauty spots that "refresh us, renew us." The landscape supplies a history of this continuing process.

Composing these poems after he had seen Godwin's photographs, Hughes inherited some of his images from her subjects. In earlier collaborations, most notably with Leonard Baskin, Hughes successfully fused his poems with the work of the other artist while simultaneously developing his own unique vision. Such is the case in *Remains of Elmet* where Hughes translates Godwin's photographs of crumbling lumb chimneys, abandoned mills, and church ruins into a poetic image of the misfortune wrought in Yorkshire by the twin forces of Christianity and technology. In a review of Max Nicholson's *The Environmental Revolution*, Hughes explains the impetus behind this image:

> The story of the mind exiled from Nature is the story of Western Man. It is the story of his progressively more desperate search for mechanical and rational and symbolic securities, which will substitute for the spirit-confidence of the Nature he has lost. . . . It is a story of decline.[8]

If effect, modern European civilization, as evidenced in the Calder Valley, has invested its values, hopes, and lives in the spirit of the machines housed in the valley's mills. But this spirit, unlike those that inhabit the natural world, may vanish in the strategic manuevers of technological warfare. "Mill Ruins" records such a disappearance:

> One morning
> The shuttle's spirit failed to come back
> (Japan had trapped it
> In a reconstructed loom

> Cribbed from smiling fools in Todmorden).
>
> Cloth rotted, in spite of the nursing.
> Its great humming abbeys became tombs.

As this poem illustrates, children "Roaming for leftovers" then smashed these tombs and trailed "homeward aimlessly / Like the earliest / Homeless Norsemen." Such invasions and battles, echoing the early invasions of Britain, continue until all that remains are the ruins scattered across the landscape's corpse.

This same battle has been carried on, on another front, by English Christianity which ritualizes abstraction while it "deposes Mother Nature,"[9] worshipping paracletes instead of real birds. Christianity evolved into one of its most extreme forms in the Methodism of Yorkshire, a religion Keith Sagar describes as a repressive Calvinism which "bred strong values" but also produced "a self-righteous and self-denying puritanism, and an aggressive self-congratulatory materialism and philistinism"[10]—fertile ground indeed for the fruits of the Industrial Revolution. Hughes reveals his own response to this religion in the poem "Mount Zion" where the speaker describes his early sense of deprivation: the blackness of the church wall blocking the moon above the kitchen window. Marched off to church, the speaker remembers the "mesmerized commissariat" whose cry "Beat itself numb again against Wesley's foundation stone." The final image of this poem highlights the Church's suppression of the natural world. A cricket, hidden in the church wall, sends out a cry—nature's song rising above the congregation's hymn. But this disturbing noise must be silenced, and the speaker remembers:

> Long after I'd been smothered in bed
> I heard them
> Riving at the religious stonework
> With screwdrivers and chisels.

Recurring images of blocking and smothering make concrete Hughes's condemnation of the Church's success in denying worshippers the beauty and sustenance nature can offer.

For Hughes, however, human force will be conquered as nature asserts its power. In the upper reaches of Top Withens, as Godwin's photograph reveals, the pioneers' stone dwellings are crumbling, "And the swift glooms of purple / Are swabbing the human shape from the freed stones." The wild heather, spreading across the moors, recovers the hills that men had built on, burying the very stones with which the hill walls and human dreams were realized. And in battles like this, another poem tells us, "Heather only toughens" . . . "listening / . . . For the star-drift / Of the returning ice." In lines like these, Hughes suggests that the heather, in its battle with the other elements, also faces annihilation when the returning ice, another glacier or equivalent disaster, bears down again upon the Calder Valley. This cyclical history of gain and loss, dominated by uncontrollable forces which must always be respected, encompasses not only the landscape, but also, in Yeatsian terms, the rise and fall of civilizations that live in that landscape. While Hughes admires, celebrates even, the remarkable power and indifference of the natural elements, he does not ignore the toll of human loss and suffering inherent in such a cycle.

The major effects on the valley of the combined force of technology and organized religion are pictured in *Remains of Elmet* in two major patterns of imagery, both describing vividly the battle between the wildness and freedom of the natural world and the restrictions imposed by the rational application of abstract principles—this battle another reflection of the Celtic-Christian-Anglo-Saxon conflict. Images of enclosure and subsequent paralysis prevail: the walling-in of land, whether hill walls which fence in farms, mill walls where machines governed human life, or church walls which both literally and metaphorically close off nature and the instinctive life. "Hill Walls" documents the first stages of this struggle, where the early farmers, "Exhilarated men," tamed the hills of the Calder Valley as they carved their farms across the body of the land:

> The great adventure had begun—
> Even the grass
> Agreed and came with them,
> And crops and cattle—

But now, as Godwin's pictures of crumbling hill walls show, only the remnants of those enclosures remain: "No survivors./Here is the hulk, every rib shattered." And even while these farmers lived, Hughes insists in another poem, walls restricted them; "Spines that wore into a bowed/Enslavement" only temporarily mastered the hills:

> Their lives went into the enclosures
> Like manure. Embraced those slopes
> Like summer cloud-shadows. Left
>
> This harvest of long cemeteries.

As the most recent example of that historical process of enclosure which fenced in the English countryside, the Yorkshire mills and chapels become for Hughes a fitting symbol of the disastrous effects of such action.

To develop the imagery of enclosure, Hughes uses, again and again, the square, a geometric figure imposed by the human mind on nature. This figure appeared across the Yorkshire landscape as "pioneer hope" squared stone: "To be cut, to be carted / And fixed in its new place." The stone "let itself be conscripted / Into mills. And it stayed in position / Defending this slavery against all." Inside those mills, however, workers soon also "Stayed in position, fixed like stones" until "they too became four-cornered, stony," hardened against "the guerrilla patience / Of the soft hill-water" by the work that the mills demanded. The very rocks of the valley, free and wild in the natural landscape, imprisoned the valley inhabitants within the walls of the textile mills until they became:

> A people fixed
> Staring at fleeces, blown flames.
>
> A people converting their stony ideas
> To woven weave, thick worsteds, dense fustians
>
> Between their bones and the four trembling quarters.

That enclosing, squared stoniness tainted not only the mills but also the churches. In a poem facing Godwin's photograph of Heptonstall Old Church, Hughes chronicles the history of the church's influence upon the people of the valley:

> A great bird landed here.
>
> Its song drew men out of rock,
> Living men out of bog and heather.
>
> Its song put a light in the valleys
> And harness on the long moors.

Like the hill walls, however, the "hard foursquare scriptures" eventually "fractured" and the "cracks filled with soft rheumatism."

Enclosure and imprisonment paralyzed the valley, a condition reflected in Hughes's metaphors of arthritic and rheumatic diseases, the final, crippling impotence before the inevitable demise of the present generation. Throughout the volume, Hughes pictures the valley as the gullet of the glacier which continues to swallow settlements which have sprung up there. The trench that the valley has become holds now the remnants of the paralytic life of the mill towns: "The arthritic remains/Of what had been a single strength." This paralysis appears most vividly in the lonely people of the valley, cut off from the land and waiting for the end:

> The mantel clock ticks in the lonely parlor
> On the heights road, where the face
> Blue with arthritic stasis

And heart good for nothing now
Lies deep in the chair-back, angled
From the window-skylines
Letting time moan its amnesia
Through the telegraph wires

As the fragments
Of the broken circle of the hills
Drift apart.

The telegraph wire, symbol of technological advancements in communication, isolates these people from the land, accelerating the debilitation that has set in. People like these, "angled / From the window-skylines," suggest a parallel with the defeated Celts, who were also "angled" and trapped as English history moved along.

The disastrous effects of technological progress recur in the images of *Remains of Elmet*: lorries rumbling over a shaky canal bridge, silenced sewing machines and shuttles, jets overhead, acid rain from "Manchester's rotten lung." In "When Men Got to the Summit," Hughes juxtaposes allusions to historic victories for control of the valley (men reaching the summit symbolizing at least temporary control and success) with the modern feat of anchoring a television antenna high on the summit of a hill rock. Such juxtapositions present ironic victories, however, for the men who reach the summit are inevitably defeated. The television set, which "blinked from the wolf's lookout," represents progress, but it also shuts people off from the beneficial effects of daily intercourse with the natural environment and traps them in those four-squared houses now beginning to crumble.

Hughes has sounded this note in his earlier poetry, and Stuart Hirschberg explains the poet's analysis of the cause of the problem:

A man first determines the laws by which nature governs herself and then invents "numbers and equations and laws" which direct nature's laws against nature herself. In the process of exploiting the earth for her material wealth and beating her into submission man has undermined and poisoned his own existence. . . . But, of course, mother-earth's revenge is that when she goes, man goes with her.[11]

Progress which led ultimately to collapse victimized the Calder Valley, and the landscape now absorbs the arthritic remains of a culture lulled into paralysis by the sound of machines, a people

That fell asleep

Under migraine of headscarves and clatter
Of clog-irons and looms

> And gutter-water and clog-irons
> And clog-irons and biblical texts.

When the looms shut down, however, the ancient energy of the earth re-emerges, freeing rock that had been cut and tamed for mills and churches, tumbling down the enclosing walls, resurrecting and renewing a dead land. Counterpointing the images of disease, decay, and death in *Remains of Elmet*, those of birth and regeneration bring one into a reborn kingdom and a new church, a free and wild natural world where walls and squares no longer prevail. This world has been continually developing in Hughes's poetry: it is one where the goddess Nature presides. Hughes has described it in an earlier poem, "A Riddle," as the "changed, unchangeable world / Of wind and of sun, of rock and water." These four images again create in *Remains of Elmet* a world which, free from the limitations of technology and religion, furnishes the only antidote to the world of abstractions. In a 1967 review of the poetry of Vasko Popa, Hughes warns that we must invest our hopes in something deeper than what is lost if civilization disappears,[12] and he illustrates in *Remains of Elmet* that that something is the beauty and permanence of the natural world. Against the backdrop of the prototypical Elmet, a kingdom over which nature spirits presided, Hughes pictures a timeless Calder Valley, a place of "a hill beyond a hill beyond a hill" and "a day beyond a day beyond a day beyond a day."

In *Remains of Elmet* Hughes presents this world, as he has done in *Gaudete, Cave Birds*, and *Crow*, in the imagery of Christian ritual. By secularizing Christian symbols, Hughes creates a non-Christian paradise centered in the natural world. The sacramental value of this world unfolds in the image patterns. An alternative to the abstractions of Christianity, and to the death and destruction produced by the scientific mind, a sacrosanct world of light, stone, water, and wind will, Hughes argues, sustain the soul when all else fails:

> They are
> The armour of bric-à-brac
> To which your soul's caddis
> Clings with all its courage.

Caddis, a fabric binding, ironically evokes the looms and mills to which the spirit of the Calder Valley has clung too long, and Hughes offers here, in place of that spirit, a new kind of binding to the earth. Drawing once again on the image of battle, Hughes pictures the combatants courageously holding on, like the last Celts in Elmet, armoured with nature's "bric-à-brac." Even though they eventually face death, these people participate in natural process rather than subvert that process through machines which exploit the land and then rust from disuse.

The celebratory tone developed by this imagery balances the bleakness created by the images of enclosure and decay, and the continual juxtaposition of contrasted images and tones energizes *Remains of Elmet*. Counterpointing the disintegrating world of the Calder mills and churches is an earthly paradise centered in "Bridestones": "Holy of holies—a hill-top chapel. / Actually a crown of outcrop rock—/ Earth's heart-stuff laid bare." This world furnishes all the necessities for religious celebration. "The Big Animal of Rock" (captured in Godwin's photograph of a giant rock jutting out of the landscape) offers tribute to the great Earth-Mother whose power over human life must be witnessed:

> Here
>
> At the Festival of Unending
> In the fleshly faith
> Of the Mourning Mother
> Who eats her children
>
> The cantor
> The rock,
> Sings.

Likewise, the tree, "A priest from another land," suffering in an endless battle against heather, stone, and wild water, offers itself as a testament to the physical and spiritual energy in the landscape: "Transfigured, bowed—/ The lightning conductor / Of a maiming glimpse—The new prophet." Quiet, natural enclosures like Hardcastle Crags serve as this world's temples in a paleolithic, silent valley where "the god lives" amid the "Meditation of conifers" and "the beech-tree solemnities."

Over and over again in this volume, Hughes invests trees, wind, water, and rock with sacramental value, the rock and stone symbolizing endurance ("a world / Of busy dark atoms / Inside the live wreathed stone"), the water, fluidity. In this changing, unchanging world, energy circulates to recharge the receptive landscape. Moving "out of nothingness into nothingness," the landscape undergoes a perpetual cycle of sacrifice, as "The light, opening younger, fresher wings / Holds this land up again like an offering," and resurrection, as it "Stretches awake, out of Revelations / And returns to itself."

Hughes leaves no doubt that the grandeur of such a world far surpasses the paradises of organized religions and indeed can be a compensation for death and destruction. The poem, "The Long Tunnel Ceiling," illustrates such compensation. A lorry carrying wool and cotton rumbles over the canal bridge, dislodging a brick, the first hint of the bridge's inevitable collapse suggesting also the decline of the entire valley. But as the brick hits the water and disappears below the surface, a trout appears—a miraculous emissary from another world. The fish, which had been carried from the upper hill streams into the town canal, provides a momentary, natural vision: an "ingot," a "treasure" of another kind. The trout displaces the brick, as it were, bringing with it the possibility of new life: "A seed / Of the wild god now flowering for me / Such a tigerish, dark, breathing lily / Between the tyres, under the tortured axles." Here the canal provides the speaker with a vision of another world, a world beneath the surface, under the soon-to-collapse bridge. Such moments are Hughes's epiphanies.

As these images demonstrate, water symbolizes permanence, connecting past to present. The water in the town canals recalls the glacier which inundated the valley, and, even though presently, as evidenced by Godwin's photographs, that water may be reduced to rivulets over cobblestone streets, the canal still offers trout and loach, remains of the "Prehistory of the canal's masonry." From the disastrous fullness of the glacier to the trickle in the street, water endures, linking the past to the present even as it foreshadows the inevitable disaster of the future:

> Heather is listening
> Past hikers, gunshots, picnickers
> For the star-drift
> Of the returning ice.

For Hughes the earth provides more gratification than the human mind can invent, the magical sound of cock-crows over the whole valley, the "time-long Creation" of hills, the high sea light which "Heaven glows through." The Word of this paradise becomes "The Word that Space Breathes," the sounds of the natural world and the singers therein. Gods and demons co-exist in this landscape, and visions come in moments when the world reveals its "beauty spots."

Revelations also come in dreams, as the last poem in the volume, "The Angel," demonstrates. In this poem Hughes draws on the imagery of the book of Revelation where the angels illustrate both the effects of God's wrath and his promise of salvation. The dreamer in Hughes's poem, however, sees not the Christian messenger of God, but rather an omen for the human loss that death represents. When the dreamer asks his mother if the angel is a blessing, her answer turns "the beauty to terror," and his ultimate revelation is of the finality of death, not the possibility of an afterlife:

> When next I stood where I stood in my dream
> Those words of my mother,
> Joined with earth and engraved in rock,
> Were under my feet.

The angel in this final poem does not reveal St. John's New Jerusalem, the heavenly city gained after a struggle on earth (and a city St. John describes as "foursquare"). For Hughes the earthly struggle and the recognition of death are the dark side of a physical world which continually renews itself. Hughes's mother's spirit lies buried under his feet, in the Calder Valley, not in St. John's city of God. Allusions to a dead mother in this last poem recall the opening poem in the volume, dedicated to Hughes's mother, where the poet sees her image in his uncle's face:

> He has brought me my last inheritance,
> Archeology of the mouth,
> Treasures that crumble at the touch of day—

His uncle's approaching death foretells the loss of his inheritance; it will be buried with all the preceding generations of Yorkshire: "Any moment now, a last kick / And the dark river will fold it away."

The poet, then, must accept this inheritance, hear the Word, capture the last songs of the present singers of a "lost kingdom" before they disappear as natural process claims human lives. In so doing he will "save" them and preserve with his voice the voices of the past. Writing in 1970, Hughes argued that artists could create their own paradises from the world around them:

a vision of the real Eden, "excellent as at the first day," the draughty radiant Paradise of the animals, which is the actual earth, in the actual Universe: he may see Pan, whom Nietzsche mistook for Dionysus, the vital, somewhat terrible spirit of natural life, which is new in every second. Even when it is poisoned to the point of death, its efforts to be itself are new in every second. [13]

As the poems in *Remains of Elmet* show, Hughes's vision of paradise includes change, loss, and death. One of the most beautiful poems in the volume, opposite a photograph of an old hill man looking down over the smokey valley, reverberates with Hughes's typical ambivalence, capturing the beauty of a dying generation's song:

> The map of their lives, like the chart of an old game,
> Lies open before them.
> Their yarning moves over it, this way and that,
> Occupying the blanks.
> Mills are missing. Chapels are missing.
> But what has escaped the demolisher
> Clings inside their masks—
> Puppets of the graveyard's dream.

> Attuned to each other, like the strings of a harp,
> They are making mesmerising music.
> Each one bowed at his dry bony profile, as at a harp.
> Singers of a lost kingdom.
>
> Wild melody, wilful improvisations.
> Stirred to hear still the authentic tones
> The reverberations their fathers
> Drew from these hill-liftings and hill-hollows
> Furthered in the throats.

Continually in *Remains of Elmet* Hughes associates words with stone, the durability of both counteracting the series of changes the valley has gone through. In this poem the singers of a lost kingdom are the poet's links to the past, the "authentic tones" of their ancestors and their "yarning" surviving long after the mills and chapels are gone, preserving some sense of permanence in the midst of change and handing on their inheritance to the future. In a poem like this one, Hughes confirms Yeats's judgment that "an aged man is but a paltry thing unless . . . Soul clap its hand and sing."

In confronting death and destruction, Hughes has always believed, as his earliest poems illustrate, that the imagination brings the outer and inner worlds into harmony:

> The inner world, separated from the outer world, is a place of demons. The outer world, separated from the inner world, is a place of meaningless objects and machines. The faculty that makes the human being out of these two worlds is called divine. [14]

Writing of János Pilinszky, whose poetry exposes the violence and terror of post-war Europe, Hughes insists that out of Pilinszky's poetic confrontation with horror, redemption is won:

> The very symbols of the horror are the very things he has redeemed. They are not redeemed in any religious sense. They are redeemed, precariously, in some all-too-human sense, somewhere in the pulsing mammalian nervous-system, by a feat of human consecration: a provisional, last-ditch "miracle" which we recognize, here, as poetic. [15]

Hughes's use of religious terminology is telling: miracles, redemption, are not only possible but also more meaningful when achieved through poetry. "Ghastliness and bliss are strangely married" in Pilinszky's poetry, but of this marriage, healing is born.

Hughes's judgment of Pilinszky's work gives some clues to both the motivation and the method of *Remains of Elmet*. Pilinszky's is a deeply personal response to a social situation which could easily give rise to despair, one to which silence might serve as the best comment. But Hughes's response to this poet serves to illustrate his faith in the redemptive value of poetry. With words "manifestly crammed with meaning," a "Universe of Death" can be redeemed. When we look at what Hughes has done in *Remains of Elmet*, we realize that these words apply to his poetry as well as to Pilinszky's.

There is no doubt that Hughes's personal sense of the Calder Valley adds a humanizing element to these poems. When the cemetery is not only symbolically the valley that consumes everything that grows in it, but also the family graveyard where "Thomas and Walter and Edith . . . Esther and Sylvia" are buried, personal loss heightens the community tragedy. This volume focuses on a landscape and a people faced with annihilation, but it is a place and people Hughes knows well, and this personal connection with the valley underpins his artistic expression of the tragedy taking place. Yet the time he spent in the valley also put him in touch with the wild beauty of the Yorkshire hills, allowing him to see beyond the surface to the enduring value of all that remains in the landscape. *Remains of Elmet* is a transitional volume in this respect; it falls between *Gaudete* whose mythic structure plots, in perhaps too detached a way, the downfall of Reverend Lumb, an Anglican minister who dies at the hands of forces he tries to repress, and the more successful elegies in *Moortown*, which memorialize the death of Jack Orchard, Hughes's father-in-law and a Devon farmer. In confronting so personal an outer world, by imagining the Calder Valley as a vast repository of lives spent in continuous battle, and the history of the valley as the social dimension of the natural cycle of birth, growth, and destruction, Hughes does indeed create a complex volume of poems.

The appropriate metaphor here is poet as archeologist, not surprising given Hughes's training at Cambridge in archeology and anthropology. One of the poems in *Remains of Elmet*, "The Ancient Briton Lay Under His Rock," focuses on the problem involved in the need to uncover the past and the corresponding impossibility of completely discovering it. The poem pictures a group that goes digging because they "needed that waft from the cave / The dawn dew-chilling of emergence, / The hunting grounds untouched all around us." Like the others buried in the Calder landscape, the Ancient Briton is a testament to his own time, an enduring witness to the past. Though his body cannot be recovered, "his pig-headed rock existed. / A slab of time, it surely did exist. / Loyal to the day, it did not cease to exist." Typically, the rock, the natural marker, survives the man, anchored in the landscape long after the human body disintegrates. As the searchers dig, however, the rock falls into the hole: "It escaped us, taking its treasure down." In the final lines of the poem, the searchers are left, laboring in "the prison" of their eyes, their sun, their "Sunday bells."

This poem recapitulates the predominant images of the volume: treasures and people buried in the landscape, the mysteries of rock and sun, the enclosing prison, the "stinging brows" laboring within range of the church bells, the people in the valley whose faces and voices hint of earlier generations. Ironically what is confirmed here is the mystery; all the digging leads the group to a typical Hughes paradox: a past which "did not cease to exist" but "lay beyond us." Out of this paradox, the structure of *Remains of Elmet* emerges.

The mysteries of time and death lie at the heart of this volume; they are introduced in the dedicatory poem where Hughes's mother's memory lives in his uncle's hands, "Keeping their last eighty years alive and attached to me." But the image of the uncle simultaneously signals the end, a theme repeated in the final poem where the Angel of Death appears "Low over Hathershelf" only to disappear "behind Stoodley, / Under the moor." The ominous words of the speaker's mother in this last poem, not specified though nevertheless understood, are that "something disastrous" which the entire volume reveals. The words of the dreamer's mother are engraved in rock under his feet, and her tombstone becomes the modern equivalent of that rock that marks the burial place of the Ancient Briton. Both of these, moreover, are linked to all the others in the graveyard that the Calder Valley has become, including those last Celts who died at Elmet. People are attached thus in *Remains of Elmet*, and the message from the past, for the present and the future, the overwhelming mystery human beings must confront, is their own death. To accept this is to acknowledge their part in the drama of natural process, and for this acceptance, nature offers as compensation a worldly paradise before death.

The tension Hughes maintains between two views of Calder, a dying valley in the last siege of the current battle, and a land stretching itself awake while the ancient energy renews it, creates the ambivalence central to an understanding of these poems. In achieving this, Hughes avoids the one-sided response which gave rise to the accusation that his earlier poetry celebrated violence, and deals with the complexity of living in a world where dynamic energy creates and destroys. In drawing upon the personal dimensions of life in the Calder Valley, Hughes can see the human abuse of the earth and the tragic helplessness of people at the mercy of natural forces. Not only do machines destroy nature, but nature destroys itself: "lets what happens to it happen." But Hughes can also reveal the wild, natural beauty of the Yorkshire valley that he knows so well, and it is important to notice that "what happens" can also give us a vision of the earthly divine. While Hughes sings of many lost kingdoms, his song celebrates what remains in the Calder Valley and in the world beyond that valley.

Notes

1. *Remains of Elmet* (London: Faber and Faber, 1979).
2. Bede, *The Ecclesiastical History of the English Nation*, trans. Michael Maclagan (Oxford: Basil Blackwell, 1949), 2:175–77.

3. *Listener*, 19 March 1964, 484–85.

4. Ekbert Faas, "Two Interviews Conducted by the Author," *The Unaccommodated Universe* (Santa Barbara: Black Sparrow Press, 1980), 205.

5. Faas, 202.

6. *New York Review of Books*, 10 June 1982, 38–40.

7. Ted Hughes, "Writing About Landscape," *Poetry in the Making* (London: Faber and Faber, 1967), 76.

8. *Your Environment* 1 (1970): 81–83.

9. *Your Environment*, 81–83.

10. Keith Sagar, *The Art of Ted Hughes* (New York: Cambridge Univ. Press, 1975), 7.

11. Stuart Hirschberg, *Myth in the Poetry of Ted Hughes* (Totowa, New Jersey: Barnes and Noble Books, 1981), 110–11.

12. *Tri-Quarterly* 9 (1967): 201–205.

13. *Your Environment*, 81–83.

14. Ted Hughes, "Myth and Education," in *Writers, Critics, and Children*, ed. Geoff Fox et al. (New York: Agathon Press, 1976), 77–94.

15. Ted Hughes, "Introduction," *János Pilinszky, Selected Poems*, trans. Ted Hughes and János Csokits (Manchester: Carcanet New Press, 1977).

"How Precisely the Job Can Be Done": Ted Hughes's *Moortown*

Carol Bere

At fifty, Ted Hughes is no longer the wunderkind of British poetry, the angry young man squaring off against the patricians of the literary establishment. But whether personal tragedy or the natural attritions of time have— or could—pacify him is another issue. He has been likened to Lear stalking the heath, his blistering rage challenging the quixotic elements. And everything about Hughes gives shape to this image: the towering physical presence; the resonant voice, a seeming fount of power only marginally contained; the outsized linguistic gifts—at times, stamped with unmistakable authority; at other times, a turbulent avalanche of overwrought images.

It is not surprising, then, that critics rarely harbor neutral feelings toward Hughes's poetry. He has been dismissed as a connoisseur of the habits of animals, his disgust with humanity barely disguised; labeled a "voyeur of violence," attacked for his generous choreographing of gore; and virtually written off as a cult poet, the private preserve of those specialized in arcane areas of mythology and Jungian psychology. Still others consider him to be the best poet writing today—admired for the originality and command of his approach; the scope and complexity of his mythic enterprise; and the apparent ease and freshness with which he can vitalize a landscape, free of any mitigating sentimentality.

And the poetry provides sufficient corroborating evidence for all of these claims. For what we are faced with in Hughes is a poet whose very strengths generate their own built-in possibilities for excess. It is precisely the wide range of his risk-taking—his constant assault on what Geoffrey Hill calls the "recalcitrance of language"—that makes works such as the highly original *Crow* and even such unwieldy endeavors as *Gaudete* both provocative as well as problematic. Hughes's despair with the ability of language to convey varied states of feeling is self-evident and, at times, the poetry may founder on the "titanic extravagance" of his verbal gymnastics. Still, to read the compelling title sequence of the recently published *Moortown* is to be reminded once again of his remarkable ability to suggest the interrelationships between all areas of life—the beauty and the tragedy inherent in the simple

Reprinted from *Literary Review* 24 (Spring 1981): 427–34, by permission of the author and the journal.

fact of existence. When Hughes writes like this, I wonder if anyone could have said things better.

Since the publication of *Wodwo* in 1967, Hughes's poetry seems to have developed along two relatively distinct lines, although obviously both are the product of the same complex poetic vision, the "same knot of obsessions" as Hughes would say. These lines express Hughes the mythmaker embarked on what has been referred to as a large-scale spiritual quest and the English nature poet who is very much of his time and his place. Although Hughes's mythology is far too large a subject to explore here—and presently there is much toiling in the vineyards of criticism unraveling Hughes's complicated handling of myth—I might mention that the working out of his mythological undertaking begins in some of the poems in *Wodwo* such as "Logos" and moves through *Crow, Gaudete, Cave Birds* and, perhaps, more glancingly, *Prometheus on His Crag*. The nature and animal poems, clearly inscribed with Hughes's preoccupations and often charged with a volatile restlessness, emerge in the early volumes, *The Hawk in the Rain, Lupercal* and *Wodwo* as well as in the later more fully-developed sequences: the magnificent *Season Songs* (ostensibly written for children but should be required reading for all adults); *Remains of Elmet* and, now, the Moortown sequence.

The recently published Moortown volume includes sequences that Hughes has written over the last decade or more: *Prometheus on His Crag*, a twenty-one poem sequence that was published in a limited edition in 1973 and reissued here with only minor revisions; *Earth Numb; Adam and the Sacred Nine*; and the later "Moortown" sequence. With the exception of occasional poems, "Moortown" and the *Prometheus* sequence seem to be the more fully realized works—as well as representative illustrations of the two veins of Hughes's poetry.

There is a new compelling generosity to Hughes's writing in the Moortown sequence, thirty-four poems that center on his farming experiences in Devon. Hughes has always had an enviable ability to dramatize nature, to isolate the vital spirit of life frequently submerged in the routine cares of everyday existence. But often there was a discordant note—a deliberate comouflaging of feeling. In the Moortown poems, though, there is an intense feeling of personal involvement and Hughes's descriptive powers are at their best in poems that open out to comment on the movements of natural process, the life and death cycles of the universe.

Recently, Stephen Spender remarked on what he considers to be the American and English qualities of Hughes's writing: "The American to me would be the kind of turned-on, confessional aspect of Hughes, the violence really. The English would be that he is still very much a nature poet. . . . Of course American poets write nature poetry, but not in the same way. English nature poetry has a more rooted quality, more the feeling that the poet lives in the landscape, has always lived in the landscape."[1] Leaving aside Spender's debatable assignment of violence, I might comment that this feeling of familiarity, of belonging, informs much of Hughes's most powerful nature poetry. It is not a vision of nature as a healing, restorative power in the Wordsworthian sense; rather, it is a feeling of at-oneness, of a developing sense of the equal susceptibility of both man and nature to the seemingly unknowable movements of the higher forces of the universe. The stark opening poem, "Rain," dramatizes the painful vulnerability of the almost defenseless farmland and its inhabitants, perpetual victims of the tireless assaults of wind and rain:

> Rains. Flood. Frost. And after frost, rain.
> Dull roof-drumming. Wraith-rain pulsing across purple-bare woods
> Like light across heaved water. Sleet in it.
> And the poor fields, miserable tents of their hedges.
> Mist-rain off-world. Hills wallowing
> In and out of a gray or silvery dissolution. A farm gleaming.
> Then all dull in the near drumming. At field corners
> Brown water backing and brimming in grass.
> Toads hop across rain-hammered roads. Every mutilated leaf there
> Looks like a frog or a rained-out mouse. Cattle
> Wait under blackened backs. We drive post holes.
> They half-fill with water before the post goes in.

Or, consider "March Morning Unlike Others" with its sympathetic portrait of the earth, fragile in its recuperation from the grim ravages of winter:

> The earth invalid, dropsied, bruised, wheeled
> Out into the sun,
> After the frightful operation.
> She lies back, wounds undressed to the sun,
> To be healed.
> Sheltered from the sneapy chill creeping north wind,
> Leans back, eyes closed, exhausted, smiling
> Into the sun. Perhaps dozing a little.
> While we sit, and smile, and wait, and know
> She is not going to die.

And the bludgeoning strokes that characterize some of Hughes's animal poems are gone as he describes the difficult process of "Dehorning," the painful death-in-life struggle of the lamb in "February 17th," or the child's sighting of the dead lamb in "Ravens." Here, a potential occasion for sentimentality is forestalled by a quick shift of perspective and the poem concludes with an observation that seems exactly right:

> "Did it cry?" you keep asking, in a three-year-old field-wide
> Piercing persistence. "Oh, yes," I say, "it cried."

Though this one was lucky insofar
As it made the attempt into a warm wind
And its first day of death was blue and warm
The magpies gone quiet with domestic happiness
And skylarks not worrying about anything
And the blackthorn budding confidently
And the skyline of hills, after millions of hard years,
Sitting softly.

Certainly, as I have already intimated, the most striking quality of "Moortown" is the personal strain, Hughes's own sense of the passing of time. The recent *Remains of Elmet*, set in his native Yorkshire, recalls a steady catalogue of deterioration—of the erosion of the land and the inevitable loss of personal relationships. Here, again, the sense of the relentless encroachments of time with its attendant personal losses is urgent. In "Coming Down Through Somerset," for instance, Hughes's response as he spies a dead badger on the road is uncharacteristically plaintive:

                    I want him
To stay as he is. Sooty gloss-throated,
With his perfect face. Paws so tired,
Power-body relegated. I want him
To stop time. His strength staying, bulky,
Blocking time. His rankness, his bristling wildness,
His thrillingly painted face.
A badger on my moment of life.
Not years ago, like the others, but now.
I stand
Watching his stillness, like an iron nail
Driven, flush to the head,
Into a yew post. Something
Has to stay.

Perhaps the most stirring evocation of loss can be found in the beautifully crafted final cluster of poems that form the elegy to Jack Orchard, Hughes's father-in-law and farming partner. Written with a quiet simplicity and candor, the poems are ways of remembering—ways of being in touch with a man whose seeming indestructibility was leveled ironically by the singled-minded incursions of cigarettes. In "The Day He Died," feelings of loss are all-inclusive:

The bright fields look dazed.
Their expression is changed.
They have been somewhere awful
And come back without him.
The trustful cattle, with frost on their back,

Waiting for hay, waiting for warmth.
Stand in a new emptiness.

From now on the land
Will have to manage without him.
But it hesitates, in this slow realization of light,
Childlike, too naked, in a frail sun,
With roots cut
And a great blank in its memory.

And I am taken with the sad muted note of "Hands," the moving concluding poem of the sequence:

Hands more of a piece with your tractor
Than with their own nerves,
Having no more compunction than dung forks,
But suave as warm oil inside the wombs of ewes,
And monkey delicate

At that cigarette
Which glowed patiently through all your labors
Nursing the one in your lung
To such strength, it squeezed your strength to water
And stopped you.

Your hands lie folded, estranged from all they have done
And as they have never been, and startling—
So slender, so taper, so white,
Your mother's hands suddenly in your hands—
In a final strangeness of elegance.

To move from Hughes's affecting elegy to *Prometheus on His Crag* (the sequence immediately following "Moortown") requires an emotional shift in gears that seems far too abrupt. Perhaps one should only read the volume at designated intervals. For *Prometheus* is a complex, demanding—sometimes problematic—work that also asks some knowledge of Hughes's treatment of myth. The obvious question of exotic specialization surfaces again and the only defense can be that, despite some vagaries of structure, *Prometheus* is rewarding. Basically, the sequence is an outgrowth of Hughes's collaboration with director Peter Brook's group, the International Center for Research in 1971. At that time, he wrote *Orghast*, an experimental dramatic piece that was both the title of the work as well as the composite language to be spoken by the actors at the Shiraz Festival in Persepolis. Like Hughes, Brook had long been preoccupied by the inability of the English language to convey shared emotions. Thus, *Orghast*, was conceived as a one-time experiment: an attempt to explore the roots and physiology of speech and, hopefully, abridge the tenuous relationship between dramatic presentation of a work and audience response.

Hughes began with a narrative that was something of a mosaic: myths such as the Prometheus story, philosophical writings, and interpolations of other dramatic pieces—works that, like *Prometheus*, probe the complex choices involved in notions of freedom and imprisonment. Clearly, the Prometheus myth with its story of the acquisition of fire, man's route to deliverance—or liberation through knowledge—is the connective tissue of the themes. Hughes had been working on the *Prometheus* poems at the same time that he was writing *Orghast* and the two works seem to be linked by his complicated approach to myth itself. A.C.H. Smith, a writer who accompanied Brook and Hughes to Persia, has commented that Hughes envisioned the story as being enacted within the physiology of man:[2] in short, a direct endorsement of the relationship between poetry and biology. An elaborate diagram sketched by Hughes indicates the parts of Prometheus' body in which the events of the myth took place. And, if I take Hughes correctly, the lyric sequence seems to closely parallel the conception of myth outlined in *Orghast*. Also, many of the concerns of Hughes's poetry over the years can be found in his treatment of the Prometheus myth: the threatening bird of prey, similar to Crow, who must be confronted; the concentration on the female principle; the notion that the birth of the son threatens the position of the father. And the idea of the divided self, or mind at war with nature can be found in Hughes's early animal poems as well as in the later more fully-articulated sequences. Hughes's Prometheus is not particularly introspective. He has none of the fury or hate of Aeschylus' Prometheus who rages at his fate. Nor does he have the majestic sweep of Shelley's Prometheus. Rather, he assesses his condition squarely with neither rancor nor recrimination; he raises the eternal Promethean questions about the relative nature of power and wisdom, or good and evil in the universe; and with neither assurances nor clear-cut resolutions, he makes the necessary leap of faith, toward reintegration, toward a positive transcendence of the self.

Although connected thematically, the lyrics appear to be spare, self-enclosed units which are occasionally undermined by jarring syntactical constructions—the blending of the abstract and the concrete that has become something of a trademark of the later poetry. Interior monologues of Prometheus interweave in a somewhat arbitrary fashion with more explanatory lyrics that comment on or describe the evolving movements of the myth. Hughes has described the sequence as a "limbo . . . a numb poem about numbness." It is this, but it is also inexact to rest with this definition. For Prometheus also intimates possibilities of reintegration, of rebirth into a higher form. The final poem, for instance, with its beautiful combination of visual and aural effects movingly dramatizes Prometheus' transfiguration—his rebirth and the consequent renewal of all nature. Most striking, perhaps, is the powerful contrast between the marvelous vision of a world sprung alive by the rebirth of Prometheus (in language reminiscent of *Crow*) and the muted, mystical vision of the final stanzas. I quote this lyric in its entirety to suggest once again Hughes's sense of the possibilities of the human spirit:

> His mother covers her eyes.
> The mountain splits its sweetness.
> The blue fig splits its magma.
>
> And the cry bulges.
> And the veiny mire
> Bubbles scalded.
>
> The mountain is uttering
> Blood and again blood.
> Puddled, blotched newsprint.
>
> With crocus evangels.
> The mountain is flowering
> A gleaming man.
>
> And the cloudy bird
> Tearing the shell
> Midwifes the upfalling crib of flames.
>
> And Prometheus eases free.
> He sways to his stature.
> And balances. And treads
>
> On the dusty peacock film where the world floats.

Hughes has spoken of the experiments of *Orghast*, of "trying to teach an actor to become the vehicle for a spirit . . . for those powers much closer to the source, who supply everything that we really want and need. . . ." It is, I think, the acceptance of this spirit that catalyzes Prometheus' transcendence. "When we hear it," remarks Hughes, "we understand what a strange thing is living in this Universe and somewhere at the core of us—strange, beautiful, pathetic, terrible. Some animals and birds express this being pure and without effort, and then you hear the whole desolate, final actuality of existence in a voice, a tone. There we really do recognize a spirit, a truth under all the truths. Far beyond human words. And the startling quality of this 'truth' is that it is terrible. It is for some reason harrowing, as well as being the utterly beautiful thing."[3]

There is no reason to assume that Hughes's direction will change measurably in the future: the mythological quest seems to be in full progress while the nature poems continue to appear in scattered periodicals. His reach is wide, his production formidable. Perhaps what Hughes has written of the poet Laura Riding's efforts to forge a distinct poetic voice can best be said of him, "her poems embody both a search and a discovery of how precisely the job can be done."

Notes

1. *Paris Review*, Winter–Spring, 1980, pp. 142–43.
2. A.C.H. Smith, *Orghast in Persepolis* (New York: Viking Press, 1972), pp. 94–97.
3. Smith, pp. 244–45; quoted from Ted Hughes, "Orghast: Talking Without Words," *Vogue* (UK edition), December, 1971.

Ted Hughes' Quest for a Hierophany:
A Reading of *River*

BO GUSTAVSSON

Ted Hughes is a mythic poet of the first rank. He uses myth in order to penetrate into the central problems of our age. He sees the poet above all as a mythic quester or shamanistic healer and in his poetry he makes himself into the mythic quester-shaman of our age. His ambition is to diagnose the ills of modern man and to offer a way of healing those ills. In this sense he can be seen as the heir of Yeats and Eliot who both in their own special ways diagnosed the discontents of modern civilization. As many critics have noted, Hughes' poetry is essentially ritual in character: as the shaman or mythic quester the poet embarks on a ritual journey of initiation and regeneration. The function of myth is precisely to reintegrate man through ritual into the sacred order of the universe, and this is also the goal of Hughes' art. *River*, published in 1983, therefore stands as the fulfillment and logical outcome of his whole career because here Hughes finally succeeds in his enterprise to reestablish contact with the sacred order of the universe.

When Hughes was fifteen he read for the first time the book that was to have a decisive influence on his whole career: Robert Graves' *The White Goddess*, first published in 1946. Graves helped Hughes understand the role of myth in poetry and the need to write a new kind of mythic poetry for our age. At Cambridge he studied anthropology and it was during these years that his lifelong interest in myth and folklore started. Later he read such works as Joseph Campbell's *The Hero with a Thousand Faces* and Mircea Eliade's *Shamanism*, two works that profoundly influenced his thinking about the function of myth and ritual. And he repeatedly expressed his ideas about the need for a new mythic poetry in his interviews and essays.

Following Graves, and confirmed in his belief by reading Joseph Campbell and Mircea Eliade, Hughes argues that, living in a materialistic and secular civilization, modern man has lost touch with his spiritual roots. He is spiritually lost, or worse still, he is spiritually dead. By exiling himself into his own intellect, the modern version of the Fall according to such

Reprinted from *Studia Neophilologica* 59, no. 2 (1987): 209–16, by permission of the author and the journal.

cultural anthropologists as Campbell and Eliade, man has caused the alienation and the death of his own soul. This is the disease of modern life that the poet as shaman or mythic quester somehow has to heal by reestablishing contact between man and nature, between the mental and the spiritual, the conscious and the unconscious.

It is then possible to understand the impetus behind Hughes' work as the mythic quest for the sacred ground of being. The myths that he wants to revitalize are the oldest myths of mankind dealing with the Great Goddess or the Great Mother. These myths concern the initiation into the mysteries of the Great Goddess, the Earth Mother, who represents the archetypal ground of being. In *The Hero with a Thousand Faces* Campbell argues that there is a mythic pattern, he calls it "the monomyth," underlying all mythologies and religions: the mythic quester's descent into the underworld, his initiation, and return.[1] The hero descends into the underworld, where he goes through a series of difficult initiations on "the road of trials," whereupon he finally returns to this world with the redemptive knowledge for his community. There is a close parallel here with the shaman's descent into the underworld in search of a cure for the sick soul of an individual or a whole community.[2] Campbell's mythic pattern of descent, initiation, and return serves very well for understanding the mythic enterprise in Hughes' poetry. Seeking to regain contact with the sacred Hughes descends in his early work into the unconscious and into nature, and in his later work he goes through a series of initiations that finally lead to the long-sought for illumination in *River*.[3] The mythic pattern of descent, initiation, and return therefore helps us better grasp the development of Hughes' mythic poetry.

In his first three books, *The Hawk in the Rain* (1957), *Lupercal* (1960), and *Wodwo* (1967), Hughes descends into the archetypal realm of nature and the unconscious. It must be emphasized that the mythic journey takes place on two planes simultaneously; it is both an inner journey and a journey into nature. In this poetry of mythic descent the poet as shaman or mythic quester enters a desolate, elemental landscape of stones, wind, and rain that seems to exist beyond man, inasmuch as man here is reduced to nothingness. This archetypal landscape is of course a landscape of the soul where the mythic quester meets a series of animals, representatives of the elemental forces of nature and the unconscious. He meets among others a hawk, an otter, a bear, and a wolf. These animals represent different aspects of the Great Goddess as "the Lady of the Beasts," to adopt Erich Neumann's terminology in his study of the archetype of the Great Mother.[4] The wonderful thing about these animals is that they are at one with their environment and their own nature: they are pure instinct in action. But they are also terrifying and it is through terror and awe that the mythic quester first glimpses the mystery of being. The poem "Hawk Roosting" presents the destructive, predatory nature of existence, the death instinct or Thanatos:

> I kill where I please because it is all mine.
> There is no sophistry in my body:
> My manners are tearing off heads—
>
> The allotment of death.
> For the one path of my flight is direct
> through the bones of the living.
> No arguments assert my right:
>
> The sun is behind me.

The poem "An Otter," on the other hand, expresses the gracious, fluid character of existence, the life instinct or Eros:

> Brings the legend of himself
> From before wars or burials, in spite of hounds and vermin-poles;
> Does not take root like the badger. Wanders, cries;
> Gallops along land he no longer belongs to;
> Re-enters the water by melting.
>
> Of neither water nor land. Seeking
> Some world lost when first he dived, that he cannot come at since,
> Takes his changed body into the holes of lakes;

The difficulty lies in reconciling these two opposing views of life, and Hughes did not succeed in doing so until the writing of *River*.

Crow, published in 1970, stands as the culmination of Hughes' early career. The creation of the Crow-figure is a unique imaginative achievement. Through the Crow-figure the mythic quester in Hughes' poetry takes on the qualities of the trickster, a common character in folklore and myth all over the world. As the trickster Crow, that supreme master of survival, the mythic quester manages to live in the destructive, elemental realm of nature and the unconscious. But the Crow-figure cannot gain redemptive knowledge, he cannot be illuminated because he lacks the ability to change and develop spiritually. To become illuminated the mythic quester must go beyond mere survival by undergoing the painful ritual of the purgation of the soul. According to Campbell, this stage in the mythic quest represents the nadir of the mythical round and it is moreover a necessary preliminary before entering on the sacred ground of being.[5] In mystical terms this stage corresponds to the mystic's Dark Night of the soul, a stage in the mystic journey when the mystic feels wholly abandoned by God enduring the purgation of his will prior to his union with the divine.[6] In the two books published after *Crow*, *Cave Birds* (1978) and *Gaudete* (1977), Hughes as mystic quester undergoes the ritual of the purgation of the soul. The aim of this ritual is the spiritual transformation of the poet: the death of his old self and the birth of a new spiritual self. However, it takes yet another group of poems, the title sequence of *Moortown* published in 1979, before Hughes has finally undergone the ritual purgation of the soul that will lead to spiritual illumination in *River*. "Moortown" is written in the form of a diary recording the events on a farm in Devon. The poet here participates in the natural ritual of the cycle of seasons as acted out by the work on the farm. By participating in this ritual round of farming he becomes attuned to the ultimately harmonious rhythms of life.

If *Crow* stands as the culmination of Hughes' early career, *River* can be said to form the culmination of his later career. A comparison of the two books throws light on Hughes' development since the publication of *Crow*. The tone of the Crow-poems is of a desperation shot through by a wry humor and irony. The combination of desperation and humor is new in Hughes, as shown for instance in this poem ("Crow Tyrannosaurus"):

> Creation quaked voices—
> It was a cortege
> Of mourning and lament
> Crow could hear and he looked around fearfully . . .
>
> Crow thought 'Alas
> Alas ought I
> To stop eating
> And try to become the light?'
>
> But his eye saw a grub. And his head, trapsprung, stabbed.
> And he listened
> And he heard
> Weeping
>
> Grubs grubs He stabbed he stabbed
> Weeping
> Weeping
>
> Weeping he walked and stabbed
>
> Thus came the eye's
>   roundness
>   the ear's
>   deafness.

The tone of *River*, on the other hand, is reverential, almost devotional as if Hughes here composes a hymn to life. The poems in *Crow* describe scenes of ruthless violence and amazing feats of survival, whereas in *River* Hughes contemplates the natural flow of life while seeking to approach the sanctuary of existence. The wonder of life is celebrated again and again in these poems and in this they recall an earlier book by Hughes written for children, *Season Songs* published in 1975. *Season Songs* also foreshadows *River* in structure since the book is patterned on the cycle of the seasons.

The deeper motivation of *River* is a search for a hierophany: the manifestation of the sacred in time. This search progresses with the course of the solstitial year or the cycle of the seasons from December to January the following year. The poems of *River* are then structured according to the solstitial year, that archetypal round of existence underlying most mythologies and religions. In *The White Goddess* Graves asserts that the great theme of poetry concerns the birth, life, death, and resurrection of the Spirit or the God of the Year and his relationship with the Great Goddess as the archetypal principle of being.[7] Hughes in *River* takes part in the ritual of the solstitial year in order to gain the redeeming knowledge of his mythic quest. As the title of the book indicates, these poems can be seen to form a contemplation of water which is preeminently the element of spirit. Earlier Hughes in a sense wrote a poetry of earth dealing with the elemental forces of nature and the unconscious, but now he comes to write a poetry of water dealing with the life of the spirit. Water, as Peter Redgrove observes in his review of *River*, symbolizes the secret elixir of life, in fact without water there would not be any life at all.[8] It is therefore very appropriate that the search for a hierophany should be undertaken through a contemplation of water.

In *River* Hughes wins new triumphs as a nature poet. Here he writes poems that in beauty and power surpass anything that he has written before. The content of the book also feels wholly convincing; there is not a trace of contrivance in these poems. Otherwise Hughes' greatest weakness as a poet is a tendency to overdramatize his feelings, which give his poems a certain air of theatricality. But in *River* he simply records his own observations and musings as an enthusiastic fisher of salmon, while becoming on a deeper level a fisher of the sacred. His special achievement is that he uses natural symbols that in an effortless way fuse the natural and spiritual realms. Take for instance the key symbol of the salmon. The book traces the life cycle of the salmon but as a symbol the salmon also stands for the soul's journey to the source of being. Hughes' deep knowledge and love of the salmon serve as a means for attaining a new spiritual awareness that has both personal and general implications. In our secular age Hughes has the courage as well as the ability to take on the archetypal role of the hierophant: the revealer of the sacred. And by so doing he opens up a source of spiritual renewal for modern man.

By following the life of the river and the wanderings of the salmon the poems of *River* recapitulate the different stages of the mythic quest on a higher plane: the mystic journey toward union with the divine. This *unio mystica* stands as the goal of both the mystic way and the mythic quest; the *unio mystica* is usually presented as a sacred marriage, and so it is in *River*. The opening poem of the book celebrates the miracle of the birth of the mythical New Year. Hughes here introduces the light and river imagery, with strong religious connotations, that will recur throughout the book. The beginning of the new solstitial year appears almost as a sacred event or sacred birth and both in tone and imagery the first poem looks forward to the last poem of *River* where another miraculous birth will take place: the birth of salmon. In "The Morning Before Christmas" the poet as mystic quester undergoes an important initiation. Together with eight other men he participates in the semi-religious rite of milking dying salmon for their eggs and milt, a kind of fertility rite.

> A world
> Wrought in wet, heavy gold. Treasure-solid.
> That morning
> Dazzle-stamped every cell in my body
> With its melting edge, its lime-bitter brightness.

The husbandry of these men—they are pictured as priest-like obstetricians— then ensures the continuance of the life cycle of the salmon. By participating in the rite of milking dying salmon the poet is initiated into the life rhythms of the mythic New Year as manifested in the miraculous world of water.

In fact the whole of *River* can be read as one long ritual: the difficult search for a hierophany following the cycle of the seasons. The close observations of nature, that abound in the book, then form part of this ritual quest. Hughes has an intimate knowledge of the life of the river and nothing seems to escape his observant eye. His month-by-month recordings of the life of the river gradually become stages in his quest for illumination because, as Eliade points out, to the questing soul the processes of nature assume spiritual significance.[9] But, as in all quests, there are sudden setbacks followed by as sudden leaps forward in awareness when the illumination sought just seems on the point of occurring. At Easter the poet experiences such a moment of revelation when catching sight of the first salmon cock minnows of the year.

> A stag-party, all bridegrooms, all in their panoply— . . .
>
> In the clatter of the light loom of water
> All singing and
> Toiling together,
> Wreathing their metals
> into the warp and weft of the lit water— . . .
>
> Labouring at earth
> In the wheel of light—

He sees them as part of the sacred order of the universe, picturing them as bridegrooms married to their fate. The image of the marriage of fate will be further developed later on in the book. Fate or destiny is here the bride who turns out to be no other than the Great Goddess in her character as the Goddess of the Wheel of Life or the Goddess of the Great Round. In "Go Fishing" the poet as mystic quester acquires as it were a soul of water in order better to understand the mysteries of the realm of water:

> Join water, wade in underbeing
> Let brain mist into moist earth
> Ghost loosen away downstream
> Gulp river and gravity

His spiritual guide has been a cormorant, a bird that has both a soul of water and a soul of air, in that, diving into water, it becomes a fish, while reemerging again it becomes a bird. In a similar manner the mystic quester must be able to enter the sphere of the spirit to gain redemptive knowledge and then return again to the world of daily life.

Hughes' aim in the poems of *River* is precisely to open himself up to his own deep Self both in Jungian terms and in terms of Hindu thought. This Self represents the center of one's being and, as the Atman of Hindu thought, it also represents divine and absolute reality. Hughes then wants to penetrate below the layers of ordinary consciousness to reach the archetypal Self or the Atman. As a mythico-mystic poet in a secular world he cannot but be syncretic in his enterprise to find the regenerative knowledge for modern man, drawing on the ideas and concepts of widely differing religions and mythologies. In one poem, for example, he roams along a Jungian bogland river looking for salmon in hidden, deep pools. In another poem he watches sea-trout standing in trance-like stillness under the roots of an oak "in a near emptiness of sunlight" ("Strangers"). And he muses to himself: "this is the real samadhi—worldless, levitated." Samadhi is an important concept in yoga, referring to the transcendence of the human condition and an experience of the Absolute. To Hughes the sea-trout become an emblem of self-transcendence through the union with the deep Self or the Atman. The paradox is that in order to achieve union with the deep Self it is first necessary to free oneself from one's superficial, rational self according to the mythico-mystic formula: he who loses his life shall find it. But this is one of the hardest things for modern secular man to do because it goes against the grain of his whole way of life.

At the center of *River* stand two poems, "That Morning", and "The Gulkana", that record two crucial experiences in Hughes' spiritual quest. The occasion of these two poems is a fishing trip in Alaska that Hughes made in 1980. In "That Morning" the poet-quester has a vision of the sheer abundance of spirit when he comes upon a river teeming with salmon. It is a sacred moment of illumination: "So we stood, alive in the river of light / Among the creatures of light, creatures of light." In terms of the mystic way it is the illumination preceding the last phase of the mystic's journey toward union with the divine. This moment also corresponds, in Campbell's mythic scheme, to the mythic quester's vision of the elixir of life, that ultimate goal of his quest. The power of the spirit furthermore shows itself by the fact that two bears, symbolizing the destructive, elemental aspects of nature and the unconscious, here are transformed into child-like creatures swimming in the river eating salmon in some kind of sacred meal. Spirit, then, is a power that can transform and even sacralize the destructive and elemental forces of life.

In "The Gulkana" the poet moves through an inner landscape of fear and threat where he finally meets his own spiritual Other or doppelganger face to face. The motif of the doppelganger actually runs throughout Hughes' work but it is not until in "The Gulkana" that he comes to accept his own spiritual Other. The doppelganger can be said to express the split in modern man's psyche, his denial and repression of his own deep Self or soul. Even the Indians of Alaska, the poem suggests, no longer have any spiritual life as a result of the onslaught of modern civilization. Now the poet at last manages to reconcile himself with his inner doppelganger, in the guise of a mythic "King Salmon", a fact that alone can ensure psychic and spiritual wholeness.[10] Recognizing the mythic "King Salmon" as his spiritual Other he also sees that self-sacrifice, the ritual dance of death performed by the salmon, is a necessary prerequisite for spiritual renewal:

> There, on some stony platform of water,
> Aboriginal Americans,
> High among rains, in an opening of the hills,
> They will begin to dance
>
> With shufflings and shudders,
> Shedding their ornaments, male by female,
> They will dance their deaths . . .
>
>   ecstasy dissolving
> In the mercy of water, at the star of the source,
> Devoured by revelation

This ritual dance of death points forward to the mystic marriage of death that will prove to be the crowning insight of the concluding poem of *River*.

In a very beautiful poem called "In the Dark Violin of the Valley" Hughes imagines the unifying and harmonizing power of spirit as a kind of night music. This is a music both for the living and the dead since spirit transcends the limits of life and death. Later the music of the spirit will soar triumphantly in full daylight, but as yet it only sings in the dark:

> All night a music
> Like a needle sewing body

> And soul together, and sewing soul
> And sky together and sky and earth
> Together and sewing the river to the sea.

Repeatedly in these poems the river is imaged as a beautiful woman, a goddess who presides over her own mystery cult administering a "love-potion" ("Low Water") to her initiates, whether they be sea-trout, an eel, "The nun of water" ("An Eel"), or salmon. It is of course the Great Goddess who as the Goddess of fate appears both in her gentle and terrifying characters ruling over the ritual drama of the mythic round of the year, a drama that involves the whole of nature and ultimately man as well. In fact the last part of *River* focuses on the poet-quester's experiences as an initiate of the mystery cult of the Great Goddess.

Approaching the sacred, Hughes draws on several religious traditions in order to describe his experience. The river, for example, becomes a Dervish dancer whirling in his "own music"; in the same poem it is also imaged as "The yell of the Muezzin / Or the 'Bismillah!' " ("Riverwatcher"). The Muezzin is the caller to prayer in Islam and the Bismillah is an Islamic formula of ritual blessing. In the concluding poem Hughes moreover refers to the Christian mass as a way of suggesting the presence of the divine. By referring to different religious traditions he wants to imply that the sacred ground of being is common to all religions and that the task of the mystic quester in a secular age is to recover that common sacred ground. And in *River* he does so by enacting the ritual death of the salmon, the mystagogues of the Great Goddess as the Goddess of the Great Round or the Goddess of life and death. In fact the whole life cycle of the salmon follows the archetypal order of nature and now this life cycle is to be consummated by a ritual death.

And so in the final poem of *River*, "Salmon Eggs," the poet-quester at last succeeds in gaining his hierophanic vision. It is a hierophany of water involving the salmon as the mystagogues of the sacred. In erotic ecstasy the salmon consummate their marriage of death so as to ensure the continuance of their life cycle. In mystical terms they sacrifice themselves through a ritual death before entering holy ground with a purified soul. By this act they lead the poet-quester on to the archetypal source of being, the holy of holies, "the altar" of being. Here the mystery of being is acted out as the wonder of birth, as a rite of continual birth, and the poet-quester exclaims in joy: "Only birth matters." This is the crowning insight of his long quest for the sacred: the sacred is revealed as the source of perpetual birth transcending and incorporating life as well as death. The source of overflowing spirit flows through both man and the cosmos and by partaking of the overflowing life of the spirit the poet-quester finally achieves his goal: the *unio mystica* or union with the Divine:

> Sanctus Sanctus
> Swathes the blessed issue.
> Perpetual mass
> Of the waters
> Wells from the cleft.
> It is the swollen vent
> Of the nameless
> Teeming inside atoms—and inside the haze
> And inside the sun and inside the earth.
>
> It is the font, brimming with touch and whisper
> Swaddling the egg.

By alluding to the Christian mass, and specifically to the Sanctus of the Eucharistic Prayer, Hughes implies that the rite of perpetual birth celebrated at the source of being is a rite of spiritual regeneration. As Eliade points out, water is the archetypal source of being since all things issue from and return to water.[11] The Great Goddess therefore manifests herself here in her most fundamental character as the Uroboros, in Erich Neumann's terminology: the Universal Mother as the primordial water of the universe.[12]

It is no exaggeration to say that the hierophany that concludes *River* represents the fulfillment of Hughes' whole career. Through his vision of the sacred he can at last propose a remedy to the spiritual disease of modern man pointing the way back to the archetypal source of being and to spiritual regeneration. Hughes' future development as a poet, if it is all possible to speculate about such matters, will probably be in the direction of a poetry returning to everyday life. He will still be a mythic poet but a mythic poet who returns, like Campbell's questing hero, with the elixir of life or regenerative knowledge to share the life of ordinary people. Hughes will then write a poetry of mythic return to everyday life and by so doing he will complete his career as the foremost mythic poet of our age. The aim of this new phase of his career, following the two earlier phases of mythic descent and mythico-mystic initiation, will be to anchor his hierophanic awareness in everyday reality and so further broaden and clarify his awareness of the sacred.

Notes

1. Joseph Campbell, *The Hero with a Thousand Faces* (New York: Pantheon Books, 1949), pp. 245 ff.
2. Mircea Eliade, *Shamanism* (New York: Pantheon Books, 1964), p. 182.
3. In an interesting essay, "Fourfold Vision in Hughes," Keith Sagar argues that Hughes' career is determined by the quest for a Blakean fourfold vision, i.e. a vision of the

sacredness of the universe. See *The Achievement of Ted Hughes*, ed. Keith Sagar (Athens: The Univ. of Georgia Press, 1983), pp. 285–312.

4. Erich Neumann, *The Great Mother* (New York: Princeton Univ. Press, 1963), pp. 268 ff.

5. Campbell, p. 246.

6. See Evelyn Underhill's classic study *Mysticism* (London: Methuen, 1962), pp. 380 ff.

7. Robert Graves, *The White Goddess* (London: Faber and Faber, 1948), p. 20.

8. Peter Redgrove, "Windings and Conchings," *The Times Literary Supplement*, 11 (1983), 1238.

9. Eliade, *Patterns in Comparative Religion* (New York: Meridian Books, 1963), p. 425.

10. Thomas West aptly calls this acceptance of the archetypal self, leading to psychic and spiritual wholeness, "a sort of biological self-lessness." See *Ted Hughes* (London: Methuen, 1985), p. 120.

11. Eliade, *Patterns in Comparative Religion*, pp. 188 ff.

12. Neumann, pp. 18 ff.

Wolf-Masks: From *Hawk* to *Wolfwatching*

Ann Skea

Of all the symbols that Hughes uses, the wolf is almost unique in the lasting power of its attraction for him, in the ambiguity of its nature as he describes it, and in the way in which he extends the scope of its symbolism from personal to universal applicability. Hughes's wolves embody the contradictory qualities of the natural energies: they have beauty of form, an economical directness of function, the instinctive voracity of appetite for which wolves are renowned, and a predatory cunning that has allowed them to survive in the harshest of environments. It is no surprise, therefore, that Hughes's latest book of poetry should be called *Wolfwatching*.

In many ways *Wolfwatching* sums up the major concerns of Hughes's artistic career. It deals with the natural energies in all their complexity, and it repeatedly shows the distortion of these energies that humans have brought about both in animals (like the caged wolf and the macaw) and in themselves. Adopting the wolf mask, which has long been one of his shamanic guises, Hughes looks again at the familiar features of his world, and records once more in his poetry the paradoxical combination of beauty and horror that, for him, defines the natural energies.

Appropriately, the eighteenth century netsuke that adorns the cover of *Wolfwatching* conveys just such paradoxical energies. The crafty, falsely humble attitude of the figure, which stands, humanlike, on two legs just as fairy-story wolves do, belies the natural predatory instincts of the creature. Both the benign and the predatory aspects of the wolf, however, are described in the title poem, which forms a pivotal node to the book—a sort of wolf-lair from which Hughes makes hunting forays into his world to capture the poem-animals which he once described in *Poetry in the Making*.[1]

In the *Wolfwatching* poems, Hughes, now an old wolf, looks again at the creatures and people that have been so important to him. The distancing effect of time has allowed him to look more closely at members of his family than he has been able to do before, and the emotions aroused are often painfully intense, but the clarity of his vision is expressed in the poems with all the knowledge, skill, and power of his maturity. His vision comprehends a historical panorama which extends from "A Sparrow Hawk," in which he

This essay was written specifically for this volume and appears here for the first time.

looks again at the hawks of his earliest poetry, to "A Dove," which depicts the turbulent and varied emotions of love that color the poems throughout this present book.

Hughes's choice of the wolf as a poetic mask is not new, and it is one that connects *Wolfwatching* with some of his earliest and most enduring beliefs. Mircea Eliade, in his study of Shamanism,[2] wrote that "the Shaman is indispensable in any ceremony that concerns the experiences of the human soul," and from Hughes's own discussions about his poetry it is obvious that he regards poetry as just such a ceremony.[3] Hughes believes that poetry gives access to the world of the spirit, and that certain powerful poetic symbols (like Blake's Tiger and Yeats's "rough beast" in "The Second Coming") have a summoning force that invokes what he calls "the elemental power circuit of the Universe" (Faas, 9). Using the rhythms of his poetry like a shaman's magic drum, Hughes, too, uses symbolic creatures to summon these powerful energies. He contains their potentially dangerous powers within the framework of his poems, and "flies" with them to the world of imagination and spirit for the healing that he finds there.[4]

In the undertaking of these poetic/shamanic journeys, Hughes's creatures not only have summoning powers, they frequently serve, also, as his shamanic costume. Eliade writes that "the Shaman's costume tends to give the Shaman a new, magical body in animal form" (Eliade, 16). It is a "mask" through which the shaman is "transubstantiated . . . into a superhuman being" (Eliade, 168) in order to undertake his journey. In *Poetry in the Making*, Hughes instructs aspiring young poets to "imagine what you are writing about. . . . Just look at it, touch it, smell it, listen to it, turn yourself into it" (18), and "The Thought Fox"[5] was, perhaps, the first of his published poems to demonstrate (and describe) his own use of this masking procedure. It is a technique Hughes adopts quite frequently, and one animal mask with which he has particular affinities and through which he has sometimes expressed some very personal emotions is that of the wolf.

To Hughes, the instinctive, predatory, wild energies that wolves exemplify are part of our own nature: they are part of the uncivilized prehistoric inheritance that is still present in our instincts and emotions.[6] Such fecund energies connect us with our roots and feed our imagination, balancing our rationality and our "sophistries" ("Egg-Head," in *Hawk*, 35), and so, Hughes believes, they are necessary. But suppressed and denied by our society's mores, he believes they become threatening and dangerous.

It is wolf-energies such as these that inhabit Hughes's poem "February" (*Lupercal*, 13),[7] where a ravening dream-wolf is conjured into his protagonist's world by a photograph of "the hairless knuckled feet / Of the last wolf killed in Britain." For Hughes, as for his protagonist, the wolf-energies that inhabit this poem exert a powerful fascination. They may "siege all thought," and threaten to "choose his head" as their home, but their attraction is such that no mythical or fairy-story wolves will now "suffice" him. So, Hughes creates his own poetic wolf-masks (such as this poem) through which he can more safely allow expression to the powerful energies that fuel his imagination.

It is typical of the care with which Hughes constructs his poetic masks that the poem's title, "February," evokes the wintery bleakness into which his wolves are summoned, and also, through its Latin origin, recalls the purifying rituals of the Feralia (the festival of the dead) and the Lupercalia which were held in Rome at this time of year. Thus, through the allusive power of a single word, Hughes conveys the ambivalence he feels in dealing with the wolf-energies, for the Lupercalia was both a purification ceremony and an invocation of fertility.

In *Lupercal*, the book of poems in which "February" appears, Hughes undertakes his own celebration of the Lupercalia. All of the poems in this book are, as Hughes told Ekbert Faas, "invocations to writing."[8] And although the title poem, "Lupercalia," partly describes the ancient Roman festival, it is, more importantly, a ritual evocation of fecund brute energies, and it ends with the poet's own prayer for renewal: "Maker of the world, / Hurrying the lit ghost of man / Age to age while the body hold, / Touch this frozen one."

"February," and the other poems in *Lupercal*, celebrate the sort of wild, primitive energies that Hughes's dream-wolf represents, but they show them as energies that have been caged, suppressed, or modified by our society until they only appear in an indirect, sterile form in "stories" or "pictures." Just as the wolf-spirit in "February" becomes a dangerous disembodied spirit that searches the world for its vanished head and "for the world / Vanished with the head," so Hughes believes that our own brute energies, suppressed by the dictates of our society, can only precariously be held in check. Sooner or later they, like the spirit-wolf, will re-emerge with potentially dangerous consequences.

Hughes has used such savage wolf imagery before with similar implications. An earlier poem, "A Modest Proposal" (*Hawk*, 25), was written at a time when many of his poems were inspired by the new, intense relationship between himself and Sylvia Plath. In it, he writes, seemingly autobiographically: "There is no better way to know us / Than as two wolves, come separately to a wood."[9] The desire these wolves have for each other creates a terrifying atmosphere of danger: it is an all-consuming distraction in which each competes against the other for "a mad final satisfaction" which will be achieved by making "the other's body and the whole wood . . . its own."

Although the wolf is a common symbol for the predatory male in the human hunt for a mate, the female, conventionally, is a submissive, unequal partner in the game. In the relationship between Ted Hughes and Sylvia Plath there was no such inequality. Sylvia wrote to her mother of Ted's effect on her: "I have never known anything like it. For the first time in my life I can use ALL of my knowing and laughing and force and writing to the hilt all the time, everything. . . . I feel a growing strength. I do not merely idolize, I see right into the core of him."[10] And Hughes's poetry at this period of his life celebrates the woman who does not "sweeten smiles, peep, cough," but

> . . . sees straight through bogeyman,
> The crammed cafes, the ten thousand
> Books packed end to end, even my gross bulk,
> To the fiery star coming from the eye itself,
> And while she can grabs of them what she can.
> —"Billet-Doux," *Hawk*, 24

The dangers of such an intense relationship as theirs were apparent to both. In "Billet-Doux" Hughes depicts such a relationship between equals not as love, which he describes as "a spoiled appetite for some delicacy," but as a condition of compulsive "desperation" in which each struggles not only to possess the other, but to avoid the surrender of self. Similarly, the lovers in "A Modest Proposal" are equal in their predatory intent, and the voracious violence of each wolf-like "skirmish" leaves both torn and exhausted.

In the "thicket" of these lovers' emotions, the wren, the prophetic bird of the English god Bran, "shrieks out" in terror at its glimpsed vision of "the red smelting of hatred" that is so close beneath the surface in these two wolves. Through the bloody "rents" in the animals' hides and the chinks of their over-bright eyes it sees the uncontrollable passions that threaten to emerge. In the light of this description of his aggressive wolf-self, the "modest proposal" Hughes makes is an ironic self-effacement, and the link this title-phrase makes with Jonathan Swift's appallingly simplistic solution to the Irish famine of 1727[11] suggests the satirical nature of Hughes's final stanzas and, perhaps, of the whole poem. Suggesting that the lovers may avoid disaster by substituting cooperation for competition, Hughes pictures an alternative mode of behavior that is essentially just another mask for the voracious wolf-instincts:

> And there rides by
> The great lord from hunting. His embroidered
> Coat floats, the tail of his horse pours,
> And at his stirrup the two great-eyed greyhounds
> That day after day bring down the towering stag
> Leap like one, making delighted sounds.

Since Hughes and Plath were both compulsive writers of poetry (it was in a sense their "master"), it is possible to see the "great lord" of this poem as a masculine version of their poetic muse. And the stag, a creature of Cernunnos, the horned Celtic god of fertility, also figures in some of the earliest pre-Celtic song/poems as a deity responsible for poetic inspiration. Robert Graves, for example, gives a version of the "Song of Amergin" (an encrypted bardic chant that is reputed to date from at least 1268 B.C.) in which the God is both the "stag of seven tines" and the inspiration of poets. [12]

The proposal that the lovers' "wolf" natures may be tamed, controlled, and put to productive use by submission to an artificial but socially acceptable ritual, is conveyed through the formal and ornate language of Hughes's last stanza and through the romantic and chivalric conventions that underlie the subject and content of his "picture." [13] At the same time the word "proposal" hints at one ritual through which this may be achieved—namely, marriage. Hughes and Plath, of course, did marry and work together, and their cooperation was an important element in their individual poetic development and success.

Despite the conventional facade, however, the couple led an unusual and intense life until Sylvia's suicide in February 1963. And there is little doubt that Sylvia's death had a stunning impact on Ted Hughes, causing a hiatus in his writing that lasted for three years.

In "The Howling of Wolves," [14] which was written within a few weeks of Sylvia's death (Sagar, 61), Hughes adopts the wolf-mask again in a poem that is full of bleakness and anguish. The title of the poem comes from one of Blake's "Proverbs of Hell": "The roaring of lions, the howling of wolves, the raging of the stormy sea, and the destructive sword, are portions of eternity too great for the eye of man." [15] This proverb expresses the incomprehensible nature of the emotions and impulses that cause the anguish in Hughes's poem.

The initial image of howling wolves "dragging" their "long leashes of sound" "up and out" of themselves into a freezing and silent forest, is cold, mournful, and eerie, and the near paranomasia between "world" and "word" in the first line suggests the inexplicable enormity of their pain. The wolves' instinctive, driven behavior and their cold "mineral" innocence are sharply contrasted with the gentle, innocent warmth of the baby's cries; and the delicacy of the violin's notes, and the urgency of the wolves' hunger for such warmth is emphasized by the repetition of the word "running": "Then crying of a baby, in this forest of starving silences / Brings the wolves running. / Tuning of a violin, in this forest delicate as an owl's ear, / Brings the wolves running—."

In the linked antitheses of the lines—the howling that "dissolves" in the silence; the "furred" steel; the small, gentle sounds that bring the wolves running, jaws "clashing and slavering"; and the attribution of innocence to these steely instruments—Hughes suggests the paradoxes of the wolves' existence. Because he believes that we, too, harbor barely controlled wolf-energies, similar paradoxes are part of the human condition. And in the slight difference between lines 11 and 12 of the poem: "That they must live like this, / That they must live," Hughes establishes two related but separate questions: that of the nature of this life, and that of the reason for life itself.

The isolation of the second of these lines in the poem's text indicates the relative importance of this latter question for Hughes at this time.

In the second half of the poem, the focus narrows from that of the wolf pack to a view of a single wolf hunched and shivering in the wind. To the observer, the wolf's howls could equally well be of joy or agony. But this wolf is driven by the "dead weight" of the powerful forces that inhabit its body and rely on that body for existence, so that the wolf MUST "feed its fur." As part of the cycles of Nature, "small" but necessary, "comprehending little" and miserably subservient to its compulsions, the wolf survives through momentous events. The picture of the night snowing stars and the sound of the earth's creaking gives a vivid impression of the workings of all-powerful natural forces, and the unwilling nature of the wolf's survival is suggested by the "dead weight" of the earth it bears. It is "living for the earth," the earth is "under its tongue" and "trying to see through its eyes," and eventually it will come to nourish the earth through death and decomposition. These images of death, compulsion, pain, and bleakness, together with onomatopoeic words like "slavering," "cracking," "whimpering," and "howling," leave the reader with an overriding impression of misery and helplessness, and this surely must have been Hughes's own emotions at this time.

Hughes's use of the wolf as a symbol does not always have this element of self-portraiture about it, but the association he makes between the wolf and the forces of Nature to which we ourselves are subject is constant. Alongside the predatory aspects of Hughes's wolves there is, also, their energy and the elements of freedom in their existence that can seem highly desirable in a regulated and restrictive society. In the story "Sunday" (Wodwo, 56–70) the child, Michael, escapes from the minister's sermon and from "situations of constraint in school, in waiting rooms, with visitors," by shutting his eyes and imagining "a wolf galloping through snow-filled, moonlit forest" (Wodwo, 56). In this case, imagination succeeds in counter-acting repressive forces, but, in the Calder Valley as Hughes describes it in Remains of Elmet,[16] the wolf has become a ghost—a "wraith" among the "foundering valleys" and the "graves full of eternal silence." Driven out of the twentieth-century world like the wolf in "February" (Lupercal, 13), she "cannot any longer in all these hills / Find her pelt."

The ambivalent nature of Hughes's wolves and the mixed feelings of attraction and fear they arouse, are matched by the role the wolf plays as a symbol in mythology and folklore, where it has a rich and varied history. As an archetypal symbol, Hughes's wolves share this history, but specific reference to such sources in his work is unusual. In "February" he does refer to two well-known fairy tales, and to the ancient epic "Song of the Nibelungs," in order to activate his reader's own fund of wolf-knowledge and to help establish the mood of the poem. In "Lupercalia" (Lupercal, 61–63), too, he makes reference to a specific myth. But one poem in which he uses a particular mythological association more fully is "The Green Wolf" (*Wodwo*, 40).

The Green Wolf was a central figure in the midsummer ceremonies that took place in Normandy in the early part of the century. During these ceremonies "a man clad all in green, who bore the title of the Green Wolf, was pursued by his comrades, and when they caught him they feigned to fling him upon the midsummer bonfire."[17] Fraser, in *The Golden Bough*, associates the Green Wolf with vegetation gods that were ritually burned each year to ensure fertility in the coming season (Fraser, 870). It is this cyclical aspect of death and rebirth, this ability of Nature to "unmake and remake" the dying man, that is the subject of Hughes's poem.

The poem is almost certainly based on personal experience. In September 1961 the Hughes family moved to a small village in Devon. The following April, when their neighbor, Percy B, suffered a stroke, Ted was called on for help by Percy's wife, Rose. The events of the following few months, until Percy's death in early July, were recorded by Sylvia in journal form, and incidental to these events is her record of the natural richness of that early spring and summer. On 7 June she wrote:

> Well, Percy B is dying. That is the verdict. Poor old Perce, says everybody. Rose comes up almost every day. "Te-ed" she calls in her hysterical, throbbing voice. And Ted comes, from the study, the tennis court, the orchard, wherever, to lift the dying man from his armchair to his bed. He is very quiet afterwards. He is a bag of bones, says Ted. I saw him in one "turn" or "do", lying back on the bed, toothless, all beakiness of nose and chin, eyes sunken as if they were not shuddering and blinking in a fearful way. And all about the world is gold and green, dripping with laburnum and buttercups and the sweet stench of June.[18]

"The Green Wolf" appears to be Ted's record of this time, and the same abundance of Nature fills the last four stanzas of his poem, carrying with it portents of death. The blood clot that paralyzes his neighbor's body "moves in" through a "dark heaven" with the inevitability with which "the punctual evening star" heralds the night. The evening star is the Star-Son of the Moon-Goddess, who is responsible for birth, fertility, and death, and the wolf itself is linked with her because of its habit of howling to the moon, and because it feeds on corpse-flesh. The white masses of hawthorn blossom with their heavy palls of "deathly perfume" are traditionally associated with the Goddess in her destructive form, and are banned from the house in many parts of England lest they bring bad luck. The bean, too, is her flower, and its "badged" jet markings, "like the ear of a tiger," suggest dangerous and deathly powers. The Green Wolf, in this poem, is the Goddess herself, and these symbols of her deathly powers also have a fertile warmth and beauty. They "unmake and remake you," just as the midsummer fires once devoured the Green Wolf in "one smouldering annihilation" to bring renewed fertility to the earth. So, "old brains, old bowels, old bodies" are devoured to make way for the new in a process that "you cannot fear" because of its natural inevitability. And, despite the powerful presence of death that pervades the summer abundance of this poem, Hughes's final images are moist, gentle ones that capture the sadness of farewell to a spirit "frozen" in a frail, crude, failing body.

In marked contrast to this poem is one published in *Moortown* in 1979 as part of "Seven Dungeon Songs" (Moortown, 123). In 1971, while working on *Orghast* with Peter Brook's Experimental Theatre Company in Persia, Hughes was asked by Brook to help him find a fresh path into the Prometheus myth, on which the experimental work *Orghast* was based. Hughes turned for inspiration to Manichaeanism (a Persian religion founded by Mani in 3 A.D.), in which the fundamental symbols are derived from the "identification of moral will, order, life and love with Light, evil, chaos and hatred with Darkness."[19] This symbolism, which has survived in the Christian teachings of the Western world, also incorporates ideas of "illumination" and emergence from darkness and imprisonment to enlightened freedom. Hughes wrote the experimental language that the actors spoke, and he constructed a mythological framework for the performance. His series of poems, "Seven Dungeon Songs," draws on this Manichaean symbolism to deal with the creation of mankind, with the human struggle against the darkness in and around us, and with our frustrated straining toward the healing power of light.

The first of these "Songs" is a vivid illustration of Hughes's belief in the wolf-component in human nature. In it, the "gangrenous breath" of a spirit wolf is shown as clouding the "tabula rasa" of human nature from birth. The babe of the poem, in its innocence, is attracted by the wolf and reaches toward it in "soft-brained" ignorance of its own position of danger. And all the time the wolf's blood drips "On to the babe's hands," suggesting, from the first, mankind's murderous potential.

Behind the images of the last six lines of the poem there lurks the shadow of the mythical she-wolf that suckled Romulus and Remus, legendary founders of Rome and sons of the god, Mars, to whom the wolf was also sacred. The milky tits of Hughes's wolf also feed and nourish a human babe, but, although she can transport this babe from its earthly home and run with it "among the stars," the journey is perilous with "precipices." So, Hughes suggests the succor and the danger that derive from the Universal Wolf[20] in human nature. And the wolf's bloody wound, linked as it is with blood on human hands, perhaps results from our own fearful efforts to destroy it, just as the last wolf in Britain was destroyed and just as our society tries to destroy any wild, animal energies in its people. The position of this poem, however, as the first of this sequence dealing with mankind's struggle with darkness and light, shows the influence of the wolf to be fundamental and unavoidable.

In keeping with his beliefs in the supernatural powers of poetry, Hughes makes his own attempt to control the power of the wolf by constructing a poetic charm to contain its predatory energies with the poem "Amulet," first published in *Moon Bells and Other Poems*,[21] and reprinted as the prefatory poem in *Under the North Star*.[22]

The form and rhythm of the poem are those of a magical incantation. By the repetition of the word "inside," the physical form of the summoned Wolf spirit with its fang, fur, tongue, blood, and eye, is enclosed within its surroundings. And the circularity, which brings the Wolf's fang into the first and the last lines of the poem, ensures that the Wolf's power is contained within the poem. While the wolf in this poem is a symbolic representative of wolf-nature everywhere (the word is given a capital letter each time it is used), Hughes has made its surroundings a realistic duplication of the natural wolf habitats, which are also the natural surroundings of mankind.

In each line of the poem, the associated images have a progression and suitability that is enhanced by visual clues. The purple fang, for example, is linked with the mountain heather, which in turn suggests the coarse wolf-fur, which is linked with the ragged forest. The Wolf's foot leads the Wolf along the stony horizon so that its tongue may taste the Doe. And by linking the Wolf's tongue and the Doe's tears, Hughes specifies and contains the Wolf's carnivorous appetites. The Doe's tears become part of the frozen swamp and of the Wolf's blood, which is chilled by the snow-wind as the Wolf prowls through that wind with gleaming eyes. The final link between the Wolf's eye and the North Star is the most powerfully magical link of all, tethering the Wolf to the Earth's axis and completing the encircling magic of the charm.

Symbolic creatures like the wolf, which "tap the elemental power circuit of the Universe," may not always behave predictably, nor can they always be controlled. In the volume *Earth-Moon*, first published in a limited edition in 1976,[23] there are suggestions that Hughes's use of wolf-masks may not always be entirely voluntary. The poem "Moon-marriage" describes powerful dream animals whose arrival and "marriage" to the dreamer is "nothing you can arrange," and whose influence survives into the dreamer's waking life. "Maybe a smiling wolf comes up close / While you doze off, in your chair, and gives you a kiss, / A cold wet doggy kiss," Hughes writes, describing once again an ambiguous fairy-tale wolf. But the predatory nature of this wolf, too, soon becomes apparent, for the dreamer becomes a captive: "You have been CHOSEN, and it's no good flailing awake bawling 'No!' / Wherever the wolf is, she just goes on smiling—." In a "Moon-marriage," the "only offspring" of the involuntary possession of the dreamer by a dream animal "are poems," and Hughes's early poem "The Thought Fox" describes just such a marriage and birth.

The "lunatic" influence of the moon over human imagination, the "madness" and inconsistency of shamanic/poetic flight, the involuntary nature of a shaman/poet's possession by his or her spirit guides (or familiars), and the wolf's long association with all these things in myth, folklore, and fairy tales, all come together in "Moon-marriage" and in another *Earth-Moon* poem called "Moon-theatre." Although the shamanic trance in which the "Moon-theatre" performance is viewed is self-induced ("tap a drum, and fix your eyes in a glassy stare"), the images that are seen, including that of the captive princess unwillingly coerced into wolfskin so that "She is a wolf, and she must howl and rave," are uncontrollable. Clearly, the spirit wolf, whether it enters the mind voluntarily or not, must be treated with caution.

Whatever the provenance of the symbolic wolf in Hughes's earlier poetry, however, his use of the wolf mask in *Wolfwatching* is not surprising given the very personal nature of many of the poems in the book and his consequent need to protect himself from the strong emotions aroused. It is also hard not to identify Hughes himself with the old wolf whose picture he draws for us in the title poem.

The temptation to make such an identification becomes irresistible when one looks at the photograph of Hughes that was published with his notes on *Wolfwatching* in the *Poetry Society Bulletin* of Autumn 1989.[24] There, we can see for ourselves the benign "Woolly-bear white" creature, with "black peepers" "withered in under the white wool," just as Hughes describes the old wolf in his poem. Other phrases in the poem seem loaded with ambiguity, but they offer a less comforting picture, for this old wolf feels the constraints of his aging body, the fraying, wearying effects of a lifetime of caged energies, and the changed image that "children's gazings" have effected—converting his predatory power to "a lumpish comfort of woolly play-wolf."[25] His heart is a "cooling stone," his weight "useless," and now "All his power is a tangle of old ends, / A jumble of leftover scraps and bits of energy / And bitten-off impulses and dismantled intuitions."

This pathetic creature yearns for the "anaesthetic" that "has already taken his strength, his beauty / And his life," and one is reminded of Hughes's description in *Poetry in the Making* of the "special kind of excitement, the slightly mesmerised and quite involuntary concentration with which you make out the stirrings of a new poem in your mind" (Poetry, 17). Is this the "anaesthetic" for which he waits? Is the power of poetic inspiration the power he has lost? For Hughes, water has always been the interface between this world and the Otherworld of the energies, and many of his poems, especially in *River*, demonstrate this fact. Is this the reason that "water / Just might help and ease" the old wolf? And can we really believe that Hughes now lies curled "In a trembling wolf-pelt he no longer / Knows how to live up to"?

No. If there really is an element of identification between Hughes and the old wolf of his poem, then the poem itself belies the self-image that he offers there. Its lines are no "few tottering steps" born of old poetic habits. Through them Hughes's ability to evoke the wolf-energies, old and young, is demonstrably as strong as ever. And, in the disparate subjects and styles of the poems that make up this volume, there is ample evidence of Hughes's continuing skill and power. Clearly, it behooves the reader to keep in mind the deceptive character of benign-looking wolves, especially if they walk on two legs like the one on the *Wolfwatching* volume's cover. One must remember, too, that a mask for which Hughes has an equally personal attachment,[26] and which he links closely with imagination and survival, is that of the fox, and, unlike the wolf, the artful fox still lives and flourishes in Britain.

In his notes on *Wolfwatching*, Hughes describes this collection of poems as "a kind of totem-pole," and certainly each poem can be seen as a carefully crafted representation of wolf-energy in one of its many forms. Many of these forms we have met before: the Macaw; the Sparrow-hawk; members of Hughes's family; the predatory deep-sea fish. Hughes calls them his "familiars," and wonders why he should consult "just these familiars at just this time." It is a question we cannot answer, but one hopes that it is not just the old-wolf trying "to find again / That warm position he had." The volume, as a whole, does not have the sustained power and impact of sequences like *Cave Birds* and *River*, and probably one should not expect this, but there is a pervasive bleakness to the overall picture that it presents of trapped and thwarted energies, and this reflects the description of the young wolf that makes up the last two-thirds of Hughes's title poem.

"And here / Is a young wolf, still intact." Here, in all its effortless power and beauty is the perfect creature to take up "the iron inheritance / The incredibly rich will" bequeathed to him by his ancestry. But here, too, is the cage, the hopeless "neurotic boredom," and the keeper bringing his water. He has no compulsive hunger to drive him, and no freedom to practice and perfect his hunting skills. He has lost touch with Nature, and, in this city environment, he is doomed to become a cipher like the Hanged Man in the tarot-pack, but without the promise of renewal that this card usually holds.

In the final lines of the poem, Hughes sums up all that he has ever said about the dangers of caging up the wolf-energies and denying them freedom of expression. In whatever form they exist in our world they are our link with Nature: without them our inner and outer worlds will be empty and hopeless, and our eyes, like those of the young wolf in the poem, will be "Like doorframes in a desert / Between nothing and nothing."

Nevertheless, in a volume where many of the poems seem to demonstrate that such a bleak future is inevitable, Hughes characteristically ends with a poem in which the energies flow with power and freedom, creating for the top of his totem pole a dove of love, and spirit, and hope.

Notes

1. Ted Hughes, *Poetry in the Making* (London: Faber & Faber, 1967), 17; hereafter cited by title.

2.   Mircea Eliade, *Shamanism* (Princeton: Princeton University Press, 1964), 182; hereafter cited as Eliade.

3.   Hughes expressed his views at length in an interview with Ekbert Faas, published as "Ted Hughes and Crow," *London Magazine* 10 (January 1971): 5–20; hereafter cited as Faas.

4.   Hughes first spoke of the healing energies of poetry in a BBC broadcast for children on 27 September 1963, since published in *Poetry in the Making*, 51.

5.   Hughes, *The Hawk in the Rain* (London: Faber & Faber, 1957), 14; hereafter cited as *Hawk*.

6.   See Hughes's discussion of wild landscape, in *Hawk*, 76.

7.   Hughes, *Lupercal* (London: Faber & Faber, 1960); hereafter cited by title.

8.   Ekbert Faas, *Ted Hughes: The Unaccommodated Universe* (Santa Barbara: Black Sparrow, 1980), 209.

9.   Stuart Hirschberg identifies these wolves with Hughes and Plath in his note in *Myth in the Poetry of Ted Hughes* (Dublin: Wolfhound Press, 1981), 220, note 111.

10.   Aurelia Plath, ed., *Sylvia Plath: Letters Home* (New York: Harper & Row, 1985), letter of 4 July 1956.

11.   Swift's satirical tract *A Modest Proposal* presents a serious, detached, and plausible argument that treats people (particularly children) like farm animals, to be exploited, marketed, and consumed.

12.   Robert Graves, *The White Goddess* (London: Faber & Faber, 1977), 212.

13.   This point is made by Keith Sagar in *The Art of Ted Hughes* (London: Cambridge University Press, 1978), 22; hereafter cited as Sagar.

14.   Hughes, *Wodwo* (London: Faber & Faber, 1967), 178; hereafter cited by title.

15.   This proverb is usually identified as no. 27 of the "Proverbs of Hell" in Blake's *The Marriage of Heaven and Hell*. See William Blake, *The Poems and Prophecies* (London: Dent, 1970), 45.

16.   Hughes, *Remains of Elmet* (London: Faber & Faber, 1979), 94.

17.   James O. Fraser, *The Golden Bough: A Study in Magic and Religion* (London: Macmillan, 1974), 854; hereafter cited as Fraser.

18.   Sylvia Plath, *Johnny Panic and the Bible of Dreams* (London: Faber & Faber, 1979), 241.

19.   A. C. Smith, *Orghast at Persepolis* (London: Eyre & Methuen, 1972), 38.

20.   Hughes refers to this phrase from Shakespeare's *Troilus and Cressida* (I.iii.121) in his review of Vitus Droscher's *Mysterious Senses*, in *New Statesman*, 27 November 1964.

21.   Ted Hughes, *Moon Bells and Other Poems* (London: Chatto & Windus, 1978).

22.   Hughes, *Under the North Star* (London: Faber & Faber, 1981).

23.   Hughes, *Earth-Moon* (London: Rainbow Press, 1976). Published in the USA as part of *Moon-Whales and Other Moon Poems* (New York: Viking, 1976).

24.   *The Poetry Society Bulletin*, no. 142 (Autumn 1989): 1–3.

25.   A great deal of Hughes's work has always been for, and with, children.

26.   Hughes tells of his early identification with a fox, and of a dreamed fox/man that changed his Cambridge study pattern. He discussed this most recently in a Thames TV production, September 1986.

FROM THE POET

◆

Myth and Education

TED HUGHES

Somewhere in *The Republic*, where he describes the constitution of his ideal State, Plato talks a little about the education of the people who will live in it. He makes the famous point that quite advanced mathematical truths can be drawn from children when they are asked the right questions in the right order, and his own philosophical method, in his dialogues, is very like this. He treats his interlocutors as children and by small, simple, logical, stealthy questions gradually draws out of them some part of the Platonic system of ideas—a system which has in one way or another dominated the mental life of the Western world ever since. Nevertheless he goes on to say that a formal education—by which he means a mathematical, philosophical and ethical education—is not for children. The proper education for his future ideal citizens, he suggests, is something quite different: it is to be found in the traditional myths and tales of which Greece possessed such a huge abundance.

Plato was nothing if not an educationalist. His writings can be seen as a prolonged and many-sided debate on just how the ideal citizen is to be shaped. It seemed to him quite possible to create an elite of philosophers who would also be wise and responsible rulers, with a perfect apprehension of the Good. Yet he proposed to start their training with the incredible fantasies of these myths. Everyone knows that the first lessons, with human beings just as with dogs, are the most important of all. So what would be the effect of laying at the foundations of their mental life this mass of supernatural figures and their impossible antics? Later philosophers, throughout history, who have come near often enough to worshipping Plato, have dismissed these tales as absurdities. So how did he come to recommend them?

They were the material of the Greek poets. Many of them had been recreated by poets into works that have been the model and despair of later writers. Yet we know what Plato thought about poets. He wanted them suppressed—much as it is said he suppressed his own poems when he first encountered Socrates. If he wanted nothing of the poets, why was he so respectful of the myths and tales which formed the imaginative world of the poets?

Reprinted from *Writers, Critics, and Children*, ed. Geoff Fox et al. (New York: Agathon, 1976), by permission of the author.

He had no religious motives. For Plato, those Gods and Goddesses were hardly more serious, as religious symbols, than they are for us. Yet they evidently did contain something important. What exactly was it, then, that made them in his opinion the best possible grounding for his future enlightened, realistic, perfectly adjusted citizen?

Let us suppose he thought about it as carefully as he thought about everything else. What did he have in mind? Trying to answer that question leads us in interesting directions.

Plato was preceded in Greece by more shadowy figures. They are a unique collection. Even what fragments remain of their writings reveal a cauldron of titanic ideas, from which Plato drew only a spoonful. Wherever we look around us now, in the modern world, it is not easy to find anything that was not somehow prefigured in the conceptions of those early Greeks. And nothing is more striking about their ideas than the strange, visionary atmosphere from which they emerge. Plato is human and familiar; he invented that careful, logical step-by-step style of investigation, in which all his great dialogues are conducted, and which almost all later philosophers developed, until it evolved finally into the scientific method itself. But his predecessors stand in a different world. By comparison they seem like mythical figures, living in myth, dreaming mythical dreams.

And so they were. We find them embedded in myth. Their vast powerful notions are emerging, like figures in half-relief, from the massif of myth, which in turn is lifting from the human/animal darkness of early Greece.

Why did they rise in Greece and not somewhere else? What was so special about early Greece? The various peoples of Greece had created their own religions and mythologies, more or less related but with differences. Further abroad, other nations had created theirs, again often borrowing from common sources, but evolving separate systems, sometimes gigantic systems. Those supernatural seeming dreams, full of conflict and authority and unearthly states of feeling, were projections of man's inner and outer world. They developed their ritual, their dogma, their hierarchy of spiritual values in a particular way in each separated group. Then at the beginning of the first millennium they began to converge, by one means or another, on Greece. They came from Africa via Egypt, from Asia via Persia and the Middle East, from Europe and from all the shores of the Mediterranean. Meeting in Greece, they mingled with those rising from the soil of Greece itself. Wherever two cultures with their religious ideas are brought sharply together, there is an inner explosion. Greece had become the battleground of the religious and mythological inspirations of much of the archaic world. The conflict was severe, and the effort to find solutions and make peace among all those contradictory elements was correspondingly great. And the heroes of the struggle were those early philosophers. The struggle created them, it opened the depths of spirit and imagination to them, and they made sense of it. What was religious passion in the religions became in them a special sense of the holiness and seriousness of existence. What was obscure symbolic mystery in the mythologies became in them a bright, manifold perception of universal and human truths. In their works we see the transformation from one to the other taking place. And the great age which immediately followed them, in the fifth century BC, was the culmination of the activity.

It seems proper, then, that the fantastic dimension of those tales should have appeared to Plato as something very much other than frivolous or absurd. We can begin to guess, maybe, at what he wanted, in familiarizing children with as much as possible of that teeming repertoire.

To begin with, we can say that an education of the sort Plato proposes would work on a child in the following way.

A child takes possession of a story as what might be called a unit of imagination. A story which engages, say, earth and the underworld is a unit correspondingly flexible. It contains not merely the space and in some form or other the contents of those two places; it reconciles their contradictions in a workable fashion and holds open the way between them. The child can re-enter the story at will, look around him, find all those things and consider them at his leisure. In attending to the world of such a story there is the beginning of imaginative and mental control. There is the beginning of a form of contemplation. And to begin with, each story is separate from every other story. Each unit of imagination is like a whole separate imagination, no matter how many the head holds.

If the story is learned well, so that all its parts can be seen at a glance, as if we looked through a window into it, then that story has become like the complicated hinterland of a single word. It has become a word. Any fragment of the story serves as the 'word' by which the whole story's electrical circuit is switched into consciousness, and all its light and power brought to bear. As a rather extreme example, take the story of Christ. No matter what point of that story we touch, the whole story hits us. If we mention the Nativity, or the miracle of the loaves and fishes, or Lazarus, or the Crucifixion, the voltage and inner brightness of the whole story is instantly there. A single word of reference is enough—just as you need to touch a power-line with only the tip of your finger.

The story itself is an acquisition, a kind of wealth. We only have to imagine for a moment an individual who knows nothing of it at all. His ignorance would shock us, and, in a real way, he would be outside our society. How would he even begin to understand most of the ideas which are at the roots of our culture and appear everywhere among the branches? To follow the meanings behind the one word Crucifixion would take us through most of European history, and much of Roman and Middle Eastern too. It would take us into every corner of our private life. And before long, it would compel us to acknowledge much more important meanings than merely informative ones. Openings of spiritual experience, a dedication to final realities which might well stop us dead in our tracks and demand of us personally a sacrifice which we could never otherwise have conceived. A word of that sort has magnetized our life into a special pattern. And behind it stands not just the crowded breadth of the world, but all the depths and intensities of it too. Those things have been raised out of chaos and brought into our ken by the story in a word. The word holds them all there, like a constellation, floating and shining, and though we may draw back from tangling with them too closely, nevertheless they are present. And they remain, part of the head that lives our life, and they grow as we grow. A story can wield so much! And a word wields the story.

Imagine hearing, somewhere in the middle of a poem being recited, the phrase 'The Crucifixion of Hitler'. The word 'Hitler' is as much of a hieroglyph as the word 'Crucifixion'. Individually, those two words bear the consciousness of much of our civilization. But they are meaningless hieroglyphs, unless the stories behind the words are known. We could almost say it is only by possessing these stories that we possess that consciousness. And in those who possess both stories, the collision of those two words, in that phrase, cannot fail to detonate a psychic depth-charge. Whether we like it or not, a huge inner working starts up. How can Hitler and Crucifixion exist together in that way? Can they or can't they? The struggle to sort it out throws up ethical and philosophical implications which could absorb our attention for a very long time. All our static and maybe dormant understanding of good and evil and what opens beyond good and evil is shocked into activity. Many unconscious assumptions and intuitions come up into the light to declare themselves and explain themselves and reassess each other. For some temperaments, those two words twinned in that way might well point to wholly fresh appraisals of good and evil and the underground psychological or even actual connections between them. Yet the visible combatants here are two stories.

Without those stories, how could we have grasped those meanings? Without those stories, how could we have reduced those meanings to two words? The stories have gathered up huge charges of reality, and illuminated us with them, and given us their energy, just as those colliding worlds in early Greece roused the philosophers and the poets. If we argue that a grasp of good and evil has nothing to do with a knowledge of historical anecdotes, we have only to compare what we felt of Hitler's particular evil when our knowledge of his story was only general with what we felt when we learned more details. It is just those details of Hitler's story that have changed the consciousness of modern man. The story hasn't stuck onto us something that was never there before. It has revealed to us something that was always there. And no other story, no other anything, ever did it so powerfully. Just as it needed the story of Christ to change the consciousness of our ancestors. The better we know these stories as stories, the more of ourselves and the world is revealed to us through them.

The story of Christ came to us first of all as two or three sentences. That tiny seed held all the rest in potential form. Like the blueprint of a city. Once we laid it down firmly in imagination, it became the foundation for everything that could subsequently build and live there. Just the same with the story of Hitler.

Are those two stories extreme examples? They would not have appeared so for the early Greeks, who had several Christs and several Bibles and quite a few Hitlers to deal with. Are Aesop's fables more to our scale? They operate in exactly the same way. Grimm's tales are similar oracles.

But what these two stories show very clearly is how stories think for themselves, once we know them. They not only attract and light up everything relevant in our own experience, they are also in continual private meditation, as it were, on their own implications. They are little factories of understanding. New revelations of meaning open out of their images and patterns continually, stirred into reach by our own growth and changing circumstances.

Then at a certain point in our lives, they begin to combine. What happened forcibly between Hitler and the Crucifixion in that phrase, begins to happen naturally. The head that holds many stories becomes a small early Greece.

It does not matter, either, how old the stories are. Stories are old the way human biology is old. No matter how much they have produced in the past in the way of fruitful inspirations, they are never exhausted. The story of Christ, to stick to our example, can never be diminished by the seemingly infinite mass of theological agonizing and insipid homilies which have attempted to translate it into something more manageable. It remains, like any other genuine story, irreducible, a lump of the world, like the body of a new-born child. There is little doubt that if the world lasts pretty soon someone will come along and understand the story as if for the first time. He will look back and see two thousand years of somnolent fumbling with the theme. Out of that, and the collision of other things, he will produce, very likely, something totally new and overwhelming, some whole new direction for human life. The same possibility holds for the ancient stories of many another deity. Why not? History is really no older than that new-born baby. And every story is still the original cauldron of wisdom, full of new visions and new life.

What do we mean by 'imagination'? There are obviously many degrees of it. Are there different kinds?

The word 'imagination' usually denotes not much more than the faculty of creating a picture of something in our heads and holding it there while we think about it. Since this is the basis of nearly everything we do, clearly it's very important that our imagination should be strong rather than weak. Education neglects this faculty completely. How is the imagination to be strengthened and trained? A student has imagination, we seem to suppose, much as he has a face, and nothing can be done about it. We use what we've got.

We do realize that it can vary enormously from one person to the next, and from almost non-existent upwards. Of a person who simply cannot think what will happen if he does such and such a thing, we say he has no imagination. He has to work on principles, or orders, or by precedent, and he will always be marked by extreme rigidity, because he is after all moving in the dark. We all know such people, and we all recognize that they are dangerous, since if they have strong temperaments in other respects they end up by destroying their environment and everybody near them. The terrible thing is that they are the planners, and ruthless slaves to the plan—which substitutes for the faculty they do not possess. And they have the will of desperation: where others see alternative courses, they see only a gulf.

Of the person who imagines vividly what will happen if he acts in a certain way, and then turns out to be wrong, we say he is dealing with an unpredictable situation or else, just as likely, he has an inaccurate imagination. Lively, maybe, but inaccurate. There is no innate law that makes a very real-seeming picture of things an accurate picture. That person will be a great nuisance, and as destructive as the other, because he will be full of confident schemes and solutions, which will seem to him foolproof, but which will simply be false, because somehow his sense of reality is defective. In other words, his ordinary perception of reality, by which the imagination regulates all its images, overlooks too much, or misinterprets too much. Many disturbances can account for some of this, but simple sloppiness of attention accounts for most of it.

Those two classes of people contain the majority of us for much of the time. The third class of people is quite rare. Or our own moments of belonging to that class are rare. Imagination which is both accurate and strong is so rare, that when somebody appears in possession of it they are regarded as something more than human. We see that with the few great generals. Normally, it occurs patchily. It is usually no more than patchy because accurate perceptions are rarely more than patchy. We have only to make the simplest test on ourselves to reconfirm this. And where our perceptions are blind, our speculations are pure invention.

This basic type of imagination, with its delicate wiring of perceptions, is our most valuable piece of practical equipment. It is the control panel for everything we think and do, so it ought to be education's first concern. Yet whoever spent half an hour in any classroom trying to strengthen it in any way? Even in the sciences, where accurate perception is recognizably crucial, is this faculty ever deliberately trained?

Sharpness, clarity and scope of the mental eye are all-important in our dealings with the outer world, and that is plenty. And if we were machines it would be enough. But the outer world is only one of the worlds we live in. For better or worse we have another, and that is the inner world of our bodies and everything pertaining. It is closer than the outer world, more decisive, and utterly different. So here are two worlds, which we have to live in simultaneously. And because they are intricately interdependent at every moment, we can't ignore one and concentrate on the other without accidents. Probably fatal accidents.

But why can't this inner world of the body be regarded as an extension of the outer world—in other words why isn't the sharp, clear, objective eye of the mind as adequate for this world as it is for the other more obviously outer world? And if it isn't, why isn't it?

The inner world is not so easily talked about because nobody has ever come near to understanding it. Though it is the closest thing to us—though it is, indeed, us—we live in it as on an unexplored planet in space. It is not so much a place, either, as a region of events. And the first thing we have to confess is that it cannot be seen objectively. How does the biological craving for water turn into the precise notion that it is water that we want? How do we 'see' the make-up of an emotion that we do not even feel—though electrodes on our skin will register its presence? The word 'subjective' was invented for a good reason—but under that vaguest of general terms lies the most important half of our experience.

After all, what exactly is going on in there? It is quite frightening, how little we know about it. We can't say there's nothing—that 'nothing' is merely the shutness of the shut door. And if we say there's something—how much more specific can you get?

We quickly realize that the inner world is indescribable, impenetrable, and invisible. We try to grapple with it, and all we meet is one provisional dream after another. It dawns on us that in order to look at the inner world 'objectively' we have had to separate ourselves from what is an exclusively 'subjective' world, and it has vanished. In the end, we acknowledge that the objective imagination, and the objective perceptions, those sharp clear instruments which cope so well with the outer world, are of very little use here.

By speculating backwards from effects, we can possibly make out a rough plan of what ought to be in there. The incessant bombardment of raw perceptions must land somewhere. And we have been able to notice that any one perception can stir up a host of small feelings, which excite further feelings not necessarily so small, in a turmoil of memory and association. And we do get some evidence, we think, that our emotional and instinctive life, which seems to be on a somewhat bigger scale and not so tied to momentary perceptions, is mustering and regrouping in response to outer circumstances. But these bigger and more dramatic energies are also occasionally yoked to the pettiest of those perceptions, and driven off on some journey. And now and again we are made aware of what seems to be an even larger drama of moods and energies which it is hard to name—psychic, spiritual, cosmic. Any name we give them seems metaphorical, since in that world everything is relative, and we are never sure of the scale of magnification or miniaturization of the signals. We can guess, with a fair sense of confidence, that all these intervolved processes, which seem like the electrical fields of our body's electrical installations—our glands, organs, chemical transmutations and so on—are striving to tell about themselves. They are all trying to make their needs known, much as thirst imparts its sharp request for water. They are talking incessantly, in a dumb radiating way, about themselves, about their relationships with each other, about the situation of the moment in the main overall drama of the living and growing and dying body in which they are assembled, and also about the outer world, because all these *dramatis personae* are really striving to live, in some way or other, in the outer world. That is the world for which they have been created. That is the world which created them. And so they are highly concerned about the doings of the individual behind whose face they hide. Because they are him. And they want him to live in the way that will give them the greatest satisfaction.

This description is bald enough, but it is as much as the objective eye can be reasonably sure of. And then only in a detached way, the way we think we are sure of the workings of an electrical circuit. But for more intimate negotiations with that world, for genuine contact with its powers and genuine exploration of its regions, it turns out that the eye of the objective imagination is blind.

We solve the problem by never looking inward. We identify ourselves and all that is wakeful and intelligent with our objective eye, saying, 'Let's be objective'. That is really no more than saying 'Let's be happy'. But we sit, closely cramped in the cockpit behind the eyes, steering through the brilliantly crowded landscape beyond the lenses, focussed on details and distinctions. In the end, since all our attention from birth has been narrowed into that outward beam, we come to regard our body as no more than a somewhat stupid vehicle. All the urgent information coming towards us from that inner world sounds to us like a blank, or at best the occasional grunt, or a twinge. Because we have no equipment to receive it and decode it. The body, with its spirits, is the antennae of all perceptions, the receiving aerial for all wavelengths. But we are disconnected. The exclusiveness of our objective eye, the very strength and brilliance of our objective intelligence, suddenly turns into stupidity—of the most rigid and suicidal kind.

That condition certainly sounds extreme, yet most of the people we know, particularly older people, are likely to regard it as ideal. It is a modern ideal. The educational tendencies of the last three hundred years, and especially of the last fifty, corresponding to the rising prestige of scientific objectivity and the lowering prestige of religious awareness, have combined to make it so. It is a scientific ideal. And it is a powerful ideal, it has created the modern world. And without it, the modern world would fall to pieces:

infinite misery would result. The disaster is, that it is heading straight towards infinite misery, because it has persuaded human beings to identify themselves with what is no more than a narrow mode of perception. And the more rigorously the ideal is achieved, the more likely it is to be disastrous. A bright, intelligent eye, full of exact images, set in a head of the most frightful stupidity.

The drive towards this ideal is so strong that it has materialized in the outer world. A perfect mechanism of objective perception has been precipitated: the camera. Scientific objectivity, as we all know, has its own morality, which has nothing to do with human morality. It is the morality of the camera. And this is the prevailing morality of our time. It is a morality utterly devoid of any awareness of the requirements of the inner world. It is contemptuous of the 'human element'. That is its purity and its strength. The prevailing philosophies and political ideologies of our time subscribe to this contempt, with a nearly religious fanaticism, just as science itself does.

Some years ago in an American picture magazine I saw a collection of photographs which showed the process of a tiger killing a woman. The story behind this was as follows. The tiger, a tame tiger, belonged to the woman. A professional photographer had wanted to take photographs of her strolling with her tiger. Something—maybe his incessant camera—had upset the tiger, the woman had tried to pacify it, whereupon it attacked her and started to kill her. So what did that hero of the objective attitude do then? Among Jim Corbett's wonderful stories about man-eating tigers and leopards there are occasions when some man-eater, with a terrifying reputation, was driven off its victim by some other person. On one occasion by a girl who beat the animal over the head with a digging stick. But this photographer—we can easily understand him because we all belong to this modern world—had become his camera. What were his thoughts? 'Now that the tiger has started in on her it would be cruelty to save her and prolong her sufferings', or 'If I just stand here making the minimum noise it might leave her, whereas if I interfere it will certainly give her the death bite, just as a cat does when you try to rescue its mouse', or 'If I get involved, who knows what will happen, then I might miss my plane,' or 'I can't affect the outcome of this in any way. And who am I to interfere with the cycles of nature? This has happened countless millions of times and always will happen while there are tigers and women,' or did he just think 'Oh my God, Oh my God, what a chance!'? Whatever his thoughts were he went on taking photographs of the whole procedure while the tiger killed the woman, because the pictures were there in the magazine. And the story was told as if the photographer had indeed been absent. As if the camera had simply gone on doing what any camera would be expected to do, being a mere mechanical device for register-ing outer appearances. I may be doing the photographer an injustice. It may be I have forgotten some mention that eventually when he had enough pictures he ran in and hit the tiger with his camera or something else. Or maybe he was just wisely cowardly as many another of us might be. Whatever it was, he got his pictures.

The same paralysis comes to many of us when we watch television. After the interesting bit is over, what keeps us mesmerized by that bright little eye? It can't be the horrors and inanities and killings that jog along there between the curtains and the mantelpiece after supper. Why can't we move? Reality has been removed beyond our participation, behind that very tough screen, and into another dimension. Our inner world, of natural impulsive response, is safely in neutral. Like broiler killers, we are reduced to a state of pure observation. Everything that passes in front of our eyes is equally important, equally unimportant. As far as what we see is concerned, and in a truly practical way, we are paralyzed. Even people who profess to dislike television fall under the same spell of passivity. They can only free themselves by a convulsive effort of will. The precious tool of objective imagination has taken control of us there. Materialized in the camera, it has imprisoned us in the lens.

In England, not very long ago, the inner world and Christianity were closely identified. Even the conflicts within Christianity only revealed and consolidated more inner world. When religious knowledge lost the last rags of its credibility, earlier this century, psychoanalysis appeared as if to fill the gap. Both attempt to give form to the inner world. But with a difference.

When it came the turn of the Christian Church to embody the laws of the inner world, it made the mistake of claiming that they were objective laws. That might have passed, if Science had not come along, whose laws were so demonstrably objective that it was able to impose them on the whole world. As the mistaken claims of Christianity became scientifically meaningless, the inner world which it had clothed became incomprehensible, absurd and finally invisible. Objective imagination, in the light of science, rejected religion as charlatanism, and the inner world as a bundle of fairy tales, a relic of primeval superstition. People rushed towards the idea of living without any religion or any inner life whatsoever as if towards some great new freedom. A great final awakening. The most energetic intellectual and political movements of this century wrote the manifestos of the new liberation. The great artistic statements have recorded the true emptiness of the new prison.

The inner world, of course, could not evaporate, just because it no longer had a religion to give it a visible body. A person's own inner world cannot fold up its spirit wings, and shut down all its tuned circuits, and become a mechanical business of nuts and bolts, just because a political or intellectual ideology requires it to. As the religion was stripped away, the defrocked inner world became a waif, an outcast, a tramp. And denied its one great health—acceptance into life—it fell into a huge sickness. A huge collection of deprivation sicknesses. And this is how psychoanalysis found it.

The small piloting consciousness of the bright-eyed objective intelligence had steered its body and soul into a hell. Religious negotiations had formerly embraced and humanized the archaic energies of instinct and feeling. They had conversed in simple but profound terms with the forces struggling inside people, and had civilized them, or attempted to. Without religion, those powers have become dehumanized. The whole inner world has become elemental, chaotic, continually more primitive and beyond our control. It has become a place of demons. But of course, insofar as we are disconnected anyway from that world, and lack the equipment to pick up its signals, we are not aware of it. All we register is the vast absence, the emptiness, the sterility, the meaninglessness, the loneliness. If we do manage to catch a glimpse of our inner selves, by some contraption of mirrors, we recognize it with horror—it is an animal crawling and decomposing in a hell. We refuse to own it.

In the last decade or two, the imprisonment of the camera lens has begun to crack. The demonized state of our inner world has made itself felt in a million ways. How is it that children are so attracted towards it? Every new child is nature's chance to correct culture's error. Children are most sensitive to it, because they are the least conditioned by scientific objectivity to life in the camera lens. They have a double motive, in attempting to break from the lens. They want to escape the ugliness of the despiritualized world in which they see their parents imprisoned. And they are aware that this inner world we have rejected is not merely an inferno of depraved impulses and crazy explosions of embittered energy. Our real selves lie down there. Down there, mixed up among all the madness, is everything that once made life worth living. All the lost awareness and powers and allegiances of our biological and spiritual being. The attempt to re-enter that lost inheritance takes many forms, but it is the chief business of the swarming cults.

Drugs cannot take us there. If we cite the lofty religions in which drugs did take the initiates to where they needed to go, we ought to remember that here again the mythology was crucial. The journey was undertaken as part of an elaborately mythologized ritual. It was the mythology which consolidated the inner world, gave human form to its experiences, and connected them to daily life. Without that preparation a drug carries its user to a prison in the inner world as passive and isolated and meaningless as the camera's eye from which he escaped.

Objective imagination, then, important as it is, is not enough. What about a 'subjective' imagination? It is only logical to suppose that a faculty developed specially for peering into the inner world might end up as specialized and destructive as the faculty for peering into the outer one. Besides, the real problem comes from the fact that outer world and inner world are interdependent at every moment. We are simply the locus of their collision. Two worlds, with mutually contradictory laws, or laws that seem to us to be so, colliding afresh every second, struggling for peaceful coexistence. And whether we like it or not our life is what we are able to make of that collision and struggle.

So what we need, evidently, is a faculty that embraces both worlds simultaneously. A large, flexible grasp, an inner vision which holds wide open, like a great theatre, the arena of contention, and which pays equal respects to both sides. Which keeps faith, as Goethe says, with the world of things and the world of spirits equally.

This really is imagination. This is the faculty we mean when we talk about the imagination of the great artists. The character of great works is exactly this: that in them the full presence of the inner world combines with and is reconciled to the full presence of the outer world. And in them we see that the laws of these two worlds are not contradictory at all; they are one all-inclusive system; they are laws that somehow we find it all but impossible to keep, laws that only the greatest artists are able to restate. They are the laws, simply, of human nature. And men have recognized all through history that the restating of these laws, in one medium or another, in great works of art, are the greatest human acts. They are the greatest acts and they are the most human. We recognize these works because we are all struggling to find those laws, as a man on a tightrope struggles for balance, because they are the formula that reconciles everything, and balances every imbalance.

So it comes about that once we recognize their terms, these works seem to heal us. More important, it is in these works that humanity is truly formed. And it has to be done again and again, as circumstances change, and the balance of power between outer and inner world shifts, showing everybody the gulf. The inner world, separated from the outer world, is a place of demons. The outer world, separated from the inner world, is a place of meaningless objects and machines. The faculty that makes the human being out of these two worlds is called divine. That is only a way of saying that it is the faculty without which humanity cannot really exist. It can be called religious or visionary. More essentially, it is imagination which embraces both outer and inner worlds in a creative spirit.

Laying down blueprints for imagination of that sort is a matter of education, as Plato divined.

The myths and legends, which Plato proposed as the ideal educational material for his young citizens, can be seen as large-scale accounts of negotiations between the powers of the inner world and the stubborn conditions of the outer world, under which ordinary men and women have to live. They are immense and at the same time highly detailed sketches for the possibilities of understanding and reconciling the two. They are, in other words, an archive of draft plans for the kind of imagination we have been discussing.

Their accuracy and usefulness, in this sense, depend on the fact that they were originally the genuine projections of genuine understanding. They were tribal dreams of the highest order of inspiration and truth, at their best. They gave a true account of what really happens in that inner region where the two worlds collide. This has been attested over and over again by the way in which the imaginative men of every subsequent age have had recourse to their basic patterns and images.

But the Greek myths were not the only true myths. The unspoken definition of myth is that it carries truth of this sort. These big dreams only become the treasured property of a people when they express the real state of affairs. Priests continually elaborate the myths, but what is not true is forgotten again. So every real people has its true myths. One of the first surprises of mythographers was to find how uncannily similar these myths are all over the world. They are as alike as the lines on the palm of the human hand.

But Plato implied that all traditional stories, big and small, were part of his syllabus. And indeed the smaller stories come from the same place. If a tale can last, in oral tradition, for two or three generations, then it has either come from the real place, or it has found its way there. And these small tales are just as vigorous educational devices as the big myths.

There is a long tradition of using stories as educational implements in a far more deliberate way than Plato seems to propose. Steiner has a great deal to say about the method. In his many publications of Sufi literature, Idries Shah indicates how central to the training of the sages and saints of Islam are the traditional tales. Sometimes no more than small anecdotes, sometimes lengthy and involved adventures such as were collected into the Arabian Nights.

As I pointed out, using the example of the Christ story, the first step is to learn the story, as if it were laying down the foundation. The next phase rests with the natural process of the imagination.

The story is, as it were, a kit. Apart from its own major subject—obvious enough in the case of the Christ story—it contains two separable elements: its pattern and its images. Together they make that story and no other. Separately they set out on new lives of their own.

The roads they travel are determined by the brain's fundamental genius for metaphor. Automatically, it uses the pattern of one set of images to organize quite a different set. It uses one image, with slight variations, as an image for related and yet different and otherwise imageless meanings.

In this way, the simple tale of the beggar and the princess begins to transmit intuitions of psychological, perhaps spiritual, states and relationships. What began as an idle reading of a fairy tale ends, by simple natural activity of the imagination, as a rich perception of values of feeling, emotion and spirit which would otherwise have remained unconscious and languageless. The inner struggle of worlds, which is not necessarily a violent and terrible affair, though at bottom it often is, is suddenly given the perfect formula for the terms of a truce. A simple tale, told at the right moment, transforms a person's life with the order its pattern brings to incoherent energies.

And while its pattern proliferates in every direction through all levels of consciousness, its images are working too. The image of Lazarus is not easily detached by a child from its striking place in the story of Christ. But once it begins to migrate, there is no limiting its importance. In all Dostoevsky's searching adventures, the basic image, radiating energies that he seems never able to exhaust, is Lazarus.

The image does not need to be so central to a prestigious religion for it to become so important. At the heart of King Lear is a very simple Fairy Tale King in a very simple little tale—the Story of Salt. In both these we see how a simple image in a simple story has somehow focussed all the pressures of an age—collisions of spirit and nature and good and evil and a majesty of existence that seemed uncontainable. But it has brought all that into a human pattern, and made it part of our understanding.

Index

♦

Abse, Dannie, 31
Achievement of Ted Hughes, 6, 25
Ackroyd, Peter, 19
Acteon, 26
Adam, 25–27, 30, 150, 155, 157, 223
Adonis, 62, 64, 149
Adorno, Theodor W., 90
Aesop, 259
Aethelfrith, 205
Aggression. *See* Hughes, Ted, and aggression, violence
Aitchison, James, 31
Ajax, 167
Alvarez, Alfred, 7, 9, 10–11, 14, 18–19, 50, 53, 61, 68, 83
Amis, Kingsley, 7, 45
Arabian Nights, 267
Aristophanes, 16, 156–57
Ashbery, John, 29
Auden, Wystan Hugh, 6, 42, 123, 133

B, Percy. *See* Key, Percy
Bardo Thödol. *See Tibetan Book of the Dead.*
Bardon, Franz, 87
Bashō, 85, 92–93
Baskin, Leonard, 22, 27, 49, 50–53, 55, 59, 163–64, 188–89, 191–92, 196, 198, 202, 209
Bayley, John, 19, 25
Beckett, Samuel, 17, 51
Bede, the Venerable, 206
Bedient, Calvin, 4, 18, 22, 24, 28, 50n
Beethoven, Ludwig von, 115
Bere, Carol, 23, 26, 29, *222–29*
Berger, John, 178–79

Betty, 181
Bible, The, 20, 42, 91, 110, 113, 155, 194, 201, 217, 256–59, 267–68
Bishop, Nicholas, 32, 104, 106
Blake, William, 1, 25, 28, 41, 84, 93, 113, 242, 245
Bly, Robert, 183
Bohr, Niels, 94
Bolt, Sidney, 13
Booth, Martin, 2, 22, 25, 28
Bradshaw, Graham, 6, 17
Bran, 244
Brandes, Rand, 21, *172–87*
Brock, Edwin, 19
Brook, Peter, 92, 111, 226, 248
Brownjohn, Alan, 8, 9, 141n
Bruno, Giordano, 93
Buile Suibhne, 184
Burns, Robert, 113

Caedmon, 44
Calvin, John, 151
Campbell, Joseph, 30, 163, 165–66, 174, 230–32, 237, 239
Carey, John, 25
Carlyle, Thomas, 102
Carmina Gadelica, 184
Carr, W. I., 8
Carruth, Hayden, 15
Castaneda, Carlos, 23, 100, 174
Castillego, Irene Claremont de, 184
Cernunnos, 244
Certic, 206
Challenge of Ted Hughes, The, 6
Chamberlain, Neville, 30

Chaucer, Geoffrey, 134
Christianity. *See* Hughes, Ted, and religion
Chuang Tzu, 90
Clare, John, 43
Conquest, Robert, 82, 145
Conrad, Joseph, 15, 115
Cooley, Peter, 14
Corbitt, Jim, 263
Cowper, William, 134
Cox, C. Brian, 11–12, 135
Crabbe, George, 134
Crane, Stephen, 151
Cushman, Keith, 6

Davis, Dick, 25, 27–28
Davison, Peter, 8
Diana, 26
Dickinson, Emily, 64–65
Dionysus, 21, 175
Donne, John, 83, 123, 125, 134, 201
Donoghue, Denis, 30
Dorbin, Stanford, 14
Dostoevsky, Fyodor, 268
Douglas, Keith, 64, 83, 151–52
Duffy, Carol Ann, 31
Dunworth, 117
Dyson, A. E., 9, 11–12, *123–30*

Eagleton, Terry, 15, 21, 25, 175
Edwin, 205–6
Ehrenpreis, Irvin, 20
Eliade, Mircea, 12, 30, 148–49, 174,
    230–31, 235, 239, 242
Eliot, Thomas Stearns, 1, 6, 68, 82, 111,
    139, 149, 152, 195, 230
Empson, William, 133, 141n
Eskimos, 63, 154–55, 161
Estridge, Commander, 115, 117
Estridge, Janet, 178–79
Estridge, Jennifer, 179–80, 185
Evans, Mrs., 177–78
Eve, 150, 156–57

Faas, Ekbert, 5–6, 21, *82–98*, 153–54,
    173–75, 177, 179, 183, 204,
    242–43
Faust, 163
Felicity, 116, 179, 182
Fenollosa, Ernest, 91, 111
Feralia, 243
Fernandez, Charles, 15–16, *153–62*
Forbes, Peter, 31
Forster, E. M., 134n, 139

Frazer, Sir James, 247
Freud, Sigmund, 12, 165
Frost, Robert, 144
Frye, Northrop, 12
Fuller, John, 7, 14

Garfitt, Roger, 30
Garten, Joe, 177, 181, 185
Gawaine, 143, 149, 152
Gifford, Terry, 5–6, 22, 30, 184,
    188–204
Gilgamesh, 63, 149
Gioia, Dana, 24
Ginsberg, Alan, 92, 172
Gitzen, Julian, 17
Godwin, Fay, 27, 205, 209–12, 215–16
Goethe, Johann Wolfgang von, 82, 93,
    96, 266
Golding, William, 129
Graham, A. C., 88
Graves, Robert, 7, 14, 21, 57, 112, 119,
    147, 149, 164, 174, 230, 234,
    244–45
Greenway, John, 163–64
Grigson, Geoffrey, 24
Grimm, Brothers, 259
Group, The, 146
Grubb, Frederick, 9, *131–42*
Gunn, Thom, 57, 67, 131, 133–34
Gustavsson, Bo, 29–31, *230–40*

Haberstroh, Patricia Boyle, 23, 29, 30,
    205–21
Hagen, Major, 176–77
Hagen, Pauline, 176–78
Hamilton, Ian, 14, 49
Hardy, Thomas, 43
Harvey, John, 24
Heaney, Seamus, 6, 17, *45–46*
Hecht, Anthony, 13
Heidegger, Martin, 21
Heraclitus, 165, 183
Herbert, Zbigniew, 51, 90
Hercules, 21, 63, 149, 174
Hill, Geoffrey, 222
Hirschberg, Stuart, 5, 23, 213
Hitler, Adolf, 258–59
Hobsbaum, Philip, 11, 146
Hoffman, Daniel, 13, 50, 58, *143–52*
Hoffmannsthal, Hugo von, 90
Holbrook, David, 4, 11, 18, 28
Holdfast, 20, 112
Holmes, John, 8, 14

Holroyd, Mrs., 181
Holub, Miroslav, 51, 90
Homberger, Eric, 24
Hopkins, Gerard Manley, 7, 123
Hough, Graham, 7–9
Hughes, Edith, 219–20
Hughes, Glyn, 23, 28
Hughes, Olwyn, 3
Hughes, Ted, and agression, violence,
    8–9, 13–14, 16–18, 22, 32, 33, 50,
    72–81, 95–96, 123–24, 128–29,
    137, 146–47, 150, 153–62, 164–71,
    220, 222–23, 231–33, 241–43, 245,
    247–49, 260; and alchemy, 188,
    196–98; and animals, 9–10, 13, 24,
    31–32, 53–54, 56–57, 75–78,
    80–81, 92–93, 111, 117, 129, 132,
    136, 143–44, 147, 149–50,
    190–204, 222–3, 230–40, 241–52;
    and Arvon Foundation, 2; and BBC,
    2, 25, 105, 164, 188, 191; at
    Cambridge, 4, 8, 46, 63, 230;
    childhood, 53, 86, 89; and children's
    literature, 1–2, 5–6, 20, 62, 113,
    255, 257, 265; and the environment,
    2, 6, 28, 30–32, 42–43, 163–71,
    209, 217; and the feminine, 22, 30,
    42, 112, 148, 172–87, 190,
    193–94, 197, 200–201, 230–40; and
    history, 10, 16, 23, 60, 67–81, 176;
    and language, 3, 6, 15, 17, 19, 21,
    41–42, 52, 56, 60–62, 65, 76,
    89–92, 99–108, 110–19, 125, 144,
    146, 151–52, 161, 166, 183, 186,
    188, 201, 208, 222, 248, 257–59,
    266–68; and the Movement, 6, 9,
    10, 22, 30, 123, 145–46; and myth,
    4, 12, 14, 15, 23–26, 43, 93–94,
    112, 115–16, 118, 144–62, 163–64,
    174–75, 179, 181–82, 206, 222–23,
    228, 230–40, 247–48, 255–68; and
    nature, 3, 9, 17–18, 21, 23, 28–30,
    32, 41–44, 46, 50, 102, 112, 132,
    135, 138, 145, 152–53, 190, 193,
    200, 205–40, 247, 251, 263; and
    postmodernism, 3; and the New
    Criticism, 4, 6, 7, 82; as Poet
    Laureate, 2, 29, 41–46; and
    psychology, 12, 16, 30, 57, 62, 77,
    87, 93–96, 148–49, 174–75, 222,
    231–32, 236, 258, 261–62; and
    religion, 15–16, 23, 46, 108, 110,
    112–13, 117–18, 140, 150–51,
    153–86, 206–11, 214–15, 217, 231,
    239, 256–59, 264–65, 267–68; and
    science, technology, 15–17, 20, 23,
    159–72, 209–11, 214, 256, 262–64,
    266; and shamanism, 4–6, 12, 14,
    30, 49–50, 54, 61–65, 95, 103,
    148–52, 174, 230–31, 242, 249;
    and surrealism, 4, 6, 12, 24, 63–65,
    88, 114, 146–49, 184; and Taoism,
    88, 90; and trickster folklore, 4–6,
    15, 163–71, 232; and Upanishads, 4,
    64, 90, 168, 236; and White
    Goddess, 5, 14, 21, 56, 112–13,
    119, 149, 164, 173–74, 184, 230,
    234; and Zen Buddhism, 4, 14, 85,
    87, 90, 94, 168–70

DRAMA
Eat Crow, 189
Orghast, 20, 85, 91–93, 111–13,
    226–27, 248
Seneca's Oedipus, 60–61, 176
Wound, The, 14, 147–50, 189

POETRY
"accused, The," 189–90
"Acteon," 26
"Adam and the Sacred Nine," 25–27,
    30, 223
"After there was nothing there was a
    woman," 201
"Amulet," 249
"Anatomy of Crow, The," 163
"Ancient Briton Lay Under His Rock,
    The," 219–220
"Ancient Heroes and the Bomber Pilot,
    The," 79, 136
"Angel, The," 216–17, 220
"Apple Tragedy," 158
"As I came, I saw a wood," 199–200
"Battle of Osfrontalis, The," 160–61
"Bayonet Charge," 135
"Bear, The," 14
"Bedtime Story, A," 109
"Big Animal Of Rock, The," 215
"Billet-Doux," 125, 244
"Black Beast, The," 169
"Black Rhino, The," 43n
"Boom," 150
"Bride and groom lie hidden for three
    days," 22, 188–89, 201
"Bridestones," 215
"Bull Moses, The," 140

"Bullfrog," 137–38
Burning of the Brothel, The, 64
"Canal's Drowning Black, The," 213
"Casualty, The," 128, 135
Cave Birds, 5–6, 22–23, 26–27, 30,
  100, 172, 184, 188–204, 214, 223,
  232, 251
"Childbirth," 114
"Childish Prank, A," 156–58, 167
"Cock-Crows," 23
"Coming Down Through Somerset," 225
"Conjuring in Heaven," 158
"Contender, The," 161
"Conversion of the Reverend Skinner,
  The," 79
"Cormorant, A," 236
"Crag Jack's Apostasy," 8, 140
"Criminal Ballad," 162
Crow, 5, 14–20, 26, 29–30, 50–53,
  56, 61, 65, 109–16, 119, 151–73,
  188, 214, 222–23, 226, 228,
  232–33
"Crow Alights," 161, 166
"Crow and the Birds," 166
"Crow and Mama," 165
"Crow Blacker than Ever," 157–58, 168
"Crow Communes," 158, 167
"Crow Frowns," 168
"Crow Hears Fate Knock at the Door,"
  167
"Crow Hill," 140
"Crow Improvises," 168
"Crow Lore," 151–52
"Crow on the Beach," 169
"Crow Sickened," 169
"Crow Tries the Media," 111, 164, 168
"Crow Tyrannosaurus," 51, 112, 166,
  233
"Crown Point Pensioners," 217–18
"Crow's Account of St. George," 63,
  160, 166–67
"Crow's Fall," 169
"Crow's First Lesson," 151, 156, 158,
  167
"Crow's Last Stand," 169
"Crow's Playmates," 159, 169
"Crow's Song of Himself," 155–59,
  167
"Crow's Theology," 159–60, 168
"Crow's Undersong," 164, 168
"Crow's Vanity," 195
"Dawn's Rose," 110
"Day He Died, The," 225–26

"Decay of Vanity, The," 83, 125,
  134–35
"Dehorning," 224
"Dick Straightup," 60, 139
"Disaster, A," 110, 161
"Door, The," 156
"Dove, A," 43, 242, 251
"Dove Breeder, The," 80
Earth-Moon, 249–50
"Earth-Numb," 223
"Eel, An," 238
"Egg-Head, The," 100–01, 131–32,
  242
"Esther's Tomcat," 78
"executioner, The," 188, 194
"Fallgrief's Girl-Friends," 79, 134
"Famous Poet," 77, 123, 128, 132–
  33
"February," 58, 80–1, 242–43, 246
"February 17th," 224
"Finale," 190, 204
"First, the doubtful charts of skin," 195
"flayed crow in the hall of judgment,
  A," 188, 190, 197–99
"Fourth of July," 140–41
"Full Moon and Little Frieda," 105
"gatekeeper, The," 189, 197
Gaudete, 18–22, 26, 30, 111–19,
  172–87, 214, 219, 222–23, 232
Gaudete "Epilogue," 1, 5, 19–22, 26,
  30, 111, 115–16, 118–19, 173,
  183–86
"Ghost Crabs," 150
"Glimpse," 20, 109–10, 119
"Gnat Song," 150
"Go Fishing," 103–04, 236
"Golden Boy, The," 113–14, 118
"Good Life, The," 138
"green mother, A," 199–201
"Green Wolf, The," 247–48
"Griefs for Dead Soldiers," 80, 127–29,
  135
"guide, The," 22, 30, 100, 199,
  201–03
"Gulkana, The," 236
"Hag, The," 134
"Hands," 226
"Hardcastle Crags," 215
Hawk In the Rain, The, 4, 6–8, 18, 31,
  53, 56, 58, 60–62, 72–73, 75–80,
  83, 99–101, 104, 112, 114,
  123–30, 131–36, 138, 143, 145–46,
  223, 231, 242–44, 249

"Hawk in the Rain, The," 53, 58,
  60–61, 72–73, 99, 104, 126, 131,
  138, 147
"Hawk Roosting," 9–10, 14, 50,
  71–73, 126, 137, 150, 153, 231–32
"High Sea-Light," 215–16
"His legs ran about," 201
"Heather," 210–11
"Heptonstall," 212–13
"Heptonstall Cemetery," 219
"Heptonstall Old Church," 212
"Hill-Stone Was Content," 212
"Hill Walls," 211
"Horrible Religious Error, A," 159–169
"Horses, The," 133
"Howling of Wolves, The," 105, 150,
  245–46
"In The Dark Violin Of The Valley,"
  237–38
"Incompatibilities," 125
"interrogator, The," 189, 192, 197
"Invitation to the Dance," 134
"Jaguar, The," 10, 56, 61, 75–76,
  124, 153
"judge, The," 192–93
"Karma," 13
"Kill, A," 155, 164–66
"knight, The," 188, 196
"Leaves," 113
"Lineage," 155, 158
"Logos," 91, 113, 223
"Long Tunnel Ceiling, The," 215–16
"Low Water," 238
Lupercal, 4, 8–10, 18, 31, 54–58,
  61–62, 71–73, 78–81, 83, 94,
  101–03, 112, 126, 136–42, 143,
  147, 150, 176, 223, 231–32, 242,
  246
"Lupercalia," 246
"Macaw, A," 251
"Macaw and Little Miss," 10, 58,
  76–77
"Magical Dangers," 168
"March Morning Unlike Others," 224
"Martyrdom of Bishop Farrar, The," 79,
  124
"Mayday on Holderness," 101–02,
  139–40
"Meeting," 62
"Mill Ruins," 209–10
"Modest Proposal, A," 83, 124–25,
  134, 143–45
Moon Bells and Other Poems, 249

"Moon-marriage," 249–50
"Moon-theatre," 250
Moortown, 5, 24–29, 30–31, 43, 219,
  222–29, 233, 248
"Moortown," 223–26, 233
Moortown Diaries, 31
"Morning Before Christmas, The," 235
"Mount Zion," 210
"Nicholas Ferrer," 8, 139
"Notes for a Little Play," 159
"November," 8, 54, 56, 138
"October Dawn," 131
"Otter, An," 58, 78, 137, 232
"Out," 13, 150
"owl flower, The," 189–90
"Parlour Piece," 80, 133
"Pennines in April," 139
"Perfect Forms, The," 140
"Phaetons," 131
"Pibroch," 69–70, 105
"Pike," 53–54, 62, 79, 103, 137, 150
"plaintiff, The," 189, 193–94, 197,
  200, 202
"Prometheus on His Crag," 25–27, 30,
  223, 226–28
"Rain," 224
"Ravens," 224–25
"Relic," 138
Remains of Elmet, 4, 23–24, 27, 30,
  205–21, 223, 225, 246
"Retired Colonel, The," 8, 56, 138–39,
  176
"Reveille," 150
"Revenge Fable," 160
"riddle, A," 197, 200, 202, 214
"risen, The," 188, 202–03
River, 1, 5, 27–31, 184, 230–40,
  250–51
"Riverwatcher," 238
"Roarers in a Ring," 131, 147
"Robin Song," 168
"Salmon Eggs," 238–39
"scream, The," 190–91, 193
Season Songs, 20, 113–14, 118, 223–34
"Second Glance at a Jaguar," 14, 56,
  153
"Secretary," 134
"September," 125, 131–32
"Seven Dungeon Songs," 248
"She seemed so considerate," 192, 195
"Six years into her posthumous life,"
  217
"Six Young Men," 79–80, 126–27, 136

"Skylarks," 60, 106, 150
"Snake Hymn," 157–58
"Soliloquy of a Misanthrope," 79, 134
"Something was happening," 197
"Song," 125
"Song of a Rat," 105, 150
"Sparrow Hawk, A," 43, 241, 251
"Still Life," 105
"Strangers," 236
"Strawberry Hill," 57, 102, 140
"summoner, The," 189, 191–92
"Telegraph Wires," 31, 44
"That Moment," 162
"That Morning," 236–37
"Theology," 150
"These Grasses Of Light," 214
"Thistles," 144–46
"Thought-Fox, The," 54, 132, 242, 249
"Thrushes," 43, 61, 138, 150
"To Paint a Water Lily," 57–58, 79, 102–03
"Top Withens," 210–11
"Trance Of Light, The," 213–15
"Tree," 215
"Tree, A," 220
"Truth Kills Everybody," 167
"Two Legends," 154
"Two Wise Generals," 134
"Under the Hill of Centurions," 235
Under the North Star, 249
"Vampire," 134
"View of a Pig," 136
"Walking bare," 202
"Walls," 211
"Warriors of the North, The," 151
"Weasels We Smoked Out Of The Bank, The," 216
"When Men Got To The Summit," 212–13
"Widdop," 215
"Wind," 62, 99–100, 131
"Wind Flashes the Grass, A," 106
"Wings," 60
"Witches," 94, 140–41
Wodwo, 12–14, 17–18, 32, 54, 61, 91, 104–06, 112, 140–41, 143–52, 223, 231, 246–48
"Wodwo," 14, 61, 104, 143
Wolfwatching, 3, 6, 31–32, 42, 186, 241–42, 250–51
"Wolfwatching," 250–51

"Woman Unconscious, A," 8, 73–75, 141
"Word That Space Breathes, The," 216

PROSE
"Context," 84
"Harvesting, The," 147
"Introduction to Janos Pilinszky," 85, 89, 91, 107–08, 218–19
"Myth and Education I," 170
"Myth and Education II," 3, 30, 82, 93, 96, 218, 255–68
"Notes on the Chronological Order of Sylvia Plath's Poems," 87, 95–96
Poetry in the Making, 88–89, 96, 241–42, 250
Poetry Is, 56
"Poetry of Keith Douglas, The," 64, 83
"Rain Horse, The," 54, 147
"Review of *Astrology*, by Louis MacNeice," 94–95
"Review of *The Environmental Revolution*, by Max Nicholson," 165, 209, 217
"Review of *Myth and Religion of the North*, by E.O. G. Turville-Petre," 146, 206
"Review of *Shamanism*, by Mircea Eliade," 95, 148–49, 152, 164
"Rock, The," 23
"Sunday," 54, 57, 64, 147, 150, 246
"Ted Hughes Writes," 83, 99
"Vasco Popa," 51, 86, 90, 95, 107, 214
"Wolfwatching," 250–51

Ilkley Literature Festival, 188–89
Imiah, Mick, 31
Isis, 21, 153
Islam, 238, 267

Jacobs, Fred Rue, 6
Jeffers, Robinson, 42
Johnson, Manley, 28
Jones, Jim, 172
Joyce, James, 49, 163
Jung, Carl Gustav, 12, 16, 30, 63, 82, 87–88, 93, 95, 165–67, 174, 188, 197–98, 222, 236

Kafka, Franz, 4, 12, 60
Keats, John, 62, 84–85, 127, 149, 152
Keen, Peter, 27
Kessler, Jascha, 15

Key, Percy, 247
Key, Rose, 247
King, Peter, 20
Kinzie, Mary, 27
Kipling, Rudyard, 139
Korzybski, Alfred, 166
Kramer, Lawrence, 17

Laing, R. D., 12
Langland, William, 43, 134
Lao Tzu, 90, 94
Larkin, Philip, 7, 29–30, 45, 67–68, 145
Larrissy, Edward, 20
Lask, Thomas, 15, 19
Lawrence, David Herbert, 9, 13, 41–43, 85, 91, 111, 131, 135–36, 143, 198, 206
Leary, Timothy, 172
Lethbridge, T. C., 94–95
Libby, Anthony, 17
Locke, John, 166–67
Lodge, David, 17
Longley, Edna, 31
Lorca, Federico Garcia, 12, 140
Lowell, Robert, 8, 68, 145
Lu Chi, 84, 88
Lucie-Smith, Edward, 146
Lumb, Reverend, 19, 116–18, 174–83
Lupercalia, 101, 243

Malory, Sir Thomas, 46
Manichaeanism, 248
Manson, Charles, 172
Marcuse, Herbert, 10, 68–69
Mars, 248
Martin, Graham, 13, 30
Marvell, Andrew, 83
Mary, 113, 118, 155
Maslin, Elizabeth, 27–29
Materer, Timothy, 37n83
Maud, 116, 182–83
May, Derwent, 12–13, 15
McClatchy, J. D., 29
McGinley, Bernard, 31
McKay, Don, 20, *109–20*
Megerle, Brenda, 17, 29
Melville, Herman, 101, 103
Merleau-Ponty, Maurice, 166
Merwin, William Stanley, 4, 7–8, 63
Milosz, Czeslaw, 1, 49
Mirandola, Pico della, 93
Modern Language Association, 29, 37n83

Mole, John, 28
Molesworth, Charles, 15
Molière, Jean Baptiste Poquelin de, 15
Mollema, A., 12
Moore, Marianne, 6, 123
Morrison, Blake, 25
Motion, Andrew, 24
Moyle, Geraldine, 19
Mozart, Wolfgang Amadeus, 61, 138
Muir, Edwin, 7
Murphy, Richard, 22–23, 183, 208

Neumann, Eric, 231, 239
Newton, Sir Isaac, 167
Newton, J. M., 9, 13–14, 20
Nye, Robert, 22

Oates, Joyce Carol, 19
Oedipus, 60–61, 176
Odysseus, 63
Olson, Charles, 8, 85–86, 91, 111
Orchard, Jack, 219, 225
Orpheus, 63, 149
Orwell, George, 10
Osborne, John, 7
Owen, Wilfred, 135

Parisi, Joseph, 25
Parker, Michael, 6
Parzival, 163, 175
Penelope, 184
Perloff, Marjorie, 15, 37n83
Pilinszky, János, 1, 85, 89, 91, 107–08, 218–19
Pinsky, Robert, 19
Plath, Sylvia, 5–6, 8, 21, 29, 32, 42, 64, 86–87, 183–85, 219, 243–45, 247
Plato, 16, 23, 91, 153, 156–57, 161, 255–57, 266–67
Poe, Edgar Allan, 147
Popa, Vasco, 51, 61, 86, 90, 95, 107, 214
Porter, David, 16, 49–66
Porter, Peter, 24, 131
Porterfield, Christopher, 14
Pound, Ezra, 68, 111
Press, John, 7, 9
Pritchard, William H., 19
Prometheus, 25–27, 30, 161, 223, 226–28
Proteus, 167
Pynchon, Thomas, 15, 163

Raine, Craig, 22
Ramsey, Jarold, 6
Ransom, John Crowe, 7, 57, 82
Raudive, 93
Redgrove, Peter, 6, 28, 234
Reid, Christopher, 22
Remus, 248
Rich, Adrienne, 8
Ricks, Christopher, 25
Riding, Laura, 91, 229
Ries, Lawrence, 17
Rimbaud, Jean Nicolas, 84–85
Ripley, Pvt., 148, 150
Roberts, Neil, 5–6, 14, 22, 30, 32, 184,
    188–204
Robinson, Craig, 5–6, 21, 25, 27
Robinson, Ian, 14
Robinson, P. F., 25–26
Robson, Jeremy, 12–13
Romulus, 248
Ronan, 184
Rosenthal, M. L., 4
Rothenberg, Jerome, 95
Rousseau, Dounier, 131

Sagar, Keith, 5–6, 16, 20–21, 99–108,
    154–56, 210, 245
Sartre, Jean Paul, 60
Scannell, Vernon, 136
Schofield, Annie, 6
Schopenhauer, Arthur, 18
Scigaj, Leonard, 1–38 (esp. 5, 14–15, 21,
    25–28, 31), 163–71
Scupham, Peter, 24–25
Seneca, 60–61, 176
Serios, Ted, 93
Sexton, Anne, 8
Sergeant, Howard, 12
Sewell, Elizabeth, 28
Shah, Idries, 149, 267
Shakespeare, William, 1, 7–8, 18, 32, 46,
    60, 62, 64, 95, 108, 134, 138, 146,
    198, 222, 248, 268
Shapcott, Jo, 31
Shelley, Percy Bysshe, 199, 227
Sillitoe, Alan, 7
Simms, David, 14
Skea, Ann, 29, 32, 241–52
Skelton, Robin, 7, 9, 13
Smith, A. C. H., 227
Smith, Dave, 23
Smith, Ron, 28

Smith, Stan, 10, 16, 67–81
Snyder, Gary, 4, 88
Socrates, 90, 153, 156–57, 255
"Song of Amergin," 245
"Song of the Nibelungs," 246
Spender, Stephen, 6, 15, 51, 123, 223
Stanford, Derek, 14, 19
Steiner, George, 267
Stevens, Wallace, 28
Strauss, P., 14
Stuart, Dabney, 15
Sweeting, Michael, 6
Swift, Jonathan, 244

Taliesin, 119
Talmud, 156
Tennyson, Alfred Lord, 134
Thomas, Dylan, 7, 9, 10, 64, 113, 118,
    123, 130, 145
Thomas, Edward, 42
Thomas, R. S., 139
Tiamat, 167
Tibetan Book of the Dead, 87–88, 148,
    168–69, 200
Tobias, Richard, 22
Tomlinson, Charles, 67–68
Tristan, 163
Tung Yu, 85
Turville-Petre, E. O. G., 146, 206

Urizen, 113
Utz, Steve, 14

Vendler, Helen, 28–29
Venus, 62, 64, 149
Violence. See Hughes, Ted, and agression,
    violence

Wagner-Martin, Linda, 37n83
Wain, John, 7
Walcott, Derek, 29, 41–44
Wallenstein, Barry, 15
Walsall, Mrs. 180–81
Weatherhead, A. K., 17
Webster, John, 123
Westlake, Dr., 176, 178–80
Westlake, Mrs., 114, 117, 177–80
Wevill, Assia Gutmann, 5, 21
White Goddess. See Hughes, Ted, and
    White Goddess
Whitman, Walt, 43, 84

Who, The, 172
Whorf, Benjamin L., 91
Wilbur, Richard, 82
Williams, Heathcote, 31
Wilson, Angus, 129
Wordsworth, William, 41, 83–84, 101, 142

Yeats, William Butler, 1, 7, 45, 62, 64, 68, 83, 93, 124, 149, 152, 207, 211, 218, 230, 242
Yoga, 236

Zeus, 156
Zosimos, 198